THIS BIBLE BELONGS TO:

....

GIVEN BY:

....

DATE:

....

OCCASION:

....

"Tell the greatness of the
Lord with me. Let us praise
his name together." *Psalm 34:3*

MAGNiFY™

OLD TESTAMENT STORIES

A Nelson Biblezine™

International Children's Bible®

A Division of Thomas Nelson, Inc.
www.tommynelson.com

TABLE OF CONTENTS

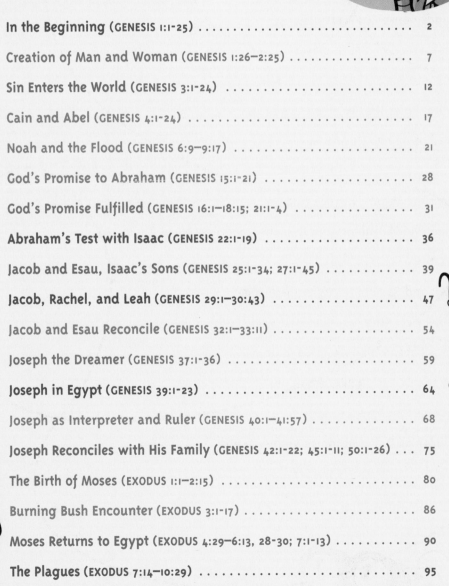

TABLE OF CONTENTS CONTINUED

INTRODUCTION

The title says it—Magnify™—both in discovering the secrets and truths of the Bible and in magnifying and honoring God!

This newest Biblezine™ gives you a super cool new way to read the stories of the Bible. You'll have a blast while learning about God's Word. You can find out how fun getting to know the Bible can be!

Magnify™ Old Testament Stories is a collection of some of the best stories from the Bible using actual scriptures from the International Children's Bible® translation. The stories will come alive as you uncover facts that help you learn how the Bible is meaningful in your life today. There's even some handy 3-D glasses to help make many fun images and games pop off the page!

JUMP IN AND EXPLORE GREAT FEATURES LIKE:

WILD WORLD FACTS

Awesome and true facts about God's wonderful creation. Sometimes gross, often weird, but always amazing to see how God's hand is in everything in the world around us!

BIBLE BASICS

Just the facts—pure and simple—about great Bible truths that you need to know.

LIVIN' IT!

Great articles to show you how to live your life based on the wisdom, promises, and truths from the Bible. Livin' your life according to God's Word will help you be the best you can be!

CALENDARS

One for January through December . . . each one with its own focus on a special Christian trait such as Repentance, Patience, Goodness and many more. Also included are suggestions for fun activities you can do to help others!

GET CONNECTED

Ever wonder how to get along with family and friends or how to have a strong relationship with God? Read the Get Connected articles to learn "tried and true" ways to help you in your relationships with God and the people around you.

DIG THIS!

Dig up amazing facts about the world of the Bible, its history and geography.

CRAFTS

INCREDIBLE EDIBLES

Fun recipes you can make and eat and simple crafts to do on your own—all related to the Bible stories!

TOP TEN

Cool lists of things to do or trivia facts for you to know, like the Top 10 Ways to Encourage Your Parents, Top 10 Ways to Grow a Happy Heart, or Top 10 Ways to Turn Food into Fun!

REAL SUPER HEROES

Yep, that's right! There were Real Super Heroes in the Bible . . . people like Adam & Eve, Moses, Joseph and many more! Learn about some of these awesome people that made a difference.

BLAST FROM THE PAST

Amazing facts about the ancient world in Bible times.

Games & Quizzes

Tons of creative and fun games and quizzes to color, decipher, decode, and solve. Find out things you may have never known before, and have a great time learning them!

Bible Critters

Love animals? Now you can learn wild and crazy things you may have never known about God's awesome Bible critters.

History Highlights

↱ Timeline tidbits to help you figure out when something happened and what was going on in the world at that time.

3-D

Punch out your free 3-D glasses, and start the fun on almost every page. Many images seem blurry or out of focus . . . but look again with your 3-D glasses! Pictures, games and much more jump off the page (look for the 3-D symbol). *Remember: DON'T try to read the Bible verses or the articles with your 3-D glasses on unless you want to go cross-eyed for life!*

FROM THE PUBLISHERS OF

MAGNiFY™

God never intended for the Bible to be too difficult for his people to understand. To make sure God's message was clear, the authors of the Bible wrote it down in everyday language. These books brought a message that the original readers could understand. These first readers knew that God spoke through these books. Down through the centuries, many people wanted a Bible so badly that they copied different Bible books by hand!

Today, now that the Bible is so easy to get, many Christians do not read it every day. Many people feel that it is too hard to understand or doesn't have any answers for their life.

The International Children's Bible® translation speaks in a clear and simple message that even young readers can understand. The ICB® presents God's Word in a clear and dynamic way.

A team of scholars from the World Bible Translation Center worked together with twenty-one other experienced Bible scholars from around the world to translate the verses from the best available Hebrew and Greek texts. You can trust that this Bible accurately presents God's Word as it came to us in the original languages.

Translators kept sentences short and simple. They tried to stay away from difficult words and worked hard to make the verses easier to read. They used more modern words for places and measurements. They put figures of speech and expressions in language that even children could understand. Also included within the text are small "d's" (to refer you to a dictionary in the back of full ICB® versions) and small "n's" that refer you to a footnote found at the bottom of the Bible page.

It is with great humility and prayerfulness that this Bible is presented to God's children. We acknowledge the infallibility of God's Word and our own human frailty. We pray that God will use this Bible to help you understand his rich truth for your life. We magnify God's holy name, and for his glory this Bible is given.

The Publisher

MAGNIFY ™

OLD TESTAMENT STORIES

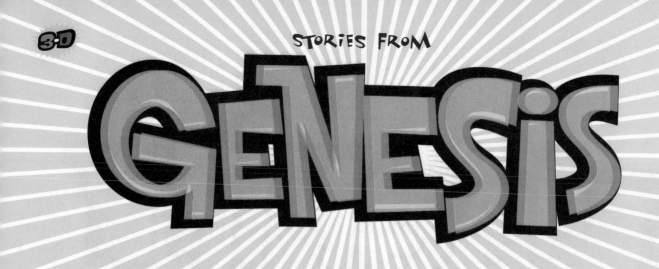

STORIES FROM
GENESIS

In the BeGinNiNg

GENESIS 1:1-25

THE BEGINNING OF THE WORLD

1 In the beginning God created the sky and the earth. ²The earth was empty and had no form. Darkness covered the ocean, and God's Spirit*d* was moving over the water.

³Then God said, "Let there be light!" And there was light. ⁴God saw that the light was good. So he divided the light from the darkness. ⁵God named the light "day" and the darkness "night." Evening passed, and morning came. This was the first day.

⁶Then God said, "Let there be something to divide the water in two!" ⁷So God made the air to divide the water in two. Some of the water was above the air, and some of the water was below it. ⁸God named the air "sky." Evening passed, and morning came. This was the second day.

⁹Then God said, "Let the water under the sky be gathered together so the dry land will appear." And it happened. ¹⁰God named the dry land "earth." He named the water that was gathered together "seas." God saw that this was good.

¹¹Then God said, "Let the earth produce plants. Some plants will make grain for seeds. Others will make fruit with seeds in it. Every seed will produce more of its own kind of plant." And it happened. ¹²The earth produced plants. Some plants had grain for seeds. The trees made fruit with seeds in it. Each seed grew

DIG THIS!

A lot of time passed between the time when God created the world and when people figured out how to write down and record what they knew. The period of time before writing began is called "pre-history." Back then, they passed on information and stories by word of mouth. Recorded history as we know it began around 3000 B.C.

LIVIN' IT!

MARVELOUS MASTERPIECE
GENESIS 1:1-25

With a word, God put the stars in place. He spoke, and the world came to be. Trees, birds, fish, mountains, oceans—once only ideas were now an incredible creation! And at the center of it, in charge of it, he made us—people created in his very image. And do you know what God said? He said, "It is very good."

So here you are, thousands of years later. When you look in the mirror, what do you see? Do you notice hair that's not quite right? A crooked smile? Clothes that don't fit today's fashion? Take a look again, and see with God's eyes. He still smiles at you. You are his special creation, planned and loved way before the world was ever made. Because of Christ, you are beautiful in his sight, and God's divine plan in you is still very good. Enjoy your uniqueness, and celebrate the truth that you were made perfectly to fulfill God's very special plan for your life.

BLAST FROM THE PAST

its own kind of plant. God saw that all this was good. ¹³Evening passed, and morning came. This was the third day.

¹⁴Then God said, "Let there be lights in the sky to separate day from night. These lights will be used for signs, seasons, days and years. ¹⁵They will be in the sky to give light to the earth." And it happened.

¹⁶So God made the two large lights. He made the brighter light to rule the day. He made the smaller light to rule the night. He also made the stars. ¹⁷God put all these in the sky to shine on the earth. ¹⁸They are to rule over the day and over the night. He put them there to separate the light from the darkness. God saw that all these things were good. ¹⁹Evening passed, and morning came. This was the fourth day.

²⁰Then God said, "Let the water be filled with living things. And let birds fly in the air above the earth."

²¹So God created the large sea animals. He created every living thing that moves in the sea. The sea is filled with these living things. Each one produces more of its own kind. God also made every bird that flies. And each bird produces more of its own kind. God saw that this was good. ²²God blessed them and said, "Have many young ones and grow in number. Fill

BIBLE BASICS

WHAT IS CREATION?

Unlike what you may have read in your science textbook, the world did not happen by chance. God planned it long before time even existed. He is so powerful that all he had to do was speak the words to create light and darkness, planets and moons, water and land, animals and people. Creation is simply everything that exists, and it all comes from God's incredible creativity.

SCIENTISTS AND BIBLE SCHOLARS DON'T ALWAYS AGREE on timelines. Fact is, it's pretty tricky to figure out how far back life goes. But many scholars believe people first started forming communities around 7,000–8,000 years before Christ was born.

the water of the seas, and let the birds grow in number on the earth." ²³Evening passed, and morning came. This was the fifth day.

BiBLe BaSiCS

What is an agreement or covenant?

An agreement is a contract or a promise. In the Old Testament, God made an agreement with his people, Israel. He promised to protect them, provide for their needs, and bless them if they kept his commands. Even though Israel failed their part of the plan, God stayed faithful and provided a Savior, Jesus, who would obey the law for us and save his people from their sins.

BiBLe CRitteRS — WINGING IT

When the Bible talks about eagles, it's most likely referring to the **GOLDEN EAGLE**, which can be found in North America, Eurasia, and Northern Africa. It is a powerful bird of prey with more than 7,000 feathers and a wing span of up to 7 feet! It uses large, yellow talons (claws) on its feet to capture large rodents, small mammals, birds, reptiles—almost anything. They build their nests out of twigs and place them high in trees or on cliffs. Both parents care for their young. In the wild, they live around 18 years, but under the protection of captivity, they can live as long as 45 years.

3-D

²⁴Then God said, "Let the earth be filled with animals. And let each produce more of its own kind. Let there be tame animals and small crawling animals and wild animals. And let each produce more of its kind."

And it happened.

²⁵So God made the wild animals, the tame animals and all the small crawling animals to produce more of their own kind. God saw that this was good.

BLAST FROM THE PAST

HISTORIANS BREAK UP PERIODS OF HISTORY BY MILLENNIUMS—a period of 1,000 years—to help make understanding history easier. It also helps to remember that, at first, the timeline goes backwards until it reaches zero. Then it goes forward. The time of the patriarchs (founding fathers) happens around the end of the 3rd millennium B.C., with the rest of the Old Testament history continuing on through most of the first millennium.

CRAFTS

PAPER-MACHÉ WORLD

3-D

INSTRUCTIONS

DAY 1: Blow up the balloon as large as you can. Tie it shut.

Pour liquid starch in a plastic bowl that has a lid.

Wet the newspaper strips in the liquid starch, and cover the balloon with the strips. When you have the balloon fully covered, set it aside to dry overnight.

DAY 2: Cover the balloon with a second layer of newspaper strips. Let dry overnight.

DAY 3: Cover the balloon with a third layer of newspaper strips. Let dry overnight.

DAY 4: Paint your world.

DAY 5: Hang your world in your room to remind you of our awesome and powerful God.

ALL ABOUT IT:

"In the beginning God created the sky and the earth. The earth was empty and had no form. Darkness covered the ocean, and God's Spirit was moving over the water" (Genesis 1:1-2). How awesome to think that God created the Universe out of nothing! In one day God created the whole earth and sky. The next day light, and so on. Today make your own world using a balloon, newspaper, paste, and paint, then marvel at the power God displayed when he created the world.

TEST YOUR CREATION KNOWLEDGE!

1 HOW WAS THE WORLD MADE?

A God spoke the word, and it was.
B Molecules bumped together and made it.
C Aliens came and created it.
D God thought it, and it was.

2 HOW MANY DAYS DID IT TAKE FOR GOD TO MAKE THE WORLD?

A 1   B none
C 7   D 6

3 WHAT WAS CREATED FIRST?

A plants   B animals
C people   D light

4 WHAT DID GOD MAKE ADAM OUT OF?

A nothing   B trees
C dust   D animals

5 WHAT DID GOD SAY WHEN HE LOOKED AT HIS CREATION?

A "Oops."
B "It is good."
C "Not bad."
D "It is a mistake."

6 WHERE DID EVE COME FROM?

A dirt   B nothing
C a bone   D another world

7 WHAT DID GOD COMMAND ADAM TO DO WITH THE WORLD?

A Take care of it.
B Use it.
C Fill it and rule it.
D All of the above.

8 WHAT HAPPENED ON THE FIFTH DAY?

A God made the sun and stars.
B God made the trees.
C God made man.
D God made the sea creatures.

9 HOW DID GOD WATER THE GARDEN?

A a sprinkler system
B fog
C rain
D a river

10 WHAT HAPPENED ON THE SEVENTH DAY?

A Man and woman were created.
B God rested from his work.
C God told Adam to get to work.
D Eve was tricked by the serpent.

Score 9-10: Congratulations, you know your stuff!
Score 7-8: You were awake in class, but not taking notes. Grab your pencil!
Score 5-6: Wake up! You must have been sleeping.
Score 4 or below: You must have cut class altogether! Get in the Word!

Answers: 1.a; 2.d; 3.d; 4.c; 5.b; 6.c; 7.d; 8.d; 9.d; 10.b

Creation of Man & Woman
GENESIS 1:26–2:25

DiG THiS!

Here's the breakdown of time before recorded (or written) history began:

Old Stone Age — before 10,000 B.C.

Middle Stone Age — 10,000 to 8000 B.C.

New Stone Age — 8000 to 4000 B.C.

Copper-Stone Age — 4000 to 3000 B.C.

Early Bronze Age — 3000 to 2000 B.C.

1 Then God said, "Let us make human beings in our image and likeness. And let them rule over the fish in the sea and the birds in the sky. Let them rule over the tame animals, over all the earth and over all the small crawling animals on the earth."

27So God created human beings in his image. In the image of God he created them. He created them male and female. 28God blessed them and said, "Have many children and grow in number. Fill the earth and be its master. Rule over the fish in the sea and over the birds in the sky. Rule over every living thing that moves on the earth."

29God said, "Look, I have given you all the plants that have grain for seeds. And I have given you all the trees whose fruits have seeds in them. They will be food for you. 30I have given all the green plants to all the animals to eat. They will be food for every wild animal, every bird of the air and every small crawling animal." And it happened. 31God looked at everything he had made, and it was very good. Evening passed, and morning came. This was the sixth day.

THE SEVENTH DAY—REST

2 So the sky, the earth and all that filled them were finished. 2By the seventh day God finished the work he had been doing. So on the seventh day he rested from all his work. 3God blessed the seventh day and made it a holy day. He made it holy because on that day he rested. He rested from all the work he had done in creating the world.

THE FIRST PEOPLE

4This is the story of the creation of the sky and the earth. When

LiViN' iT!

SLEEP ON IT GENESIS 2:2

No doubt, creating the universe is tough stuff. But did God really need to take a break when it was all said and done? Did creation tire him out before it even got started?

No. The Bible says that God never sleeps. So why did he rest on the seventh day? He rested for us. He was creating a picture for us so that we would follow in his footsteps. Unlike God, people do need rest. Work and productivity are good things, and God wants us to take care of the world he created. But he also wants us to set aside time from the regular routine to focus on him.

It's like a time out to regroup and remember what and who is really important in life, and to worship him with other believers. It's a special blessing that God gives to his people. This Sunday, ask God how he would like you to rest—and enjoy your day with him.

GENESIS 2:5-13

the Lord God made the earth and the sky, ⁵there were no plants on the earth. Nothing was growing in the fields. The Lord God had not yet made it rain on the land. And there was no man to care for the ground. ⁶But a mist often rose from the earth and watered all the ground.

⁷Then the Lord God took dust from the ground and formed man from it. The Lord breathed the breath of life into the man's nose. And the man became a living person. ⁸Then the Lord God plant-ed a garden in the East, in a place called Eden. He put the man he had formed in that garden. ⁹The Lord God caused every beautiful tree and every tree that was good for food to grow out of the ground. In the middle of the garden, God put the tree that gives life. And he put there the tree that gives the knowledge of good and evil.

¹⁰A river flowed through Eden and watered the garden. From that point the river was divided. It had four streams flowing into it. ¹¹The name of the first stream is Pishon. It flows around the whole land of Havilah, where there is gold. ¹²That gold is good. Bdellium and onyx" are also there. ¹³The name of the sec-

2:12 **bdellium and onyx** Bdellium is an expensive, sweet-smelling resin like myrrh. And onyx is a gem.

History Highlights

↗ **7000 B.C.**
Stone tools were shaped by grinding from Europe.

7000 5000 3000 1000 0 1000 NOW

REAL SUPER HEROES

ADAM

It might seem easier to remember Adam as the first guy who messed things up. After all, he had the beautiful garden, all the animals, and a wonderful wife. Did he really need to eat from that tree, too? How could Adam ever gain hero status after that fatal sin?

Before the Fall, Adam was a hero. He walked with God every day. He named all the animals. He protected Eve. But when sin entered the picture, Adam became a fallen hero. Broken and faced with the consequences of his sin, Adam could have given up hope. He could have left God altogether. But he didn't. Instead, he admitted that he had done wrong. He was ashamed, but still humble enough to receive God's help. He knew enough about God to understand his love. He was learning about receiving forgiveness. Adam was a hero after the Fall, because he shows us how to let God fix the lives we have broken.

BLAST FROM THE PAST

YOU'VE HEARD A LOT ABOUT IRAQ AND IRAN IN THE NEWS. But did you know that those countries were a part of Mesopotamia, the very first place where scholars think life began? No one knows where the Garden of Eden was, but from the Bible's descriptions, life began somewhere in the ancient Near East.

ond river is Gihon. It flows around the whole land of Cush. [14]The name of the third river is Tigris. It flows out of Assyria toward the east. The fourth river is the Euphrates.

[15]The Lord God put the man in the garden of Eden to care for it and work it. [16]The Lord God commanded him, "You may eat the fruit from any tree in the garden. [17]But you must not eat the fruit from the tree which gives the knowledge of good and evil. If you ever eat fruit from that tree, you will die!"

THE FIRST WOMAN

[18]Then the Lord God said, "It is not good for the man to be alone. I will make a helper who is right for him."

[19]From the ground God formed every wild animal and every bird in the sky. He brought them to the man so the man could name them. Whatever the man called each living thing, that became its name. [20]The man gave names to all the tame animals, to the birds in the sky and to all the wild animals. But Adam[n] did not find a helper that was right for him. [21]So the Lord God caused the man to sleep very deeply. While the man was asleep, God took one of the ribs from the man's body. Then God closed the man's skin at the place where he took the rib. [22]The Lord God used the rib from the man to make a woman. Then the Lord brought the woman to the man.

LIVIN' IT!

HOLD YOUR BREATH
GENESIS 2:7

How long can you hold your breath? Even the most trained person can only hold their breath for so long until they feel their lungs will explode. Fact is, we've got to breathe.

Have you ever noticed how God brought Adam to life? After he formed him from the dust, God breathed on him. It was God's breath that brought life. Our every breath that we breathe—every single one—comes from God. Without him, not a moment of life would be possible.

Now think about how often you breathe. That's how close God wants to be with us. He wants us to look to him to provide every need, fill every moment, and provide the strength of life to do those things he has called us to do.

2:20 Adam This is the name of the first man. It also means "humans," including men and women.

INCREDIBLE EDIBLES

FRUIT SALAD

INGREDIENTS

apples
oranges
pineapple
bananas

strawberries
(or you can use any fruit you have at home)

HERE'S THE SCOOP:

After God created people he said, "Look, I have given you all the plants that have grain for seeds. And I have given you all the trees whose fruits have seeds in them. They will be food for you" (Genesis 1:29). Prepare a fruit salad for your family today, using the foods that God made just for us to eat.

TO MAKE FRUIT SALAD

1. Wash and cut the fruit into bite-size pieces.

2. Mix the fruit together in a bowl.

3. Serve it as a snack or a salad for the family dinner meal.

BLAST FROM THE PAST

WHILE DIFFERENT PEOPLE GROUPS HAD THEIR OWN LANGUAGES, Aramaic was the official language in ancient Bible areas from the 8th century on. It became so popular that other countries began using it to help make talking between different groups easier, especially for trade and business. The Old Testament was originally written in Hebrew and Aramaic.

[23]And the man said,
"Now, this is someone
  whose bones came from
    my bones.
  Her body came from
    my body.
I will call her 'woman,'
  because she was taken out
    of man."

[24]So a man will leave his father and mother and be united with his wife. And the two people will become one body.

[25]The man and his wife were naked, but they were not ashamed.

DIG THIS!

Did you know that before Abraham became known as the father of the Hebrew people, he was most likely an Amorite? Amorites and Elamites were ancient peoples who conquered Sumeria and slowly came into that area from the west.

"The Lord God used the rib from the man to make a woman."

Genesis 2:22

GENESIS 3:1-10

Sin Enters the World
GENESIS 3:1-24

THE BEGINNING OF SIN

3 Now the snake was the most clever of all the wild animals the Lord God had made. One day the snake spoke to the woman. He said, "Did God really say that you must not eat fruit from any tree in the garden?"

²The woman answered the snake, "We may eat fruit from

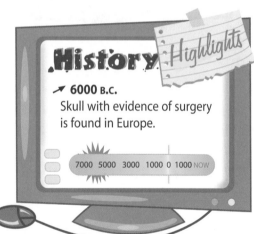

History Highlights

↗ **6000 B.C.**
Skull with evidence of surgery is found in Europe.

7000 5000 3000 1000 0 1000 NOW

the trees in the garden. ³But God told us, 'You must not eat fruit from the tree that is in the middle of the garden. You must not even touch it, or you will die.'"

⁴But the snake said to the woman, "You will not die. ⁵God knows that if you eat the fruit

from that tree, you will learn about good and evil. Then you will be like God!"

⁶The woman saw that the tree was beautiful. She saw that its fruit was good to eat and that it would make her wise. So she took some of its fruit and ate it. She also gave some of the fruit to her husband who was with her, and he ate it.

⁷Then, it was as if the man's and the woman's eyes were opened. They realized they were naked. So they sewed fig leaves together and made something to cover themselves.

⁸Then they heard the Lord God walking in the garden. This was during the cool part of the day. And the man and his wife hid from the Lord God among the trees in the garden. ⁹But the Lord God called to the man. The Lord said, "Where are you?"

LIVIN' IT!

ALL TRICK AND NO TREAT
GENESIS 3:6

Eve knew the rules. But there she was, right where she shouldn't have been. Whatever kind of fruit hung from the Tree of the Knowledge of Good and Evil, it was the most beautiful fruit Eve had ever seen. *Surely God is holding out on me,* she must have thought. *Why doesn't God want me to have the very best?*

Sin sneaks up on us today the same way it did on Eve thousands of years ago. It begins with a heart that doesn't really believe that God is good. As we doubt him, the sinful choices around us—being mean to our sister, lying to our parents, watching a TV show we know we shouldn't—start to look really good. We begin to believe that if we don't follow what we want, we won't be happy. So we cave.

Then sin stings our souls just like it did for Eve. It separates us from fellowship with our Father. We need to stand guard against Satan's tricky schemes. When you're tempted to do wrong, remember that Satan is a liar, but God is good. Choose what is right. And if you fail, remember to confess it right away to God, because he always forgives a repentant heart.

¹⁰The man answered, "I heard you walking in the garden. I was afraid because I was naked. So I hid."

CONNECT THE DOTS

God gave Adam and Eve a choice. Their decision brought sin, so God sent a Savior to the world. Connect the dots to see the symbol that asks us the same question today: Will you choose life or death? Then write the verse below.

_____

_____

_____

Genesis 3:17

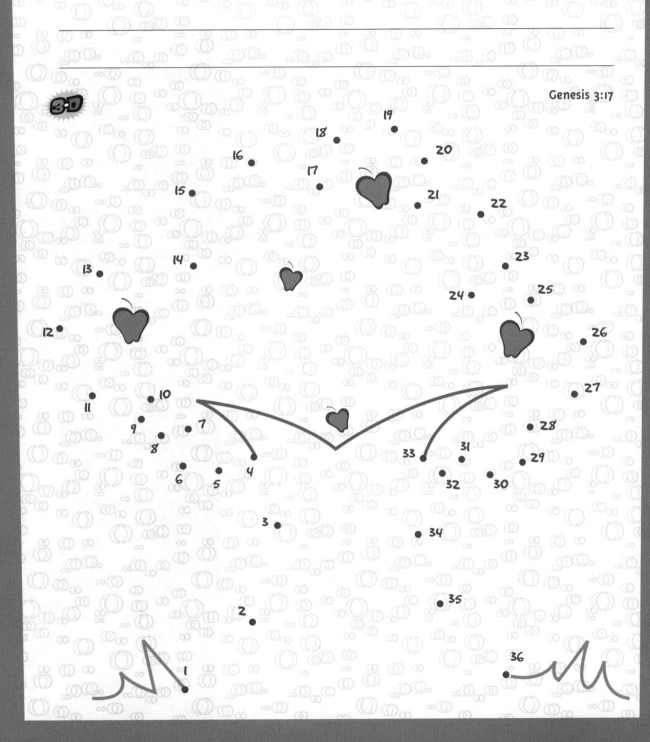

GENESIS 3:11-20

¹¹God said to the man, "Who told you that you were naked? Did you eat fruit from that tree? I commanded you not to eat from that tree."

> **"The Lord God made clothes from animal skins for the man and his wife. And so the Lord dressed them."**
> *Genesis 3:21*

¹²The man said, "You gave this woman to me. She gave me fruit from the tree. So I ate it."

¹³Then the Lord God said to the woman, "What have you done?"

She answered, "The snake tricked me. So I ate the fruit."

¹⁴The Lord God said to the snake,

"Because you did this,
 a curse will be put on you.
 You will be cursed more
  than any tame animal or
  wild animal.
 You will crawl on your
  stomach,
 and you will eat dust all the
  days of your life.
¹⁵I will make you and the woman
  enemies to each other.
Your descendants*ᵈ* and her
  descendants
 will be enemies.
 Her child will crush your head.
  And you will bite his heel."

¹⁶Then God said to the woman,
"I will cause you to have
  much trouble
 when you are pregnant.
And when you give birth
  to children,
 you will have great pain.
You will greatly desire
  your husband,
 but he will rule
  over you."

¹⁷Then God said to the man, "You listened to what your wife said. And you ate fruit from the tree that I commanded you not to eat from.
"So I will put a curse
  on the ground.
 You will have to work
  very hard for food.
In pain you will eat its food
  all the days of your life.
¹⁸The ground will produce thorns
  and weeds for you.
 And you will eat the plants
  of the field.
¹⁹You will sweat and work hard
  for your food.
Later you will return to the
  ground.

This is because you were
  taken from the ground.
You are dust.
 And when you die, you will
  return to the dust."
²⁰The man named his wife Eve.*ⁿ*
This is because she is the mother

LIVIN' IT!

DOMINOES
GENESIS 3:13-19

Every sin we commit has a consequence. It may have a really big effect, like when someone kills another person, or when husbands and wives are not faithful to one another. Or it may have seemingly smaller effects in certain situations—like when you hurt someone's feelings, or when you yell at your little brother for annoying you.

Whatever the case, when we choose to disobey God, several things happen. We lose our close connection with God. Our souls become a little more used to doing wrong, which makes the next wrong thing seem not so bad. And we keep hurting the people around us.

When Adam sinned, it affected all of humankind. We were all born into sin after him. The good news is that Jesus said that when we belong to him, we can choose what is right. He gives us his Holy Spirit to make good decisions. And he offers forgiveness when we mess up. When you want to sin, remember the results. Instead, turn to Jesus for help.

3:20 Eve This name sounds like the Hebrew word meaning "alive."

GET CONNECTED

RELATIONSHIPS WITH FRIENDS

Bad Apple Eve knew what Adam had said. God said no fruit from that tree. But she had tasted it, and she wanted Adam to try it out, too. Of course, he did, and the rest of creation fell with Adam's terrible choice.

As Christians today, we still feel the same kind of temptation that Eve did. When we've done something wrong—or are thinking about doing something wrong—we often want our friends to join us. Though company makes us feel less guilty, really, our guilt is even greater. We've hurt our own souls, but we've also caused others to sin, as well. When you're tempted to sin, don't look for others to help you get away with it. Instead, ask others to pray for you, and turn your heart back to God.

> "God put angels on the east side of the garden. He also put a sword of fire there."
>
> *Genesis 3:24*

of everyone who ever lived.

²¹The Lord God made clothes from animal skins for the man and his wife. And so the Lord dressed them. ²²Then the Lord God said, "Look, the man has become like one of us. He knows good and evil. And now we must keep him from eating some of the fruit from the tree of life. If he does, he will live forever." ²³So the Lord God forced the man out of the garden of Eden. He had to work the ground he was taken from. ²⁴God forced the man out of the garden. Then God put angels on the east side of the garden. He also put a sword of fire there. It flashed around in every direction. This kept people from getting to the tree of life.

REAL SUPER HEROES

EVE

Eve was the first woman, the first mother of the entire human race. She didn't choose her place in history, but God did—and for that we recognize her as a hero. She worked with Adam in the garden, tended the fields, and kept him company as they explored this new world that God had created for them.

Of course, the ending wasn't a happy one—at least not at the beginning. Eve got tricked by Satan. He fooled her into thinking God created a world that held something more desirable than closeness with God. Eve was tricked. Adam outright disobeyed. And together they began a new age of sin that would haunt every human to be born after them. She realized she was wrong. Like Adam, she looked to God for help. So he clothed them, gave them children, and ultimately provided a Savior to rescue them. God gave Eve's life a happy ending, but it happened in heaven instead of the garden.

APPLESAUCE

INGREDIENTS

6 apples
3/4 cup water
Sugar and cinnamon to taste
blender

HERE'S THE SCOOP:

Before you start making your applesauce, ask your parent or grandparent to cut one of the apples in half through the center, dividing the top of the apple from the bottom. When you open the apple halves, you will see two stars inside the apple. In the Bible, God used stars to tell Abraham how many children he would have. He also used a star to lead the shepherds and the wise men to the baby Jesus. The star represents hope and guidance.

There were consequences for Adam and Eve's sin, but God showed them his love even when they sinned. "The Lord God made clothes from animal skins for the man and his wife. And so the Lord dressed them" (Genesis 3:21). When you sin, ask God to forgive you and for his help to resist temptation the next time. Remember the apple and the promise of hope and guidance God hid inside the apple.

RECIPE

1. Ask a parent or grand-parent to peel and cut 6 apples into chunks.

2. Place 12 chunks in the blender with 3/4 cup of water and blend.

3. Continue to add the apples until all are blended and soft.

4. Add sugar and cinnamon to taste.

Cain & Abel

GENESIS 4:1-24

THE FIRST FAMILY

4 Adam had sexual relations with his wife Eve. She became pregnant and gave birth to Cain.[*] Eve said, "With the Lord's help, I have given birth to a man." [2]After that, Eve gave birth to Cain's brother Abel. Abel took care of sheep. Cain became a farmer.

[3]Later, Cain brought a gift to God. He brought some food from the ground. [4]Abel brought the best parts of his best sheep. The Lord accepted Abel and his gift. [5]But God did not accept Cain and his gift. Cain became very angry and looked unhappy.

[6]The Lord asked Cain, "Why are you angry? Why do you look so unhappy?

[7]If you do good, I will accept you. But if you do not do good, sin is ready to attack you. Sin wants you. But you must rule over it."

[8]Cain said to his brother Abel, "Let's go out into the field." So Cain and Abel went into the field. Then Cain attacked his brother Abel and killed him.

[9]Later, the Lord said to Cain, "Where is your brother Abel?"

Cain answered, "I don't know.

GET CONNECTED

RELATIONSHIPS WITH FRIENDS

Stuck Like Glue It's a good thing Adam and Eve didn't believe in divorce! If they had given up on each other, the rest of the world would never have happened.

In today's society, people tend to stick up only for themselves. When times get tough with friends or family, they just leave instead of working through their problems. God says that he wants us to stick together. He even allows the hard times in our lives to develop the kind of character we need to become more like Jesus.

The world will see a difference in our lives if we remain committed to our families and the body of Christ around us, even in very difficult circumstances. Ask God to help you, your family, and your church to stay close to him.

 4:1 Cain This name sounds like the Hebrew word for "I have given birth."

REAL SUPER HEROES

ENOCH

Several men had lived before him. The Bible records it quite matter-of-factly. Adam, Seth, Enosh, Kenan, Mahalalel, Jared—all men who lived on earth, had sons, and died. Then comes Enoch. He had lived for 65 years when he had Methuselah, and something changed in his heart. He didn't just live out his days as everyone before him had done. The description changes. Enoch had changed. He began to walk with God.

What does it mean to walk with God? The Bible doesn't give us specifics into Enoch's life. We just know that, at a special time in his life, he changed from just simply living life to becoming God's friend. He loved God so much and got so close to him that he didn't even have to die before he went to heaven. As God's children, we should ask God to give us hearts like Enoch's, so we, too, would walk with him all of our days on this earth.

Is it my job to take care of my brother?"

¹⁰Then the Lord said, "What have you done? Your brother's blood is on the ground. That blood is like a voice that tells me what happened. ¹¹And now you will be cursed in your work with

¹³Then Cain said to the Lord, "This punishment is more than I can stand! ¹⁴Look! You have forced me to stop working the ground. And now I must hide from you. I will wander around on the earth. And anyone who meets me can kill me."

BLAST FROM THE PAST

ABRAHAM WAS THE FIRST PATRIARCH (meaning "father") of the Jewish record. Genesis 1—11 tells about time before Abraham, which scholars call "Primeval History." It describes what the world was like before the patriarchs came.

> **"if you do good, i will accept you. But if you do not do good, sin is ready to attack you."** *Genesis 4:7*

the ground. It is the same ground where your brother's blood fell. Your hands killed him. ¹²You will work the ground. But it will not grow good crops for you anymore. You will wander around on the earth."

¹⁵Then the Lord said to Cain, "No! If anyone kills you, I will punish that person seven times more." Then the Lord put a mark on Cain. It was a warning to anyone who met him not to kill him.

GET CONNECTED

RELATIONSHIPS WITH GOD

Spirit and Truth Have you ever heard someone say, "I like to think that God is. . . ." and then they fill in the blank with whatever they hope God to be? What do you think God is like? It's very tempting to make God fit whatever ideal we hold in our minds. But our image may not be completely true.

God corrected Cain because Cain brought an offering that he thought was pretty good. The problem was that he didn't follow God's standard of what was good. Worshiping God isn't something that we can make up and do however we want. God is true, so we must worship him according to what is true. It is a good thing to think about God. But let his Word guide your thoughts so that you understand who he really is and worship him in the way he says we should.

CAIN'S FAMILY

¹⁶Then Cain went away from the Lord. Cain lived in the land of Nod," east of Eden. ¹⁷Cain had sexual relations with his wife. She became pregnant and gave birth to Enoch. At that time Cain was building a city. He named it after his son Enoch. ¹⁸Enoch had a son named Irad. Irad had a son named Mehujael. Mehujael had a son named Methushael. And Methushael had a son named Lamech.

¹⁹Lamech married two women. One wife was named Adah, and the other was Zillah. ²⁰Adah gave birth to Jabal. He

4:16 **Nod** This name sounds like the Hebrew word for "wander."

LIVIN' IT!

A KILLER COMPARISON
GENESIS 4:1-15

So you and your brother just got your report cards. Like always, his is filled with A's. Yours carries a few more letters of the alphabet. And you feel that burning sensation that makes your eyes squint and your jaw clench tight. Why does everything come easy for him? Why do you have to work so hard just to stay average?

Watch out! The sin of envy is right at the door of your heart, just where it was for Cain when he compared himself with Abel. When we compare ourselves with others, we always seem to come up short. Comparing makes us think others have it better than us, and it makes us bitter and angry. It destroys our relationship with others and with God. We must guard against it by growing thankful hearts. Next time you feel like you're missing out on something you need, stop to pray. Ask God to help you see all the good in your life, and tell God out loud that you appreciate the work he's doing in you.

was the first person to live in tents and raise cattle. ²¹Jabal's brother was Jubal. Jubal was the first person to play the harp and flute. ²²Zillah gave birth to Tubal-Cain. He made tools out of bronze and iron. The sister of Tubal-Cain was Naamah.

²³Lamech said to his wives:

"Adah and Zillah, hear my voice!
 You wives of Lamech, listen to what I say.
I killed a man for wounding me.
I killed a young man for hitting me.
²⁴Cain's killer may be punished 7 times.
 Then Lamech's killer will be punished 77 times."

History Highlights

↗ **5000 B.C.**
Copper is melted and cast in the Near East.

7000 5000 3000 1000 0 1000 NOW

FROM THE BLAST PAST

FROM THE VERY BEGINNING, God wanted his people to offer him the first of whatever they produced, called a tithe. Many cultures tithed, though they gave money to kings, not God. Tablets from the ancient city of Ugarit, on the Mediterranean coast, describe tithing where a king would pay a ten-percent tax for his city to show loyalty to the regional ruler who would offer protection in return. Israelites tithed their money and possessions to God as a sign of loyalty to him and to receive his protection.

CRAFTS

GIFTS OF ♥LOVE

In presenting their gifts to God, Cain "brought some food from the ground. Abel brought the best parts of his best sheep. The Lord accepted Abel and his gift" (Genesis 4:3-4). Cain gave a gift to God, but Abel gave God his best.

God has gifted you uniquely. There is nobody else like you—never has been, never will be! You may have a talent for singing, writing, making arts and crafts, playing sports, helping friends, or listening. When you do your best in the talents God has given you, it is an act of worship to God. Use the ideas below (or your own) to offer a gift of love to God today.

IDEAS

1. Singing: Sing your favorite song out loud for God to hear.

2. Writing: Write a love letter to God. Pour out your heart to him in thanksgiving.

3. Arts and Crafts: Make a creation using your talents to honor God.

4. Sports: Devote time to practicing and improving your skills to be the best team player you can be for God.

5. Helping: Find someone who needs help in your family or neighborhood, and thank God for the opportunity to serve them.

6. Listening: Listen to your friends as they share about their joys and struggles, and pray for them.

3-D

NoAh the FlooD

GENESIS 6:9—9:17

NOAH AND THE GREAT FLOOD

6 This is the family history of Noah. Noah was a good man. He was the most innocent man of his time. He walked with God. ¹⁰Noah had three sons: Shem, Ham and Japheth.

¹¹People on earth did what God said was evil. Violence was everywhere. ¹²And God saw this evil. All people on the earth did only evil. ¹³So God said to Noah,

"People have made the earth full of violence. So I will destroy all people from the earth. ¹⁴Build a boat of cypress wood

bring a flood of water on the earth. I will destroy all living things that live under the sky. This includes everything that has the breath of life. Everything on the earth will die. ¹⁸But I will make an agreement with you. You, your sons, your wife and your sons' wives will all go into the boat. ¹⁹Also, you must bring into

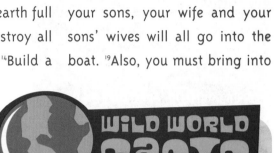

Genesis 6:9—9:17
TORRENTiAL TROUBLE

Noah didn't know what to expect. The people of his day were unfamiliar with rain, not to mention floods. But today we know a lot more about this devastating event. Each year in America alone, more than 100 people die in floods, with damages costing more than 2 billion dollars. Flash floods in the U.S. are the number one weather-related killer, and more than 90% of all natural disasters in the U.S. involve flooding of some kind. Because of technology, though, we are better able to predict when a flood will occur. Each time we hear in the news about a flood that has happened, we can remember God's promise to us that he is in control, and he will never again destroy the whole earth in that way.

BLAST FROM THE PAST

THE BiBLE iSN'T THE ONLY RECORD THAT SAYS the world was created and then almost destroyed by a worldwide flood. We also have ancient Mesopotamian and Egyptian writings that tell the same kind of stories in their own words.

for yourself. Make rooms in it and cover it inside and outside with tar. ¹⁵This is how big I want you to build the boat: 450 feet long, 75 feet wide and 45 feet high. ¹⁶Make an opening around the top of the boat. Make it 18 inches high from the edge of the roof down. Put a door in the side of the boat. Make an upper, middle and lower deck in it. ¹⁷I will

the boat two of every living thing, male and female. Keep them alive with you. ²⁰There will be two of every kind of bird, animal and crawling thing. They will come to you to be kept alive. ²¹Also gather some of every kind of food. Store it on the boat as food for you and the animals."

²²Noah did everything that God commanded him.

LIVIN' IT!

AGAINST THE TIDE
GENESIS 6:9-22

Ever feel like you're the only one who knows what's right and wants to do it? It's not easy going against what everybody else is doing. We all have a desire to fit in and be like everybody else. And let's face it. Obeying God is often not the popular choice.

Noah knew the pain and difficulty of being different. Apart from his own family, he really was the only one in the whole world who wanted to please God. And think of the insults he endured when he began to build a boat in a place where they had never even seen rain. It took Noah 150 years to build the boat (sometimes called an ark). That's 150 years of hearing people say how crazy he was; 150 years of not fitting in, but obeying God.

You know the rest. The world was lost, but Noah and his family were saved. When others are laughing at you because of your faith, the rewards of obedience may not seem so great. But hold on. God's blessings always outshine our darkest moments of testing.

THE FLOOD BEGINS

7 Then the Lord said to Noah, "I have seen that you are the best man among the people of this time. So you and your family go into the boat. ²Take with you seven pairs, each male with its female, of every kind of clean[d] animal. And take one pair, each male with its female, of every kind of unclean animal. ³Take seven pairs of all the birds of the sky, each male with its female. This will allow all these animals to continue living on the earth after the flood. ⁴Seven days from now I will send rain on the earth. It will rain 40 days and 40 nights. I will destroy from the earth every living thing that I made."

⁵Noah did everything that the Lord commanded him.

⁶Noah was 600 years old when the flood came. ⁷He and his wife and his sons and their wives went into the boat. They went in to escape the waters of the flood. ⁸The clean animals, the unclean animals, the birds and everything that crawls on the ground ⁹came to Noah. They went into the boat in groups of two, male and female. This was just as God had commanded Noah. ¹⁰Seven days later the flood started.

¹¹Noah was now 600 years old. The flood started on the seventeenth day of the second month of that year. That day the under-

Bible Critters "COO"OOL BIRDS

As small and seemingly insignificant as they are, **DOVES** have played a major role in Jewish history from the time when Noah used a dove to find dry land, to the sacrifices made for sin, to the time when the Holy Spirit descended from heaven in the form of a dove. White doves, also called Ringneck Dove, Mourning Dove, Capes, Zebra Dove, White Fantail, White Winged Dove, Turtledove, and Australian Crested Dove, are migratory birds—they travel to different locations depending on the season. They eat mainly seeds and nothing else and can suck up water with their beaks instead of scooping it up like most birds. They also make gentle cooing sounds and can travel very long distances. If you want to see a picture of one, visit Gotpetsonline.com.

INCREDIBLE EDIBLES

RAINBOW IN THE CLOUDS

INGREDIENTS

paper plates
whipped topping (in a can)
Froot Loops® cereal

HERE'S THE SCOOP:

Noah followed God's laws and talked with him, even when everyone else sinned and did whatever they wanted. Have you ever been in a place where it seemed you were the only one doing what was right? Can you imagine how hard it was for Noah to build a boat in a desert while the people around him laughed at him?

Noah obeyed God, and God saved Noah and his family from the flood. After the flood, God talked to Noah again. He made a promise to Noah: "When I bring clouds over the earth, a rainbow appears in the clouds. Then I will remember my agreement. It is between me and you and every living thing. Floodwaters will never again destroy all life on the earth" (Genesis 9:14-15).

When you feel all alone because you are doing the right thing, remember the story of Noah and the promise God gave him after the flood.

TO MAKE A RAINBOW

1. Squirt out "clouds" of whipped cream onto a paper plate.

2. Next, sprinkle Froot Loop cereal into the whipped cream, or arrange the colored loops into a rainbow shape in the "clouds."

3. Grab a spoon, and enjoy your tasty rainbow treat!

4. Add sugar and cinnamon to taste.

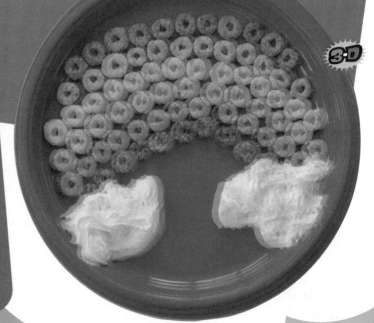

3-D

GENESIS 7:12-24

SOMETHING STINKS
GENESIS 7:16

Have you ever wondered how Noah felt when he heard the door of the ark close behind him? He knew his world was about to change forever. He knew that he was locked in a boat with some family and a whole lot of animals, and it probably wasn't going to be fun.

Sometimes obeying God may make you feel like you're getting on your own ark. You don't know where you are going. And, at times, the circumstances around you stink. But remember Noah and God when life gets you down. Though Noah didn't know what was going to happen, God did. It's not important for us to plan our lives just how we think they should be. Instead, we just obey God and trust him to make life turn out the way he wants it to. He promises to use every single moment for good purposes in our lives. Even in the stink, look to the sky. God's rainbow of promise is shining over you the whole time.

ground springs split open. And the clouds in the sky poured out rain. [12]The rain fell on the earth for 40 days and 40 nights.

[13]On that same day Noah and his wife, his sons Shem, Ham and Japheth and their wives went into the boat. [14]They had every kind of wild animal and tame animal. There was every kind of animal that crawls on the earth. Every kind of bird was there. [15]They all came to Noah in the boat in groups of two. There was every creature that had the breath of life. [16]One male and one female of every living thing came. It was just as God had commanded Noah. Then the Lord closed the door behind them.

[17]Water flooded the earth for 40 days. As the water rose, it lifted the boat off the ground. [18]The water continued to rise, and the boat floated on the water above the earth. [19]The water rose so much that even the highest mountains under the sky were covered by it. [20]The water continued to rise until it was more than 20 feet above the mountains.

[21]All living things that moved on the earth died. This included all the birds, tame animals, wild animals and creatures that swarm on the earth. And all human beings died. [22]So everything on dry land died. This means everything that had the breath of life in its nose. [23]So God destroyed from the earth every living thing that was on the land. This was every man, animal, crawling thing and bird of the sky. All that was left was Noah and what was with him in the boat. [24]And the

REAL SUPER HEROES

NOAH

Everyone around him had forgotten about God and was sinning in some really bad ways. But not Noah. He remembered God's goodness, and he continued to obey him, even though it wasn't a popular thing to do. When God told him to build a boat—even though it had never rained before—he obeyed. Everyone around him made fun of him through the many years it took to build it. But no one laughed when the rains came. Noah and his family were safe in the ark, and everyone else drowned in the flood.

People may make fun of you for obeying God, too. But that's okay, because following God is right and best. Just like Noah, you will be safe and rewarded in the end.

BLAST FROM THE PAST

THOUSANDS OF SMELLY ANIMALS . . . dark rooms . . . the sound of rain. It's amazing that Noah didn't go crazy! According to the dates given in the Bible, he and his family were in the ark for 371 days. That's over a year!

waters continued to cover the earth for 150 days.

THE FLOOD ENDS

8 But God remembered Noah and all the wild animals and tame animals with him in the boat. God made a wind blow over the earth. And the water went down. ²The underground springs stopped flowing. And the clouds in the sky stopped pouring down rain. ³⁻⁴The water that covered the earth began to go down. After 150 days the water had gone down so much that the boat touched land again. It came to rest on one of the mountains of Ararat.ⁿ This was on the seventeenth day of the seventh month. ⁵The water continued to go down. By the first day of the tenth month the tops of the mountains could be seen.

⁶Forty days later Noah opened the window he had made in the boat. ⁷He sent out a raven. It flew here and there until the water had dried up from the earth. ⁸Then Noah sent out a dove. This was to find out if the water had dried up from the ground. ⁹The dove could not find a place to land because water still covered the earth. So it came back to the boat. Noah reached out his hand and took the bird. And he brought it back into the boat.

¹⁰After seven days Noah again sent out the dove from the boat. ¹¹And that evening it came back to him with a fresh olive leaf in its mouth. Then Noah knew that the ground was almost dry. ¹²Seven days later he sent the dove out again. But this time it did not come back.

¹³Noah was now 601 years old. It was the first day of the first month of that year. The water was dried up from the land. Noah removed the covering of the boat and saw that

GET CONNECTED

RELATIONSHIPS WITH GOD

Promise Keepers We've heard the story so many times we often take it for granted. God told Noah to build a big boat (sometimes called an ark), and he did it. The rains fell. People died. Noah was saved. End of story. But have you ever thought how hard it must have been for Noah to believe God in the first place? Without having ever seen rain as we know it, Noah worked for years because he trusted God to keep his word.

Noah could trust God because he has a perfect record when it comes to promises. He has never failed to do what he says. What about you? Are you a person of your word? When you say you will do something, do you follow through? As children of God, we need to speak the truth and follow up what we say with actions. Ask God to help you only commit to what he has asked you to do, and then for strength to complete it.

⭐ **8:3-4 Ararat** The ancient land of Urartu, an area in Eastern Turkey.

GENESIS 8:14-22

the land was dry. ¹⁴By the twenty-seventh day of the second month the land was completely dry.

¹⁵Then God said to Noah, ¹⁶"You and your wife, your sons and their wives should go out of the boat. ¹⁷Bring every animal out of the boat with you—the birds, animals and everything that crawls on the earth. Let them have many young ones and let them grow in number."

¹⁸So Noah went out with his sons, his wife and his sons' wives. ¹⁹Every animal, everything that crawls on the earth and every bird went out of the boat. They left by families.

²⁰Then Noah built an altar to the Lord. Noah took some of all the clean^d birds and animals. And he burned them on the altar as offerings to God. ²¹The Lord was pleased with these sacrifices. He said to himself, "I will never again curse the ground because of human beings. Their thoughts are evil even when they are young. But I will never again destroy every living thing on the earth as I did this time.
²²"As long as the earth continues, there will be

> planting and
> harvest.

Cold and hot,

summer and winter,
day and night
will not stop."

THE NEW BEGINNING

9 Then God blessed Noah and his sons. He said to them, "Have many children. Grow in number and fill the earth. ²Every animal on earth and every bird in the sky will respect and fear you. So will every animal that crawls on the ground and every fish in the sea respect and fear you. I have given them to you.

³"Everything that moves, everything that is alive, is yours for food. Earlier I gave you the green plants. And now I give you everything for food. ⁴But you must not eat meat that still has blood in it, because blood gives life. ⁵I will demand your blood for your lives. That is, I will demand the life of any animal that kills a person. And I will demand the life of anyone who takes another person's life.

⁶"Whoever kills a human being
    will be killed by a human
    being.
This is because God made humans
    in his own image.

⁷"Noah, I want you and your family to have many children. Grow in number on the earth and become many."

⁸Then God said to Noah and his sons, ⁹"Now I am making my agreement with you and your people who will live after you. ¹⁰And I also make it with every living thing that is with you. It is with the birds, the tame animals and the wild animals. It is with all that came out of the boat with you. I make my agreement with every living thing on earth. ¹¹I make this agreement with you: I will never again destroy all living things by floodwaters. A flood will never again destroy the earth."

¹²And God said, "I am making an agreement between me and you and every living creature that is with you. It will continue from now on. This is the sign: ¹³I am putting my rainbow in the clouds. It is the sign of the agreement between me and the earth. ¹⁴When I bring clouds over the earth, a rainbow appears in the clouds. ¹⁵Then I will remember my agreement. It is between me and you and every living thing. Floodwaters will never again destroy all life on the earth. ¹⁶When the rainbow appears in the clouds, I will see it. Then I will remember the agreement that continues forever. It is between me and every living thing on the earth."

¹⁷So God said to Noah, "That rainbow is a sign. It is the sign of the agreement that I made with all living things on earth."

GET CONNECTED

RELATIONSHIPS WITH FAMILY

Don't Miss the Boat It's hard to imagine what Noah was thinking all those years he had to endure insults, even while he was obeying God. But as hard as it was for Noah, think about his three sons, Shem, Ham, and Japheth!

When the culture around you is used to making fun of authority and disrespecting parents, it's easy to start to think like them. Isn't it normal for kids to turn into teens and think their parents aren't cool anymore? While it may seem normal for the world, it is not acceptable to God. He wants us to respect our parents, even if they have a weird job or a quirky personality. We respect them because they are God's gift of protection and love for us.

When you're tempted to second-guess your parents, remember Noah's sons. Because they stood by their dad, they got to get in the boat and be saved. God keeps us safe, too, when we honor our parents.

God's Promise to Abraham
GENESIS 15:1-21

GOD'S AGREEMENT WITH ABRAM

15 After these things happened, the Lord spoke his word to Abram in a vision. God said, "Abram, don't be afraid. I will defend you. And I will give you a great reward."

²But Abram said, "Lord God, what can you give me? I have no son. So my slave Eliezer from Damascus will get everything I own after I die." ³Abram said, "Look, you have given me no son. So a slave born in my house will inherit everything I have."

⁴Then the Lord spoke his word to Abram. He said, "That slave will not be the one to inherit what you have. You will have a son of your own. And your son will inherit what you have."

⁵Then God led Abram outside. God said, "Look at the sky. There are so many stars you cannot count them. And your descendants[d] will be too many to count."

⁶Abram believed the Lord. And the Lord accepted Abram's faith, and that faith made him right with God.

⁷God said to Abram, "I am the Lord who led you out of Ur of Babylonia. I did that so I could give you this land to own."

⁸But Abram said, "Lord God, how can I be sure that I will own this land?"

GET CONNECTED

RELATIONSHIPS WITH GOD

Amazing Grace Have you ever wondered what was so special about Abraham? What caused God to notice him, to make him the father of God's chosen people? Was he spectacular in some way?

If he was, the Bible doesn't mention it. The only remarkable thing about Abraham was that he believed God and trusted him to do what he said. God's selection was what made him special.

Do you ever wonder about yourself? Why do you get to have a relationship with your Creator? Just like Abraham, the answer lies in God, not you. He chose you because he loved you before you were ever made. We can't understand why, but when we understand the truth of God's love, we are forever grateful for his grace and mercy toward us.

REAL SUPER HEROES

ABRAM/ABRAHAM

Abraham was amazing, but it wasn't because of his looks or his job. He didn't come from an impressive or wealthy family. In fact, there was nothing on the outside that would make him stand out in the crowd. Abraham did have an encounter with God—and that was special. But beyond even that, the most incredible fact about Abraham was that he believed God.

Doesn't sound like that big of a deal? It is. Ever since Adam and Eve doubted God's goodness in the garden, people have had a hard time believing God is who he says he is and will do what he says he will do. But Abraham never stopped believing God. God accepted Abraham's faith, and that faith made him right with God. All Abraham did was trust God, and God made him the father of his chosen people, with literally millions of descendants to follow him.

[9]The Lord said to Abram, "Bring me a three-year-old cow, a three-year-old goat and a three-year-old male sheep. Also bring me a dove and a young pigeon."

[10]Abram brought them all to God. Then Abram killed the animals and cut each of them into two pieces. He laid each half opposite the other half. But he did not cut the birds in half.

[11]Later, large birds flew down to eat the animals. But Abram chased them away.

[12]As the sun was going down, Abram fell into a deep sleep. While he was asleep, a very terrible darkness came. [13]Then the Lord said to Abram, "You can be sure that your descendants will be strangers and travel in a land they

History Highlights

↗ **4000–3000 B.C.**
Copper-Stone Age

7000 5000 3000 1000 0 1000 NOW

GAMES & QUIZZES

UNSCRAMBLE THESE KEY WORDS THAT HELPED ABRAHAM UNDERSTAND GOD'S AGREEMENT WITH HIM.

1. nvisoi _____
2. nso _____
3. intirhe _____
4. ysk _____
5. rasst _____
6. vedbeiel _____
7. escdantdens _____
8. rold _____
9. malsani _____
10. eeagrntme _____

Answers: 1. vision; 2. son; 3. inherit; 4. sky; 5. stars; 6. believed; 7. descendants; 8. Lord; 9. animals; 10. agreement

WILD WORLD FACTS

Genesis 15:1-20
BREAKING IT DOWN

God promised Abraham that he would have descendants that outnumbered the sands on the seashore. So how much sand is there? And how is it formed? In general, sand is just a specific type of soil that can be made when rocks are frozen and then thawed, breaking them up into small pieces. Wave action, ground movement (earthquakes), and other water on rocks all help the process of breaking the earth's soil into the tiny particles we know as sand.

Depending on the location, sand can have many different rock particles in it. Sand at the beach will include crushed shells, coral, and limestone. Desert sand contains quartz, along with whatever kind of soils are present in the surrounding mountains. Desert sand dunes form as the rocks from the mountains are eroded (broken down), and the dunes move over the course of time by the wind.

As far as how much sand exists, we really don't know. The number of grains is always increasing because erosion is always taking place. But that was God's point, after all. God's blessing would be too great to count. Thousands of years after God's promise to Abraham, we see that he was right.

[NPS.gov]

LIVIN' IT!

WHY ME?
GENESIS 15:1-20

There's that gentle nudge. That quiet prod from the Holy Spirit. He wants you to go to that kid over there and tell him about Jesus. "Why me?" you ask. "Why do you think I should be the one?"

Abram probably thought the same thing when God called him up out of his homeland to go to a new place he had never been. What was so special about Abram that he should be the father of God's chosen people?

On one hand, there isn't anything special about any of us. We are all sinners who constantly make bad choices and don't know what we're doing. But on the other hand, we have an incredible God who loves us, and who made each one of us distinctly different from others. We are sinful, hopeless people that God chooses to renew and restore and use in the building of his kingdom. We don't know why he chooses to love us, but he does—and that makes us very special. So when he calls us to serve him, don't wonder, *Why me?* Instead, remember that God made you exactly the way he did so that you would be able to do the work he has planned for you.

---

don't own. The people there will make them slaves. And they will do cruel things to them for 400 years. [14]But I will punish the nation where they are slaves. Then your descendants will leave that land, taking great wealth with them. [15]Abram, you will live to be very old. You will die in peace and will be buried. [16]After your great-great-grandchildren are born, your people will come to this land again. It will take that long, because the Amorites are not yet evil enough to punish."

[17]The sun went down, and it was very dark. Suddenly a smoking firepot and a blazing torch passed between the halves of the dead animals." [18]So on that day the Lord made an agreement with Abram. The Lord said, "I will give this land to your descendants. I will give them the land between the river of Egypt and the great river Euphrates. [19]This is the land of the Kenites, Kenizzites, Kadmonites, [20]Hittites, Perizzites, Rephaites,[d] [21]Amorites, Canaanites, Girgashites and Jebusites."

 15:17 **passed . . . animals** This showed that God sealed the agreement between himself and Abram.

God's Promise Fulfilled
GENESIS 16:1—18:15; 21:1-4

HAGAR AND ISHMAEL

16 Sarai, Abram's wife, had no children. She had a slave girl from Egypt named Hagar. ²Sarai said to Abram, "Look, the Lord has not allowed me to have children. So have sexual relations with my slave girl. If she has a child, maybe I can have my own family through her."

Abram did what Sarai said. ³This was after Abram lived ten years in Canaan. And Sarai gave Hagar to her husband

Abram. (Hagar was her slave girl from Egypt.)

⁴Abram had sexual relations with Hagar, and she became pregnant. When Hagar learned she was pregnant, she began to treat her mistress Sarai badly. ⁵Then Sarai said to Abram, "This is your fault. I gave my slave girl to you. And when she became pregnant, she began to

treat me badly. Let the Lord decide who is right—you or me."

⁶But Abram said to Sarai, "You are Hagar's mistress. Do anything you want to her." Then Sarai was hard on Hagar, and Hagar ran away.

⁷The angel of the Lord found Hagar beside a spring of water in the desert. The spring was by the road to Shur. ⁸The angel said, "Hagar, you are Sarai's slave girl. Where have you come from? Where are you going?"

> ## "The angel of the Lord also said, 'i will give you so many descendants they cannot be counted.'"
> *Genesis 16:10*

Hagar answered, "I am running from my mistress Sarai."

⁹The angel of the Lord said to her, "Go home to your mistress and obey her." ¹⁰The angel of the Lord also said, "I will give you so many descendants[d] they cannot be counted."

¹¹The angel also said to her,

"You are now pregnant,
   and you will have a son.

You will name him Ishmael,[n]
   because the Lord has heard
      your cries.
¹²Ishmael will be like a wild
   donkey.
   He will be against everyone.
   And everyone will be against
      him.
   He will attack all his brothers."

¹³The slave girl gave a name to the Lord who spoke to her. She said to him, "You are 'God who sees me.'" This is because she said to herself, "Have I really seen God who sees me?" ¹⁴So the well there was called Beer Lahai Roi.[n] It is between Kadesh and Bered.

¹⁵Hagar gave birth to a son for Abram. And Abram

BIBLE BASICS

WHAT'S UP WITH CIRCUMCISION?

It might seem strange for the Bible to talk about circumcision—a surgery the Israelites performed on 8-day-old boys. But God commanded that all Israelites be circumcised as a sign that they were a part of his agreement or covenant. It showed that they were different and set apart from the other nations around them. In the New Testament, God requires that our hearts be circumcised. In other words, God removes the sin in our hearts so that we can be set apart for him.

16:11 **Ishmael** The Hebrew words for "Ishmael" and "has heard" sound similar.   16:14 **Beer Lahai Roi** This means "the well of the Living One who sees me."

named him Ishmael. [16]Abram was 86 years old when Hagar gave birth to Ishmael.

PROOF OF THE AGREEMENT

17 When Abram was 99 years old, the Lord appeared to him. The Lord said, "I am God All-Powerful. Obey me and do what is right. [2]I will make an agreement between us. I will make you the ancestor of many people."

[3]Then Abram bowed facedown on the ground. God said to him, [4]"I am making my agreement with you: I will make you the father of many nations. [5]I am changing your name from Abram" to Abraham." This is because I am making you a father of many nations. [6]I will give you many descendants.[d] New nations will be born from you. Kings will come from you. [7]And I will make an agreement between me and you and all your descendants from now on: I will be your God and the God of all your descendants. [8]You live in the land of Canaan now as a stranger. But I will give you and your descendants all this land forever. And I will be the God

of your descendants."

[9]Then God said to Abraham, "You and your descendants must keep this agreement from now on. [10]This is my agreement with you and all your descendants: Every male among you must be circumcised.[d] You must obey this agreement. [11]Cut away the foreskin to show that you follow the agreement between me and you. [12]From now on when a baby boy is eight days old, you will circumcise him. This includes any boy born among your people or any who is your slave. (He would not be one of your descendants.) [13]So circumcise every baby boy. Circumcise him

whether he is born in your family or bought as a slave. Your bodies will be marked. This will show that you are part of my agreement that lasts forever. [14]Any male who is not circumcised will be separated from his people. He has broken my agreement."

ISAAC—THE PROMISED SON

[15]God said to Abraham, "I will change the name of Sarai," your wife. Her new name will be Sarah." [16]I will bless her. I will give her a son, and you will be the father. She will be the mother of many nations. Kings of nations will come from her."

[17]Abraham bowed facedown on the ground and laughed. He said to himself, "Can a man have a child

---

GET CONNECTED

RELATIONSHIPS WITH GOD

For Laughing Out Loud Picture your great grandmother. Now picture her having a baby in her old age. Does the thought make you laugh? It made Sarah laugh out loud. She was 90 years old when the Lord told her that he was going to give her a son, and that her descendants would become so great they would outnumber the grains of sand along the sea.

Sarah learned—and we should, too—that nothing is impossible for God. Think about it. If he created everything that exists, he can control it, too. So what seems impossible to you? Do you have a friend who seems too far from God to ever become a Christian? Do you want your parents to get along better? Nothing is too hard for God. Just pray and trust him to do what is right. He promises to take care of you.

> **"i am God All-Powerful. Obey me and do what is right."**
> *Genesis 17:1*

17:5 **Abram** This name means "honored father." 17:5 **Abraham** The end of the Hebrew word for "Abraham" sounds like the beginning of the Hebrew word for "many." 17:15 **Sarai** An Aramaic name meaning "princess." 17:15 **Sarah** A Hebrew name meaning "princess."

INCREDIBLE EDIBLES

SARAH'S BREAD

INGREDIENTS

1 cup salt
1 cup flour
1 tablespoon vegetable oil
water
food coloring

HERE'S THE SCOOP:

When Abraham met his guests, he immediately offered them bread to eat and water to wash their feet. Sarah was in the kitchen. Abraham told her to use the best flour and make bread. Making bread or a meal for guests was common in the Bible. Sharing a meal with someone signifies the desire to spend time with them and make them comfortable while they are with you.

Follow the recipe below to make a different kind of dough—playdough! Invite a friend to come over and make the playdough with you, then play with it together, sharing and enjoying each other's company.

DOUGH RECIPE

1. Mix the salt and flour together.

2. Add the oil, and mix well.

3. Mix your favorite color of food coloring with the water.

4. Slowly add the colored water a little at a time, until the dough is the right texture.

when he is 100 years old? Can Sarah give birth to a child when she is 90?" [18]Then Abraham said to God, "Please let Ishmael be the son you promised."

LIVIN' IT!

THE HAGAR BROUHAHA
GENESIS 16:1-15

She knew God had promised her a son. But now she was getting pretty old. What should she do? Sarah did what we all are often guilty of doing—she took matters into her own hands. She figured God must need a little help getting his plan to come together. But what she ended up doing cost her a friendship, divided her marriage, and messed up the lives of those around her.

For some reason, we often think we know more than God. We figure we can fix the broken relationships around us by forcing others to act the way we want them to act. But it doesn't work. Like Sarah, we have forgotten that God alone is in control. When we need help or direction, the very first thing we need to do is pray. Talk to God about it. Ask him what he would like us to do. Then search his Word for answers. Wait for God to show up in your life. He always will— at just the right time, to finish his work in you.

[19]God said, "No. Sarah your wife will have a son, and you will name him Isaac." I will make my agreement with him. It will be an agreement that continues forever with all his descendants. [d]

[20]"You asked me about Ishmael, and I heard you. I will bless him. I will give him many descendants. And I will cause their numbers to grow very greatly. He will be the father of 12 great leaders. I will make him into a great nation. [21]But I will make my agreement with Isaac. He is the son whom Sarah will have at this same time next year." [22]After God finished talking with Abraham, God rose and left him.

[23]Then Abraham gathered Ishmael and all the males born in his camp. He also gathered the slaves he had bought. So that day Abraham circumcised every man and boy in his camp. This was what God had told him to do. [24]Abraham

was 99 years old when he was circumcised. [25]And Ishmael, his son, was 13 years old when he was circumcised. [26]Abraham and his son were circumcised on that same day. [27]Also on that day all the men in Abraham's camp were circumcised. This included all those born in his camp and all the slaves he had bought from other nations.

THE THREE VISITORS

18 Later, the Lord again appeared to Abraham near the great trees of Mamre. At that time Abraham was sitting at the door of his tent. It was during the hottest part of the day. [2]He looked up and saw three men standing near him. When Abraham saw them, he ran from his tent to meet them. He bowed facedown on the ground before them. [3]Abraham said, "Sir, if you think well of me, please stay awhile with me, your servant. [4]I will

 17:19 Isaac The Hebrew words for "he laughed" (vs. 17) and "Isaac" sound the same.

REAL SUPER HEROES

SARAH

It probably wasn't easy being married to Abraham. Life was all well and good until he said he had spoken with this God they had not known before. Now they had to pack up everything and move to some strange foreign land. Later, some strangers would tell her and her husband that, after almost a century of being childless, her old body would bear a son. Later still, after the promise came true, she'd have to watch her husband walk off with her precious son to obey a command that could end his life.

Sarah's life wasn't easy, but it was an adventure. Through the trials, she learned to trust Abraham's God who had called them to a better place. Just as Abraham believed, so did Sarah. Together they became the parents of the Jewish race, and received the incredible blessing that comes from believing—a real relationship with God.

BLAST FROM THE PAST

WAS SARAH OUT OF HER MIND? Why would she want her husband to have a baby with another woman? It was actually something her culture said she had to do. Ancient marriage contracts found in the city of Nuzi, dating from the middle of the 2nd millennium B.C., said that if the wife was unable to have a boy baby, then she had to provide one through a female servant.

bring some water so all of you can wash your feet. You may rest under the tree. [5]I will get some bread for you, so you can regain your strength. Then you may continue your journey."

The three men said, "That is fine. Do as you said."

[6]Abraham hurried to the tent where Sarah was. He said to her, "Hurry, prepare 20 quarts of fine flour. Make it into loaves of bread." [7]Then Abraham ran to his cattle. He took one of his best calves and gave it to a servant. The servant hurried to kill the calf and to prepare it for food. [8]Abraham gave the three men the calf that had been cooked. He also gave them milk curds and milk. While the three men ate, he stood under the tree near them.

[9]The men asked Abraham, "Where is your wife Sarah?"

"There, in the tent," said Abraham.

[10]Then the Lord said, "I will certainly return to you about this time a year from now. At that time your wife Sarah will have a son."

Sarah was listening at the entrance of the tent which was behind him. [11]Abraham and Sarah were very old. Sarah was past the age when women normally have children. [12]So she laughed to herself, "My husband and I are too old to have a baby."

[13]Then the Lord said to Abraham, "Why did Sarah laugh? Why did she say, 'I am too old to have a baby'? [14]Is anything too hard for the Lord? No! I will return to you at the right time a year from now. And Sarah will have a son."

[15]Sarah was afraid. So she lied and said, "I didn't laugh."

• • •

A BABY FOR SARAH

21 The Lord cared for Sarah as he had said. He did for her what he had promised. [2]Sarah became pregnant. And she gave birth to a son for Abraham in his old age. Everything happened at the time God had said it would. [3]Abraham named his son Isaac. Sarah gave birth to this son of Abraham. [4]Abraham circumcised[d] Isaac when he was eight days old as God had commanded.

GET CONNECTED

RELATIONSHIPS WITH GOD

Best Friends Isn't it cool how the Lord and Abraham just sat and talked! God appeared as a man and had conversations—even ate food at one point—with Abraham and treated him as a close friend.

Do you ever wish that God still worked the same way today? No doubt, it is harder to have a deep friendship with someone you can't see. But God has asked us to trust him. We don't have to see a face, because the Bible shows us his heart. As we believe what he says, we realize that he is a part of every moment of our day. We don't have to give formal prayers all the time. We can talk to him just like we would our best friend. Let him know what you're thinking. What you need. And listen in your heart for him to answer. Like Abraham, you'll discover that you have the God of creation as your very best friend.

Abraham's
Test with Isaac
GENESIS 22:1-19

GOD TESTS ABRAHAM

22 After these things God tested Abraham's faith. God said to him, "Abraham!"

And he answered, "Here I am."

²Then God said, "Take your only son, Isaac, the son you love. Go to the land of Moriah. There kill him and offer him as a whole burnt offering. Do this on one of the mountains there. I will tell you which one."

³Early in the morning Abraham got up and saddled his donkey. He took Isaac and two servants with him. He cut the wood for the sacrifice. Then they went to the place God had told them to go. ⁴On the third day Abraham looked up and saw the place in the distance. ⁵He said to his servants, "Stay here with the donkey. My son and I will go over there and worship. Then we will come back to you."

⁶Abraham took the wood for the sacrifice and gave it to his son to carry. Abraham took the knife and the fire. So Abraham and his son went on together.

⁷Isaac said to his father Abraham, "Father!"

Abraham answered, "Yes, my son."

Isaac said, "We have the fire and the wood. But where is the lamb we will burn as a sacrifice?"

⁸Abraham answered, "God will give us the lamb for the sacrifice, my son."

So Abraham and his son went on together. ⁹They came to the place God had told him about. There, Abraham built an altar. He laid the wood on it. Then he tied up his son Isaac. And he laid Isaac on the wood on the altar. ¹⁰Then Abraham took his knife and was about to kill his son.

¹¹But the angel of the Lord called to him from heaven. The angel said, "Abraham! Abraham!"

Abraham answered, "Yes."

LIVIN' IT!

ON THE ALTAR
GENESIS 22:1-19

Imagine how Isaac must have felt. He had offered sacrifices with his father before. He knew the routine. But this time was different. He was building the altar, but where was the lamb to sacrifice? As Abraham pulled out the rope and bound him to the wood, Isaac knew.

Imagine, now, the joy Isaac must have felt when God told Abraham to stop. When they looked around and saw the ram to sacrifice in Isaac's place. Both father and son are united, and life goes on.

We, too, get to experience the pain and joy that Isaac felt. Like Isaac, we have been bound by sin. We deserved death to pay the price for our disobedience. But instead, God provided a better sacrifice—his own Son. Jesus got on an altar (the cross) for us, and because he did, we are united with our heavenly Father. Because Jesus gave his life for us, we can have life that goes on forever.

BiBLE BaSiCS

WHAT IS FORGIVENESS?

Forgiveness is a decision to no longer hold another person guilty or want to punish them for what they did wrong. In Old Testament times, the Israelites had to offer animal sacrifices to pay for their sins and earn God's forgiveness. Now, because Jesus has paid the full price for our sins on the cross, we can receive God's forgiveness simply by asking for it and turning from our sin. Likewise, we need to be ready to forgive others who wrong us.

History Highlights

➚ **3300 B.C.**
Domestication of the Horse

7000 5000 3000 1000 0 1000 NOW

[12]The angel said, "Don't kill your son or hurt him in any way. Now I can see that you respect God. I see that you have not kept your son, your only son, from me."

[13]Then Abraham looked up and saw a male sheep. Its horns were caught in a bush. So Abraham went and took the sheep and killed it. He offered it as a whole burnt offering to God. Abraham's son was saved. [14]So Abraham named that place The Lord Gives. Even today people say, "On the mountain of the Lord it will be given."

[15]The angel of the Lord called to Abraham from heaven a second time. [16]The angel said, "The Lord says, 'You did not keep back your son, your only son, from me. Because you did this, I make you this promise by my own name: [17]I will surely bless you and give you many descendants.[d] They will be as many as the stars in the sky and the sand on the seashore. And they will capture the cities of their enemies. [18]Through your descendants all the nations on the earth will be blessed. This is because you obeyed me.'"

[19]Then Abraham returned to his servants. They all traveled back to Beersheba, and Abraham stayed there.

GET CONNECTED

RELATIONSHIPS WITH GOD

A Tough Choice How could Abraham do the unthinkable—kill his only son—to obey God? Why would God even ask him to do such a thing? He was friends with God. He understood enough about God's character to trust him, even when the situation looked hopeless. He knew God would be faithful to his promise, even if it meant giving up what he cared about the most—his son Isaac.

How strong is your desire for God? Is there anything in your life that you would not be willing to give up if God asked it of you? It is very tempting to grow attached to the people and things of this world. But God is all we really need. Ask him to create a stronger desire for him alone in your heart, and to show you areas in your life where you need to let go of the things in this world and cling to your relationship with God.

REAL SUPER HEROES

ISAAC

Isaac had to know that, from day one, he was something special. Sure, there was Ishmael, his half brother born to Hagar. But Isaac was the child of promise, the miracle baby whom God said he would use to father a nation for himself. He would receive the greater share of his father's inheritance because God said so.

He learned faith from his father. He was so certain of God's promise that he was willing to let his father tie his hands and feet and lay him on the altar in obedience to God's command. Just like his dad, Isaac trusted God to make good on his promise, even if it meant God having to resurrect him from the dead.

But he wasn't perfect, either. Out of fear, he lied to his neighbors about his wife Rebekah, telling them that she was his sister (the same sin his dad had committed). Because of our fallen nature, sometimes our faith wavers. God, however, is always faithful. His blessing remained on Isaac and passed down on through the generations after him. God was paving the way for the promised Messiah.

CLOSE CALL

God had asked the unthinkable, but Abraham was ready to obey. Fill in this crossword puzzle to find out the facts of this amazing story from Genesis 22.

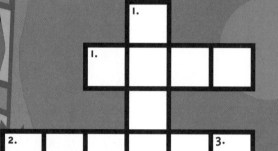

ACROSS:

1. What Isaac hoped his dad planned to sacrifice.
2. God did this to Abraham's faith.
3. What God told Abraham to do to his son.
4. The practice of offering something to God.
5. The father known for his great faith.

DOWN:

1. What it takes to believe and trust God.
2. The one who told Abraham to stop.
3. How they carried the wood.
4. What Isaac was to Abraham.
5. The name of Abraham's only son.

ANSWER KEY: ACROSS: 1. lamb; 2. tested; 3. kill; 4. sacrifice; 5. Abraham • DOWN: 1. faith; 2. angel; 3. donkey; 4. son; 5. Isaac.

Jacob & Esau, Isaac's Sons

GENESIS 25:1-34; 27:1-45

ABRAHAM'S FAMILY

25 Abraham married again. His new wife was Keturah. ²She gave birth to Zimran, Jokshan, Medan, Midian, Ishbak and Shuah. ³Jokshan was the father of Sheba and Dedan. Dedan's descendants*d* were the people of Assyria, Letush and Leum. ⁴The sons of Midian were Ephah, Epher, Hanoch, Abida and Eldaah. All these were descendants of Keturah. ⁵Abraham left everything he owned to Isaac. ⁶But before Abraham died, he did give gifts to the sons of his other wives. Abraham sent them to the East to be away from Isaac.

⁷Abraham lived to be 175 years old. ⁸He breathed his last breath and died at an old age. He had lived a long and satisfying life. ⁹His sons Isaac and Ishmael buried him in the cave of Machpelah. This cave is in the field of Ephron east of Mamre. Ephron was the son of Zohar the Hittite. ¹⁰This is the same field that Abraham had bought from the Hittites. Abraham was buried there with his wife Sarah. ¹¹After Abraham died, God blessed his son Isaac. Isaac was now living at Beer Lahai Roi.

¹²This is the family history of Ishmael, Abraham's son. (Hagar, Sarah's Egyptian servant, was Ishmael's mother.) ¹³These are the names of Ishmael's sons in the order they were born. The first son was Nebaioth. Then came Kedar, Adbeel, Mibsam, ¹⁴Mishma, Dumah, Massa, ¹⁵Hadad, Tema, Jetur, Naphish and Kedemah. ¹⁶These were Ishmael's sons. And these are the names of the tribal leaders. They are listed according to their settlements and camps. ¹⁷Ishmael lived 137 years.

DIG THIS!

Mount Seir is another name for Edom. The Edomites descended from Esau and lived in the mountains south and east of the Dead Sea. The King's Highway ran through the country of Edom, which meant that Israel had to interact with Edomites from time to time, even though they weren't friendly to one another. God did warn the Israelites, though, to respect the Edomites because of their connection to Esau.

GET CONNECTED

RELATIONSHIPS WITH FAMILY

A Sneaky Secret It seems a little strange for a Bible story. A mother and son, Rebecca and Jacob, work together to trick Isaac, the husband and father. God had chosen to give his blessing to Jacob, and he accomplished his will through the secret plans of the mother.

What this story doesn't mean is that you should try to trick your parents. What it does mean is that you should listen to them, just like Jacob listened to his mom. Even if you don't understand why they want you to do what they ask, you should still obey (as long as it doesn't mean disobeying God). In Jacob's case, obedience meant receiving an incredible inheritance. Likewise, God promises to bring great blessings to kids who obey their parents.

INCREDIBLE EDIBLES

JACOB'S SOUP

INGREDIENTS

1 can corn
1 can sliced carrots
1 can potatoes
2 cans chicken broth
1 can peas or green beans

HERE'S THE SCOOP:

When Esau came home from working in the fields, he was very hungry. He was so hungry, in fact, that he let his appetite control his thinking. Esau allowed Jacob to talk him out of his rights as the firstborn son—all for a bowl of vegetable soup!

Have you ever done something you knew was wrong, but the immediate reward was so tempting, you did it anyway? Maybe you've watched a movie or played a video game you know your parents wouldn't approve, but you watched or played it anyway. Don't let Satan turn your eyes away from God in a moment of temptation.

After you've finished making your vegetable soup, bring your family together for a great family meal and time of discussion. Talk about some weaknesses you have that sometimes tempt you to give up something God has given you. Help each other learn how to resist temptation, and ask for God's help.

RECIPE

Open the cans. Pour all the ingredients into a crockpot. Ask your mom to cook the soup on high for 2-3 hours or low for 4-6 hours. Enjoy your hot soup together at dinner time!

BLAST FROM THE PAST

PEOPLE DID NOT EVOLVE from one life form to another (as evolutionists believe). But science and technology did change and grow. Genesis talks a lot about how the early people groups changed from being only shepherds and farmers to becoming great builders, as well.

Then he breathed his last breath and died. [18]Ishmael's descendants lived from Havilah to Shur. This is east of Egypt stretching toward Assyria. Ishmael's descendants often attacked the descendants of his brothers.

ISAAC'S FAMILY

[19]This is the family history of Isaac. Abraham had a son named Isaac. [20]When Isaac was 40 years old, he married Rebekah. Rebekah was from Northwest Mesopotamia. She was Bethuel's daughter and the sister of Laban the Aramean. [21]Isaac's wife could not have children. So Isaac prayed to the Lord for her. The Lord heard Isaac's prayer, and Rebekah became pregnant.

[22]While she was pregnant, the babies struggled inside her. She asked, "Why is this happening to me?" Then she went to get an answer from the Lord.

[23]The Lord said to her,

"Two nations are in your body.
    Two groups of people will
        be taken from you.
One group will be stronger
        than the other.
    The older will serve the
        younger."

[24]And when the time came, Rebekah gave birth to twins. [25]The first baby was born red. His skin was like a hairy robe. So he was named Esau. [26]When the second baby was born, he was holding on to Esau's heel. So that baby was named Jacob. Isaac was 60 years old when they were born.

[27]When the boys grew up, Esau became a skilled hunter. He loved to be out in the fields. But Jacob was a quiet man. He stayed among the tents. [28]Isaac loved Esau. Esau hunted the wild animals that Isaac enjoyed eating. But Rebekah loved Jacob.

[29]One day Jacob was boiling a pot of vegetable soup. Esau came in from hunting in the fields. He was weak from hunger. [30]So Esau said to Jacob, "Let me eat some of that red soup. I am weak with hunger." (That is why people call him Edom.")

BIBLE BASICS

WHAT'S THE BIG DEAL ABOUT BEING THE FIRSTBORN?

Being the first son born into a Jewish family was good news for the boy. It meant that he would receive an inheritance two times bigger than what the other siblings received. It also meant that he would be the leader of the family once the father died. As a whole, the Israelites were considered God's firstborn because of the special privileges they had. Jesus is also called God's firstborn Son.

#1

25:25 Esau This name may mean "hairy." **25:26 Jacob** This name sounds like the Hebrew word for "heel." "Grabbing someone's heel" is a Hebrew saying for tricking someone. **25:30 Edom** This name sounds like the Hebrew word for "red."

JACOB GOT THE BLESSING, BUT HIS LIFE WASN'T EXACTLY EASY. HELP HIM UNSCRAMBLE THESE WORDS TO STRAIGHTEN OUT HIS MESSED-UP RELATIONSHIPS.

1. nalab _____
2. peehs _____
3. lrchae _____
4. heal _____
5. duatghesr _____
6. rramy _____
7. nnatpegr _____
8. hahlib _____
9. drenchli _____
10. dramankes _____

[31]But Jacob said, "You must sell me your rights as the firstborn son."[n]

[32]Esau said, "I am almost dead from hunger. If I die, all of my father's wealth will not help me."

[33]But Jacob said, "First, promise me that you will give it to me." So Esau made a promise to Jacob. In this way he sold his part of their father's wealth to Jacob. [34]Then Jacob gave Esau bread and vegetable soup. Esau ate and drank and then left. So Esau showed how little he cared about his rights as the firstborn son.

JACOB TRICKS ISAAC

27 When Isaac was old, his eyes were not good. He could not see clearly. One day he called his older son Esau to him.

Isaac said, "Son."

Esau answered, "Here I am."

[2]Isaac said, "I am old. I don't know when I might die. [3]So take your bow and arrows, and go hunting in the field. Kill an animal for me to eat. [4]Prepare the tasty food that I love. Bring it to me, and I will eat. Then I will bless you

before I die." [5]So Esau went out in the field to hunt.

Rebekah was listening as Isaac said this to his son Esau. [6]Rebekah said to her son Jacob, "Listen, I heard your father talking to your brother Esau. [7]Your father said, 'Kill an animal. Prepare some tasty food for me to eat. Then I will bless you before the Lord before I die.'

> "Kill an animal. Prepare some tasty food for me to eat. Then i will bless you before the Lord before i die."
>
> *Genesis 27:7*

[8]So obey me, my son. Do what I tell you. [9]Go out to our goats and bring me two young ones. I will prepare them just the way your father likes them. [10]Then you will take the food to your father. And he will bless you before he dies."

[11]But Jacob said to his mother Rebekah, "My brother Esau is a hairy man. I am smooth! [12]If my father touches me, he will know I am not Esau. Then he will not bless me. He will place a curse on me because I tried to trick him."

[13]So Rebekah said to him, "If your father puts a curse on you, I will accept the blame. Just do what I said. Go and get the goats for me."

[14]So Jacob went out and got two goats and brought them to his

⭐ **25:31 rights...son** Usually the firstborn son had a high rank in the family. The firstborn son usually became the new head of the family.

REAL SUPER HEROES

JACOB

Through Jacob we begin to see God's promise taking shape. Son of Isaac, twin with Esau, Jacob became the one to receive God's blessing after his father Jacob. But the blessing didn't come without some effort. After all, he was born with a disadvantage. He started off in second place. The birthright belonged to his twin brother Esau. But by scheming and deceiving, Jacob seemed to steal the birthright (though in truth, God had already chosen him to be the one to receive the blessing).

Then came the true test. Jacob had it out with God. He wrestled, not in his mind, but with his flesh. He literally fought the angel of the Lord all night long in order to receive God's blessing. In the end, he got what he wanted. His name was changed to Israel, marking the beginning of the Jewish people. But he also received an injury. The angel hurt his hip, and he walked with a limp for the rest of his life. It was his reminder of his encounter with God, the hard-fought battle of faith, and the fact that an all-powerful God had shown him mercy.

> "Come near so i can touch you, my son. if i can touch you, i will know if you are really my son Esau."
>
> *Genesis 27:21*

LIVIN' IT!

NO SOUP FOR YOU
GENESIS 25:1-34

Imagine if Publisher's Clearinghouse called you up to announce that you had won a million dollars? Would you be excited, or would you pass on the offer and ask for a Big Mac instead? Believe it or not, Esau was actually guilty of passing up his right to a double portion of his father's inheritance because he wanted some soup instead. He wanted to satisfy himself right away, instead of waiting for something much better.

As Christians, we need to understand what an incredible inheritance we have through Jesus. He has given us everything we need to live holy lives that please God. Like Esau, though, we are tempted to give up. We are willing to let the desires of this world become more important to us than our desire for God—and our laziness produces very bad results. We need to thank Jesus for the sacrifice he made for us, and ask him for strength to live every moment knowing that we are God's children. And we must use the gifts and talents he gives us for his glory.

mother. Then she cooked them in the special way Isaac enjoyed. ¹⁵She took the best clothes of her older son Esau that were in the house. She put them on the younger son Jacob. ¹⁶She took the skins of the goats. And she put them on Jacob's hands and neck. ¹⁷Then she gave Jacob the tasty food and the bread she had made.

¹⁸Jacob went in to his father and said, "Father."

And his father said, "Yes, my son. Who are you?"

¹⁹Jacob said to him, "I am Esau, your first son. I have done what you told me. Now sit up and eat some meat of the animal I hunted for you. Then bless me."

²⁰But Isaac asked his son, "How did you find and kill the animal so quickly?"

Jacob answered, "Because the Lord your God led me to find it."

²¹Then Isaac said to Jacob, "Come near so I can touch you, my son. If I can touch you, I will know if you are really my son Esau."

²²So Jacob came near to Isaac his father. Isaac touched him and said, "Your voice sounds like Jacob's voice. But your hands are hairy like the hands of Esau." ²³Isaac did not know it was Jacob, because his hands were hairy like Esau's hands. So Isaac blessed Jacob. ²⁴Isaac asked, "Are you really my son Esau?"

Jacob answered, "Yes, I am."

²⁵Then Isaac said, "Bring me the food. I will eat it and bless you." So Jacob gave him the food, and Isaac ate. Jacob gave him wine, and he drank. ²⁶Then Isaac said to him, "My son, come near and kiss me." ²⁷So Jacob went to his father and kissed him. Isaac smelled Esau's clothes and blessed him. Isaac said,

"The smell of my son
    is like the smell of the field
        that the Lord has blessed.
²⁸May God give you plenty of
    rain and good soil.

Then you will have plenty of grain and wine.

²⁹May nations serve you.
May peoples bow down
  to you.
May you be master over your
  brothers.
  May your mother's sons
    bow down to you.
May everyone who curses you
    be cursed.
  And may everyone who
    blesses you be blessed."

³⁰Isaac finished blessing Jacob. Then, just as Jacob left his father Isaac, Esau came in from hunting. ³¹Esau also prepared some tasty food and brought it to his father. He said, "Father, rise and eat the food that your son killed for you. Then bless me."

³²Isaac asked, "Who are you?"

He answered, "I am your son—your firstborn^d son—Esau."

³³Then Isaac trembled greatly. He said, "Then who was it that hunted the animals and brought me food before you came? I ate it, and I blessed him. And it is too late now to take back my blessing."

³⁴When Esau heard the words of his father, he let out a loud and bitter cry. He said to his father, "Bless me—me, too, my father!"

³⁵But Isaac said, "Your brother came and tricked me. He has taken your blessing."

³⁶Esau said, "Jacob^n is the right name for him. He has tricked me these two times. He took away my share of everything you own. And now he has taken away my blessing." Then Esau asked, "Haven't you saved a blessing for me?"

³⁷Isaac answered, "I gave Jacob the power to be master over you. And all his brothers will be his servants. And I kept him strong with grain and wine. There is nothing left to give you, my son."

³⁸But Esau continued, "Do you have only one blessing, Father? Bless me, too, Father!" Then Esau began to cry out loud.

³⁹Isaac said to him,
  "You will live far away from
    the best land,

Genesis 25:1-34; 27:1-45

WILD WORLD FACTS

DOUBLE TROUBLE

Jacob and Esau were twins, born to compete with one another, it seems. Jewish culture placed a lot of importance on the firstborn son, so it mattered to them who actually came into the world first.

What people in Bible times didn't understand about twins is that they were conceived at exactly the same time. Their life began when their mother's egg either split in half making identical twins with the same genetic makeup, or when two eggs were released at the same time and fertilized, making fraternal twins. Since Jacob and Esau looked so different, they were most likely fraternal twins.

Sometimes problems can occur in the womb which causes the growing cells to be connected. This causes congenitally united twins (when two people are joined together at birth). God says that he is the one who forms us in the womb and knows everything about us, even before we were conceived. Because we are God's creation, each of us is unique and special to him.

[Oracle Think Quest]

27:36 Jacob This name sounds like the Hebrew word for "heel." "Grabbing someone's heel" is a Hebrew saying for tricking someone.

far from the rain.

⁴⁰You will live by using
   your sword
   and be a slave to your
      brother.
But when you struggle,
   you will break free
      from him."

⁴¹After that Esau hated Jacob because of the blessing from Isaac. Esau thought to himself, "My father will soon die, and I will be sad for him. After that I will kill Jacob."

⁴²Rebekah heard about Esau's plan to kill Jacob. So she sent for Jacob. She said to him, "Lis-ten, your brother Esau is comforting himself by planning to kill you. ⁴³So, son, do what I say. My brother Laban is living in Haran. Go to him at once! ⁴⁴Stay with him for a while, until your brother is not so angry. ⁴⁵In time, your brother will not be angry. He will forget what you did to him. Then I will send a servant to bring you back. I don't want to lose both of my sons on the same day."

DIG THIS!

In more ways than one, Abraham was a trendsetter. He even made caves more popular as a good place to bury the dead. He purchased a cave from a Hittite to bury Sarah in, and later he was buried in that same cave, the Cave of Machpelah. Until then, caves were used as storage areas or places to hide from enemies. Many Jewish descendants followed his example by burying their dead in caves.

jaCob, Rachel, & LeAh

GENESIS 29:1—30:43

JACOB ARRIVES IN NORTHWEST MESOPOTAMIA

29 Then Jacob continued his journey. He came to the land of the people of the East. ²He looked and saw a well in the field. Three flocks of sheep were lying nearby, because they drank water from this well. A large stone covered the mouth of the well. ³All the flocks would gather there. The shepherds would roll the stone away from the well and water the sheep. Then they would put the stone back in its place.

⁴Jacob said to the shepherds there, "My brothers, where are you from?"

They answered, "We are from Haran."

⁵Then Jacob asked, "Do you know Laban grandson of Nahor?"

They answered, "We know him."

⁶Then Jacob asked, "How is he?"

They answered, "He is well. Look, his daughter Rachel is coming now with his sheep."

⁷Jacob said, "But look, it is still the middle part of the day. It is not time for the sheep to be gathered for the night. So give them water and let them go back into the pasture."

⁸But they said, "We cannot do that until all the flocks are gathered. Then we will roll away the stone from the mouth of the well and water the sheep."

⁹While Jacob was talking with the shepherds, Rachel came with her father's sheep. It was her job to take care of the sheep. ¹⁰Then Jacob saw Laban's daughter Rachel and Laban's sheep. So he went to the well and rolled the stone from its mouth. Then he watered Laban's sheep. Now Laban was the brother of Rebekah, Jacob's mother. ¹¹Then Jacob kissed Rachel and cried. ¹²He told her that he was from her father's family. He said that he was the son of Rebekah. So Rachel ran home and told her father.

¹³When Laban heard the news about his sister's son Jacob, Laban ran to meet him. Laban hugged him and kissed him and brought him to his house. Jacob told Laban

REAL SUPER HEROES

LeAh

She wasn't beautiful. She wasn't even okay. Leah was just downright plain looking, and her husband didn't want her. He had been tricked into marrying her, and he really loved her sister. Leah had child after child, hoping to gain his love, but never could.

It sounds like a pitiful story. How could Leah be a hero? Because she learned that God loved her. Even though her life was never easy, God took care of her. She cried out to God for help and found a friendship with him that she couldn't find anywhere else. In the end, it was through her children that the promised Messiah would come. Her name would be remembered forever.

Do you ever feel unloved? Unwanted? Rejected? Remember Leah and the love of God. You're not alone. He sees you, knows you, and loves you more than you'll ever know. Take hope in his friendship, and let his love strengthen your heart.

everything that had happened. [14]Then Laban said, "You are my own flesh and blood."

JACOB IS TRICKED

So Jacob stayed there a month. [15]Then Laban said to Jacob, "You are my relative. But it is not right for you to keep on working for me without pay. What would you like me to pay you?"

[16]Now Laban had two daughters. The older was Leah, and the younger was Rachel. [17]Leah had weak eyes, but Rachel was very beautiful. [18]Jacob loved Rachel. So he said to Laban, "Let me marry your younger daughter Rachel. If you will, I will work seven years for you."

[19]Laban said, "It would be better for her to marry you than someone else. So stay here with me." [20]So Jacob worked for Laban seven years so he could marry Rachel. But they seemed to him like just a few days. This was because he loved Rachel very much.

[21]After seven years Jacob said to Laban, "Give me Rachel so that I may marry her. The time I promised to work for you is over."

[22]So Laban gave a feast for all the people there. [23]That evening Laban brought his daughter Leah to Jacob. Jacob and Leah had sexual relations together. [24](Laban gave his slave girl Zilpah to his daughter to be her servant.) [25]In the morning Jacob saw that he had had sexual relations with Leah! He said to Laban, "What have you done to me? I worked hard for you so that I could marry Rachel! Why did you trick me?"

[26]Laban said, "In our country we do not allow the younger daughter to marry before the older daughter. [27]But complete the full week of the marriage ceremony with Leah. I will give you Rachel to marry also. But you must serve me another seven years."

[28]So Jacob did this and completed the week with Leah. Then Laban gave him his daughter

> **"So Jacob worked for Laban seven years so he could marry Rachel."**
>
> *Genesis 29:20*

LIVIN' IT!

WORTH THE WAIT
GENESIS 29:1-30

The movie producers couldn't have written it any better. Jacob saw Rachel, and it was love at first sight. So he did what any decent guy would do, and asked permission to marry her. Laban said, "Sure—but you have to work for it." Jacob had to agree to wait seven years, working hard to serve Laban in order to win Rachel's hand in marriage. But he loved her so much that the time seemed like only a few days to him.

One look at the magazines, TV shows, and maybe even the friends around you, and it becomes really obvious that waiting for true love is not a popular decision. Because of the sin in their hearts, people want whatever and whoever they want right away, and they aren't willing to wait. But God is equally clear. We must wait on him. Until the time is right for you to get married, you should be busy working for your Master and Savior. Then, in God's right time, he will provide the one for you who will best help you to know God better and carry out his work together as a team.

Rachel as a wife. [29](Laban gave his slave girl Bilhah to his daughter Rachel to be her servant.) [30] So Jacob had sexual relations with Rachel also. And Jacob loved Rachel more than Leah. Jacob worked for Laban for another seven years.

She named him Simeon." She said, "The Lord has heard that I am not loved. So he gave me this son."

[34] Leah became pregnant again and gave birth to another son. She named him Levi." Leah said, "Now, surely my husband will be close to me. I have given him three sons."

[35] Then Leah gave birth to another son. She named him Judah." Leah named him this because she said, "Now I will praise the Lord." Then Leah stopped having children.

WILD WORLD FACTS

Genesis 30:1-24

THE OTHER APPLE

Ever wonder why Rachel was so desperate for Leah's mandrakes? Mandrakes are a type of plant that still grows in regions all across Europe. In Bible times—and even today—they are believed by certain people to have a special power that helps people have babies. They are a perennial plant (meaning they come back each year), and grow fruit similar to a melon that many people call "love apples." It is bland to the taste, but it contains a poison that can cause sleep, hallucinations, and even death.

Rachel believed that if she could get some of Leah's mandrakes, she would be able to feed them to Jacob and, in turn, would be able to become pregnant, just as Leah had done. What she didn't realize was that God was in control of her ability to have children, not a plant. He chose the time when she would have children.

[www.barr-family.com]

JACOB'S FAMILY GROWS

[31] The Lord saw that Jacob loved Rachel more than Leah. So the Lord made it possible for Leah to have children. But Rachel did not have any children. [32] Leah became pregnant and gave birth to a son. She named him Reuben," because she said, "The Lord has seen my troubles. Surely now my husband will love me."

[33] Leah became pregnant again and gave birth to another son.

30 Rachel saw that she was not giving birth to children for Jacob. So she envied her sister Leah. Rachel said to Jacob, "Give me children, or I'll die!"

[2] Jacob became angry with her. He said, "Can I do what only God can do? He is the one who has kept you from having children."

[3] Then Rachel said, "Here is my slave girl Bilhah. Have sexual relations with her so she can give birth to a child for me. Then I can have my own family through her."

[4] So Rachel gave Bilhah, her slave girl, to Jacob as a wife. And he had sexual relations with her. [5] She became pregnant and gave Jacob a son. [6] Rachel said, "God has declared me innocent. He has listened to my prayer and has given me a son." So Rachel named this son Dan."

[7] Bilhah became pregnant again and gave Jacob a second son. [8] Rachel said, "I have struggled hard with my sister. And I have won." So she named that son Naphtali."

[9] Leah saw that she had stopped having children. So she gave her slave girl Zilpah to Jacob as a wife. [10] Then Zilpah had a son. [11] Leah said, "I am lucky."

 29:32 Reuben This name sounds like the Hebrew word for "he has seen my troubles." **29:33 Simeon** This name sounds like the Hebrew word for "has heard." **29:34 Levi** This name sounds like the Hebrew word for "be close to." **29:35 Judah** This name sounds like the Hebrew word for "praise." **30:6 Dan** This name means "he has declared innocent." **30:8 Naphtali** This name sounds like the Hebrew word for "my struggle."

So she named her son Gad.[n] [12]Zilpah gave birth to another son. [13]Leah said, "I am very happy! Now women will call me happy." So she named that son Asher.[n]

[14]During the wheat harvest Reuben went into the field and found some mandrake[n] plants. He brought them to his mother Leah. But Rachel said to Leah, "Please give me some of your son's mandrakes."

[15]Leah answered, "You have already taken away my husband. Now you are trying to take away my son's mandrakes."

But Rachel answered, "If you will give me your son's mandrakes, you may sleep with Jacob tonight."

[16]When Jacob came in from the field that night, Leah went out to meet him. She said, "You will have sexual relations with me tonight. I have paid for you with my son's mandrakes." So Jacob slept with her that night.

[17]Then God answered Leah's prayer, and she became pregnant again. She gave birth to a fifth son. [18]Leah said, "God has given me what I paid for, because I gave my slave girl to my husband." So Leah named her son Issachar.[n]

[19]Leah became pregnant again and gave birth to a sixth son. [20]She said, "God has given me a fine gift. Now surely Jacob will honor me, because I have given him six sons." So Leah named the son Zebulun.[n]

[21]Later Leah gave birth to a daughter. She named her Dinah.

[22]Then God remembered Rachel and answered her prayer. God made it possible for her to have children. [23]She became pregnant and gave birth to a son. She said, "God has taken away my shame." [24]She named him Joseph.[n] Rachel said, "I wish the Lord would give me another son."

JACOB TRICKS LABAN

[25]After the birth of Joseph, Jacob said to Laban, "Now let me go to my own home and country. [26]Give me my wives and my children, and let me go. I have earned them by working for you. You know that I served you well."

[27]Laban said to him, "If I have pleased you, please stay. I know the Lord has blessed me because of you. [28]Tell me what I should pay you, and I will give it to you."

[29]Jacob answered, "You know that I have worked hard for you. Your flocks have grown while I cared for them. [30]When I came, you had little. Now you have much. Every time I did something for you, the Lord blessed you. But when will I be able to do something for my own family?"

> "Then God answered Leah's prayer, and she became pregnant again. She gave birth to a fifth son."
>
> *Genesis 30:17*

History Highlights

➤ **3200 B.C.**
Earliest Picture of a Boat with a Sail

7000 5000 3000 1000 0 1000 NOW

30:11 Gad This name may mean "lucky." **30:13 Asher** This name may mean "happy." **30:14 mandrake** A plant which was believed to cause a woman to become pregnant. **30:18 Issachar** This name sounds like the Hebrew word for "paid for." **30:20 Zebulun** This name sounds like the Hebrew word for "honor." **30:24 Joseph** This name sounds like the Hebrew word for "he adds."

[31]Laban asked, "Then what should I give you?"

Jacob answered, "I don't want you to give me anything. Just do this one thing. Then I will come back and take care of your flocks. [32]Today let me go through all your flocks of white sheep and black goats. I will take every spotted or speckled lamb. I will take every black lamb and every spotted or speckled goat. That will be my pay. [33]In the future you can easily see if I am honest. You can come to look at my flocks. If I have any goat that isn't speckled or spotted or any sheep that isn't black, you will know I stole it."

[34]Laban answered, "Agreed! We will do what you ask." [35]But that day Laban took away all the male goats that had streaks or spots. And he took all the speckled and spotted female goats (all those that had white on them). And he took all the black sheep. He told his sons to watch over them. [36]Laban took these animals to a place that was three days' journey away from Jacob. Jacob took care of all the animals that were left.

[37]So Jacob cut green branches from poplar, almond and plane trees. He peeled off some of the bark so that the branches had white stripes on them. [38]He put the branches in front of the flocks at the watering places. When the animals came to drink, they also mated there. [39]So the goats mated in front of the branches. Then the young that were born were streaked, speckled or spotted. [40]Jacob separated the young animals from the others. And he made them face the streaked and dark animals in Laban's flock. Jacob kept his animals separate from Laban's. [41]When the stronger animals in the flock were mating, Jacob put the branches before their eyes. This was so the animals would mate near the branches. [42]But when the weaker animals mated,

GET CONNECTED

RELATIONSHIPS WITH FAMILY

The First to Be Last "I'm going to finish my dinner first so I can get on the computer!" shouts your younger sister. "Well, I'm going to get on it now so you can't get on it later!" you scream back, before you even realize what you're saying. No matter how hard we try (or don't try), we all naturally want to have the best for ourselves. We want our needs met first, and maybe we'll let others have their turn later.

Cain and Abel. Jacob and Esau. Leah and Rachel. The list of family members in the Bible fighting for their rights to be first goes on and on. But God wants more from us. He wants us to be like his Son, Jesus, who was willing to put aside the glory he truly deserved in order to serve others—even unto death. Next time your sibling tries to get one up on you, let it happen. Even encourage him with a happy heart. Then remember to thank God for Jesus' servant heart, and ask him to make you more like him.

> "if i have pleased you, please stay. i know the Lord has blessed me because of you."
>
> *Genesis 30:27*

Jacob did not put the branches there. So the animals born from the weaker animals were Laban's. And the animals born from the stronger animals were Jacob's. [43]In this way Jacob became very rich. He had large flocks, many male and female servants, camels and donkeys.

GET CONNECTED

RELATIONSHIPS WITH FRIENDS

Kingdom Focus From as early as you can remember, even adults have thought it was cute to match up little boys and girls. Now, lots of kids your age think it's important to "go out" with each other, even if you really don't "go" anywhere.

Remember that God—the same one who chose you before the world was made—has already chosen the perfect person for you to marry one day. God will reveal his plan to you at the right time. But until then, our attention and efforts need to be focused on building up the body of Christ and telling others about Jesus. As you focus on God's kingdom, his character will be formed within your heart, making you into the kind of person you need to be when you meet the one he has for you.

JANUARY REPENTANCE

1

Prayer Pointer:
Take 10 minutes to pray, and give the New Year to God.

2

Make a snowball, and put it in the freezer . . . or cut out a paper snowflake.

3

4

Hide-It-in-Your-Heart:
Take away my sin, and I will be clean. Wash me, and I will be whiter than snow (Psalm 51:7).

5

6

Make a card of construction paper, and mail it to a friend.

7

8

Put on ear muffs and coat, and take a jog around the block.

9

10

Plan a family outing to the ice skating rink.

11

12

13

Prayer Pointer:
Ask God to fill your family with peace and heal broken relationships.

14

15

16

Religious Freedom Day

17

Martin Luther King Jr.'s Birthday

18

19

Call your grandmother just to talk.

20

21

Make snowmen Jello® jigglers.

22

23

Make hot chocolate and marshmallows with your mom, and serve your brothers and sisters.

24

25

26

Australia Day

27

Hide-It-in-Your-Heart:
Create in me a pure heart, God. Make my spirit right again (Psalm 51:10).

28

29

30

Take some blankets to the local home-less shelter.

31

Prayer Pointer:
Ask God to help your dad be a strong leader for your family.

3-D

Jacob & Esau Reconcile
GENESIS 32:1—33:11

JACOB MEETS ESAU

32 When Jacob also went his way, the angels of God met him. [2]When Jacob saw them, he said, "This is the camp of God!" So Jacob named that place Mahanaim.[n]

[3]Jacob's brother Esau was living in the area called Seir in the country of Edom. Jacob sent messengers to Esau. [4]Jacob told the messengers, "Give this message to my master Esau: 'This is what Jacob, your servant, says: I have lived with Laban and have remained there until now. [5]I have cattle, donkeys, flocks, and male and female servants. I send this message to you and ask you to accept us.'"

[6]The messengers returned to Jacob and said, "We went to your brother Esau. He is coming to meet you. And he has 400 men with him."

[7]Then Jacob was very afraid and worried. He divided the people who were with him into two camps. He also divided all the flocks, herds and camels into two camps. [8]Jacob thought, "Esau might come and destroy one camp. But the other camp can run away and be saved."

[9]Jacob said, "God of my father Abraham! God of my father Isaac! Lord, you told me to return to my country and my family. You said that you would do good to me. [10]I am not worthy of the kindness and continual goodness you have shown me. The first time I traveled across the Jordan River, I had only my walking stick. But now I own enough to have two camps. [11]Please save me from my brother Esau. I am afraid he will come and kill all of us, even the mothers with the children. [12]You said to me, 'I will do good to you. I will make your children as many as the sand of the seashore. There will be too many to count.'"

[13]Jacob stayed there for the night. He prepared a gift for Esau from what he had with him. [14]It was 200 female goats and 20 male goats, 200 female sheep and 20 male sheep. [15]There were

32:2 **Mahanaim** This name means "two camps."

10

Ways to Grow a Happy Heart

1. Pray before you get out of bed.

2. Write a poem about God's love.

3. Think of 3 good things about today, and share them with a friend.

4. Smile.

5. Laugh out loud.

6. Surprise your sister with a special treat.

7. Play with the younger kids at recess.

8. Tell your parents you love them and appreciate them.

9. Play with a puppy.

10. Roll down a grassy hill.

30 female camels and their young, 40 cows and 10 bulls, 20 female donkeys and 10 male donkeys. [16]Jacob gave each separate flock of animals to one of his servants. Then he said to them, "Go ahead of me and keep some space between each herd." [17]Jacob gave them their orders. To the servant with the first group of animals he said, "My brother Esau will come to you. He will ask you, 'Whose servant are you? Where are you going? Whose animals are these?' [18]Then you will answer, 'These animals belong to your servant Jacob. He sent them as a gift to you my master, Esau. And Jacob also is coming behind us.'"

[19]Jacob ordered the second servant, the third servant and all the other servants to do the same thing. He said, "Say the same thing to Esau when you meet him. [20]Say, 'Your servant Jacob is coming behind us.'" Jacob thought, "If I send this gift ahead of me, maybe Esau will forgive me. Then when I see him, perhaps he will accept me." [21]So Jacob sent the gift to Esau. But Jacob stayed that night in the camp.

JACOB WRESTLES WITH GOD

[22]During the night Jacob rose and crossed the Jabbok River at the crossing. He took his 2 wives, his 2 slave girls and his 11 sons with him. [23]He sent his family and everything he had across the river. [24]But Jacob stayed behind alone. And a man came and wrestled with him until the sun came up. [25]The man saw that he could not defeat Jacob. So he

Genesis 32:1-32

A STRONG REMINDER

WILD WORLD FACTS

Jacob had fought with God. Not many people can say that. But the incident didn't happen without injury. God touched the muscle of Jacob's hip and put it out of commission. Jacob would walk with a limp ever after.

God gave us our muscles to help hold our bodies together and to provide the mechanism we need to move. Muscles attach to our bones through tendons and other tissues, and convert the chemical energy we have in our blood into physical action. More than 600 muscles, made of millions of tiny protein filaments, work together to help us move, breath, pump blood to our bodies, and live.

We need to remember the incredible creation of God as we look at our own gifts and abilities. While his work is amazing, we would still be nothing without him. Like Jacob, we need to seek to know God with every muscle and bone in our bodies.

[Innerbody.com]

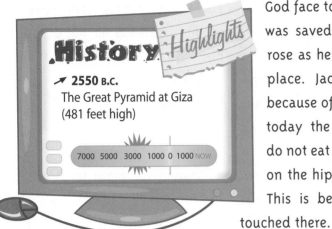

History Highlights

↗ **2550 B.C.**
The Great Pyramid at Giza
(481 feet high)

7000 5000 3000 1000 0 1000 NOW

God face to face. But my life was saved." ³¹Then the sun rose as he was leaving that place. Jacob was limping because of his leg. ³²So even today the people of Israel do not eat the muscle that is on the hip joint of animals. This is because Jacob was touched there.

struck Jacob's hip and put it out of joint. ²⁶Then the man said to Jacob, "Let me go. The sun is coming up."

But Jacob said, "I will let you go if you will bless me."

²⁷The man said to him, "What is your name?"

And he answered, "Jacob."

²⁸Then the man said, "Your name will no longer be Jacob. Your name will now be Israel,ⁿ because you have wrestled with God and with men. And you have won."

²⁹Then Jacob asked him, "Please tell me your name."

But the man said, "Why do you ask my name?" Then he blessed Jacob there.

³⁰So Jacob named that place Peniel.ⁿ He said, "I have seen

JACOB SHOWS HIS BRAVERY

33 Jacob looked up and saw Esau coming. With him were 400 men. So Jacob divided his children among Leah, Rachel and the two slave girls. ²Jacob put the slave girls with their children first. Then he put Leah and her children behind them. And he put Rachel and Joseph last. ³Jacob himself went out in front of them. He bowed down flat on the ground seven times as he was walking toward his brother.

⁴But Esau ran to meet Jacob. Esau put his arms around him and hugged him. Then Esau kissed him, and they both cried. ⁵Esau looked up and saw the women and children. He asked, "Who are these people with you?"

Jacob answered, "These are the children God has given me.

WILD WORLD FACTS

Genesis 25:19-34

SEE THE NEED

It drove Esau to sell his birthright. It forced thousands of Israelites to travel to Egypt for relief. It's one of the most powerful forces we know. Hunger—our body's cry for food—can make everything else in our lives seem unimportant until we have that basic need met.

Even today, more than 1 billion people suffer from hunger and malnutrition. About 24,000 people die each day from hunger and hunger-related illnesses, many of whom are children under the age of five. Many organizations have been formed to help take food to starving people, and their joint efforts have made an impact. Lives can change when we think beyond ourselves and help others in need. Ask your pastor what your church is doing to help meet the basic needs of the needy people in your area or around the world. And ask how you can help, too. Meet their physical needs first, then the door to treating their spiritual needs will be opened, as well.

[TheHungerSite.com]

 32:28 Israel This name means "he wrestles with God." **32:30 Peniel** This name means "the face of God."

Bible Critters

3-D

DESERT DWELLERS

Did you know that the **DROMEDARY CAMEL** is able to drink 30 gallons of water in 10 minutes?! In fact, God made camels with several unique characteristics that help them handle the harsh climate in the Middle East. Their humps are filled with fat, which helps provide energy over a long period of time. Their body temperature also rises and falls between 97°F and 107°F to keep them from wasting any water by sweating. And camels are kind to the environment. They eat only a few leaves from each plant so that food is left over for other animals and so that the plants won't die.

GENESIS 33:6-11

LIVIN' IT!

RIGHTING WRONGS
GENESIS 33:1-11

Jacob had tricked him. Esau had fallen for it. Now brothers—twins, no less—had parted ways. They had decided to live life apart because of their fight.

Despite the hurt in their relationship, Jacob wanted to become friends again. He thought long and hard about how to heal their friendship. Using gifts and very kind words, he approached his brother—only to find out that his brother had already forgiven him!

Is there someone in your life whose feelings or friendship you've hurt? Can you think of ways to reach out to that person to let them know that you're sorry? Ask God to give you wisdom and an opportunity. Then, when God gives you the right moment, ask for forgiveness, and work hard to not let another argument ever separate you again.

God has been good to me, your servant."

[6]Then the two slave girls and their children came up to Esau. They bowed down flat on the earth before him. [7]Then Leah and her children came up to Esau. They also bowed down flat on the earth. Last of all, Joseph and Rachel came up to Esau. And they, too, bowed down flat before him.

[8]Esau said, "I saw many herds as I was coming here. Why did you bring them?"

Jacob answered, "They were to please you, my master."

[9]But Esau said, "I already have enough, my brother. Keep what you have."

[10]Jacob said, "No! Please! If I have pleased you, then please accept the gift I give you. I am very happy to see your face again. It is like seeing the face of God because you have accepted me. "So I beg you to accept the gift I give you. God has been very good to me. And I have more than I need." And because Jacob begged, Esau accepted the gift.

DIG THIS!

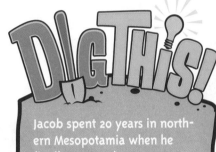

Jacob spent 20 years in northern Mesopotamia when he finally returned to Canaan. He met the angels of God at Mahanaim and wrestled with the angel of the Lord at Peniel.

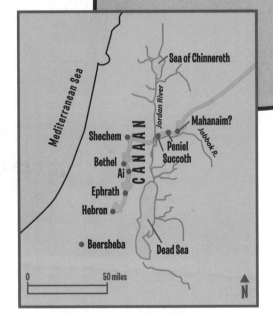

Joseph the Dreamer
GENESIS 37:1-36

JOSEPH THE DREAMER

37 Jacob lived in the land of Canaan, where his father had lived. [2]This is the family history of Jacob.

Joseph was a young man, 17 years old. He and his brothers cared for the flocks. His brothers were the sons of Bilhah and Zilpah, his father's wives. Joseph gave his father bad reports about his brothers. [3]Joseph was born when his father Israel, also called Jacob, was old. So Israel loved Joseph more than his other sons. He made Joseph a special robe with long sleeves. [4]Joseph's brothers saw that their father loved Joseph more than he loved them. So they hated their brother and could not speak to him politely.

[5]One time Joseph had a dream. When he told his brothers about it, they hated him even more. [6]Joseph said, "Listen to the dream I had. [7]We were in the field tying bundles of wheat together. My bundle stood up, and your bundles of wheat gathered around mine. Your bundles bowed down to mine."

[8]His brothers said, "Do you really think you will be king over us? Do you truly think you will rule over us?" His brothers hated him even more now. They hated him because of his dreams and what he had said.

[9]Then Joseph had another dream. He told his brothers about it also. He said, "Listen, I had another dream. I saw the sun, moon and 11 stars bowing down to me."

[10]Joseph also told his father about this dream. But his father scolded him, saying, "What kind of dream is this? Do you really believe that your mother, your brothers and I will bow down to you?" [11]Joseph's brothers were jealous of him. But his father thought about what all these things could mean.

WILD WORLD FACTS

Genesis 37:5-11
NIGHT LIFE

What did you dream last night? Can't remember? Of course, we can't call on Joseph to help us out. In his day he had an amazing God-given ability not only to interpret dreams, but also to figure out what people had dreamed in the first place. Even though we may not remember them, we do dream every night. Dreams are actually a part of the sleep cycle that God has given to us.

Scientists still don't agree about what causes dreams. Some say the neurons in our brains weren't finished sending their messages, so at night as we rest, the chemical processes in our brains keep going. Others say it's our body's way of resolving issues. What they do agree on is the fact that we forget 95-99% of everything we dream. If you'd like to get better at remembering, keep a journal by your bed. If you wake up in the middle of the night after a dream, write it down so you'll remember it the next morning.

[Yahooligans: Ask Earl]

GENESIS 37:12-22

¹²One day Joseph's brothers went to Shechem to herd their father's sheep. ¹³Jacob said to Joseph, "Go to Shechem. Your brothers are there herding the sheep."

Joseph answered, "I will go."

¹⁴His father said, "Go and see if your brothers and the sheep are all right. Then come back and tell me." So Joseph's father sent him from the Valley of Hebron.

When Joseph came to Shechem, ¹⁵a man found him wandering in the field. He asked Joseph, "What are you looking for?"

¹⁶Joseph answered, "I am looking for my brothers. Can you tell me where they are herding the sheep?"

¹⁷The man said, "They have already gone. I heard them say they were going to Dothan." So Joseph went to look for his brothers and found them in Dothan.

JOSEPH SOLD INTO SLAVERY

¹⁸Joseph's brothers saw him coming from far away. Before he reached them, they made a plan to kill him. ¹⁹They said to each other, "Here comes that dreamer. ²⁰Let's kill him and throw his body into one of the wells. We can tell our

LIVIN' IT!

DIVINE DEEDS
GENESIS 37:1-36

They sure made his brothers angry. Even his parents were perturbed—though it did make them think. Joseph just had a crazy thing about dreams, and it drove everyone around him batty.

Do you have a quirky personality trait? Do you tend to like things most people don't, or say things that don't quite fit in? Do you sometimes just feel weird? Joseph probably did, too. After all, no one else was dreaming dreams like he was. But the truth is, the dreams came from God. They were a divine gift that showed that Joseph was called to do a very special job. He eventually ruled over Egypt, second only to the king, and saved thousands of lives because he could interpret dreams.

Even if you think you don't fit in, remember Joseph. God made you just the way you are so that you will be perfectly suited one day to carry out the good works he has planned just for you to do.

GET CONNECTED

RELATIONSHIPS WITH FRIENDS

Good Riddance They thought they were getting rid of him. Toss him in a well. Sell him as a slave. Whatever—just get Joseph out of here!

Joseph's brothers had a bigger problem than a pesky little brother. They had let the sin of jealousy grow in their hearts. They wanted to be the favorite. They wanted the special treatment. But since they couldn't get it, they wanted to get rid of the one who was being favored.

Jealousy always kills our relationships with other people. It also crushes our own souls. Instead of wishing for what other people have, we need to remember God's goodness toward us already. Make a list of your blessings, and then thank God for them. Then ask him to help you trust him to provide all that you need.

father that a wild animal killed him. Then we will see what will become of his dreams."

²¹But Reuben heard their plan and saved Joseph. He said, "Let's not kill him. ²²Don't spill any blood. Throw him into this well

CRAFTS

JOSEPH'S COAT

SUPPLIES

Coffee filters
spray bottle of water
bold-tip markers

ALL ABOUT IT:

The first time Joseph is mentioned in the Bible, we are told about the love his father Jacob had for him. Jacob loved Joseph more than all his brothers because Joseph was born in Jacob's old age. Because he loved him so much, he made him a special colorful robe.

"Joseph's brothers saw that their father loved Joseph more than he loved them. So they hated their brother" (Genesis 37:4).

Everything in life is not fair or even. However, as much as possible, we need to think about other people's feelings and include them. Today make rainbow filters for your family and friends—and maybe even someone who is not your friend. Give the rainbow filters away with a smile, and let the people around you know how special you think they are.

RAINBOW FILTERS INSTRUCTIONS

Flatten out the coffee filters to make them completely round. Using your markers, make designs and squiggles on the filters, covering them with ink. When you are finished, lay each coffee filter, one at a time, on two stacked paper towels. Squirt the coffee filters with water, and watch the marker colors blend together.

Hang your coffee filters to dry, using more paper towels underneath them. When they are dry, share your rainbow filters with others to help brighten their day!

Bible Critters

GOT YOUR GOAT?

GOATS played a big role in animal sacrifices, as well as in common uses for milk and meat—in Bible times and today. The Nubian goat is a well-known breed that began in Egypt long ago. Just like sheep, Nubian goats have four-chambered stomachs that help them break down the simple plant foods they eat. They are also able to eat a lot of food very quickly, in order to avoid being out in the open where predators can attack them. You'll find Nubian goats on the savannah, in the desert, scrub, or mountains—and probably on the menu at some restaurants.

3-D

here in the desert. But don't hurt him!" Reuben planned to save Joseph later and send him back to his father. [23]So when Joseph came to his brothers, they pulled off his robe with long sleeves. [24]Then they threw him into the well. It was empty. There was no water in it.

[25]While Joseph was in the well, the brothers sat down to eat. When they looked up, they saw a group of Ishmaelites. They were traveling from Gilead to Egypt. Their camels were carrying spices, balm[d] and myrrh.[d]

[26]Then Judah said to his brothers, "What will we gain if we kill our brother and hide his death? [27]Let's sell him to these Ishmaelites. Then we will not be guilty of killing our own brother. After all, he is our brother, our own flesh and blood." And the other brothers agreed. [28]So when the Midianite traders came by, the brothers took Joseph out of the well. They sold him to the Ishmaelites for eight ounces of silver. And the Ishmaelites took him to Egypt.

[29]Reuben was not with his brothers when they sold Joseph to the Ishmaelites. When Reuben came back to the well, Joseph was not there. Reuben tore his clothes to show he was sad. [30]Then he went back to his brothers and said, "The boy is not there! What will I do?" [31]The brothers killed a goat and

REAL SUPER HEROES

JOSEPH

He just didn't get it. You don't tell your eleven other brothers that you have dreams about them some day bowing down to you. In fact, Joseph didn't understand jealousy and envy at all—until he ended up in the bottom of a well and then sold to slave traders. That was more than just kids making fun of him at school. More than just wearing the wrong clothes. Joseph's own family hated him, and they were willing to get rid of him to prove it.

Stronger than his brothers' hate, Joseph discovered love. The kind of devotion that stays, even when you say the wrong thing. Joseph discovered that God was capable of turning even the very worst situation into something wonderful, when he put his trust in him. Joseph learned—and so did his father and brothers—that God is more in control than we ever thought possible. God is able to make use out of years that seem wasted.

BLAST FROM THE PAST

EGYPT MUST HAVE BEEN HARD AT WORK. As far back as 2700 B.C. they began building a number of pyramids to serve as burial places for their rulers when they died. The Step Pyramid of Pharaoh Djoser was the first to be built, and many others copied it. The Great Pyramid is over 480 feet high, and is 756 feet wide on each side!

dipped Joseph's long-sleeved robe in its blood. ³²Then they brought the robe to their father. They said, "We found this robe. Look it over carefully. See if it is your son's robe."

³³Jacob looked it over and said, "It is my son's robe! Some savage animal has eaten him. My son Joseph has been torn to pieces!" ³⁴Then Jacob tore his clothes and put on rough cloth to show that he was sad. He continued to be sad about his son for a long time. ³⁵All of Jacob's sons and daughters tried to comfort him. But he could not be comforted. Jacob said, "I will be sad about my son until the day I die." So Jacob

cried for his son Joseph.

³⁶Meanwhile the Midianites who had bought Joseph had taken him to Egypt. There they sold him to Potiphar. Potiphar was an officer to the king of Egypt and captain of the palace guard.

DIG THIS!

Mesopotamia is the general name of the land where many of the events in the Old Testament happened. It is located between the Tigris and Euphrates rivers.

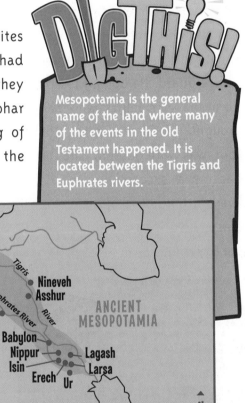

Joseph in Egypt

GENESIS 39:1-23

JOSEPH IS SOLD TO POTIPHAR

39 Now Joseph had been taken down to Egypt. An Egyptian named Potiphar was an officer to the king of Egypt. He was the captain of the palace guard. He bought Joseph from the Ishmaelites who had brought him down there. ²The Lord was with Joseph, and he became a successful man. He lived in the house of his master, Potiphar the Egyptian.

³Potiphar saw that the Lord was with Joseph. He saw that the Lord made Joseph successful in everything he did. ⁴So Potiphar was very happy with Joseph. He allowed Joseph to be his personal servant. He put Joseph in charge of the house. Joseph was trusted with everything Potiphar owned. ⁵So Joseph was put in charge of the house. He was put in charge of everything Potiphar owned. Then the Lord blessed the people in Potiphar's house because of Joseph. And the Lord blessed everything that belonged to Potiphar, both in the house and in the field. ⁶So Potiphar put Joseph in charge of everything he owned. Potiphar was not concerned about anything, except the food he ate.

JOSEPH IS PUT INTO PRISON

Now Joseph was well built and handsome. ⁷After some time the wife of Joseph's master began to desire Joseph. One day she said to him, "Have sexual relations with me."

⁸But Joseph refused. He said to her, "My master trusts me with everything in his house. He has put me in charge of every-

History Highlight

↗ **2450 B.C.**
Smelted Iron from Mesopotamia

7000 5000 3000 1000 0 1000 NOW

thing he owns. ⁹There is no one in his house greater than I. He has not kept anything from me, except you. And that is because you are his wife. How can I do such an evil thing? It is a sin against God."

¹⁰The woman talked to Joseph every day, but he refused to have

BIBLE BASICS

WHO IS GOD?

God is the Creator and Sustainer of the universe. He is one Spirit who exists in three different persons: God the Father, God the Son, and God the Holy Spirit. God the Son, also called Jesus, is the only person of the Godhead to take on a human body. All three persons are eternal—they had no beginning and will have no end. Though God is all-powerful, he is also all-loving and desires to have a deep relationship with the people he created.

> "My master trusts me with everything in his house."
> *Genesis 39:8*

BLAST FROM THE **PAST**

PEOPLE iN BiBLE TiMES DiDN'T HAVE THE KiND OF MEDiCiNE WE ENJOY TODAY. They did, however, discover that certain plants could help heal some of their sicknesses. Ancient balm is a kind of resin (thick, gummy stuff) taken from trees by cutting the bark. When it wasn't used as a medicine, it made a pretty good perfume.

sexual relations with her or even spend time with her.

¹¹One day Joseph went into the house to do his work as usual. He was the only man in the house at that time. ¹²His master's wife grabbed his coat. She said to him, "Come and have sexual relations with me." But Joseph left his coat in her hand and ran out of the house.

¹³She saw what Joseph had done. He had left his coat in her hands and had run outside. ¹⁴So she called to the servants in her house. She said, "Look! This Hebrew slave was brought here to shame us. He came in and tried to have sexual relations with me. But I screamed. ¹⁵My scream scared him, and he ran away. But he left his coat with me."

¹⁶She kept his coat until her husband came home. ¹⁷And she told her husband the same story. She said, "This Hebrew slave you brought here came in to shame me! ¹⁸When he came near me, I screamed. He ran away, but he left his coat."

¹⁹When Joseph's master heard what his wife said Joseph had done, he became very angry. ²⁰So Potiphar arrested Joseph and put him into prison. This prison was where the king's prisoners were put. And Joseph stayed there in the prison.

GET CONNECTED

RELATIONSHIPS WITH AUTHORITY

In God's Service Do you have a teacher that just seems to get under your skin? A parent whose personality clashes with yours? You know that God wants you to honor those in authority over you. But how?

Take note of Joseph. In his lifetime, he worked for a number of different rulers. Some were kind; others were not. But it really didn't matter what kind of ruler he served. Joseph considered himself working for God, and everything he did was with God's glory in mind.

No matter who God places over you, you can always show the respect to them that God requires. You might need to pray for help, but you can always remember that it is actually Jesus that you are serving when you obey those in authority over you.

Homework? You bet!

JOURNEY with JOSEPH

Joseph had to go a long way to find God's fulfilled promise. His journey wasn't easy—and neither is this quiz, if you don't know the facts! Test your Old Testament trivia knowledge as Joseph travels through trials to triumph, as Egypt's ruler and Israel's preserver.

1 WHO TOOK JOSEPH TO EGYPT?

A Moabites
B Ishmaelites
C His brothers
D No one; he just wandered there.

2 WHAT DID HIS BROTHERS TELL THEIR DAD HAD HAPPENED TO JOSEPH?

A "Merchants came and bought him from us."
B "He ran away."
C "A wild animal must have eaten him."
D "We don't know."

3 WHO WAS POTIPHAR?

A the baker
B the cupbearer
C an officer to the king of Egypt
D Joseph's younger brother

4 WHY WAS JOSEPH THROWN INTO PRISON?

A He was disobedient.
B He was rude to Potiphar's wife.
C He was a bad worker.
D He obeyed God.

5 HOW DID GOD SHOW KINDNESS TO JOSEPH IN PRISON?

A He made life easy for him.
B He made the warden like Joseph.
C He made everything Joseph did successful.
D Both b and c.

6 WHAT WAS JOSEPH'S SPECIAL TALENT?

A He could write poems.
B He could sing songs.
C He could interpret dreams.
D He could touch his nose with his tongue.

7 WHAT DID THE BAKER DREAM?

A Birds ate bread from the baskets on his head.
B Cows ate the birds.
C Three cows bowed to three birds.
D He fed poisonous food to the king.

8 WHO HELPED JOSEPH GET OUT OF PRISON?

A God, through the baker
B God, through the jailor
C God, through the chief officer
D God, through his dad

9 WHAT COULD JOSEPH DO THAT NO ONE ELSE COULD?

A interpret dreams
B make colorful coats
C do a dance
D tell the king what he dreamed and why

10 HOW DID THE KING REWARD JOSEPH?

A sent him home
B sent him back to Potiphar
C sent him back to jail
D made him second-in-command

Score 9-10: You rule the roost!
Score 7-8: Servant to the king.
Score 5-6: One of the ones left behind.
Score 4 or below: In danger of starvation—run to the Word for food!

ANSWERS: 1.b; 2.c; 3.c; 4.d; 5.d; 6.c; 7.a; 8.c; 9.d; 10.d

GET CONNECTED

RELATIONSHIPS WITH GOD

Forget-Me-Nots The baker had been terrified. He was having all these strange dreams. Would he ever get out of prison alive? Joseph kindly helped him. He explained his dreams and asked that the baker please remember him when he was freed.

But the baker forgot. He was so happy with his own life, that he forgot about Joseph. It's a bad habit we all seem to have, especially with our relationship with God.

When life is good, we go about our day and forget to include God in it. When something bad happens or we need help, suddenly we remember God. God wants us to remember him and the people around us all of the time. Ask God to help you to be aware of his presence and the needs of others around you.

[21]But the Lord was with Joseph and showed him kindness. The Lord caused the prison warden to like Joseph. [22]The prison warden chose Joseph to take care of all the prisoners. He was responsible for whatever was done in the prison. [23]The warden paid no attention to anything that was in Joseph's care. This was because the Lord was with Joseph. The Lord made Joseph successful in everything he did.

Joseph as Interpreter & Ruler

GENESIS 40:1—41:57

JOSEPH INTERPRETS TWO DREAMS

40 After these things happened, two of the king's officers displeased the king. These officers were the man who served wine to the king and the king's baker. [2]The king became angry with his officer who served him wine and his baker. [3]So he put them in the prison of the captain of the guard. This was the same prison where Joseph was kept. [4]The captain of the guard put the two prisoners in Joseph's care. They stayed in prison for some time.

[5]One night both the king's officer who served him wine and the baker had a dream. Each had his own dream with its own meaning. [6]When Joseph came to them the next morning, he saw they were worried. [7]Joseph asked the king's officers who were with him, "Why do you look so unhappy today?"

[8]The two men answered, "We both had dreams last night. But no one can explain the meaning of them to us."

Joseph said to them, "God is the only One who can explain the meaning of dreams. So tell me your dreams."

[9]So the man who served wine to the king told Joseph his dream. He said, "I dreamed I saw a vine. [10]On the vine there were three branches. I watched the branches bud and blossom, and then the grapes ripened. [11]I was holding the king's cup. So I took the grapes and squeezed the juice into the cup. Then I gave it to the king."

[12]Then Joseph said, "I will explain the dream to you. The three branches stand for three days. [13]Before the end of three days the king will free you. He will allow you to return to your work. You will serve the king his wine just as you did before. [14]But when you are free, remember me. Be kind to me. Tell the king about me so that I can get out of this prison. [15]I was

WILD WORLD FACTS

Genesis 41:1-36
KOOKY COWS

The king had been having strange dreams. He kept seeing skinny cows eat fat cows. Beside the fact that it's just weird to be dreaming about cows, it's even stranger that the cows in his dream were carnivores (meat eaters). Everybody knows that real cows are all herbivores (plant eaters). But why do they prefer the green stuff?

God designed a cow's body in such a special way that they can easily break down the nutrients stored up in grass. In fact, their stomachs have four different sections; each helps digest the grass. Cows that eat only grass can make up to 50 glasses of milk each day. But if you add corn, hay, and mixed feed to their diet, they can make up to 100 glasses of milk a day!

Fortunately, the king was able to make sense out of his dreams with the help of God and Joseph.

[Yahooligans: Ask Earl]

DiG THiS!

In ancient times, idols played a big role not only in worship, but also in the society as a whole. Sometimes they symbolized who had the most power in a particular family. An ancient tablet found in Nuzi (a second-millennium city) explains that, at times, household gods showed family leadership, which is why important families kept them in their home.

taken by force from the land of the Hebrews. And I have done nothing here to deserve being put in prison."

[16]The baker saw that Joseph's explanation of the dream was good. So he said to Joseph, "I also had a dream. I dreamed there were three bread baskets on my head. [17]In the top basket there were all kinds of baked food for the king. But the birds were eating this food out of the basket on my head."

[18]Joseph answered, "I will tell you what the dream means. The three baskets stand for three days. [19]Before the end of three days, the king will cut off your head! He will hang your body on a pole. And the birds will eat your flesh."

[20]Three days later it was the king's birthday. So he gave a feast for all his officers. In front of his officers, he let the chief officer who served his wine and the chief baker out of prison. [21]The king gave his chief officer who served wine his old position. Once again he put the king's cup of wine into the king's hand. [22]But the king hanged the baker on a pole. Everything happened just as Joseph had said it would. [23]But the officer who served wine did not remember Joseph. He forgot all about him.

THE KING'S DREAMS

41 Two years later the king had a dream. He dreamed he was standing on the bank of the Nile River. [2]He saw seven fat and beautiful cows come up out of the river. They stood there, eating the grass. [3]Then seven more cows came up out of the river. But they were thin and ugly. They stood beside the seven beautiful cows on the bank of the Nile. [4]The seven thin and ugly cows ate the seven beautiful fat cows. Then the king woke up. [5]The king slept again and dreamed a second time. In his dream he saw seven full and good heads of grain growing on one stalk. [6]After that, seven more heads of grain sprang up. But they were thin and burned by the hot east wind. [7]The thin heads of grain ate the seven full and good heads. Then the king woke up again.

BLAST FROM THE PAST

IT'S EASY TO THINK that people who lived so long ago must have not been very smart or developed. But by 3000 B.C., people in Mesopotamia and Egypt were already using complicated watering techniques to use the floods of the Tigris, Euphrates, and Nile rivers to their advantage.

Bible Critters — WHAT A CROC!

Bet you can't guess where **NILE CROCODILES** come from. Okay, maybe you can. But did you know that the Nile crocodile can grow up to 20 feet and weigh close to 900 pounds? Despite the scary stories, crocs aren't all bad. Mother crocodiles protect their young by tossing them into their mouths to hide. And both parents help the youngsters hatch out of their eggs by rolling the eggs in their mouths with their tongues to gently crack the shell, making the great escape easier.

And he realized it was only a dream. ⁸The next morning the king was troubled about these dreams. So he sent for all the magicians and wise men of Egypt. The king told them his dreams. But no one could explain their meaning to him.

⁹Then the chief officer who served wine to the king said to him, "I remember something I promised to do. But I had forgotten about it. ¹⁰There was a time when you were angry with me and the baker. You put us in prison in the house of the captain of the guard. ¹¹In prison we each had a dream on the same night. Each dream had a different meaning. ¹²A young Hebrew man was in the prison with us. He was a servant of the captain of the guard. We told him our dreams, and he explained their meanings to us. He told each man the meaning of his dream. ¹³Things happened exactly as he said they would: I was given back my old position, and the baker was hanged."

> **"We told him our dreams, and he explained their meanings to us."**
> *Genesis 41:12*

¹⁴So the king called for Joseph. The guards quickly brought him out of the prison. He shaved, put on clean clothes and went before the king.

¹⁵The king said to Joseph, "I have had a dream. But no one can explain its meaning to me. I have heard that you can explain a dream when someone tells it to you."

¹⁶Joseph answered the king, "I am not able to explain the meaning of dreams. God will do this for the king."

¹⁷Then the king said to Joseph, "In my dream I was standing on the bank of the Nile River. ¹⁸I saw seven fat and beautiful cows. They came up out of the river and ate the grass. ¹⁹Then I saw seven more cows come out of the river. They were thin and lean and ugly. They were the worst looking cows I have seen in all the land of Egypt. ²⁰And these thin and ugly cows ate the first seven fat cows. ²¹But after they had eaten the seven cows, no one could tell they had eaten them. They just looked as thin and ugly as they did in the

beginning. Then I woke up.

22"I had another dream. I saw seven full and good heads of grain growing on one stalk. 23Then seven more heads of grain sprang up after them. But these heads were thin and ugly. They were burned by the hot east wind. 24Then the thin heads ate the seven good heads. I told this dream to the magicians. But no one could explain its meaning to me."

GET CONNECTED

RELATIONSHIPS WITH AUTHORITY

Love Our Leaders While good things do happen in the world, there are many hard things that happen, too—like war, famine, earthquakes, crime, poverty, and countless other issues people deal with every day.

Though life can be hard, God has given us leaders to help us. Our police, the government, and our soldiers are all a part of that system that helps us keep the peace here at home. Their jobs are not easy, and they cannot do it alone. You can help them, though, by obeying the rules they give us, and by praying for them every day. Through our prayers, God can bring us peace.

JOSEPH TELLS THE DREAMS' MEANING

25Then Joseph said to the king, "Both of these dreams mean the same thing. God is telling you what he is about to do. 26The seven good cows stand for seven years. And the seven good heads of

grain stand for seven years. Both dreams mean the same thing. 27The seven thin and ugly cows stand for seven years. And the seven thin heads of grain burned by the hot east wind stand for seven years of hunger. 28This will happen as I told you. God is showing the king what he is about to do. 29You will have seven years of good crops and plenty to eat in all the land of Egypt. 30But after those seven years, there will come

seven years of hunger. All the food that grew in the land of Egypt will be forgotten. The time of hunger will eat up the land. 31People will forget what it was like to have plenty of food. This is because the hunger that fol-

> **"This will happen as i told you. God is showing the king what he is about to do."**
>
> *Genesis 41:28*

lows will be so great. 32You had two dreams which mean the same thing. This shows that God has firmly decided that this will happen. And he will make it happen soon.

33"So let the king choose a man who is very wise and understanding. Let the king set him over the land of Egypt. 34And let the king also appoint officers over the land. They should take one-fifth of all the food that is grown during the seven good years. 35They should gather all the food that is produced during the good years that are coming. Under the king's authority they should store the grain in the cities and guard it. 36That food should be saved for later. It will be used during the seven years of hunger that will come on the land of Egypt. Then the people in Egypt will not die during the seven years of hunger."

CRAFTS

JOSEPH'S DREAMS

God gave Joseph the gift of interpreting dreams. From someone's dreams he could tell what was going to happen in the future. But he always gave glory to God for being able to tell what the dreams meant.

Dreams can stir up many emotions. Make your own dream journal, and keep it close by your bed. When you wake up after a dream that you've enjoyed, write it down in your journal. It is always fun to go back and remember places we've been in dreamland.

SUPPLIES

notebook
construction paper
scissors
glue
decorations (buttons,
    sequins, stickers, etc.)

3-D

DREAM JOURNAL INSTRUCTIONS

Decorate a notebook with construction paper, stickers, etc., and label it your dream journal. Keep it in your room next to your bed to record your favorite dreams.

10

TOP TEN

Ways to Encourage Your Leaders

1. Say the pledge of allegiance.
2. Pray for our military.
3. Write a letter of support to the president.
4. Bring your teacher a small gift and card.
5. Recite a verse you learned to your Sunday school teachers.
6. Thank your parents for spending time with you.
7. Obey.
8. Be respectful.
9. Say good things about them when they're not around.
10. Try to do your very best.

JOSEPH IS MADE RULER OVER EGYPT

37This seemed like a very good idea to the king. All his officers agreed. 38And the king asked them, "Can we find a better man than Joseph to take this job? God's spirit is truly in him!"

39So the king said to Joseph, "God has shown you all this. There is no one as wise and understanding as you are. 40I will put you in charge of my palace. All the people will obey your orders. Only I will be greater than you."

41Then the king said to Joseph, "Look! I have put you in charge of all the land of Egypt." 42Then the king took off from his own finger his ring with the royal seal on it. And he put it on Joseph's finger. He gave Joseph fine linen clothes to wear. And he put a gold chain around Joseph's neck. 43The king had Joseph ride in the second royal chariot. Men walked ahead of his chariot calling, "Bow down!" By doing these things, the king put Joseph in charge of all of Egypt.

44The king said to him, "I am the king. And I say that no one in all the land of Egypt may lift a hand or a foot unless you say he may." 45The king gave Joseph the name Zaphenath-Paneah. He also gave Joseph a wife named Asenath. She was the daughter of Potiphera, priest of On. So Joseph traveled through all the land of Egypt.

46Joseph was 30 years old when he began serving the king of Egypt. And he left the king's court and traveled through all the land of Egypt. 47During the seven good years, the crops in the land grew well. 48And Joseph gathered all the food produced in Egypt during those seven years of good crops. He stored the food in the cities. In every city he stored grain that had been grown in the fields around that city. 49Joseph stored much grain, as much as the sand of the seashore. He stored so much grain that he could not measure it.

50Joseph's wife was Asenath daughter of Potiphera, the priest of On. Before the years of hunger came, Joseph and Asenath

"Joseph stored much grain, as much as the sand of the seashore. He stored so much grain that he could not measure it."

Genesis 41:49

had two sons. ⁵¹Joseph named the first son Manasseh.ⁿ Joseph said, "God has made me forget all the troubles I have had and all my father's family." ⁵²Joseph named the second son Ephraim.ⁿ Joseph said, "God has given me children in the land of my troubles."

⁵³The seven years of good crops came to an end in the land of Egypt. ⁵⁴Then the seven years of hunger began, just as Joseph had said. In all the lands people had nothing to eat. But in Egypt there was food. ⁵⁵The time of hunger became terrible in all of Egypt. The people cried to the king for food. He said to all the Egyptians, "Go to Joseph. Do whatever he tells you to do."

⁵⁶The hunger was everywhere in that part of the world. And Joseph opened the storehouses and sold grain to the people of Egypt. This was because the time of hunger became terrible in Egypt. ⁵⁷And all the people in that part of the world came to Joseph in Egypt to buy grain. This was because the hunger was terrible everywhere in that part of the world.

"The time of hunger became terrible in all of Egypt. The people cried to the king for food." *Genesis 41:55*

41:51 **Manasseh** This name sounds like the Hebrew word for "made me forget." 41:52 **Ephraim** This name sounds like the Hebrew word for "given me children."

joseph Reconciles with his Family

GENESIS 42:1-22; 45:1-11; 50:1-26

THE DREAMS COME TRUE

42 Jacob learned that there was grain in Egypt. So he said to his sons, "Why are you just sitting here looking at one another? ²I have heard that there is grain in Egypt. Go down there and buy grain for us to eat. Then we will live and not die."

³So ten of Joseph's brothers went down to buy grain from Egypt. ⁴But Jacob did not send Benjamin, Joseph's brother, with them. Jacob was afraid that something terrible might happen to Benjamin. ⁵Along with many other people, the sons of Jacob, also called Israel, went to Egypt to buy grain. This was because the people in the land of Canaan were hungry also.

⁶Now Joseph was governor over Egypt. He was the one who sold the grain to people who came to buy it. So Joseph's brothers came to him. They bowed facedown on the ground before him. ⁷When Joseph saw his brothers, he knew who they were. But he acted as if he didn't know them. He asked unkindly, "Where do you come from?"

They answered, "We have come from the land of Canaan to buy food."

⁸Joseph knew they were his brothers. But they did not know who he was. ⁹And Joseph remembered his dreams about his brothers bowing to him. He said to them, "You are spies! You came to learn where the nation is weak!"

¹⁰But his brothers said to him, "No, my master. We come as your servants just to buy food. ¹¹We are all sons of the same father. We are honest men, not spies."

¹²Then Joseph said to them, "No! You have come to learn where this nation is weak!"

¹³And they said, "We are 10 of 12 brothers. We are sons of the same father. We live in the land of Canaan. Our youngest brother is there with our father right now. And our other brother is gone."

¹⁴But Joseph said to them, "I can see I was right! You are spies! ¹⁵But I will give you a way to prove you are telling the truth. As

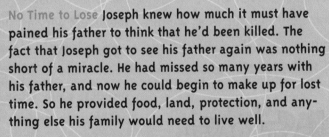

GET CONNECTED

RELATIONSHIPS WITH FAMILY

No Time to Lose Joseph knew how much it must have pained his father to think that he'd been killed. The fact that Joseph got to see his father again was nothing short of a miracle. He had missed so many years with his father, and now he could begin to make up for lost time. So he provided food, land, protection, and anything else his family would need to live well.

Have you ever thought about how you can support your parents? Of course, they don't need your money. But you can love them and show them respect by obeying with a happy heart. You can let them know you appreciate their work by helping around the house and keeping peace with your siblings. Don't wait until many precious years are gone. Make the most of every moment by saying thanks to your parents through heartfelt service and love.

surely as the king lives, you will not leave this place until your youngest brother comes here. ¹⁶One of you must go and get your brother. The rest of you will stay here in prison. We will see if you are telling the truth. If not, as surely as the king lives, you are spies." ¹⁷Then Joseph put them all in prison for three days.

¹⁸On the third day Joseph said to them, "I am a God-fearing man. Do this thing, and I will let you live: ¹⁹If you are honest men, let one of your brothers stay here in prison. The rest of you go and carry grain back to feed your hungry families. ²⁰Then bring your youngest brother back here to me. If you do this, I will know you are telling the truth. Then you will not die."

The brothers agreed to this. ²¹They said to each other, "We are being punished for what we did to our brother. We saw his trouble. He begged us to save him,

but we refused to listen. That is why we are in this trouble now."

²²Then Reuben said to them, "I told you not to harm the boy. But you refused to listen to me. So now we are being punished for what we did to him."

• • •

JOSEPH REVEALS WHO HE IS

45 Joseph could not control himself in front of his servants any longer. He cried out, "Have everyone leave me." When only the brothers were left with Joseph, he told them who he was. ²Joseph cried so loudly that the Egyptians heard him. And the people in the king's palace heard about it. ³He said to his brothers, "I am Joseph. Is my father still alive?" But the brothers could not answer him, because they were very afraid of him.

⁴So Joseph said to them, "Come close to me." So the brothers came close to him. And he said to them, "I am your

brother Joseph. You sold me as a slave to go to Egypt. ⁵Now don't be worried. Don't be angry with yourselves because you sold me here. God sent me here ahead of you to save people's lives. ⁶No food has grown on the land for two years now. And there will be five more years without planting or harvest. ⁷So God sent me here ahead of you. This was to make sure you have some descendants[d] left on earth. And it was to keep you alive in an amazing way. ⁸So it was not you who sent me here, but God. God has made me the highest officer of the king of Egypt. I am in charge of his palace. I am the master of all the land of Egypt.

⁹"So leave quickly and go to my father. Tell him, 'Your son Joseph says: God has made me master over all Egypt. Come down to me quickly. ¹⁰Live in the land of Goshen. You will be near me. Also your children, your grandchildren, your flocks and herds and all that you have will

HAVE THEY GOT MAIL? No, people back then did not have a postal service for the regular people. However, as early as 2000 B.C., the Egyptians did begin a kind of postal service, but it was only for the government and official business.

GET CONNECTED

RELATIONSHIPS WITH FAMILY

Strength in Humility If anybody had a right to be mad, it was Joseph. He was sold into slavery by his brothers. Falsely accused by a woman. Forgotten in jail. And now, after years and years of hardship, at the height of his power, his brothers—the ones who had gotten him into all that mess—come asking for help.

So what did he do? He gave it to them. He provided not only food, but land and protection, as well. Why? Joseph had a humble heart. He knew that it didn't matter what others did to him. God was in control of his life, and God was able to work out all things for his good. His humility helped rebuild his family.

Have family members hurt your feelings? Do you think they owe you something? Remember Joseph and the power of humility. Forgive them, just as your heavenly Father forgives you, and ask God to heal your family.

be near me. "I will care for you during the next five years of hunger. In this way, you and your family and all that you have will not starve.'

· · ·

JACOB'S BURIAL

50 When Jacob died, Joseph hugged his father and cried over him and kissed him. ²He commanded the doctors who served him to prepare his father's body. So the doctors prepared Jacob's body to be buried. ³It took the doctors 40 days to prepare his body. This was the usual time it took. And the Egyptians had a time of sorrow for Jacob. It lasted 70 days.

⁴When this time of sorrow had ended, Joseph spoke to the king's officers. He said, "If you think well of me, please tell this to the king: ⁵'When my father was near death, I made a promise to him. I promised I would bury him in a cave in the land of Canaan. This is a burial place that he cut out for himself. So please let me go and bury my father. Then I will return.'"

⁶The king answered, "Keep your promise. Go and bury your father."

⁷So Joseph went to bury his father. All the king's officers, the elders of his court and all the elders of Egypt went with Joseph. ⁸Everyone who lived with Joseph and his brothers went with him. And everyone who lived with his father also went. They left only their children, their flocks and their herds in the land of Goshen. ⁹Men in chariots and on horses also went with Joseph. It was a very large group.

¹⁰They went to the threshing^d floor of Atad, east of the Jordan River. There they cried loudly and bitterly for Jacob, also called Israel. Joseph's time of sorrow continued for seven days. ¹¹The people that lived in Canaan saw the sadness at the threshing floor of Atad. They said, "Those Egyptians are showing great sorrow!" So now that place is named Sorrow of the Egyptians.

¹²So Jacob's sons did what their father commanded. ¹³They carried his body to the land of Canaan. They buried it in the cave in the field of Machpelah near Mamre. Abraham had bought this cave and field from Ephron the Hittite. He bought the cave to use as a burial place. ¹⁴After Joseph buried his father,

FEBRUARY PATIENCE

1 Let your sister or brother have the first turn on the computer.

2 Prayer Pointer: Ask God to show you what it means to be patient with him, with yourself, and with others.

3

4 Hide-It-in-Your-Heart: A wise person is patient. He will be honored if he ignores a wrong done against him (Proverbs 19:11).

5

6 Invite your friends to go home with you after school to build a sky-scraper out of Legos.

7

8

9 Chinese New Year

10

11 Prayer Pointer: Ask God to help your teachers grow in patience toward the students.

12

13 Make hearts out of salt dough. Put string through a hole in the top, and make necklaces for Valentine's Day.

14 Valentine's Day!

15

16

17 Spend an afternoon playing with your younger sister or brother.

18

19 Do 10 sit-ups and 10 push-ups before breakfast.

20

21 President's Day

22 Surprise your family by making everyone's bed before school.

23 Prayer Pointer: Pray for children around the world to hear about God's love for them.

24

25 Hide-It-in-Your-Heart: It is better to be patient than to be proud (Ecclesiastes 7:8).

26

27

28 Make beef stew with your mom, and take some to a neighbor.

LIVIN' IT!

FOR GOODNESS SAKE
GENESIS 50:1-26

It was more than just the fact that they laughed at him. Worse than just being teased or ridiculed. Joseph realized his brothers actually hated him so much, they even thought about killing him. And then they sold him to become a slave in a faraway land.

Joseph had endured years of hard times, but eventually became the ruler of the Egyptian kingdom. So when all was said and done, what did he have to say to his brothers? "You meant to hurt me. But God turned your evil into good" (Genesis 50:20). He wasn't bitter. Not even angry. God had given Joseph the wisdom to see that, no matter what people try to do to us, God is the one who still controls our every moment. Like Joseph, we need to keep our eyes on God's goodness and remember that he promises to make all things work for the best in our lives.

he returned to Egypt. His brothers and everyone who had gone with him to bury his father also returned.

THE BROTHERS FEAR JOSEPH

¹⁵After Jacob died, Joseph's brothers said, "What if Joseph is still angry with us? We did many wrong things to him. What if he plans to pay us back?" ¹⁶So they sent a message to Joseph. It said, "Your father gave this command before he died. ¹⁷He said to us, 'You have done wrong. You have sinned and done evil to Joseph. Tell Joseph to forgive you, his brothers.' So now, Joseph, we beg you to forgive our wrong. We are the servants of the God of your father." When Joseph received the message, he cried.

¹⁸And his brothers went to him and bowed low before him. They said, "We are your slaves."

¹⁹Then Joseph said to them, "Don't be afraid. Can I do what only God can do? ²⁰You meant to hurt me. But God turned your evil into good. It was to save the lives of many people. And it is being done. ²¹So don't be afraid. I will take care of you and your children." So Joseph comforted his brothers and spoke kind words to them.

²²Joseph continued to live in Egypt with all his father's family. He died when he was 110 years old. ²³During Joseph's life Ephraim had children and grandchildren. And Joseph's son Manasseh had a son named Makir. Joseph accepted Makir's children as his own.

THE DEATH OF JOSEPH

²⁴Joseph said to his brothers, "I am about to die. But God will take care of you. He will lead you out of this land. He will lead you to the land he promised to Abraham, Isaac and Jacob." ²⁵Then Joseph had the sons of Israel make a promise. He said, "Promise me that you will carry my bones with you out of Egypt."

²⁶Joseph died when he was 110 years old. Doctors prepared his body for burial. Then they put him in a coffin in Egypt.

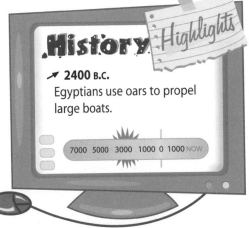

History Highlights

↗ **2400 B.C.**
Egyptians use oars to propel large boats.

7000 5000 3000 1000 0 1000 NOW

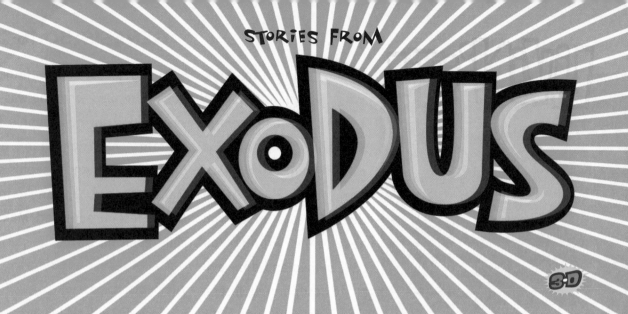

EXODUS

3-D

the Birth of MoSes

EXODUS 1:1—2:15

JACOB'S FAMILY IN EGYPT

1 When Jacob, also called Israel, went to Egypt, he took his sons. And each son took his own family with him. These are the names of the sons of Israel: ²Reuben, Simeon, Levi, Judah, ³Issachar, Zebulun, Benjamin, ⁴Dan, Naphtali, Gad and Asher. ⁵There was a total of 70 people who were descendants[d] of Jacob. Jacob's son Joseph was already in Egypt.

⁶By some time later, Joseph and his brothers had died, along with all the people who had lived at that same time. ⁷But the people of Israel had many children, and their number grew greatly. They became very strong, and the country of Egypt was filled with them.

TROUBLE FOR THE PEOPLE OF ISRAEL

⁸Then a new king began to rule Egypt. He did not know who Joseph was. ⁹This king said to his people, "Look! The people of Israel are too many! And they are too strong for us to handle! ¹⁰We must make plans against them. If we don't, the number of their people will grow even more. Then if there is a war, they might join our enemies. Then they could fight us and escape from the country!"

"So the Egyptians made life hard for the people of Israel. They put slave masters over the Israelites. The slave masters forced the Israelites to build the cities Pithom and Rameses for the king. These cities were supply centers in which the Egyptians stored things. ¹²The Egyptians forced the Israelites to work even harder. But this made the Israelites grow in number and spread

LiViN' iT!

SISTER SMARTS
EXODUS 2:1-15

Terrible times had come upon the Hebrew people. All the baby boys were being killed by the Egyptians who ruled over the Israelites. So what did Moses' mom do when he was born? She put him in a basket and sent him floating down the Nile River.

And that could have been the end of the story. But Moses' sister made sure it wasn't. She followed the basket closely and watched the miracle of the king's daughter finding—and keeping—the Hebrew baby as her own. Thinking fast, she offered to find a Hebrew woman to nurse the child. When she got the green light, she had his mother nurse him under the protection of the king himself!

Like Moses' sister, we need to be on the lookout for creative ways to reunite a lost world with our heavenly Father. Don't be afraid because you're young. Look for the right moment, and trust God to do a miracle through you!

more. So the Egyptians became more afraid of them. ¹³They forced the Israelites to work even harder. ¹⁴The Egyptians made life hard for the Israelites. They forced the Israelites to work very hard making bricks and mortar. They also forced them to do all kinds of hard work in the fields. The Egyptians were not merciful to them in all their hard work.

¹⁵There were two Hebrew nurses named Shiphrah and Puah. These nurses helped the Israelite women give birth to their babies. The king of Egypt said to the nurses, ¹⁶"When you are helping the Hebrew women give birth to their babies, watch! If the baby is a girl, let the baby live. But if it is a boy, kill it!" ¹⁷But the nurses feared God. So they did not do as the king told them. They let all the boy babies live. ¹⁸Then the king of Egypt sent for the nurses. He said, "Why did you do this? Why did you let the boys live?"

¹⁹The nurses said to him, "The Hebrew women are much stronger than the Egyptian women. They give birth to their babies before we can get there." ²⁰God was good to the nurses. And the Hebrew people continued to grow in number. So they became even stronger. ²¹Because the nurses

feared God, he gave them families of their own.

²²So the king commanded all his people: "Every time a boy is born to the Hebrews, you must throw him into the Nile River. But let all the girl babies live."

BABY MOSES

2 There was a man from the family of Levi. He married a woman who was also from the family of Levi. ²She became pregnant and gave birth to a son. She saw how wonderful the

IMAGINE HAVING TO GIVE BIRTH TO BABIES without a doctor, without a hospital, and without medicine! In Bible times (and still in some cultures today), babies were delivered by trained midwives—women who were experienced in helping mothers give birth and recognize signs of problems.

baby was, and she hid him for three months. ³But after three months, she was not able to hide the baby any longer. So she got a basket made of reeds and covered it with tar so that it would float. She put the baby in the basket. Then she put the basket among the tall grass at the edge of the Nile River. ⁴The

Ways to Encourage Your Parents

1. Pray for them.
2. Do your homework without being asked.
3. Tell them about your day.
4. Ask them how you can better help them.
5. Clean up your room without complaining.
6. Ask your parents their thoughts about your friends, and listen.
7. Put an encouraging note at your dad's place at the dinner table.
8. Read a bedtime story to your younger siblings.
9. Use your allowance to buy them a gift.
10. Tell them every day that you love them.

GET CONNECTED

RELATIONSHIPS WITH FRIENDS

Befriending Backstabbers Moses thought he would at least get a "thanks." After all, he had saved the Israelite's life by killing the cruel Egyptian. But the one he thought was his friend turned and told on him, instead. Moses had to flee the country.

Have you ever had a friend turn their back on you? Did they tell someone else your secret? Did they have a party and not invite you? In our lives, people—even the people closest to us—will let us down. It's just a part of the sin in their lives, as well as ours. We need to trust God to heal our broken hearts. Tell God about the hurt, and ask him to help you forgive the one who hurt you. Be sure to talk to your friends in love, so that your relationship can be strong again.

baby's sister stood a short distance away. She wanted to see what would happen to him.

⁵Then the daughter of the king of Egypt came to the river. She was going to take a bath. Her servant girls were walking beside the river. She saw the basket in the tall grass. So she sent her slave girl to get it. ⁶The king's daughter opened the basket and saw the baby boy. He was crying, and she felt sorry for him. She said, "This is one of the Hebrew babies."

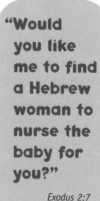

"Would you like me to find a Hebrew woman to nurse the baby for you?"

Exodus 2:7

⁷Then the baby's sister asked the king's daughter, "Would you like me to find a Hebrew woman to nurse the baby for you?"

⁸The king's daughter said, "Yes, please." So the girl went and got the baby's own mother.

⁹The king's daughter said to the woman, "Take this baby and nurse him for me. I will pay you." So the woman took her baby and nursed him. ¹⁰After the child had grown older, the woman took him to

CRAFTS

BABY MOSES' BOAT

SUPPLIES

1/4 cup light corn syrup

1/4 cup water, colored with red food coloring

1/4 cup vegetable oil

tall, thin glass, cup, or jar

ALL ABOUT IT:

Even though she knew it was for his good, it took a lot of courage for Moses' mother to put her baby in a basket and send him down the Nile River. To make the boat waterproof and to keep it from sinking, she covered the bottom of the basket with tar. Reading your Bible and obeying your parents are some things that will help you stay "afloat" in life.

FLOATING COLORS INSTRUCTIONS

1. Pour the corn syrup in the jar.

2. Slowly add the water to the corn syrup.

3. Finally, add the vegetable oil to the mixture.

What happened to the water? The same is true for you. First follow God's Word. Next follow your parents' example. Finally, live your life securely in the knowledge that God will hold you up and help you succeed.

3-D

EGYPTIANS BELIEVED THAT PHARAOH (the title given to their king or leader) was actually the sky god, named Horus, who had come to earth to rule them. From 2700 B.C. on, pharaohs became known for their pyramids.

the king's daughter. She adopted the baby as her own son. The king's daughter named him Moses,” because she had pulled him out of the water.

MOSES HELPS HIS PEOPLE

¹¹Moses grew and became a man. One day he visited his people, the Hebrews. He saw that they were forced to work very hard. He saw an Egyptian beating a He-brew man, one of Moses' own peo-ple. ¹²Moses looked all around and saw that no one was watching. So he killed the Egyptian and hid his body in the sand.

¹³The next day Moses returned and saw two Hebrew men fighting each other. He saw that one man was in the wrong. Moses said to that man, "Why are you hitting one of your own people?"

¹⁴The man answered, "Who made you our ruler and judge? Are you going to kill me as you killed the Egyptian?"

Then Moses was afraid. He thought, "Now everyone knows what I did."

¹⁵When the king heard about what Moses had done, he tried to kill Moses. But Moses ran away from the king and went to live in the land of Midian. There he sat down near a well.

2:10 **Moses** The name Moses sounds like the Hebrew word for "to pull out."

WORD SCRAMBLE

Times were confusing for the poor enslaved Israelites. Help them sort out these words relating to Moses' birth.

1. elvi _____

2. skbate _____

3. ienl revir _____

4. yabb ybo _____

5. brhewe _____

6. iantpegy _____

7. thba _____

8. vesla irgl _____

9. pteddao _____

10. semos _____

BurNing bush Encounter

EXODUS 3:1-17

THE BURNING BUSH

3 One day Moses was taking care of Jethro's sheep. Jethro was the priest of Midian and also Moses' father-in-law. Moses led the sheep to the west side of the desert. He came to Sinai, the mountain of God. ²There the angel of the Lord appeared to Moses in flames of fire coming out of a bush. Moses saw that the bush was on fire, but it was not burning up. ³So Moses said, "I will go closer to this strange thing. How can a bush continue burning without burning up?"

⁴The Lord saw Moses was coming to look at the bush. So God called to him from the bush, "Moses, Moses!"

And Moses said, "Here I am."

⁵Then God said, "Do not come any closer. Take off your sandals. You are standing on holy ground. ⁶I am the God of your ancestors. I am the God of Abraham, the God of Isaac and the God of Jacob." Moses covered his face because he was afraid to look at God.

⁷The Lord said, "I have seen the troubles my people have suffered in Egypt. And I have heard their cries when the Egyptian slave masters hurt them. I am concerned about their pain. ⁸I have come down to save them from the Egyptians. I will bring them out of that land. I will lead them to a good land with lots of

LiViN' iT!

STOP STAMMERING
EXODUS 3:1-17

God had saved him from the Egyptians. Raised him in the royal courts. Spared him from the soldiers. And now God was speaking directly to Moses from the burning bush. You would expect him to be a little nervous. And probably mutter some words of thanks. But when God asked Moses to return to Egypt to free his people, Moses made excuses! He argued that he wasn't the right fit for the job. God needed to consider someone else.

God wasn't pleased with Moses' response, and he doesn't like to hear it from us, either. Whenever God asks us to do something, he is the one who makes it possible and causes it to happen. We don't have to be spectacular people. We do have to trust in an incredible God. Next time you feel God calling you out of your comfort zone, don't be afraid! God gives us the power to obey!

BLAST FROM THE PAST

AT FIRST ANCIENT PEOPLE GROUPS had a hard time with their tools. Iron, an element found naturally in the ground, was used to make tools and weapons. The problem with iron is that it is soft and easily bent. Later they found that they could mix it with carbon to make steel, a much stronger material. A dagger with an iron blade was found in Pharaoh Tutankhamun's tomb, dating back to 1336-1327 B.C.

GET CONNECTED

RELATIONSHIPS WITH GOD

Your Own Burning Bush Sometimes God appeared in a cloud. Sometimes as a person. And sometimes as fire, such as when he spoke to Moses out of the burning bush. In the Old Testament, God was continuously making contact with his people, telling them truth and leading them in the right way.

God never changes. He still desires to speak to us today and to lead us in the truth. Most likely, you won't wake up each morning to a burning bush in your room. But because of Jesus, we can have total access to God. We can have an encounter with God just like Moses did every time we open God's Word. When we read it, we are reading the very words that God has spoken to us. They are living words that actually change our hearts and lives as we read and obey. Make sure to set aside time each day to spend with God and his Word.

room. This is a land where much food grows. This is the land of these people: the Canaanites, Hittites, Amorites, Perizzites, Hivites and Jebusites. [9] I have heard the cries of the people of Israel. I have seen the way the Egyptians have made life hard for them. [10] So now I am sending you to the king of Egypt. Go! Bring my people, the Israelites, out of Egypt!"

"But Moses said to God, "I am not a great man! Why should I be the one to go to the king and lead the Israelites out of Egypt?"

[12] God said, "I will be with you. This will be the proof that I am sending you: You will lead the people out of Egypt. Then all of you will worship me on this mountain."

[13] Moses said to God, "When I go to the Israelites, I will say to them, 'The God of your ancestors sent me to you.' What if the people say, 'What is his name?' What should I tell them?"

[14] Then God said to Moses, "I AM WHO I AM." When you go to the people of Israel, tell them, 'I AM sent me to you.'"

[15] God also said to Moses,

3:14 I . . . I AM The Hebrew words are like the name "YAHWEH." This Hebrew name for God, usually called "Lord," shows that God always lives and is always with his people.

REAL SUPER HEROES

MOSES

He had been spared, although all the other Hebrew boys his age had been killed. He had grown up in the king's courts learning the laws of the land, as well as the language. And yet, when God called him to action, Moses could see nothing but his shortcomings. He felt inadequate. He thought God had made a mistake.

But God doesn't make mistakes. God had planned on Moses before he had even made the world. Moses had his attention on what he couldn't do. But God knew what was possible through him.

God had mercy on Moses. He allowed Aaron to be his spokesman. But it was Moses who knew God. And it was through Moses that God told his people about himself.

We don't ever need to be self-conscious. Instead, we need to be aware of God. We need to know that he made us, he holds the plan, and he will make it happen.

When you're unsure of yourself, think of Moses. Remember God's grace. And rest in his power that, whatever he has called you to do, he will empower you to accomplish it.

EXODUS 3:16-17

"This is what you should tell the people: 'The Lord is the God of your ancestors. He is the God of Abraham, the God of Isaac and the God of Jacob. And he sent me to you.' This will always be my

name. That is how people from now on will know me.

[16]"Go and gather the elders and tell them this: 'The Lord, the God of your ancestors, has appeared to me. The God of Abraham, Isaac and Jacob spoke to

Exodus 3:1-17

A HOT TOPIC

If you saw a burning bush, you probably wouldn't take off your shoes. Of course, Moses did because he was having an once-in-a-lifetime encounter with God.

However, regular burning bushes are not out of the ordinary. Forest fires of many different kinds happen across the world in patterns almost as predictable as the rain. In fact, it seems as if creation was designed to allow for fires, which can actually help the vegetation that caused it. Basically, plants and trees in the forest produce leaves, branches, and bi-products that become a kind of fuel. They also give off oxygen, a required element for fire. Then all it takes is a spark—caused by lightning or a person not being careful with their campfire—and the forest fire begins. While fires can cause obvious damage, they also can clear out the way for new growth. Some plants can even take advantage of it, treating fire as a natural form of pruning that allows their roots to produce even better foliage.

Though creation can often fend for itself, we should never play with fire or test it out to see its impact. Leave the natural pruning up to God!

[Novaonline.Firewars.com]

me. He says: I care about you, and I have seen what has happened to you in Egypt. [17]I have decided that I will take you away from the troubles you are suffering in Egypt. I will lead you to the land of the Canaanites, Hittites, Amorites, Perizzites, Hivites and Jebusites. This land grows much food.'

WRITE OUT THE VERSE BELOW AND CONNECT THE DOTS.

Remember all of the amazing miracles God performed through Moses just to make a people all his own!

EXODUS 3:12

_____

_____

_____

_____

Moses Returns to Egypt

EXODUS 4:29–6:13, 28-30; 7:1-13

MOSES RETURNS TO EGYPT

4 So Moses and Aaron gathered all the elders of the Israelites. ³⁰Aaron told them everything that the Lord had told Moses. Then Moses did the miracles for all the people to see. ³¹So the Israelites believed. They heard that the Lord was concerned about them and had seen their troubles. Then they bowed down and worshiped him.

MOSES AND AARON BEFORE THE KING

5 After Moses and Aaron talked to the people, they went to the king of Egypt. They said, "This is what the Lord, the God of Israel says: 'Let my people go so they may hold a feast for me in the desert.'"

²But the king of Egypt said, "Who is the Lord? Why should I obey him and let Israel go? I do not know the Lord. And I will not let Israel go."

³Then Aaron and Moses said, "The God of the Hebrews has talked with us. Now let us travel three days into the desert. There we will offer sacrifices to the Lord our God. If we don't do this, he may kill us with a disease or in war."

THE BIBLE'S HISTORY TALKS ABOUT TWO MAIN PLACES: Mesopotamia and Egypt. It was at the southernmost part of Mesopotamia where Sumeria developed. Sumerians were known for forming the first township type of government. Unfortunately, they worshiped a false god which affected not only their money, communities, and spiritual lives, but also changed many other groups of people around them.

BLAST FROM THE PAST

⁴But the king said to them, "Moses and Aaron, why are you taking the people away from their work? Go back to your hard work! ⁵There are very many Hebrews. And now you want them to quit their hard work!"

⁶That same day the king gave a command to the slave masters and foremen. ⁷He

GET CONNECTED

RELATIONSHIPS WITH FRIENDS

Super Support Moses had all the training and experience, but he was still afraid to go to the king on behalf of God's people. Though God could have easily forced him, instead God gave him a brother with a little more guts.

Let's face it. Life is easier with friends. And obeying God comes easier when we are surrounded by other people who want to do the same thing. The Bible says that two are better than one, because one can help the other when the time for help comes.

What about you? Do you have friends who can help you serve God better? If not, ask God right now to provide what you need and to help you become the kind of friend that others need.

said, "Don't give the people straw to make bricks as you used to do. Let them gather their own straw. 8But they must still make the same number of bricks as they did before. Do not accept fewer. They have become lazy. That is why they are asking me, 'Let us go to offer sacrifices to our God.' 9Make these people work harder. Keep them busy. Then they will not have time to listen to the lies of Moses."

10So the slave masters and foremen went to the Israelites and said, "This is what the king says: I will no longer give you straw. 11Go and get your own straw wherever you can find it. But you must make as many bricks as you made before." 12So the people went everywhere in Egypt looking for dry stalks to use for straw. 13The slave masters kept forcing the people to work harder. They said, "You must make just as many bricks as you did when you were given straw." 14The king's slave masters had chosen the Israelite foremen. They had made them responsible for the work the people did. The Egyptian slave masters beat these men and asked them, "Why aren't you making as many bricks as you made in the past?"

15Then the Israelite foremen went to the king. They complained and said, "Why are you treating us, your servants, this way? 16You give us no straw. But we are commanded to make bricks. Our slave masters beat us. But it is your own people's fault."

17The king answered, "You are lazy! You don't want to work! That is why you ask to leave here and make sacrifices to the Lord. 18Now, go back to work! We will not give you any straw. But you must make just as many bricks as you did before."

DIG THIS!

If you've seen pictures of the Middle East, you might wonder how Egyptians and other people were able to grow anything in such desert-like conditions. Early on, Egyptians learned how to use the water from the Nile River for all their crops and their daily household uses. It's easy to see why turning the Nile's water into blood was such a problem for the whole country.

REAL SUPER HEROES

AARON

Sometimes, to be a good leader, you have to be a good follower. But the catch is following the right leader. Aaron, Moses' brother, was from the tribe of Levi. Unlike Moses, who continued to ask God to send someone else, Aaron was eager to do the Lord's work. So after Moses complained to God about his assigned task, God allowed Aaron to work alongside Moses.

But God didn't speak directly to Aaron. He spoke through Moses, and Moses instructed Aaron. Once when Moses was gone a long time talking to God, Aaron acted on his own and ended up leading Israel into sin when he made a golden calf to worship. But after Moses returned, Aaron returned to following what was right and, in turn, became a strong spiritual leader for Israel.

As a kid, God has also given you leaders to help you become strong. Your parents and teachers can help you understand God's ways. As you follow them, you too will become a strong leader for those around you.

[19]The Israelite foremen knew they were in trouble. This was because the king had told them: "You must make just as many bricks each day as you did before." [20]As they were leaving the meeting with the king, they met Moses and Aaron. Moses and Aaron were waiting for them. [21]So they said to Moses and Aaron,

"May the Lord punish you.

History Highlights

➚ 2166 B.C. – 1991 B.C.
Abraham's Life

7000 5000 3000 1000 0 1000 NOW

You caused the king and his officers to hate us. You have given them an excuse to kill us."

MOSES COMPLAINS TO GOD

[22]Then Moses returned to the Lord and said, "Lord, why have you brought this trouble on your people? Is this why you sent me here? [23]I went to the king and said what you told me to say. But ever since that time he has made the people suffer.

And you have done nothing to save them."

6 Then the Lord said to Moses, "Now you will see what I will do to the king of Egypt. I will use my great power against him, and he will let my people go. Because of my power, he will force them out of his country."

[2]Then God said to Moses, "I am the Lord. [3]I appeared to Abraham, Isaac and Jacob by the name, God All-Powerful. But they did not know me by my name, the Lord. [4]I also

made my agreement with them to give them the land of Canaan. They lived in that land, but it was not their own land. [5]Now I have heard the cries of the Israelites. The Egyptians are treating them as slaves. And I remember my agreement. [6]So tell the people of Israel that I say to them, 'I am the Lord. I will save you from the hard work the Egyptians force you to do. I will make you free. You will not be slaves to the Egyptians. I will free you by my great power. And I will punish the Egyptians terri-

Exodus 5:1-21

HARD-PRESSED

WILD WORLD FACTS

The Israelites weren't happy. Ever since Moses showed up, their work was becoming harder and harder. They made bricks for the king. Because the king didn't like Moses, he took away the straw the Israelites needed to make bricks.

Back then bricks were made by hand—the combination of straw, mud, and other natural products mixed together, poured into molds, and dried by the sun. Over the centuries, the process has become much easier. Today bricks are usually made from either clay or ground shale. Clay bricks can be made through the soft-mud method, where the clay is poured into molds and dried. Commercial makers use the stiff-mud process, where the clay is forced through a die and then cut into the proper shape. Once clay bricks are molded, a hydraulic press is used to make them dense and compact. Then the bricks are fired in a kiln (a special oven that gets extremely hot). When a little salt is added to the process, the bricks become more water-resistant. Then they are ready for building or making roadways.

[Wikipedia: Brick]

WHERE DID THE HEBREWS COME FROM? Many scholars believe the name comes from a group of people known as the Habiru. Other historical writings like the Armana letters, the Mari tablets, and the Nuzi documents describe them as "armed brigands" (soldiers) because of the way they traveled from place to place and formed small groups to help protect themselves.

bly. ⁷I will make you my own people, and I will be your God. You will know that I am the Lord your God. I am the One who saves you from the hard work the Egyptians force you to do. ⁸I will lead you to the land that I promised to Abraham, Isaac and Jacob. I will give you that land to own. I am the Lord.'"

⁹So Moses told this to the people of Israel. But they would not listen to him. They were discouraged, and their slavery was hard.

¹⁰Then the Lord said to Moses, ¹¹"Go tell the king of Egypt that he must let the Israelites leave his land."

¹²But Moses answered, "The Israelites will not listen to me. So surely the king will not listen to me, either. I am not a good speaker."

¹³But the Lord told Moses and Aaron to talk to the king. He commanded them to lead the Israelites out of Egyp.

•••

GOD REPEATS HIS CALL TO MOSES

²⁸The Lord spoke to Moses in the land of Egypt. ²⁹He said, "I am the Lord. Tell the king of Egypt everything I tell you."

³⁰But Moses answered, "I am not a good speaker. The king will not listen to me."

7 The Lord said to Moses, "I have made you like God to the king of Egypt. And your brother Aaron will be like a prophet^d for you. ²Tell Aaron your brother everything that I command you. Then let him tell the king of Egypt to let the Israelites leave his country. ³But I will make the king stubborn. Then I will do many miracles^d in Egypt. ⁴But he will still refuse to listen. So then I will punish Egypt terribly. And I will lead my divisions, my people the Israelites, out of that land. ⁵I will punish Egypt with my power. And I will bring the Israelites out of that land. Then they will know I am the Lord."

⁶Moses and Aaron did just as the Lord had commanded them. ⁷Moses was 80 years old, and Aaron was 83, when they spoke to the king.

"i will make you my own people, and i will be your God. You will know that i am the Lord your God."

Exodus 6:7

3-D

AARON'S WALKING STICK
BECOMES A SNAKE

3-D

[8]The Lord said to Moses and Aaron, [9]"The king will ask you to do a miracle.[d] When he does, Moses, you tell Aaron to throw his walking stick down in front of the king. It will become a snake."

[10]So Moses and Aaron went to the king as the Lord had commanded. Aaron threw his walking stick down in front of the king and his officers. And it became a snake.

[11]So the king called in his wise men and his magicians. With their tricks the Egyptian magicians were able to do the same thing. [12]They threw their walking sticks on the ground, and their sticks became snakes. But then Aaron's stick swallowed theirs. [13]But the king was stubborn. He refused to listen to Moses and Aaron, just as the Lord had said.

the Plagues

EXODUS 7:14—10:29

THE WATER BECOMES BLOOD

7 Then the Lord said to Moses, "The king is being stubborn. He refuses to let the people go. ¹⁵In the morning the king will go out to the Nile River. Go meet him by the edge of the river. Take with you the walking stick that became a snake. ¹⁶Tell him this: The Lord, the God of the Hebrews, sent me to you. He said, 'Let my people go worship me in the desert.' Until now you have not listened. ¹⁷This is what the Lord says: 'This is how you will know that I am the Lord. I will strike the water of the Nile River with this stick in my hand. And the water will change into blood. ¹⁸Then the fish in the Nile will die, and the river will begin to stink. And the Egyptians will not be able to drink the water from the Nile.'"

¹⁹The Lord said to Moses, "Tell Aaron to stretch the walking stick in his hand over the rivers, canals, ponds and pools in Egypt. The water will become blood everywhere in Egypt. There even will be blood in the wooden buckets and stone jars."

²⁰So Moses and Aaron did just as the Lord had commanded. Aaron raised his walking stick and struck the water in the Nile River. He did this in front of the king and his officers. So all the water in the Nile changed into blood. ²¹The fish in the Nile died, and the river began to stink. So the Egyptians could not drink water from it. Blood was everywhere in the land of Egypt.

²²Using their tricks, their magicians of Egypt did the same thing. So the king was stubborn and refused to listen to Moses and Aaron. This happened just as the Lord had said. ²³The king turned and went into his palace. He ignored what Moses and Aaron had done. ²⁴The Egyptians could not drink the water from the Nile. So all of them dug along the bank of the river. They were looking for water to drink.

THE FROGS

²⁵Seven days passed after the Lord changed the Nile River.

8 Then the Lord told Moses, "Go to the king of Egypt and tell him, 'This is what the Lord says: Let my people go to worship me. ²If you refuse, then I will punish Egypt with frogs. ³The Nile River will be filled with frogs. They will come from the river and enter your palace. They will be in your bedroom and your bed. The frogs will enter the houses of your officers and your people. They will enter your ovens and your baking pans. ⁴The frogs will jump up all over

> **"This is how you will know that I am the Lord. I will strike the water of the Nile River with this stick in my hand. And the water will change into blood."**
>
> *Exodus 7:17*

you, your people and your officers.'"

5Then the Lord said to Moses, "Tell Aaron to hold his walking stick in his hand over the rivers, canals and ponds. Make frogs come up out of the water onto the land of Egypt."

6So Aaron held his hand over all the waters of Egypt. The frogs came up out of the water and covered the land of Egypt. 7The magicians used their tricks to do the same thing. So even more frogs came up onto the land of Egypt.

8So the king called for Moses and Aaron. He said, "Pray to the Lord to take the frogs away from me and my people. I will let your people go to offer sacrifices to the Lord."

9Moses said to the king, "Please set the time that I should pray for you, your people and your officers. Then the frogs will

Bible Critters — FAST FORWARD FROGS

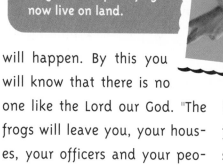

It was bad enough that Moses just spoke the word and they began crawling out of the Nile River. But **FROGS** weren't supposed to appear that fast! In fact, frogs are actually born from eggs that are laid in the water. When they hatch, they emerge as tadpoles and look nothing like frogs. Over the next couple of months though, the tail shrinks, legs and arms form, and the gills or glands that enabled the tadpole to breath in water (like a fish) gives way to lungs that help the frog now live on land.

will happen. By this you will know that there is no one like the Lord our God. "The frogs will leave you, your houses, your officers and your people. They will remain only in the Nile."

12Moses and Aaron left the king. Moses asked the Lord about the frogs he had sent to the king. 13And the Lord did as Moses asked. The frogs died in

king saw that they were free of the frogs, he became stubborn again. He did not listen to Moses and Aaron, just as the Lord had said.

THE GNATS

16Then the Lord said to Moses, "Tell Aaron to raise his walking stick and strike the dust on the

>
> **"The frogs will jump up all over you, your people and your officers."** Exodus 8:4

leave you and your houses. They will remain only in the Nile."

10The king answered, "Tomorrow."

Moses said, "What you want

the houses, in the yards and in the fields. 14The Egyptians put them in piles. The whole country began to stink. 15When the

ground. Then everywhere in Egypt the dust will change into gnats." 17They did this. Aaron raised the walking stick that was

CRAFTS

MOSES, PHARAOH, AND THE PLAGUES

bowl

milk

food coloring

dishwashing soap

ALL ABOUT IT:

Many times things are not what they appear to be. Moses warned the king about each plague before it came. As we read the account of what happened, it is hard for us to see why the king wouldn't listen to Moses or turn to God before the plagues came upon Egypt. However, when our focus is not on God and his plans for our lives, we too will make poor choices.

When the king's magicians were able to copy the first couple of the miracles Moses did, the king didn't listen to Moses. But as the plagues continued, the magicians were not able to reproduce what only the power of God could produce.

As you do the experiment below, you will see that you have the ability to erase colors. Look closely. Are they all gone or just moved? When we sin, only God has the power to cleanse and take away our sin through the blood of Jesus. Keep your eyes on God, trust his plans for your life, and be on the lookout for the "magicians" around you.

INSTRUCTIONS

1. Fill a bowl half full of milk (whole milk is best).

2. Drop ten drops of food coloring into the milk.

3. Let the colors swirl around, then drop one drop of dishwashing soap in the milk.

What happened to the colors?

Note: Do not drink the milk!

To redo the experiment, you should start with a fresh bowl of milk.

3-D

BLAST FROM THE PAST

FROM THE BEGINNING OF TIME, people have relied on different kinds of grain to live. Flax was grown for its fibers, which help make linen. Spelt is a food grain like wheat, but can grow in drier, desert places. Wheat and barley have been grown in Egypt since 5000 B.C. and in Palestine since 8000 B.C.

in his hand and struck the dust on the ground. Then everywhere in Egypt the dust changed into gnats. The gnats got on the people and animals. [18]Using their tricks, the magicians tried to do the same thing. But they could not make the dust change into gnats. The gnats remained on the people and animals. [19]So the magicians told the king that the power of God had done this. But the king was stubborn and refused to listen to them. This happened just as the Lord had said.

THE FLIES

[20]The Lord told Moses, "Get up early in the morning. Meet the king of Egypt as he goes out to the river. Tell him, 'This is what the Lord says: Let my people go so they can worship me. [21]If you don't let them go, I will send swarms of flies. I will send them into your houses. The flies will be on you, your officers and your people. The houses of Egypt will be full of flies. And they will be all over the ground, too. [22]But I will not treat the people of Israel the same as the Egyptian people. There will not be any flies in the land of Goshen, where my people live. By this you will know that I, the Lord, am in this land. [23]I will treat my people differently from your people. This miracle[d] will happen tomorrow.'"

> **"if you don't let them go, i will send swarms of flies."** *Exodus 8:21*

[24]So the Lord did as he had said. Great swarms of flies came into the king's palace and his officers' houses. All over Egypt flies were ruining the land. [25]The king called for Moses and Aaron. He told them, "Offer sacrifices to your God here in this country."

[26]But Moses said, "It wouldn't be right to do that. The Egyptians hate the sacrifices we offer to the Lord our God. They will see us offer sacrifices they hate. Then they will throw stones at us and kill us. [27]Let us make a three-day journey into the desert. We must offer sacrifices to the Lord our God there. This is what the Lord told us to do."

²⁸The king said, "I will let you go. Then you may offer sacrifices to the Lord your God in the desert. But you must not go very far away. Now go and pray for me."

²⁹Moses said, "I will leave and pray to the Lord. He will take the flies away from you, your officers and your people tomorrow. But do not try to trick us again. Do not stop the people from going to offer sacrifices to the Lord."

³⁰So Moses left the king and prayed to the Lord. ³¹And the Lord did as Moses asked. He removed the flies from the king, his officers and his people. Not one fly was left. ³²But the king became stubborn again and did not let the people go.

THE DISEASE ON THE FARM ANIMALS

9 Then the Lord told Moses, "Go to the king of Egypt. Tell him, 'This is what the Lord, the God of the Hebrews, says: Let my people go to worship me. ²You might refuse to let them go and continue to hold them. ³Then the Lord will punish you. He will send a terrible disease on all your farm animals. He will cause all of your horses, donkeys, camels, cattle and sheep to become sick. ⁴But the Lord will treat Israel's animals differently from the animals of Egypt. None of the animals that belong to the Israelites will die. ⁵The Lord has set tomorrow as the time he will do this in the land.'" ⁶The next day the Lord did as he promised. All the farm animals in Egypt died. But none of the animals belonging to Israelites died. ⁷The king sent people to see what had happened to the animals of Israel. They found that not one of them had died. But the king was still stubborn. He did not let the people go.

THE BOILS

⁸The Lord said to Moses and Aaron, "Fill your hands with the ashes from a furnace. Moses, throw the ashes into the air in front of the king of Egypt. ⁹The

WILD WORLD FACTS

Exodus 9:8-12

BAD OOZE FOR EGYPT

Imagine going to bed with the clear, smooth skin you've always enjoyed. Then you wake up to find hundreds of zitlike bumps all over your whole body! Pretty horrifying thought, isn't it? But it's basically what happened to the Egyptians.

A boil, also called a skin abscess, is an infection that happens in the skin, often surrounding the root of a hair. As the infection grows, your body sends white blood cells to fight it off—which, combined with proteins and the bacteria, is known as pus. The infected areas ooze pus until the source of the infection is removed.

Different kinds of boils require different treatments. Often hot and cold compresses can release the infection and cure it. Sometimes antibiotics are needed. And in some cases, surgery is required. In the Egyptians' case, all they needed was a king who would obey God!

[Medicinenet.com]

Boil

ashes will spread like dust through all the land of Egypt. The dust will cause boils to break out and become sores on the skin. These sores will be on people and animals everywhere in the land."

¹⁰So Moses and Aaron took ashes from a furnace. Then they went and stood before the king. Moses threw ashes into the air. It caused boils to break out and become sores on people and animals. ¹¹The magicians could not stand before Moses. This was because all the Egyptians had boils, even the magicians. ¹²But the Lord made the king stubborn. So he refused to listen to Moses and Aaron. This happened just as the Lord had said.

THE HAIL

¹³Then the Lord said to Moses, "Get up early in the morning and go to the king of Egypt. Tell him, 'This is what the Lord, the God of the Hebrews, says: Let my people go to worship me. ¹⁴If you do not do this, this time I will punish you with all my power. I will punish you, your officers and your people. Then you will know that there is no one in the whole land like me. ¹⁵By now I could have used my power and caused a bad disease. It would have destroyed you and your people from the earth. ¹⁶But I have let you live for this reason: to show you my power. In this way my name will be talked about in all the earth. ¹⁷You are still against my people. You do not want to let them go. ¹⁸So at this time tomorrow, I will send a terrible hailstorm. It will be the

> **"The dust will cause boils to break out and become sores on the skin."** *Exodus 9:9*

WILD WORLD FACTS

Exodus 9:13-35

ALL HAIL, THE WEATHER

While hail was most likely a new phenomena for the Egyptians back in Moses' day, people today across the world are well aware of its damaging impact. Each year, hail causes more than one billion dollars of damage to crops and property.

Hailstones are formed during storms where strong, warm updrafts and cold downdrafts are present. When this happens, each water droplet that begins to fall gets caught in the updraft, shooting the water up higher into the sky where the temperatures are very low. The water freezes and then falls in the downdraft, where it partially thaws. If it gets caught in another updraft, more layers of rainwater will coat the half-frozen ball, causing it to get thicker. This cycle keeps repeating itself until the hailstone breaks free and falls to the earth at speeds of up to 120 mph. The largest hailstone ever recorded was 17.5 inches and weighed almost 2 pounds!

[NOAA.gov]

PLAGUED WITH PROBLEMS!

The king wasn't a fast learner, but are you? How much do you know about the plagues God sent on Egypt? Take this quiz to see where you stand.

1 WHO WAS SENT TO TALK TO THE KING?

A Moses alone
B Moses and Miriam
C Moses and Aaron
D Moses and his wife

2 WHAT WAS THE FIRST MIRACLE MOSES DEMONSTRATED?

A a burning bush
B water into blood
C a stick turned into a snake
D frogs

3 WHAT HAPPENED TO THE MAGICIANS' SNAKES?

A They slithered off.
B They bit the magicians.
C They were eaten by Moses' snake.
D They vanished.

4 WHAT DID MOSES TURN INTO BLOOD?

A the Nile River
B all the water in the jugs and pots
C both a and b
D none of the above

5 WHICH OF THE FOLLOWING PLAGUES DID GOD NOT SEND?

A gnats
B flies
C worms
D frogs

6 WHEN GOD SENT THE PLAGUE ON EGYPT'S ANIMALS, WHAT HAPPENED TO ISRAEL'S ANIMALS?

A They got sick and died.
B They ate the Egyptian's animals.
C Nothing.
D They began complaining.

7 WHERE DID THE LOCUSTS COME FROM?

A the north
B the south
C the east
D the west

8 WHAT FINALLY GOT TO THE KING?

A the boils
B the darkness
C Moses
D the death of his child

9 HOW DID ISRAEL ESCAPE THE ANGEL OF DEATH?

A They prayed hard.
B They tried to be really good.
C They smeared lamb's blood on their doorposts.
D They hid.

10 WHEN DID THE KING GIVE MOSES THE WORD FOR THE ISRAELITES TO LEAVE?

A a week later
B the next day
C the night his child died
D he never did

Squigglty-boo!

Score 9-10: Congratulations, you know your stuff!
Score 7-8: You were awake in class, but not taking notes. Grab your pencil!
Score 5-6: Wake up! You must have been sleeping.
Score 4 or below: You must have cut class altogether! Get in the Word!

With your 3D glasses on, close your right eye to reveal what the magician made appear! **3-D**

ANSWERS: 1. c; 2. c; 3. c; 4. c; 5. c; 6. c; 7. c; 8. d; 9. c; 10. c

BiBLe CRiTTeRS

3·D

SHOO FLY

Have you ever wondered w
HOUSEFLY can be foun
made of three main parts:
really interesting. What ma
They can turn solids into li
They actually vomit up foo
That's why flies are known

worst in Egypt since it became a nation. ¹⁹Now send for your animals and whatever you have in the fields. Bring them into a safe place. The hail will fall on every person or animal that is still in the fields. If they have not been brought in, they will die.'" ²⁰Some of the king's officers respected the word of the Lord. They hurried to bring their slaves and animals inside. ²¹But others ignored the Lord's message. They left their slaves and animals in the fields.

²²The Lord told Moses, "Raise your hand toward the sky. Then the hail will start falling over all the land of Egypt. It will fall on people, animals and on everything that grows in the fields of Egypt." ²³So Moses raised his walking stick toward the sky. And the Lord sent thunder and hail. And lightning flashed down to the earth. So he caused hail to fall upon the land of Egypt. ²⁴There was hail, and there was lightning flashing as it hailed. This was the worst hailstorm in Egypt since it had become a nation. ²⁵The hail destroyed everything that was in the fields in all the land of Egypt. The hail destroyed both people and animals. It also destroyed everything that grew in the fields. It broke all the trees in the fields. ²⁶The only place it did not hail was in the land of Goshen. The people of Israel lived there.

²⁷The king sent for Moses and Aaron. He told them, "This time I have sinned. The Lord is in the right. And I and my people are in the wrong. ²⁸Pray to the Lord. We have had enough of God's thunder and hail. I will let you go. You do not have to stay here any longer."

²⁹Moses told the king, "When I leave the city, I will raise my hands to the Lord in prayer. And the thunder and hail will stop. Then you will know that the earth belongs to the Lord. ³⁰But I know that you and your officers do not yet fear the Lord God."

³¹The flax was in bloom, and the barley had ripened. So these crops were destroyed. ³²But both wheat crops ripen later. So they were not destroyed.

"Raise your hand toward the sky. Then the hail will start falling over all the land of Egypt."

Exodus 9:22

Dig This!

Ever heard of King Tut? His real name was Tutankhamun, and he was an Egyptian king who ruled Egypt very close—within 100 years—to the Israelites' escape. Though buried in 1336 B.C., archaeologists discovered his burial spot and found all of his treasures buried along with him in his pyramid.

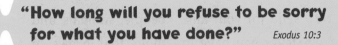

"How long will you refuse to be sorry for what you have done?" *Exodus 10:3*

³³Moses left the king and went outside the city. He raised his hands to the Lord. And the thunder and hail stopped. The rain also stopped falling to the ground. ³⁴The king saw that the rain, hail and thunder had stopped. Then he sinned again. He and his officers became stubborn again. ³⁵The king became stubborn and refused to let the Israelites go. This happened just as the Lord had said through Moses.

THE LOCUSTS

10 The Lord said to Moses, "Go to the king of Egypt. I have made him and his officers stubborn. I did this so I could show them my powerful miracles.ᵈ ²I also did this so you could tell your children and your grandchildren. Tell them how I made fools of the Egyptians. Tell them about the miracles I did among them. Then all of you will know that I am the Lord."

³So Moses and Aaron went to the king. They told him, "This is what the Lord, the God of the Hebrews, says: 'How long will you refuse to be sorry for what you have done?

Let my people go to worship me. ⁴If you refuse to let my people go, tomorrow I will bring locustsᵈ into your country. ⁵They will cover the land, and no one will be able to see the ground. They will eat anything that was left from the hailstorm. They will eat the leaves from every tree growing in the field. ⁶They will fill your palaces and all your officers' houses. They will fill the houses of all the Egyptian people. There will be more locusts than your fathers or ancestors have ever seen. There will be more locusts than there have been since people began living in Egypt.'" Then Moses turned and walked away from the king.

⁷The king's officers asked him, "How long will this man make trouble for us? Let the Israelite men go to worship the Lord their God. Don't you know that Egypt is ruined?"

⁸So Moses and Aaron were brought back to the king. He said to them, "Go and worship the Lord your God. But tell me, just who is going?"

⁹Moses answered, "We will go with our young and our old people, our sons and daughters and sheep and cattle. This is because we are going to have a feast to honor the Lord."

¹⁰The king said to them, "The Lord really will have to be with

> **"if you refuse to let my people go, tomorrow i will bring locusts into your country."**
> *Exodus 10:4*

you if ever I let you and all of your children leave Egypt. See, you are planning something evil. "No! Only the men may go and worship the Lord. That is what you have been asking for." Then the king forced Moses and Aaron out of his palace.

[12]The Lord told Moses, "Raise your hand over the land of Egypt, and the locusts will come. They will spread all over the land of Egypt. They will eat all the plants that the hail did not destroy."

[13]So Moses raised his walking stick over the land of Egypt. And the Lord caused a strong wind to blow from the east. It blew across the land all that day and night. When morning came, the east wind had brought the locusts. [14]Swarms of locusts covered all the land of Egypt and settled everywhere. There were more locusts than ever before or after. [15]The locusts covered the whole land so that it was black. They ate everything that was left after the hail. They ate every plant in the field and all the fruit on the trees. Nothing green was left on any tree or plant anywhere in Egypt.

[16]The king quickly called for Moses and Aaron. He said, "I have sinned against the Lord your God and against you. [17]Now forgive my sin this time. Pray to the Lord your God. Ask him to stop this punishment that kills."

[18]Moses left the king and prayed to the Lord. [19]So the Lord changed the wind. He made a very strong wind to blow from the west. It blew the locusts away into the Red Sea.[d] Not one locust was left anywhere in Egypt. [20]But the Lord caused the king to be stubborn again. And he did not let the people of Israel go.

LIVIN' iT!

A SORRY APOLOGY
EXODUS 10:16-20

"Well, I *said* I'm sorry!" It's a common apology among kids. The kind that has all the right words and all the wrong meaning. What does it mean to be truly sorry? The king of Egypt didn't seem to know. He did know that he didn't like the plagues God was sending on his people. He wanted them to stop. So he told Moses he was sorry for keeping the children of Israel in Egypt. But as soon as the Israelites began to leave, he took back his word. The king ordered them to stay—again.

When we see a sin in our lives, God tells us we must repent. What that means is to admit that we've done wrong, and we need God to cleanse our hearts. Then we take positive steps to not do that same sin over again. A true apology is one offered with a humble heart—a heart that understands how much we need God's forgiveness and his strength to do right the next time.

THE DARKNESS

[21]Then the Lord told Moses, "Raise your hand toward the sky, and darkness will cover the land of Egypt. It will be so dark you will be able to feel it." [22]So Moses raised his hand toward the sky. Then total darkness was everywhere in Egypt for three days. [23]No one could see anyone else.

And no one could go anywhere for three days. But the Israelites had light where they lived.

[24]Again the king of Egypt called for Moses. He said, "All of

[25]Moses said, "You must let us have animals to use as sacrifices and burnt offerings. We have to offer them to the Lord our God. [26]So we must take our animals with

We will know when we get there."

[27]But the Lord made the king stubborn again. So he refused to let them go. [28]Then he told Moses, "Get out of here! Don't

> **"You must let us have animals to use as sacrifices and burnt offerings. We have to offer them to the Lord our God."** *Exodus 10:25*

you may go and worship the Lord. You may take your women and children with you. But you must leave your sheep and cattle here."

us. Not a hoof will be left behind. We have to use some of the animals to worship the Lord our God. We do not yet know exactly what we will need to worship the Lord.

come here again! The next time you see me, you will die."

[29]Then Moses told the king, "I'll do what you say. I will not come to see you again."

the PaSSoVeR

EXODUS 11:1—12:30

THE DEATH OF THE FIRSTBORN

11 Now the Lord had told Moses, "I have one more way to punish the king and the people of Egypt. After this, the king will send all of you away from Egypt. When he does, he will force you to leave completely. ²Tell the men and women of Israel to ask their neighbors for things made of silver and gold." ³The Lord had caused the Egyptians to respect the Israelites. The king's officers and the Egyptian people already considered Moses to be a great man.

⁴So Moses said to the king, "This is what the Lord says: 'About midnight tonight I will go through all Egypt. ⁵Every firstborn[d] son in the land of Egypt will die. The firstborn son of the king, who sits on his throne, will die. Even the firstborn of the slave girl grinding grain will die. Also the firstborn farm animals will die. ⁶There will be loud crying everywhere in Egypt. It will be worse than any time before or after this. ⁷But not even a dog will bark at the Israelites or their animals.' Then you will know that the Lord treats Israel differently from Egypt. ⁸Then all your officers will come to me. They will bow facedown to the ground before me. They will say, 'Leave and take all your people with you.' After that, I will leave." Then Moses very angrily left the king.

⁹The Lord had told Moses, "The king will not listen to you and Aaron. This is so that I may do many miracles[d] in the land of Egypt." ¹⁰Moses and Aaron did all these great miracles in front of the king. But the Lord made him stubborn. And the king would not let the people of Israel leave his country.

PASSOVER

12 The Lord spoke to Moses and Aaron in the land of Egypt: ²"This month will be the first month of the year for you. ³Both of you are to tell the whole community of Israel: On the tenth day of this month each man must get one lamb. It is for the people in his house. ⁴There may not be enough people in his house to eat a whole lamb. Then he must share it with his closest neighbor. There must be enough lamb for everyone to eat. ⁵The lamb must be a one-year-old male. It must have nothing wrong with it. This animal can be either a young sheep or a young goat. ⁶Keep the

BiBLe BaSiCS

WHaT IS THe PaSSoVeR?

When the Israelites were still slaves in Egypt, God used many different plagues to convince the king to let them leave. The last plague was the angel of death that passed over the houses killing every firstborn child. The only way to save a child was to put the blood of a spotless lamb on the doorposts of the home. Jews still celebrate Passover feasts to remember that event. Christians can celebrate it, too, because we have the blood of God's spotless Lamb, Jesus Christ, covering and protecting us.

GOD'S FORGIVENESS

God has always used blood to forgive sins. This Old Testament picture points us to the ultimate sacrifice on the cross made by Jesus, the Lamb of God.

Connect the dots, color the picture, then write the verse below.

EXODUS 12:13

animal with you to take care of it until the fourteenth day of the month. On that day all the people of the community of Israel will kill these animals. They will do this as soon as the sun goes down. [7]The people must take some of the blood. They must put it on the sides and tops of the doorframes. These are the doorframes of the houses where they eat the lambs. [8]On this night they must roast the lamb over a fire. Then they must eat it with bitter herbs and bread made without yeast. [9]Do not eat the lamb raw or boiled in water. Roast the whole lamb over a fire—with its head, legs and inner organs. [10]You must not leave any of it until morning. But if any of it is left over until morning, you must burn it with fire.

[11]"This is the way you must eat it: You must be fully dressed as if you were going on a trip. You must have your sandals on, and you must have your walking stick in your hand. You must eat it in a hurry. This is the Lord's Passover.[d]

[12]"That night I will go through the land of Egypt. I will kill all the firstborn[d] of animals and people in the land of Egypt. I will punish all the gods of Egypt. I am the Lord. [13]But the blood will be a sign on the houses where you are. When I see the blood, I will pass over you. Nothing terrible will hurt you when I punish the land of Egypt.

[14]"You are always to remember this day. Celebrate it with a feast to the Lord. Your descendants[d] are to honor the Lord with this feast from now on. [15]For this feast you must eat bread made without yeast for seven days. On the first day of this feast, you are to remove all the yeast from your houses. No one should eat any yeast for the full seven days of the feast. If anyone eats yeast, then that person will be separated from Israel. [16]You are to have holy meetings on the first and last days of the feast. You must not do any work on these days. The only work you may do on these days is to prepare your meals. [17]You must celebrate the Feast[d] of Unleavened Bread. Do this because on this very day I brought your divisions of people out of Egypt. So all of your descendants must celebrate this day. This is a law that will last from now on. [18]You are to eat bread made without yeast. Start this on the evening of the fourteenth day of the first month of

BLAST FROM THE PAST

IN 1200 B.C. PEOPLE began using iron instead of bronze to make tools and weapons. Iron became known as the common symbol of war.

DIG THIS!

Change has changed over the centuries. Up until 625 B.C., people didn't have coins for money like we do today. Instead, they used silver and gold—often storing them as thick, bulky jewelry—as a way of showing wealth and holding power to trade. A necklace buried with Psusennes I (a pharaoh) in about 991 B.C. and discovered in 1940 A.D. weighs more than 42 pounds.

INCREDIBLE EDIBLES

THE PASSOVER

INGREDIENTS

boxed bread mix
(with yeast)

oven

time

HERE'S THE SCOOP:

Today Passover is still celebrated using bread that is made without yeast. Yeast causes dough to rise and makes bread soft and fluffy. Dough without yeast is thick and hard. Jesus used yeast to give us a picture of how sin can destroy our lives. It only takes a little yeast—but a lot of time—to make bread rise. Likewise a small sin, such as a "little white lie," can cause the sin to grow in our hearts and its consequences to affect many others.

INSTRUCTIONS

This week ask a parent or an older sibling to help you make the bread for your family's dinner. Follow the directions on the box of bread mix. Bread takes a long time to rise and bake, so start in the morning. As you are making your bread, you will need to pound out the yeast and have the bread rise again. God uses his Word and other Christians to help us "pound out" the sin in our lives so we can "rise" in our service to God.

3-D

your year. Eat this until the evening of the twenty-first day. ¹⁹For seven days there must not be any yeast in your houses. Anybody who eats yeast during this time must be separated from the community of Israel. This includes Israelites and non-Israelites. ²⁰During this feast you must not eat yeast. You must eat bread made without yeast wherever you live."

²¹Then Moses called all the elders of Israel together. He told them, "Get the animals for your families. Kill the animals for the Passover. ²²Take a branch of the hyssop plant and dip it into the bowl filled with blood. Wipe the blood on the sides and tops of the doorframes. No one may leave his house until morning. ²³The Lord will go through Egypt to kill the Egyptians. He will see the blood on the sides and tops of the doorframes. Then the Lord

will pass over that house. He will not let the one who brings death come into your houses and kill you.

²⁴"You must keep this command. This law is for you and your descendants from now on. ²⁵Do this when you go to the land the Lord has promised to give to you. ²⁶When your children ask you, 'Why are we doing these things?' ²⁷you will say, 'This is the Passover sacrifice to honor the Lord. When we were in Egypt, the Lord passed over the houses of Israel. The Lord killed the Egyptians, but he saved our homes.'" So now the people bowed down and worshiped the Lord. ²⁸They did just as the Lord commanded Moses and Aaron.

²⁹At midnight the Lord killed all the firstborn sons in the land of Egypt. The firstborn of the

king, who sat on the throne, died. Even the firstborn of the prisoner in jail died. Also all the firstborn farm animals died. ³⁰The king, his officers and all the Egyptians got up during the night. Someone had died in every house. So there was loud crying everywhere in Egypt.

> **"During this feast you must not eat yeast. You must eat bread made without yeast wherever you live."**
>
> *Exodus 12:20*

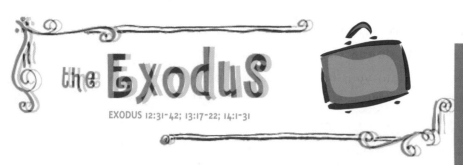

the Exodus

EXODUS 12:31-42; 13:17-22; 14:1-31

POWER IN THE BLOOD
EXODUS 12:13

The angel of death was on the move. He passed from house to house, killing the firstborn son of every family unless he saw the stain of blood on the home's doorpost. In this way, the Jews were spared, and the Egyptians awoke to the terrible news that someone in every Egyptian household had died in the night.

Though this final plague happened long ago, the picture it paints still stands today. God has always required the shedding of blood to forgive sins and to save from death. Just as the Israelites hoped in the blood of the lamb they smeared on their doorposts, we must depend on the blood of the Lamb of God, Jesus, to cover our sins and save our souls from the death we deserve. In the end, we will awake in heaven and realize God's promise was true.

ISRAEL LEAVES EGYPT

12 During the night the king called for Moses and Aaron. He said to them, "Get up and leave my people. You and your people may do as you have asked. Go and worship the Lord. ³²Take all of your sheep and cattle as you have asked. Go. And also bless me." ³³The Egyptians also

Israelites took rich gifts from the Egyptians.

³⁷The Israelites traveled from Rameses to Succoth. There were about 600,000 men walking. This does not include the women and children. ³⁸Many other people who were not Israelites went with them. A large number of

"That night the Lord kept watch to bring them out of Egypt."

Exodus 12:42

asked the Israelites to hurry and leave. They said, "If you don't leave, we will all die!"

³⁴The people of Israel took their dough before the yeast was added. They wrapped the bowls for making dough in clothing and carried them on their shoulders. ³⁵The people of Israel did what Moses told them to do. They asked their Egyptian neighbors for things made of silver and gold and for clothing. ³⁶The Lord caused the Egyptians to think well of the Israelites. So the

sheep, goats and cattle went with them. ³⁹The Israelites used the dough they had brought out of Egypt. They baked loaves of bread without yeast. The dough had no yeast in it because they had been rushed out of Egypt. So they had no time to get food ready for their trip.

⁴⁰The people of Israel had lived in Egypt for 430 years. ⁴¹On the day the 430 years ended, the Lord's divisions of people left Egypt. ⁴²That night the Lord kept

watch to bring them out of Egypt. So on this same night the Israelites are to keep watch. They are to do this to honor the Lord from now on.

A-MAZE-ING GOODBYE

Help the Israelites flee from Egypt, *through* the Red Sea, to the place of safety on the other side.

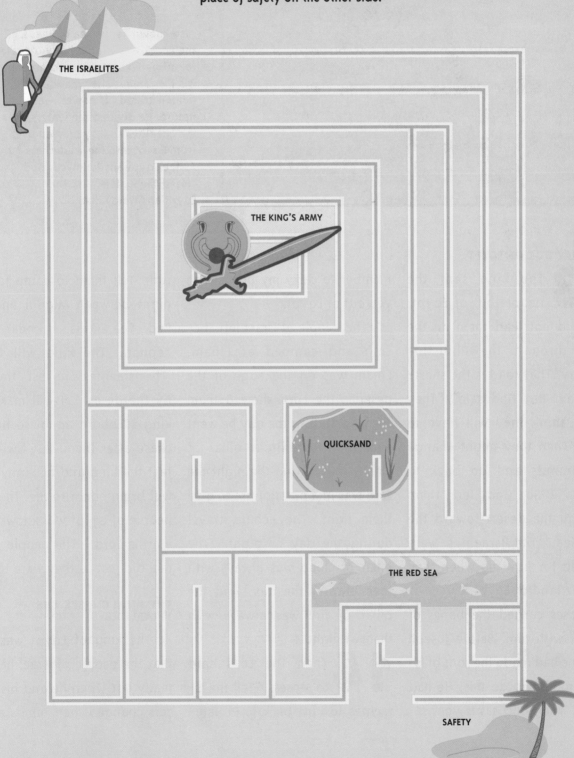

THE ISRAELITES

THE KING'S ARMY

QUICKSAND

THE RED SEA

SAFETY

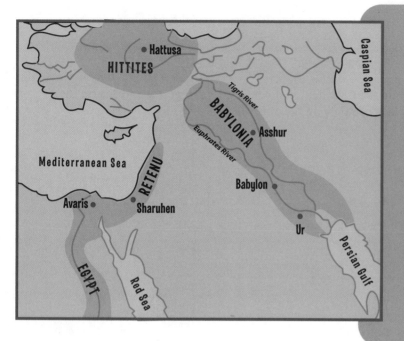

Hattusa
HITTITES
Caspian Sea
Tigris River
BABYLONIA
Asshur
Euphrates River
Mediterranean Sea
RETENU
Babylon
Avaris
Sharuhen
Ur
EGYPT
Red Sea
Persian Gulf

BiBLe BaSiCS

WHAT AND WHERE IS THE RED SEA?

Also known as the Sea of Reeds, the Red Sea is a large body of water found between Africa and Arabia. It's the famous site where God demonstrated his power over nature. He divided the waters for the Israelites as they crossed over from Egypt into the wilderness. As the Egyptians followed, God closed the waters, and the Egyptians were killed.

THE WAY OUT OF EGYPT

13 The king sent the people out of Egypt. God did not lead them on the road through the Philistine country. That road is the shortest way. But God said, "They might think they will have to fight. Then they might change their minds and go back to Egypt." [18]So God led them through the desert toward the Red Sea.[d] The Israelites were dressed for fighting when they left the land of Egypt.

[19]Moses carried the bones of Joseph with him. Before Joseph died, he had made the sons of Israel promise to do this. He had said, "When God saves you, re-member to carry my bones with you out of Egypt."

[20]The people of Israel left Suc-coth and camped at Etham. Etham was on the edge of the desert. [21]The Lord showed them the way. During the day he went ahead of them in a pillar of cloud. And during the night the Lord was in a pillar of fire to give them light. They could travel during the day or night. [22]The pillar of cloud was always with them during the day. And the pillar of fire was always with them at night.

14 Then the Lord said to Moses, [2]"Tell the Is-raelites to turn back to Pi Hahi-roth. Tell them to camp for the night between Migdol and the Red Sea. This is near Baal Zephon. [3]The king will think, 'The Israelites are lost, trapped by the desert.' [4]I will make the king stubborn again so he will chase after them. But I will de-feat the king and his army. This will bring honor to me. Then the people of Egypt will know that I am the Lord." The people of Is-rael did just as they were told.

THE KING CHASES THE ISRAELITES

[5]The king of Egypt was told that the people of Israel had al-ready left. Then he and his offi-cers changed their minds about

> "But Moses answered, 'Don't be afraid! Stand still and see the Lord save you today.'"
>
> *Exodus 14:13*

them. They said, "What have we done? We have let the people of Israel leave. We have lost our slaves!" ⁶So the king prepared his war chariot and took his army with him. ⁷He took 600 of his best chariots. He also took all the other chariots of Egypt. Each chariot had an officer in it. ⁸The Lord made the king of Egypt stubborn. So he chased the Israelites, who were leaving victoriously. ⁹The king of Egypt came with his horses, chariot drivers and army. And they chased the Israelites. They caught up with the Israelites while they were camped by the Red Sea.ᵈ This was near Pi Hahiroth and Baal Zephon.

¹⁰The Israelites saw the king and his army coming after them. They were very frightened and cried to the Lord for help. ¹¹They said to Moses, "What have you done to us? Why did you bring us out of Egypt to die in the desert? There were plenty of graves for us in Egypt. ¹²We told you in Egypt, 'Let us alone! Let us stay and serve the Egyptians.' Now we will die in the desert."

¹³But Moses answered, "Don't be afraid! Stand still and see the Lord save you today. You will never see these Egyptians again after today. ¹⁴You will only need to remain calm. The Lord will fight for you."

¹⁵Then the Lord said to Moses, "Why are you crying out to me? Command the people of Israel to start moving. ¹⁶Raise your walking stick and hold it over the sea. The sea will split. Then the people can cross the sea on dry land. ¹⁷I have made the Egyptians stubborn so they will chase the Israelites. But I will be honored when I defeat the king and all of his chariot drivers and chariots. ¹⁸I will defeat the king, his chariot drivers and chariots. Then Egypt will know that I am the Lord."

Bible Critters — SURPRISE DELIGHT

The people needed food. So what did God provide? He gave them an incredible game bird, right at their fingertips. **QUAIL**, also known as the Mediterranean quail or Japanese quail, are a familiar sight in many places around the world. Usually they live in tall grass, where they make their nests out of a scrape in the ground lined with plants. Some breeds startle easily and shoot straight up in the air when a predator comes near it. Other times, they will run and hide among the grass. They like to eat seeds and insects occasionally. They do migrate to other locations, although scientists are never sure why and where they will go because their patterns are complicated. One thing is for certain: Most cultures love the taste of quail, and they provided a great daily feast for the hungry Israelites.

3-D

MARCH GOODNESS

1 Bake a batch of cookies, and take them to the nursing home.

2

3 Hide-It-in-Your-Heart: The Lord wants to show his mercy to you. He wants to rise and comfort you. The Lord is a fair God. And everyone who waits for his help will be happy (Isaiah 30:18).

4

5 Prayer Pointer: Ask God to make you more aware of his goodness in your life.

6 Take a walk in the park, and count how many bird nests you find.

7 Sit by a different person at lunch today.

8

9 Plant tomato seeds in a paper cup, and put them in the windowsill.

10

11

12 Prayer Pointer: Pray for our country to keep showing goodness and charity to other nations who need our help.

13

14

15 Ask your grandfather to take you fishing.

16

17 Wear something green!

18

19

20 Hide-It-in-Your-Heart: Surely your goodness and love will be with me all my life. And I will live in the house of the Lord forever (Psalm 23:6).

21

22 Fill Easter baskets with candy and encouraging Bible verses, and give them to your neighbors.

23 Tape a nail near your bathroom mirror to remember how Jesus died for you.

24

25 Invite a friend to spend the night this Saturday and go to church with you on Sunday.

26

27

28 Make a list of all the ways that Jesus' death and resurrection has changed your life.

29 Prayer Pointer: Thank God for his goodness, and ask for creative ways to show goodness to others.

30

31 Help your mother clear the table and clean up the dishes when the meal is over.

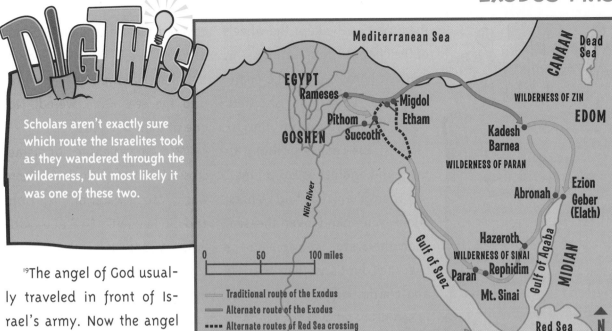

DIG THIS!

Scholars aren't exactly sure which route the Israelites took as they wandered through the wilderness, but most likely it was one of these two.

Mediterranean Sea

EGYPT
Rameses
Pithom
GOSHEN
Succoth
Migdol
Etham
Nile River
CANAAN
Dead Sea
WILDERNESS OF ZIN
EDOM
Kadesh Barnea
WILDERNESS OF PARAN
Abronah
Ezion Geber (Elath)
Hazeroth
WILDERNESS OF SINAI
Paran
Rephidim
Mt. Sinai
Gulf of Suez
Gulf of Aqaba
MIDIAN
Red Sea

0   50   100 miles

— Traditional route of the Exodus
— Alternate route of the Exodus
- - - Alternate routes of Red Sea crossing

N

¹⁹The angel of God usually traveled in front of Israel's army. Now the angel of God moved behind them. Also, the pillar of cloud moved from in front of the people and stood behind them. ²⁰So the cloud came between the Egyptians and the people of Israel. The cloud made it dark for the Egyptians. But it gave light to the Israelites. So the cloud kept the two armies apart all night.

²¹Moses held his hand over the sea. All that night the Lord drove back the sea with a strong east wind. And so he made the sea become dry ground. The water was split. ²²And the Israelites went through the sea on dry land. A wall of water was on both sides.

²³Then all the king's horses, chariots and chariot drivers followed them into the sea. ²⁴Between two and six o'clock in the

WILD WORLD FACTS

Exodus 13:20-22

CLOUD THE ISSUE

While we don't know exactly what kind of cloud God used to reveal his presence to the Israelites as he led them out of Egypt, we do know that God has created different kinds of clouds that help us understand and predict our weather.

Basically, clouds are a collection of either water droplets or ice crystals that are suspended in the sky. Stratus clouds are mostly all gray and can cover the sky. Cirrus clouds are thin and high in the sky. Cumulus clouds are lumpy and can also stretch high into the sky, often forming thunderheads (the kind that produce thunderstorms and look like a giant anvil in the sky). Mammatus clouds look like little pouches hanging down and are associated with strong thunderstorms and tornadoes.

God used a cloud to help Israel know where to go. Today God uses his Word to lead his people in the right direction.

[USAToday.com/weather]

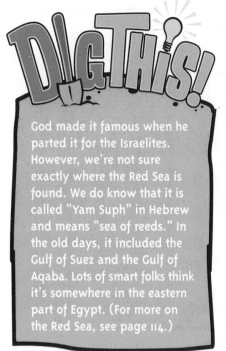

God made it famous when he parted it for the Israelites. However, we're not sure exactly where the Red Sea is found. We do know that it is called "Yam Suph" in Hebrew and means "sea of reeds." In the old days, it included the Gulf of Suez and the Gulf of Aqaba. Lots of smart folks think it's somewhere in the eastern part of Egypt. (For more on the Red Sea, see page 114.)

morning, the Lord looked down from the pillar of cloud and fire at the Egyptian army. He made them panic. [25]He kept the wheels of the chariots from turning. This made it hard to drive the chariots. The Egyptians shouted, "Let's get away from the Israelites! The Lord is fighting for them and against us Egyptians."

[26]Then the Lord told Moses, "Hold your hand over the sea. Then the water will come back over the Egyptians, their chariots and chariot drivers." [27]So Moses raised his hand over the sea. And at dawn the water became deep again. The Egyptians were trying to run from it. But the Lord swept them away into the sea. [28]The water became deep again. It covered the chariots and chariot drivers. So all the king's army that had followed the Israelites into the sea was covered. Not one of them survived.

[29]But the people of Israel crossed the sea on dry land. There was a wall of water on their right and on their left. [30]So that day the Lord saved the Israelites from the Egyptians. And the Israelites saw the Egyptians lying dead on the seashore. [31]When the people of Israel saw the great power that the Lord had used against the Egyptians, they feared the Lord. And they trusted the Lord and his servant Moses.

PHARAOH SAID, "NO!" BUT GOD SAID, "GO!"

HELP THE ISRAELITES MAKE SENSE OF THE EVENTS THAT GOT THEM OUT OF EGYPT.

1. smose nda ronaa _____

2. ym eoplep _____

3. ssovpaer _____

4. dreab _____

5. rryhu _____

6. piarll fo oucld _____

7. omiprse _____

8. riotchas _____

9. mbal _____

10. dre eas _____

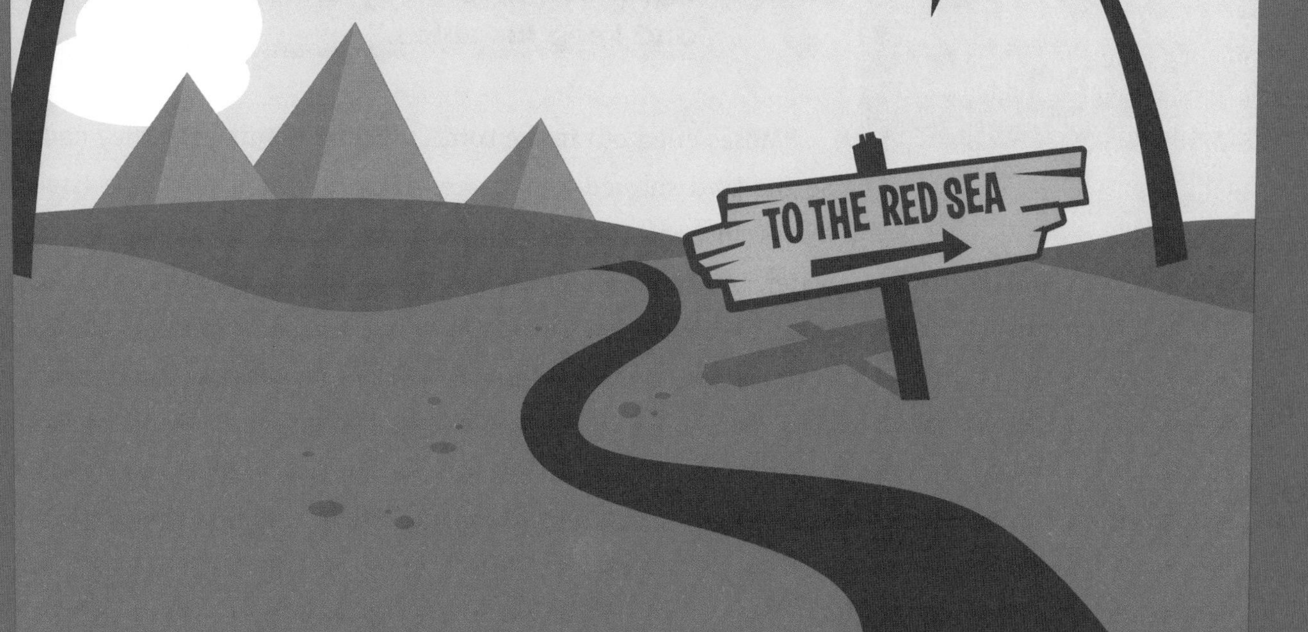

TO THE RED SEA

the WilDeRneSs

EXODUS 15:22–17:16

LIVIN' IT!

BREAD OF HEAVEN
EXODUS 16:1-36

The Israelites were in trouble. Hundreds of thousands of people were wandering around in the wilderness, and none of them had any food. So they complained to Moses—and ultimately to God—for getting them into this problem.

As outsiders reading their story, we may wonder how they could ever question God. Hadn't he already proven how good he was to them? Couldn't they trust him to provide? But the truth is, we often treat God the same way. It's easy when life is going well to trust that God has our best interests at heart. But when hard times come, we begin to wonder if he knows what he's doing. But rest assured, God will always take care of us—just like he did the Israelites in the wilderness. He himself is our daily bread, the modern-day manna that we need to live every moment of our lives.

THE BITTER WATER

15 Moses led the people of Israel away from the Red Sea.[d] The people went into the Desert of Shur. They traveled for three days in the desert but found no water. [23]Then they came to Marah, where there was water. But they could not drink it because it was too bitter. That is why the place was named Marah.[n] [24]The people grumbled to Moses. They asked, "What will we drink?"

[25]Moses cried out to the Lord. So the Lord showed him a tree. Moses threw the tree into the water. And the water became good to drink.

There the Lord gave the people a rule and a law to live by. There he also tested their loyalty to him. [26]He said, "You must

obey the Lord, your God. You must do what the Lord said is right. You must obey all his laws and keep his rules. If you do these things, I will not give you any of the sicknesses I gave the Egyptians. I am the Lord. I am the Lord who heals you."

[27]Then the people traveled to Elim. At Elim there were 12 springs of water and 70 palm trees. So the people camped there near the water.

THE PEOPLE DEMAND FOOD

16 Then the whole Israelite community left Elim. They came to the Desert of Sin. This place was between Elim and Sinai. They came to this place on the fifteenth day of the

> **"You must do what the Lord said is right. You must obey all his laws and keep his rules."** *Exodus 15:26*

second month after they had left Egypt. [2]Then the whole Israelite community grumbled to Moses and Aaron in the desert. [3]The Israelites said to them, "It would have been better if the Lord had killed us in the land of Egypt. There we had meat to eat. We had all the food we wanted. But

15:23 **Marah** This name means "bitter."

> **"At twilight you will eat meat. And every morning you will eat all the bread you want. Then you will know i am the Lord, your God."**
>
> *Exodus 16:12*

you have brought us into this desert. You will starve us to death here."

⁴Then the Lord said to Moses, "I will cause food to fall like rain from the sky. This food will be for all of you. Every day the people must go out and gather what they need for that day. I will do this to see if the people will do what I teach them. ⁵On the sixth day of each week, they are to gather twice as much as they gather on other days. Then they are to prepare it."

⁶So Moses and Aaron said to all the Israelites: "This evening you will know that the Lord is the one who brought you out of Egypt. ⁷Tomorrow morning you will see the greatness of the Lord. He has heard you grumble against him. We are nothing. You are not grumbling against us, but against the Lord." ⁸And Moses said, "Each evening the Lord will give you meat to eat. And every morning he will give you all the bread you want. He will do this because he has heard you grumble against him. You

are not grumbling against Aaron and me. You are grumbling against the Lord."

⁹Then Moses said to Aaron, "Speak to the whole community of the Israelites. Say to them, 'Meet together in front of the Lord because he has heard your grumblings.'"

¹⁰So Aaron spoke to the whole community of the Israelites. While he was speaking, they looked toward the desert. There the greatness of the Lord appeared in a cloud.

¹¹The Lord said to Moses, ¹²"I have heard the grumblings of the people of Israel. So tell them, 'At twilight you will eat meat. And every morning you will eat all the bread you want. Then you will know I am the Lord, your God.'"

¹³That evening, quail came and covered the camp. And in the morning dew lay around the camp. ¹⁴When the dew was gone, thin flakes like frost were on the desert ground. ¹⁵When the Israelites

GET CONNECTED

RELATIONSHIPS WITH GOD

Lost and Found The Israelites were feeling afraid. Even though living in Egypt was terrible, at least they knew where they were. Now they were lost in a wilderness, and they wondered if they'd ever survive.

Though they felt lost, God knew right where they were—and where they were going. We need to remember that God is with us, too. Even though we may not understand why God is allowing certain pain or problems to come into our lives, we can remember that he sees the big picture, and he knows where he is leading us. We're not lost, so don't be afraid. Just trust your loving Father to take care of you as he leads you closer to him.

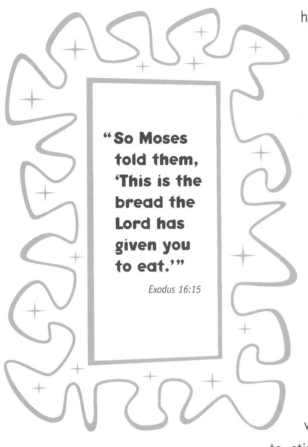

"So Moses told them, 'This is the bread the Lord has given you to eat.'"

Exodus 16:15

saw it, they asked each other, "What is that?" They asked this question because they did not know what it was.

So Moses told them, "This is the bread the Lord has given you to eat. ¹⁶The Lord has commanded, 'Each one of you must gather what he needs. Gather about two quarts for every person in your family.'"

¹⁷So the people of Israel did this. Some people gathered much, and some gathered little. ¹⁸Then they measured it. The person who gathered more did not have too much. The person who gathered less did not have too little. Each person gathered just as much as he needed.

¹⁹Moses said to them, "Don't keep any of it to eat the next day." ²⁰But some of the people did not listen to Moses. They kept part of it to eat the next morning. But it became full of worms and began to stink. So Moses was angry with these people.

²¹Every morning each person gathered as much food as he needed. But when the sun became hot, it melted away.

²²On the sixth day the people gathered twice as much food. They gathered four quarts for every person. So all the leaders of the community came and told this to Moses. ²³Moses said to them, "This is what the Lord commanded. Tomorrow is the Sabbath,ᵈ the Lord's holy day of rest. Bake what you want to bake, and boil what you want to boil today. But save the rest of the food until tomorrow morning."

The Ten Commandments

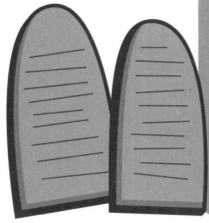

BIBLE BASICS

WHAT EXACTLY IS THE LAW?

God's commands are the Law. Once God gave Moses the Ten Commandments—as well as a ton of detailed do's and don'ts—Israel had a pretty good idea of what God expected from his people. However, no human can actually obey the whole Law. In the New Testament, God fulfills the requirements of the Law through his own Son, Jesus. Jesus obeyed the Law perfectly so that we no longer have to work to earn God's favor. Now we receive God's favor when we receive his Son as our Savior—a new agreement known as grace.

BiBLe CRiTTeRS

3-D

WRONG MOOOVE

It's easy to see why God was offended. Aaron had tried to make an idol in the image of God, so he fashioned a calf—yes, that's right, a baby **COW**—to do the job. While bulls (the adult male cow) were often used in sacrifices, they were never intended to be worshiped. Cows, often called cattle, were domesticated thousands of years ago and have been used for milk, meat, hide, and a bunch of other products like cheese, glue, gelatin, soap, and more. Just like sheep and goats, cows have a four-part stomach to help them digest the grass and plants they eat. Some cultures still use cows to pull carts, and others still worship them as spiritual beings.

EXODUS 16:24-35

[24]So the people saved it until the next morning, as Moses had commanded. And none of it began to stink or have worms in it. [25]Moses told the people, "Eat the food you gathered yesterday. Today is a Sabbath, the Lord's day of rest. So you will not find any out in the field today. [26]You should gather the food for six days. But the seventh day is a Sabbath day. On that day there will not be any food on the ground."

[27]On the seventh day some of the people went out to gather food, but they couldn't find any. [28]Then the Lord said to Moses, "How long will all you people refuse to obey my commands and teachings? [29]Look, the Lord has made the Sabbath a day of rest for all of you. So on the sixth day he will give you enough food for two days. But on the Sabbath each of you must stay where you are. Do not leave your house." [30]So the people rested on the Sabbath.

[31]The people of Israel called the food manna.[d] The manna was like small white seeds. It tasted like wafers made with honey.

[32]Then Moses said, "The Lord said, 'Save two quarts of this food for your descendants.[d] Then they can see the food that I gave you to eat. I did this in the desert when I brought you out of Egypt.'"

[33]Moses told Aaron, "Take a jar and fill it with two quarts of manna. And save this manna for your descendants." [34]So Aaron did what the Lord had commanded Moses. Aaron put the jar of manna in front of the Box[d] of the Agreement. He did this so it could be kept. [35]The Israelites ate manna for 40 years. They ate it until they came to the land where they settled. They ate

WILD WORLD FACTS

Exodus 17:1-7
NO SWEAT!

They had been wandering in the wilderness for days. They were hot, tired, and very thirsty. So God provided water out of a rock!

God knows our needs even before we do. He was the one who made our bodies need water. In fact, our bodies are approximately 65% water! When we get hot—either by the sun or by exercising—our bodies work to cool off our skin and lower our body temperature back to normal. Sweat glands kick in and release the water that normally bathes the cells to come to the surface of our skin, where it is evaporated into the air. It's actually the evaporation of our sweat—not the water itself—that cools us down. If we don't put more water back into our bodies, our cells will not be able to keep the core temperature of our body down. Then all of our cells become "tired" and unable to function at full capacity.

So next time you get thirsty, remember to drink plenty of water—and remember God, our Living Water, who meets all of our needs.

[Gatorade Sports Science Institute]

THE ISRAELITES IN THE WILDERNESS

INGREDIENTS

2 slices of bread

butter

butter knife

HERE'S THE SCOOP:

When God led the Israelites out of Egypt into the desert, he provided all their needs. The people were hungry, so God provided manna and quail for them to eat. He said, "At twilight you will eat meat. And every morning you will eat all the bread you want. Then you will know that I am the Lord, your God" (Exodus 16:12). God freely and abundantly provided all the food they needed every day for 40 years!

One day this week, skip a meal or two and see how hungry you get for food. When the hunger is too much, make this bread and butter snack to see how good bread can taste when you are really hungry.

BREAD & BUTTER RECIPE

Using a butter knife, spread soft butter on two slices of bread. Enjoy your meal with a tall glass of water, and give thanks to God for all the food you enjoy every day.

3-D

manna until they came to the edge of the land of Canaan. [36]The measure they used for the manna was two quarts. It was one-tenth of an ephah.[n]

WATER FROM A ROCK

17 The whole Israelite community left the Desert of Sin. They traveled from place to place as the Lord commanded. They camped at Rephidim. But there was no water there for the people to drink. [2]So they quarreled with Moses. They said, "Give us water to drink."

But Moses said to them, "Why do you quarrel with me? Why are you testing the Lord?"

[3]But the people were very thirsty for water. So they grumbled against Moses. They said, "Why did you bring us out of Egypt? Was it to kill us, our children and our farm animals with thirst?"

[4]So Moses cried to the Lord, "What can I do with these people? They are almost ready to kill me with stones."

[5]The Lord said to Moses, "Go ahead of the people of Israel. And take some of the elders of Israel with you. Carry with you the walking stick that you used to strike the Nile River. Now go! [6]I will stand in front of you on a rock at Mount Sinai. Hit that rock with the stick, and water will come out of it. Then the people can drink." Moses did these things as the elders of Israel watched. [7]Moses named that place Massah[n] because the Israelites tested the Lord. They asked, "Is the Lord with us or not?" He also named it Meribah[n] because they quarreled.

THE AMALEKITES FIGHT ISRAEL

[8]At Rephidim the Amalekites came and fought the Israelites. [9]So Moses said to Joshua, "Choose some men and go and fight the Amalekites. Tomorrow I will stand on the top of the hill. I will hold the stick God gave me to carry."

[10]Joshua obeyed Moses and went to fight the Amalekites. At

GET CONNECTED

RELATIONSHIPS WITH AUTHORITY

Winning the Whining Battle "Oh, no! Not again," you groan. "I don't want to eat *that* for dinner." Or maybe your parents need to run an errand when you just want to stay put and play on the computer. There's a million little things that happen through the day that demand a choice from us. Are you going to accept this turn of events with a grateful heart that trusts God's plan for you, or are you going to complain about it?

For one full day, take note of how you respond to your mom, dad, siblings, teachers, and friends. Do you obey with a happy heart, or do you moan and groan? Are you thankful for the small things, or do you constantly want more? Don't be like the Israelites who missed out on the joy of watching their Father provide. Instead, look for God's hand in everything to see what he has in store for you—and be thankful!

16:36 ephah An ephah was a measure that equaled 20 quarts. **17:7 Massah** This name sounds like the Hebrew word for "testing." **17:7 Meribah** This name sounds like the Hebrew word for "quarreled."

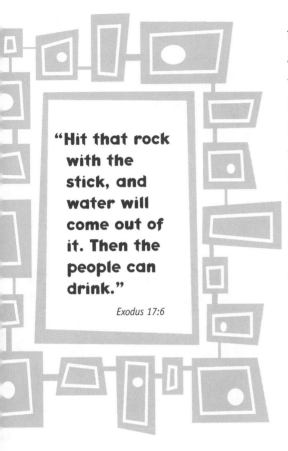

> "Hit that rock with the stick, and water will come out of it. Then the people can drink."
>
> *Exodus 17:6*

the same time Moses, Aaron and Hur went to the top of the hill. ¹¹As long as Moses held his hands up, the Israelites would win the fight. But when Moses put his hands down, the Amalekites would win. ¹²Later, Moses' arms became tired. So the men put a large rock under Moses, and he sat on it. Then Aaron and Hur held up Moses' hands. Aaron was on one side of Moses, and Hur was on the other side. They held his hands up like this until the sun went down. ¹³So Joshua defeated the Amalekites in this battle.

¹⁴Then the Lord said to Moses, "Write about this battle in a book so people will remember. And be sure to tell Joshua. Tell him because I will completely destroy the Amalekites from the earth."

¹⁵Then Moses built an altar. He named it The Lord is my Banner. ¹⁶Moses said, "I lifted my hands toward the Lord's throne. The Lord will fight against the Amalekites forever."

the TEN CoMMandMeNts

EXODUS 19:1—20:23

ISRAEL AT SINAI

19 Exactly three months after the Israelites had left Egypt, they reached the Desert of Sinai. ²They had left Rephidim and had come to the Desert of Sinai. The Israelites camped in the desert in front of Mount Sinai. ³Then Moses went up on the mountain to God. The Lord called to him from the mountain. The Lord said, "Say this to the family of Jacob. And tell this to the people of Israel:

" i will come to you in a thick cloud. i will speak to you." *Exodus 19:9*

⁴'Every one of you has seen what I did to the people of Egypt. You saw how I carried you out of Egypt. I did it as an eagle carries her young on her wings. And I brought you here to me. ⁵So now obey me and keep my agreement. Do this, and you will be my own possession, chosen from all nations. Even though the whole earth is mine, ⁶you will be my kingdom of priests. You will be a nation that belongs to me alone.' You must tell the Israelites these words."

⁷So Moses went down and called the elders of the people together. He told them all the words the Lord had commanded him to say. ⁸And all the people answered together, "We will do everything he has said." Then Moses took their answer back to the Lord.

⁹And the Lord said to Moses, "I will come to you in a thick cloud. I will speak to you. The people will hear me talking to you. I will do this so the people will always trust you." Then Moses told the Lord what the people had said.

¹⁰The Lord said to Moses, "Go to the people and have them spend today and tomorrow preparing themselves. They must wash their clothes ¹¹and be ready by the day after tomorrow. On that day I, the Lord, will come down on Mount Sinai. And all the people will see me. ¹²But you must set a limit around the mountain. The people are not to cross it. Tell the people not to go up on the mountain. Tell them not to touch the foot of it. Anyone who touches the mountain must be put to death.

LIViN' iT!

HOLY MOUNTAIN
EXODUS 19:1-25

In Moses' day, God was beginning to explain to his chosen people how a sinful people could come before a holy God. Though God wanted them to be his own people who loved him, because of his holiness they were still not allowed to go to where God was speaking with Moses. They would actually be put to death if they disobeyed.

Today we are able to come to God without fear of death because Jesus makes it possible. Because of Jesus' sacrifice on the cross, God sees only his perfection—not our sinfulness—and we are always welcome to come before his throne. But we need to remember how God dealt with the Israelites, because it helps us to understand just how perfect and holy God really is. While he is our father, he is also the God of all creation and deserves our praise and respect.

BIBLE BASICS

WHAT IS THE BOX OF THE AGREEMENT WITH THE LORD?

Sometimes called the Ark of the Covenant, this was the special box made of gold that God had the Israelites make to carry three important relics: Aaron's budded staff, the Ten Commandments, and a jar of manna. This box stayed in the holiest part of the tabernacle and became known as God's footstool. Though there was no power in the box, it did show that wherever the Israelites traveled, God was there with them.

¹³He must be put to death with stones or shot with arrows. No one is allowed to touch him. Whether it is a person or an animal, he will not live. But the trumpet will make a long blast. Only then may the people go up on the mountain."

¹⁴So Moses went down from the mountain to the people. He made them prepare themselves for service to God. And the people washed their clothes. ¹⁵Then Moses said to the people, "Be ready in three days. Do not have sexual relations during this time."

¹⁶It was the morning of the third day. There was thunder and lightning with a thick cloud on the mountain. And there was a very loud blast from a trumpet. All the people in the camp were frightened. ¹⁷Then Moses led the people out of the camp to meet God. They stood at the foot of the mountain. ¹⁸Mount Sinai was covered with smoke. This happened because the Lord came down on it in fire. The smoke rose from the mountain like smoke from a furnace. And the whole mountain shook wildly. ¹⁹The sound from the trumpet became louder. Then Moses spoke, and the voice of God answered him.

²⁰So the Lord came down on the top of Mount Sinai. Then he called Moses to come up to the top of the mountain. So Moses went up. ²¹The Lord said to Moses, "Go down and warn the people. They must not force their way through to see me. If they do, many of them will die. ²²Even the priests, who may come near me, must first prepare themselves. If they don't, I, the Lord, will punish them."

Ways to Remember the Ten Commandments

1. Write them down 10 times.
2. Pick a key word in each one, and look up the definition.
3. Recite them to your younger sister.
4. Turn them into a song.
5. Pray about a different commandment each day for 10 days.
6. Post them inside your locker at school.
7. Ask your friends to quiz you.
8. Write them on each finger.
9. Draw a picture that helps you visualize each one.
10. Explain them to your younger brother.

3-D

COMMANDMENT KEEPERS

EXODUS 20:1-17

ACROSS:

1. Fake gods.
2. To take what isn't yours.
3. Seventh-day duty.
4. God's command for couples: No ____!
5. To take someone's life.
6. The opposite of the truth.

DOWN:

1. God alone deserves this.
2. What God is . . . and what he wants from us.
3. What God made.
4. What Israel felt when they heard from God.
5. How we should treat our parents.

BiBLe BasiCS

WHat IS tHe SaBBatH?

For Jews, the Sabbath is Saturday, the seventh day of the Jewish week. The Sabbath is a special day set apart for worship, an idea that extends back to the beginning of creation when God rested from his work on the seventh day. No work is allowed for Jews on this holy day. Most Christians, however, view the Sabbath as Sunday, the day Jesus rose from the dead. While people still disagree on what exactly should or should not be done on the Sabbath, the Ten Commandments make it clear that God does want us to set aside time to remember and worship him on that day each week.

THE TEN COMMANDMENTS

20 Then God spoke all these words: [2]"I am the Lord your God. I brought you out of the land of Egypt where you were slaves.

[3]"You must not have any other gods except me.

[4]"You must not make for yourselves any idols. Don't make something that looks like anything in the sky above or on the earth below or in the water below the land. [5]You must not worship or serve any idol. This is because I, the Lord your God, am a jealous God. A person may sin against me and hate me. I will punish his children, even his grandchildren and great-grandchildren. [6]But I will be very kind to thousands who love me and obey my commands.

[7]"You must not use the name of the Lord your God thoughtlessly. The Lord will punish anyone who is guilty and misuses his name.

[8]"Remember to keep the Sabbath[d] as a holy day. [9]You may work and get everything done during six days each week. [10]But the seventh day is a day of rest to honor the Lord your God. On that day no one may do any work: not you, your son or daughter, or your men or women

[23]Moses told the Lord, "The people cannot come up Mount Sinai. You yourself told us to set a limit around the mountain. We made it holy."

[24]The Lord said to him, "Go down and bring Aaron with you. But don't allow the priests or the people to force their way through. They must not come up to the Lord. If they do, I will punish them."

[25]So Moses went down to the people and told them these things.

GET CONNECTED

RELATIONSHIPS WITH AUTHORITY

Friends for Life Have you ever wondered why God gave his people so many rules? While it might look like God was just being picky, he was really being protective. He gave his people rules to obey so that they would not sin and have to face the serious consequences that come from sinning. He knew what his people needed to do to really have joy in their lives.

Families are God's idea, too. He has set up families so that the parents are in charge and are given the task of raising up kids into adults who know and love God. Don't get angry when your parents tell you what to do. They are simply obeying God when they lead you. Instead, understand that they are God's special gift to you to protect and develop you. Your parents can become your closest friends who help you through the different times of your life—if you let them.

GET CONNECTED

RELATIONSHIPS WITH FAMILY

The Parent Plan Everyone else is getting to go. *Your* parents say no. You're embarrassed and angry, and you want to do something, but what? You could yell at your parents and say ugly things, or give them "that look," or even disobey. But if you did, you know you'd be sinning. God says that we must not only obey our parents, but we should honor them, too. That means obeying with a happy heart that trusts in God's plan. God leads us through our parents, so we must respect their decisions, even if we don't agree with them. God's commandment comes with a promise: that we may live long and well on the earth.

slaves. Neither your animals nor the foreigners living in your cities may work. "The reason is that in six days the Lord made everything. He made the sky, earth, sea and everything in them. And on the seventh day, he rested. So the Lord blessed the Sabbath day and made it holy.

¹²"Honor your father and your mother. Then you will live a long time in the land. The Lord your God is going to give you this land.

¹³"You must not murder anyone.

¹⁴"You must not be guilty of adultery.ᵈ

¹⁵"You must not steal.

¹⁶"You must not tell lies about your neighbor in court.

¹⁷"You must not want to take your neighbor's house. You must not want his wife or his men or women slaves. You must not want his ox or his donkey. You must not want to take anything that belongs to your neighbor."

¹⁸The people heard the thunder and the trumpet. They saw the lightning on the mountain and smoke rising from the mountain. They shook with fear and stood far away from the mountain. ¹⁹Then they said to Moses, "Speak to us yourself. Then we will listen. But don't let God speak to us, or we will die."

²⁰Then Moses said to the people, "Don't be afraid. God has come to test you. He wants you to respect him so you will not sin."

²¹The people stood far away from the mountain while Moses went near the dark cloud where God was. ²²Then the Lord told Moses to say these things to the Israelites: "You yourselves have seen that I talked with you from heaven. ²³You must not use gold or silver to make idols for yourselves. You must not worship these false gods in addition to me.

THE TEN COMMANDMENTS

SUPPLIES

red construction paper

scissors

hole punch

yarn

marker

ALL ABOUT IT:

God does not expect us to be perfect, but he does expect us to listen and obey his commands. When God gave the Ten Commandments to Moses, he did not give us just a list of rules. God shared his heart and showed us how he feels when we disobey his laws. "You must not worship or serve any idol. This is because I, the Lord your God, am a jealous God. . . . I will be very kind to thousands who love me and obey my commands" (Exodus 20:5-6).

Did you know that God is jealous? He loves us so much, and he wants us to love him more than we love anything or anyone else. The Ten Commandments are more than a list of laws to obey. God gave them to us because he knows that obeying them keeps us from hurting ourselves and others. They are a window into the heart of God and a recipe for us to use to grow closer to him. As you make your heart craft, think about how much God loves you and longs for you to know him better.

HEART CRAFT INSTRUCTIONS

1. Cut a large heart out of red construction paper.

2. Write the Ten Commandments on the heart.

3. Punch 10 holes, evenly spaced, around the outer edge of the heart. (These represent the Ten Commandments.)

4. Lace your heart with yarn to connect the ten holes.

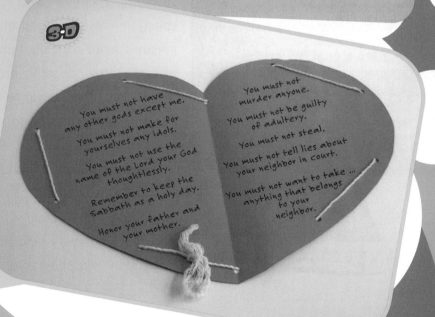

3-D

You must not have any other gods except me.
You must not make for yourselves any idols.
You must not use the name of the Lord your God thoughtlessly.
Remember to keep the Sabbath as a holy day.
Honor your father and your mother.

You must not murder anyone.
You must not be guilty of adultery.
You must not steal.
You must not tell lies about your neighbor in court.
You must not want to take ... anything that belongs to your neighbor.

the TabernAcle

EXODUS 25–28; 30

LIVIN' iT!

TOTALLY TABERNACLE
EXODUS 25:1-40

If you read all of the Old Testament description of how God wanted his tabernacle to be built, you might begin to wonder, *Why? Why did it matter exactly how each piece was to be made?* The answer is that God was using physical symbols in his Temple to paint a picture for us of what was happening spiritually in a world we cannot see.

As we study the tabernacle, we also understand God's requirements for forgiveness. And we can better understand why Christ's sacrifice was so perfect that it ripped the veil in two that had once separated God's people from him. God is a God of order. He is truth, and he wants us to worship him in spirit and truth. Just like the Israelites, we want to pay attention to what pleases God and make it our deepest pleasure to obey him—not because we're afraid of him, but because we love him and we know that he loves us.

GIFTS FOR THE LORD

25 The Lord said to Moses, ²"Tell the Israelites to bring me gifts. Receive for me the gifts each man wants to give. ³These are the gifts that you should receive from them: gold, silver, bronze, ⁴blue, purple and red thread, and fine linen. Receive cloth made of goat hair. ⁵Receive the male sheep skins that are dyed red. Receive fine leather, acacia wood ⁶and olive oil to burn in the lamps. And receive spices for sweet-smelling incense*d* and the special olive oil poured on a person's head to make him a priest. ⁷Also accept onyx stones and other jewels to be put on the holy vest*d* and the chest covering.

⁸"The people must build a holy place for me. Then I can live among them. ⁹Build this Holy Tent*d* and everything in it by the plan I will show you.

THE BOX OF THE AGREEMENT

¹⁰"Use acacia wood and build a Holy Box.*d* It must be 45 inches long, 27 inches wide and 27 inches high. ¹¹Cover the Holy Box inside and out with pure gold. And put a gold strip all around it. ¹²Make four gold rings for the Holy Box. Attach the gold rings to its four feet, two rings on each side. ¹³Then make poles from acacia wood and cover them with gold. ¹⁴Put the poles through the rings on the sides of the Box. Use these poles to carry the Holy Box. ¹⁵These poles must always stay in the rings of the Holy Box. Do not take the poles out. ¹⁶Then put the two flat stones in the Holy Box. I will give you these stones on which the commands are written.

¹⁷"Then make a lid of pure gold for the Holy Box. This lid is the mercy seat.*d* Make it 45 inches long and 27 inches wide. ¹⁸Then hammer gold to make two creatures with wings. Put one on each end of the lid. ¹⁹Put one creature with wings on one end of the lid. And put the other creature with wings on the other end. Attach the creatures with wings to the lid so that they will all be one piece.

20The creatures' wings should be spread out over the lid. The creatures are to face each other across the lid. 21Put this lid on top of the Holy Box. Also put in this Holy Box the agreement which I will make with you. 22I will meet with you there, above the lid between the two creatures with wings. These are on the Box of the Agreement. There I will give you all my commands for the Israelites.

THE TABLE

23"Make a table out of acacia wood. It must be 36 inches long, 18 inches wide and 27 inches high. 24Cover it with pure gold. Put a gold strip around it. 25Then make a frame three inches high that stands up all around the edge. Put a gold strip around the frame. 26Then make four gold rings. Attach them to the four corners of the table where the four legs are. 27Put the rings close to the frame around the top of the table. These rings will hold the poles for carrying the table. 28Make the poles out of acacia wood and cover them with gold. Carry the table with these poles. 29Make the plates and bowls for the table out of pure gold. Make the jars and cups out of pure gold. They will be used for pouring out the drink offerings. 30On this table put the bread that shows you are in my presence. It must always be there in front of me.

THE LAMPSTAND

31"Hammer pure gold to make a lampstand. Its base, stand, flower-like cups, buds and petals must all be joined together in one piece. 32The lampstand must have three branches on one side and three branches on the other. 33Each branch must have three cups shaped like almond flowers on it. Each cup must have a bud and a petal. 34And there must be four more cups made like almond flowers on the lampstand itself. These cups must also have buds and petals. 35Put a bud under each pair of branches that goes out from the lampstand. 36The branches, buds and lampstand must be one piece of pure, hammered gold.

37"Then make seven small oil lamps and put them on the lampstand. They will give light to the area in front of the lampstand. 38The wick trimmers and trays must be made of pure gold. 39Use 75 pounds of pure gold to make the lampstand and everything with it. 40Be very careful to make them by the plan I showed you on the mountain.

> **"The people must build a holy place for me. Then i can live among them. Build this Holy Tent and everything in it by the plan i will show you."**
>
> *Exodus 25:8-9*

THE HOLY TENT

26 "Make the Holy Tentd with ten pieces of cloth. These pieces must be made of fine linen and blue,

10 TOP TEN

Ways to Turn Food into Fun

1. Make playdough you can eat (look it up online!).
2. Pick a new topping to go on your peanut butter sandwich.
3. Use healthy foods to make a face on bread.
4. Cut the bottom half of a hotdog into quarters, and make it look like an octopus.
5. Bake sugar cookies from scratch.
6. Lick the bowl and beaters.
7. Try a new recipe.
8. Build a gingerbread house.
9. Build the tallest PBJ sandwich.
10. Make your own pizza.

purple and red thread. Have a skilled craftsman sew designs of creatures with wings on the pieces of cloth. ²Make each piece the same size. Each piece should be 42 feet long and 6 feet wide. ³Sew five pieces of cloth together for one set. Sew the other pieces together for the second set. ⁴Make loops of blue cloth down the edge of the end piece of each set. ⁵Make 50 loops on the end piece of the first set. And make 50 loops on the end piece of the second set. These loops must be opposite each other. ⁶And make 50 gold hooks. Use these to join the two sets of cloth. This will make the Holy Tent one piece.

⁷"Then make another tent that will cover the Holy Tent. Make this tent of 11 pieces of cloth made from goat hair.

• • •

¹⁴Make two more coverings for the Holy Tent. One should be made from male sheep skins colored red. The outer covering should be from fine leather.

¹⁵"Use acacia wood to make upright frames for the Holy Tent.

• • •

³⁰Set up the Holy Tent by the plan shown to you on the mountain.

³¹"Make a curtain of fine linen and blue, purple and red thread. Have a skilled craftsman sew designs of creatures with wings on the curtain. ³²Hang the curtain by gold hooks on four posts of acacia wood. Cover these posts with gold and set them in four silver bases. ³³Hang the curtain from the hooks in the roof. Put the Holy Box*d* containing the two flat stones behind the curtain. This curtain will separate the Holy Place from the Most Holy Place. ³⁴Put the lid on the Holy Box in the Most Holy Place.

³⁵"Outside the curtain, put the table on the north side of the Holy Tent. And put the lampstand on the south side of the Holy Tent. This will be across from the table.

THE ENTRANCE OF THE HOLY TENT

³⁶"Then make a curtain for the entrance of the Tent.*d* Make it with fine linen and blue, purple and red thread. Someone who can sew

well is to sew designs on it. [37]Make five posts of acacia wood covered with gold. Make five gold hooks on which to hang the curtain from the posts. And make five bronze bases for the five posts.

THE ALTAR

27 "Make an altar for burnt offerings out of acacia wood. Make it 4¹/2 feet high. It should be square: 7¹/2 feet long and 7¹/2 feet wide. [2]Make each of the four corners of the altar stick out like a horn. The corners with their horns must be all one piece. Then cover the whole altar with bronze.

• • •

THE COURTYARD OF THE HOLY TENT

[9]"Make a wall of curtains to form a courtyard around the Holy Tent.[d] The south side should have a wall of fine linen curtains 150 feet long.

• • •

[19]All the things used in the Holy Tent must be made of bronze. And all the tent pegs for the Holy Tent and the wall around the courtyard must be made of bronze.

OIL FOR THE LAMP

[20]"Command the people of Israel to bring you pure olive oil. It is to be made from pressed olives. This is to keep the lamps on the lampstand burning. [21]Aaron and his sons must keep the lamps burning before the Lord from evening till morning. This will be in the Meeting Tent.[d] It is outside the curtain which is in front of the Holy Box.[d] The Israelites and their descendants[d] must obey this rule from now on.

CLOTHES FOR THE PRIESTS

28 "Tell your brother Aaron to come to you. His sons Nadab, Abihu, Eleazar and Ithamar must come with him. Separate them from the other Israelites. These men must serve as priests. [2]Make holy clothes for your brother Aaron to give him honor and beauty. [3]Speak to all the people to whom I have given the ability to make

clothes. Tell these skilled craftsmen to make the clothes for Aaron. Use these clothes to make him belong to me. Then he may serve me as a priest. [4]These are the clothes they must make: a chest covering, a holy vest,[d] an outer robe, a woven inner robe, a turban and a cloth belt. The craftsmen must make these holy clothes. They are for your broth-

> **"And all the tent pegs for the Holy Tent and the wall around the courtyard must be made of bronze."**
>
> *Exodus 27:19*

er Aaron and his sons. Then Aaron and his sons may serve me as priests. [5]The craftsmen must use gold and blue, purple and red thread, and fine linen.

THE HOLY VEST

[6]"Use gold and blue, purple and red thread, and fine linen to make the holy vest.[d] The craftsmen are to make this holy vest. [7]At each top corner of this holy vest there will be a pair of shoulder straps. These are to be tied together over each shoulder.

[8]"The craftsmen will very carefully weave a belt on the holy vest. Make the belt with gold and blue, purple and red thread, and fine linen.

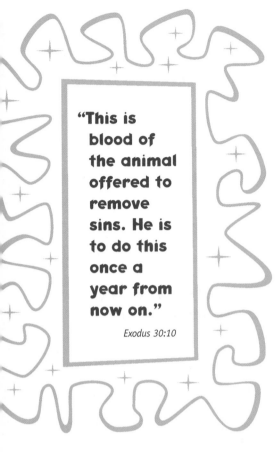

> **"This is blood of the animal offered to remove sins. He is to do this once a year from now on."**
>
> *Exodus 30:10*

⁹"Take two onyx stones. Write the name of the 12 sons of Israel on these jewels. ¹⁰Write 6 names on one stone and 6 names on the other stone. Write the names in order, from the oldest son to the youngest.

• • •

THE CHEST COVERING

¹⁵"Make a chest covering to help in making decisions. The craftsmen should make it as they made the holy vest.ᵈ They must use gold and blue, purple and red thread, and fine linen.

• • •

²⁹"When Aaron enters the Holy Place, he will wear the names of the sons of Israel over his heart. These names are on the chest covering that helps in making decisions. This will be a continual reminder before the Lord. ³⁰And put the Urim and Thummimᵈ inside the chest covering. These things will be on Aaron's heart when he goes before the Lord. They will help in making decisions for the Israelites. So Aaron will always carry them with him when he is before the Lord.

THE ALTAR FOR BURNING INCENSE

30 "Make an altar out of acacia wood for burning incense.ᵈ ²Make it square—18 inches long and 18 inches wide. It must be 36 inches high. Make the corners stick out like horns. These must be one piece with the altar. ³Cover its top, its sides and its corners with pure gold. And put a gold strip all around the altar.

⁷"Aaron must burn sweet-smelling incense on the altar every morning. He will do this when he comes to take care of the oil lamps. ⁸He must burn incense again in the evening when he lights the lamps. So incense will burn before the Lord every day from now on. ⁹Do not use this altar for offering any other incense or burnt offering. Do not use this altar to offer any kind of grain offering or drink offering. ¹⁰Once a year Aaron must make the altar ready for service to God. He will do it by putting blood on its corners. This is blood of the animal offered to remove sins. He is to do this once a year from now on. This altar belongs completely to God's service."

• • •

History Highlights

➤ **2000 B.C.**
Drains and sewers were used at Knossos, Crete; soap is known in Babylon.

7000 5000 3000 1000 0 1000 NOW

BiBLe CRitteRS

3-D

PIGGIN' OUT

The Israelites were told not to eat them. At that time, God considered them unclean. But **PIGS** do have some good qualities, despite their dirty reputation. For one, they are always there when you need them. Pigs can be found on every continent in the world, except Antarctica. People domesticated many of the breeds thousands of years ago, and we have used them ever since for their meat and hide (skin). There are some wild pigs left, including the wild boar, the bush hog, and the warthog. All pigs are very adaptable to their environment, meaning that they aren't particular about their surroundings and can eat just about anything, given the situation. They prefer plants and small animals (like worms and snakes), and they use their tusks to dig for food in the ground.

THE BRONZE BOWL

[17]The Lord said to Moses, [18]"Make a bronze bowl for washing. Build it on a bronze stand. Put the bowl and stand between the Meeting Tent[d] and the altar. Put water in the bowl. [19]Aaron and his sons must wash their hands and feet with the water from this bowl. [20]Each time, before they enter the Meeting Tent, they must wash with water. This way they will not die. They approach the altar to serve as priests. They offer a sacrifice to the Lord by fire. [21]Each time they do this, they must wash their hands and their feet so they will not die. This is a rule which Aaron and his descendants[d] are to keep from now on."

OIL FOR APPOINTING

[22]Then the Lord said to Moses, [23]"Take the finest spices: 12 pounds of liquid myrrh,[d] half that amount (that is, 6 pounds) of sweet-smelling cinnamon, 6 pounds of sweet-smelling cane [24]and 12 pounds of cassia.[d] Weigh all these by the Holy Place measure. Also take 4 quarts of olive oil. [25]Mix all these things like a perfume to make a holy olive oil. This special oil must be put on people and things. Do this to make them ready for service to God. [26]Put this oil on the Meeting Tent[d] and the Holy Box[d] with my laws in it. [27]Put this oil on the table and all its dishes. And put this oil on the lampstand and all its tools. Put the oil on the incense[d] altar. [28]Also, put the oil on the altar for burning offerings and all its tools. Put this oil on the bowl and the stand under the bowl. Put oil on all these things to prepare them for service to God. [29]You will give these things for service to God. They will be very holy. Anything that touches these things must also be holy.

[30]"Put the oil on Aaron and his sons to make them priests. Give them for service to me. Then they may serve me as priests. [31]Tell the Israelites, 'This is to be my holy olive oil from now on. It is to be put on people and things to make them ready for service to God. [32]Do not pour it on the bodies of ordinary people. Do not make perfume the same way you make this oil. It is holy, and you must treat it as holy. [33]Someone might make perfume like it. Or he might put it on someone who is not a priest. Then that person must be separated from his people.'"

WILD WORLD FACTS

Exodus 29:38-41
A BLOODY MESS

If you're squeamish at the sight of blood, be glad you didn't live in Bible times. Under the Old Agreement, God said that the Israelites had to shed blood in order to pay for their sins. So what's the big deal about blood? It's one of the main fluids that keep us alive. It is made up of four parts—red cells, white cells, platelets, and plasma—each of which serve a special role in carrying nutrients to our bodies and then carrying the waste away from our cells. Blood appears red in color because of the protein called hemoglobin that travels around in the plasma. Fortunately, the Israelites didn't have to shed their own blood for forgiveness. God allowed them to use animals' blood as a temporary payment, until Christ came to make the perfect sacrifice that took away the guilt of our sins.

[Yahooligans: Ask Earl]

BIBLE BASICS

WHY DID ISRAEL HAVE A TABERNACLE?

God is a God of order, and he had a particular way for his people to worship him. He gave the Israelites very specific instructions on how to build a place of worship that could be easily moved. At first, the tabernacle was a large, ornate tent that Israel could take with them as they traveled around in the wilderness and eventually into Canaan. Once Israel was settled in the Promised Land, Solomon built a permanent Temple for worship.

INCENSE

³⁴Then the Lord said to Moses, "Take these sweet-smelling spices: resin, onycha, galbanum and pure frankincense.ᵈ Be sure that you have equal amounts of each. ³⁵You must make incenseᵈ as a man who makes perfume would do. Add salt to it to keep it pure and holy. ³⁶Beat some of the incense into a fine powder. Put some of it in front of the Holy Boxᵈ of the Agreement in the Meeting Tent.ᵈ There I will meet with you. You must use this incense powder only for its very special purpose. ³⁷Do not make incense for yourselves the same way you make this incense. Treat it as holy to the Lord. ³⁸Whoever makes incense like this to use as perfume must be separated from his people."

NUMBERS

Balaam's Donkey

NUMBERS 22:4-35

BALAAM AND BALAK

22 Balak son of Zippor was the king of Moab at this time. ⁵He sent messengers to Balaam son of Beor at Pethor. It was near the Euphrates River in the land of Amaw. Balak said, "A nation has come out of Egypt. They cover the land. They have camped next to me. ⁶They are too powerful for me. So come and put a curse on them. Maybe then I can defeat them and make them leave the area. I know that if you bless someone, the blessings happen.

And if you put a curse on someone, it happens."

⁷The elders of Moab and Midian went with payment in their hands. They found Balaam. Then they told him what Balak had said.

⁸Balaam said to them, "Stay here for the night. I will tell you what the Lord tells me." So the Moabite leaders stayed with him.

⁹God came to Balaam and asked, "Who are these men with you?"

GET CONNECTED

RELATIONSHIPS WITH FRIENDS

Love to Listen Have you ever noticed that God gave each of us two ears, but only one mouth? It's a good visual reminder to us that listening to others is a lot more important than talking.

In fact, the best way we can get to know another person better is simply by letting them talk. Instead of thinking about the next thing you're going to say, really listen to what they're saying, and follow up with questions that help you understand them even better. Listening is also a great thing to do whenever someone is sad. It helps others to tell what they're feeling inside, and it comforts them even more than our words could.

7

8

6

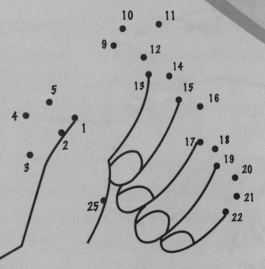

CONNECT THE DOTS

Write the verse here:

_____

_____

_____

Numbers 22:31

Like Balaam, we need to see God in the details, listen when he speaks to us, and most importantly obey!

5

4 1

2

3

10 11

9 12

14

13 15 16

17 18

19 20

21

25 22

23

24

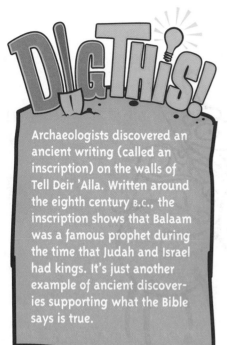

DIG THIS!

Archaeologists discovered an ancient writing (called an inscription) on the walls of Tell Deir 'Alla. Written around the eighth century B.C., the inscription shows that Balaam was a famous prophet during the time that Judah and Israel had kings. It's just another example of ancient discoveries supporting what the Bible says is true.

¹⁰Balaam said to God, "The king of Moab, Balak son of Zippor, sent them. He sent me this message: "'A nation has come out of Egypt. They cover the land. So come and put a curse on them. Then maybe I can fight them and force them out of my land.'"

¹²But God said to Balaam, "Do not go with them. Don't put a curse on those people. I have blessed them."

¹³The next morning Balaam awoke and said to Balak's leaders, "Go back to your own country. The Lord will not let me go with you."

¹⁴So the Moabite leaders went back to Balak. They said, "Balaam refused to come with us."

¹⁵So Balak sent other leaders. He sent more leaders this time. And they were more important. ¹⁶They went to Balaam and said, "Balak son of Zippor says this: Please don't let anything stop you from coming to me. ¹⁷I will pay you well. I will do what you say. Come and put a curse on these people for me."

¹⁸But Balaam answered Balak's servants, "King Balak could give me his palace full of silver and gold. But I cannot disobey the Lord my God in anything, great or small. ¹⁹You stay here tonight as the other men did. I will find out what more the Lord tells me."

²⁰That night God came to Balaam. He said, "These men have

> "The donkey saw the angel of the Lord standing in the road. The angel had a sword in his hand."
>
> Numbers 22:23

GET CONNECTED

RELATIONSHIPS WITH FAMILY

Hidden Danger Balaam couldn't believe it. Whack after whack, and still, his old faithful donkey stood still. It wasn't until the donkey spoke and Balaam's eyes were opened to see the angel in front of him that Balaam understood.

We know that our parents are supposed to discipline us. But when you are going through it, it is often hard to take. You may think, *What are they doing?* or *Why don't they let me do what I want!* or *They just don't understand me.* Just like Balaam, as kids, you often don't—and can't—see the big picture. But your parents can. When they correct you or keep you from doing something you want to do, don't resist them. Trust that they have your best interests at heart (like Balaam's faithful donkey), and thank God that he protects you through your parents.

BALAAM'S DONKEY

SUPPLIES

2-foot square piece of white fabric

3-inch styrofoam ball

one yard of white string

yellow and white pipe cleaners

black marker

old white tights

INSTRUCTIONS

1. Open your square of fabric, and place the styrofoam ball in the middle.

2. Tie the ball into the middle of the fabric with the white string, creating the angel's head. Do not cut the string tails off.

3. Cut 12 inches off the bottom of each side of the tights (like creating 2 new socks).

4. Shape the white pipe cleaners in the new "socks" to make wings for the angel.

5. Tie the wings and the bottom of a yellow pipe cleaner into the string.

6. Shape the yellow pipe cleaner into a halo for the angel.

7. Use the marker to draw a face on the angel.

8. Use the string to hang your angel on a closet door hook or over the doorknob.

ALL ABOUT IT:

Balaam could not see the angel that his donkey saw on the path. How many times have you thought you knew all about a situation, only to find out later you did not have all the facts?

God gives us the Bible and our parents to guide us on the path he has set before us. Hang this angel in your room to remind you to look to God and your parents for help as you grow in faith and follow the Lord.

APRIL service

1 April Fool's Day: Surprise your friends with something sweet!

2

3 Take out the trash each day this month.

4

5 Hide-It-in-Your-Heart: As for me and my family, we will serve the Lord (Joshua 24:15).

6 Take a walk in the park, and count how many bird nests you find.

7 Commit to walking or running a mile each week, even if it's just laps around your yard.

8 Prayer Pointer: Ask God to humble you so you will be ready to serve him in whatever way he asks.

9

10 Invite someone from the neighborhood over to play.

11

12

13 Ask your brothers and sisters how you can help them.

14

15 Prayer Pointer: Thank Jesus for being willing to come to earth to serve us, and ask him to give you the same kind of heart.

16

17 Play soccer in the park.

18

19 Spend a Saturday serving in a soup kitchen.

20

21 Write a note to your teachers thanking them for their help.

22

23 Go on a nature walk, and gather wild flowers for your mom.

24 Help your younger brother with his homework.

25

26 Help your dad prune the bushes and plant spring flowers.

27 Go climb a tree.

28

29 Hide-It-in-Your-Heart: The Lord has told you what is good. He has told you what he wants from you: Do what is right to other people. Love being kind to others. And live humbly, trusting your God (Micah 6:8).

30

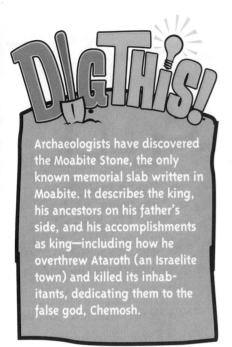

Archaeologists have discovered the Moabite Stone, the only known memorial slab written in Moabite. It describes the king, his ancestors on his father's side, and his accomplishments as king—including how he overthrew Ataroth (an Israelite town) and killed its inhabitants, dedicating them to the false god, Chemosh.

come to ask you to go with them. Go. But only do what I tell you."

BALAAM AND HIS DONKEY

²¹Balaam got up the next morning. He put a saddle on his donkey. Then he went with the Moabite leaders. ²²But God became angry because Balaam went. So the angel of the Lord stood in the road to stop Balaam. Balaam was riding his donkey. And he had two servants with him. ²³The donkey saw the angel of the Lord standing in the road. The angel had a sword in his hand. So the donkey left the road and went into the field.

Balaam hit the donkey to force her back on the road.

²⁴Later, the angel of the Lord stood on a narrow path between two vineyards. There were walls on both sides. ²⁵Again the donkey saw the angel of the Lord. So the donkey walked close to one wall. This crushed Balaam's foot against the wall. So he hit her again.

²⁶The angel of the Lord went ahead again. The angel stood at a narrow place. It was too narrow to turn left or right. ²⁷The donkey saw the angel of the Lord. So she lay down under Balaam. Balaam was very angry and hit her with his stick. ²⁸Then the Lord made the donkey talk. She said to Balaam, "What have I done to make you hit me three times?"

²⁹Balaam answered the donkey, "You have made me look foolish! I wish I had a sword in my hand! I would kill you right now!"

³⁰But the donkey said to Balaam, "I am your very own donkey. You have ridden me for years. Have I ever done this to you before?"

"No," Balaam said.

³¹Then the Lord let Balaam see the angel. The angel of the Lord was standing in the road with his sword drawn. Then Balaam bowed facedown on the ground.

³²The angel of the Lord asked Balaam, "Why have you hit your donkey three times? I have stood here to stop you. What you are doing is wrong. ³³The donkey saw me. She turned away from me three times. If she had not turned away, I would have killed you by now. But I would let her live."

³⁴Then Balaam said to the angel of the Lord, "I have sinned. I did not know you were

> **"The donkey saw the angel of the Lord. So she lay down under Balaam."** Numbers 22:27

standing in the road to stop me. If I am wrong, I will go back."

³⁵The angel of the Lord said to Balaam, "Go with these men. But say only what I tell you." So Balaam went with Balak's leaders.

STORIES FROM DEUTERONOMY

Moses' Last Days

DEUTERONOMY 31:1-8; 32:45-52

JACOB TAKES MOSES' PLACE

31 Then Moses went and spoke these words to all the Israelites: ²"I am now 120 years old. I cannot lead you anymore. The Lord told me I would not cross the Jordan River. ³The Lord your God will lead you across himself. He will destroy those nations for you. You will take over their land. Joshua will also lead you across. This is what the Lord has said. ⁴The Lord will do to these nations what he did to Sihon and Og. They were the kings of the Amorites. He destroyed them and their land. ⁵The Lord will give those nations to you. Do to them everything I told you. ⁶Be strong and brave. Don't be afraid of them. Don't be frightened. The Lord your God will go with you. He will not leave you or forget you."

⁷Then Moses called Joshua and spoke to him in front of the people. Moses said, "Be strong and brave. Lead these people

History Highlights

↗ 1876 B.C.
Jacob enters Egypt.

7000 5000 3000 1000 0 1000 NOW

BIBLE BASICS

WHAT ARE IDOLS?

As you read the Old Testament, you will discover names of idols, such as Baal, Ashtoreth, Dagon, and many more. People from other places worshiped many false gods, hoping that the statues they carved would come to life and help them in their lives. God warned the Israelites to stay away from idols—not only because they aren't real, but also because he alone deserves our worship. However, Israel often forgot the truth and worshiped idols just like the people around them. Their disobedience made God angry, and they were punished for their sins.

GET CONNECTED

RELATIONSHIPS WITH FAMILY

Parent Pep Talk In many ways, Moses was like a parent to the thousands of Israelites he had helped bring out of Egypt. For nearly 40 years, he had watched over them, prayed for them, helped them solve their problems, and taken care of them. In these last days of his life, Moses reminds them of what is most important in life—their relationship with God—and he prays they won't forget that when he's gone.

Much of the time, we treat our parents the same way the Israelites treated Moses. When we get our way, we're nice. When we don't, we complain and disobey. But don't be like the Israelites. Look at the big picture. Understand that your parents are in the same role, on a smaller scale, that Moses was. They pray for you, love you, and take care of you. Trust them. Listen to them when they speak. And when they are away, remember what you've learned, and obey.

of Moab. It is across from Jericho. Look at the land of Canaan. I am giving it to the Israelites to own. ⁵⁰You will die on that mountain that you climb. This is how your brother Aaron died on Mount Hor. ⁵¹You both sinned against me at the waters of Meribah Kadesh. That is in the Desert of Zin. You did not honor me as holy there among the Israelites. ⁵²So now you will only look at the land from far away. You will not enter the land I am giving the people of Israel."

into the land the Lord promised to give their ancestors. Help the people take it as their own. ⁸The Lord himself will go before you. He will be with you. He will not leave you or forget you. Don't be afraid. Don't worry."

32 When Moses finished speaking these words to all Israel, ⁴⁶he said to them: "Pay attention to all the words I have said to you today. Command your children to obey

carefully everything in these teachings. ⁴⁷These should not be unimportant words for you. They mean life for you! By these words you will live a long time in the land you are crossing the Jordan River to own."

MOSES GOES UP TO MOUNT NEBO

⁴⁸The Lord spoke to Moses again that same day. He said, ⁴⁹"Go up the Abarim Mountains. Go to Mount Nebo in the country

Moab was a city located on a plateau (a flat, raised place) southeast of the Dead Sea. Most Moabites were farmers who kept herds of sheep and goats and farmed wheat and barley. Even though they were the descendants of Lot, they were considered enemies of the Israelites. They also worshiped the god Chemosh instead of the one true God.

LOCATED IN THE AREA SOUTHEAST OF THE DEAD SEA, Moab was a nation that came from one of Lot's daughters. Even though they were related to the Israelites (because Lot was the son of Abraham's brother), they were not friendly to one another.

STORIES FROM JOSHUA

Joshua and the Spies

JOSHUA 1:1–2:24

GOD'S COMMAND TO JOSHUA

1 Moses was the servant of the Lord. Joshua son of Nun was Moses' assistant. After Moses died, the Lord said to Joshua: ²"My servant Moses is dead. Now you and all these people go across the Jordan River. Go into the land I am giving to the people of Israel. ³I promised Moses I would give you this land. So I will give you every place you go in the land. ⁴All the land from the desert in the south to Lebanon in the north will be yours. All the land from the great river, the Euphrates, in the east, to the Mediterranean Sea in the west will be yours. This includes the land of the Hittites. ⁵Just as I was with Moses, so I will be with you. No one will be able to stop you all your life. I will not leave you. I will never leave you alone.

⁶"Joshua, be strong and brave! You must lead these people so they can take their land. This is the land I promised their fathers I would give them. ⁷Be strong and brave. Be sure to obey all the teachings my servant Moses gave you. If you follow them exactly, you will be successful in everything you do. ⁸Always remember what is written in the Book of the Teachings. Study it day and night. Then you will be sure to obey everything that is written there. If you do this, you will be wise and successful in everything. ⁹Remember that I commanded you to be strong and brave. So don't be afraid. The Lord your God will be with you everywhere you go."

> **"Remember that I commanded you to be strong and brave. So don't be afraid. The Lord your God will be with you everywhere you go."**
>
> *Joshua 1:9*

GET CONNECTED

RELATIONSHIPS WITH GOD

No Pressure Joshua was feeling the pressure. Now he was in charge of thousands of Israelites who had a history of complaining and turning on their leaders. How could he do it? What should he do?

God knew the job was scary. That's why over and over again he told Joshua to be strong and courageous. Why? Because God was with him! God makes everything possible.

Do you ever feel like living the Christian life is impossible? Feel like you're just not up to the task of being holy? Relax! Just as Joshua drew strength by trusting in God to deliver, we become strong in God when we realize how weak we are on our own. Only God is able to produce the good work he longs to see in us. And he has promised to finish the job. We can be strong and courageous in our faith because we serve an all-powerful God.

JOSHUA'S ORDERS TO THE PEOPLE

¹⁰So Joshua gave orders to the officers of the people. He said, ¹¹"Go through the camp and tell the people, 'Get your supplies ready. Three days from now you will cross the Jordan River. You will go and take the land the Lord your God is giving you.'"

¹²Then Joshua spoke to the people of Reuben, Gad and the eastern half-tribe of Manasseh.

Joshua said, ¹³"Remember what Moses, the servant of the Lord, told you. He said the Lord your God would give you rest. And he said the Lord would give you this land. ¹⁴Now the Lord has given you this land east of the Jordan River. Your wives, your children and your animals may stay here. But your fighting men must dress for war and cross the Jordan River ahead of your brothers. You must help your brothers. ¹⁵The Lord has given you a place to rest. He will do the same for your brothers. But you must help them until they take the land. This is the land the Lord

JOSHUA & CALEB — REAL SUPER HEROES

How would you feel if you walked into your church on Sunday morning and found that all the people inside had given up their hope in God? What if they all decided that being a Christian was just too hard and too scary—what would you do?

It actually happened, though not in a sanctuary. Joshua, Caleb, and 10 other spies had been sent into the land God had promised to give them, and they came back with their report. Joshua and Caleb saw the same people as the other spies, and they were confident that God was capable of victory. But the others grew scared. They didn't think God could do it. So they persuaded the entire Jewish nation to give up hope. Only Joshua and Caleb—out of the entire Jewish family—remained strong. Forty years were spent wandering in the desert, and the unbelieving generation of Israelites died without seeing God's promise fulfilled.

However, God spared Joshua and Caleb. Because of their strong faith and obedience, God blessed them and allowed them to go into the land. Joshua took Moses' place as leader of the people, and he witnessed many miracles as God made his promise come true.

PICTURE PERFECT

3-D

The blessing was within sight!

And God had chosen Joshua to lead the Israelites into the Promised Land. But he had to follow God closely. How well would you have done remembering God's Word if you had been Joshua? Check this out and see!

1 JOSHUA WAS THE SON OF

A Noah.
B Moses.
C Nun.
D We don't know.

2 WHAT BODY OF WATER DID JOSHUA HAVE TO CROSS?

A The Jordan
B The Euphrates
C The Nile
D The Dead Sea

3 WHO WAS GOING WITH JOSHUA?

A Moses
B All the Israelites who came out of Egypt
C No one
D God, Caleb, and the new generation of Israel

4 WHO WAS SUPPOSED TO STAY BEHIND UNTIL THE LAND WAS SECURE?

A No one
B The women
C The children
D Both b and c

5 WHY DID GOD TELL THEM TO HELP EACH OTHER TAKE THE LAND?

A Because he didn't want them fighting.
B Because they didn't know where they were going.
C Because the land was full of enemies who would fight back.
D No particular reason.

6 HOW MANY SPIES DID JOSHUA SEND INTO JERICHO?

A 1
B 2
C 12
D 50

7 WHO HELPED THE SPIES?

A Ruth
B Esther
C Rahab
D Deborah

8 WHAT DID SHE HANG IN THE WINDOW TO STAY SAFE?

A a scarlet rope
B a white flag
C a flower
D a good-luck charm

9 HOW LONG DID THE MEN STAY WITH HER?

A a week
B a day
C a few hours
D three days

10 WHAT REPORT DID THE SPIES GIVE JOSHUA?

A "Don't try it. The people are way too tough."
B "The land has nice people. Let's just be friends with them."
C "The people are afraid of us because God is at work."
D "The people are ready to fight us."

Score 9-10: March into victory!
Score 7-8: Double-check your marching orders.
Score 5-6: Need to regroup.
Score 4 or below: Retreat! It's time for retraining!

3-D

Answers: 1. c; 2. a; 3. d; 4. d; 5. c; 6. b; 7. c; 8. a; 9. d; 10. c

LIVIN' IT!

AWESOME ALLY
JOSHUA 2:1-24

Have you ever felt like you messed up so badly that you can't be forgiven? Do you feel destined to just be a bad person?

Rahab could have felt like that. Even by pagan opinion, she had one of the lowest, most immoral jobs around town. But she held out hope. She had heard about the God of the Israelites, and she chose to stand with his people instead of her own.

Later, we discover that Rahab was actually used by God to not only help Israel defeat their enemies, but she was also in the royal bloodline of Jesus himself.

We are never too far away from God to return. In fact, God says that he comes after us because he loves us so much. We just need to ask for help, and he is ready and able to do much more than we could ever imagine.

their God is giving them. Then you may return to your own land east of the Jordan River. That is the land that Moses, the servant of the Lord, gave you."

[16] Then the people answered Joshua, "Anything you command us to do, we will do. Any place you send us, we will go. [17] Just as we fully obeyed Moses, we will obey you. We ask only that the Lord your God be with you just as he was with Moses. [18] Then, if anyone refuses to obey your commands or turns against you, he will be put to death. Just be strong and brave!"

SPIES SENT TO JERICHO

2 Joshua son of Nun secretly sent out two spies from Acacia. Joshua said to them, "Go and look at the land. Look closely at the city of Jericho."

So the men went to Jericho. They went to the house of a prostitute[d] and stayed there. This woman's name was Rahab.

[2] Someone told the king of Jericho, "Some men from Israel have come here tonight. They are spying out the land."

[3] So the king of Jericho sent this message to Rahab: "Bring out the men who came to you and entered your house. They have come to spy out our whole land."

[4] Now the woman had hidden the two men. She said, "They did come here. But I didn't know where they came from. [5] In the evening, when it was time to close the city gate, they left. I don't know where they went. Go quickly. Maybe you can catch them." [6] (But the woman had taken the men up to the roof.[n] She had hidden them there under stalks of flax.[d] She had spread the flax out there to dry.) [7] So the king's men went out looking for the spies from Israel. They went to the places where people cross the Jordan River.

GET CONNECTED

RELATIONSHIPS WITH FAMILY

The Big Picture Ever heard of the saying, "He can't see the forest for the trees"? It comes from the common experience people have where they get so focused on the tiny details that they are unable to see the big picture.

We often miss God's big picture because we are so distracted with the day-to-day things that happen in our lives. When your brothers and sisters are arguing with you, it seems like winning the fight is the most important thing at the time. But really God wants you to see life as he sees it. You were born to love God and his people—including siblings. When we remember why God created us, it helps us to obey him better in the little things.

2:6 roof In Bible times houses were built with flat roofs. The roof was used for drying things such as flax and fruit. And it was used as an extra room, as a place for worship and as a place to sleep in the summer.

The city gate was closed just after the king's men left the city.

8The spies were ready to sleep for the night. So Rahab went to the roof and talked to them. 9She said, "I know the Lord has given this land to your people. You frighten us very much. Everyone living in this land is terribly afraid of you. 10We are afraid because we have heard how the Lord helped you. We heard how he dried up the Red Sea[d] when you came out of Egypt. We heard how you destroyed Sihon and Og. They were the two Amorite kings who lived east of the Jordan. 11When we heard this, we became very frightened. Now our men are afraid to fight you. This is because the Lord your God rules the heavens above and the earth below! 12So now, make me a promise before the Lord. Promise that you will show kindness to my family just as I showed you kindness. Give me some proof that you will do this. 13Promise me you will allow my family to live. Save my father, mother, brothers, sisters and all of their families from death."

14The men agreed. They said, "We will trade our lives for your lives. Don't tell anyone what we are doing. When the Lord gives us our land, we will be kind to you. You may trust us."

15The house Rahab lived in was built on the city wall. So she used a rope to let the men down through a window. 16She said to

> **"Promise that you will show kindness to my family just as i showed you kindness."**
>
> *Joshua 2:12*

WILD WORLD FACTS

Joshua 2:1-7
FABULOUS FLAX FACTS

People in Bible times seemed crazy about it. Truth is, flax—also known as linseed—is still an important resource, and you might ought to know just a bit about it.

Flax is a blue-flowered crop that produces tiny seeds that are flat and oval-shaped with one pointed tip. They vary in color from yellow to dark brown and have a chewy, nutty taste. The seeds are harvested from the plant using a fine mesh screen, yielding a pure crop of flaxseed, perfect for use in cooking, making oils, and in animal feed. Adding flax to breads, cereals, or other products is an excellent idea since flax is known to reduce the risk of certain diseases like cancer, heart disease, and stroke. In fact, some farmers feed it to their chickens to produce extra-healthy eggs! Some varieties of flax—the kind that was grown in Bible regions—are also used to make linen, a kind of fabric.

[Flax Council of Canada]

INCREDIBLE EDIBLES

JOSHUA AND THE SPIES

INGREDIENTS

crescent rolls

small hotdogs or cocktail wieners

oven

HERE'S THE SCOOP:

Rahab hid the two spies under flax plants that were used to make fabric for clothes. God allowed the spies to be hidden to save their lives. Later God also allowed Rahab and her family to be hidden to save their lives.

Make this recipe for a tasty reminder of God's power to protect and save us.

A HIDDEN SURPRISE RECIPE

1. Open the package of crescent rolls and unroll them.

2. In each triangle place a small hotdog.

3. "Hide" the hotdog in the dough by rolling up the crescent roll.

4. Place them on a cookie sheet.

5. Have one of your parents to cook the rolls as directed on the packaging.

6. Enjoy your hidden surprise treat!

3-D

ANIMALGRAM

Unscramble the letters in each row to spell the name of a biblical animal. When you have unscrambled all the rows, read down the circled letters to find out God's best creatures.

MABL ___ ___ ___ ___

PAE ___ ___ ___

INOL ___ ___ ___ ___

TOAG ___ ___ ___ ___

KNASE ___ ___ ___ ___ ___

GDO ___ ___ ___

OCW ___ ___ ___

XOF ___ ___ ___

SEOUM ___ ___ ___ ___ ___

BABRIT ___ ___ ___ ___ ___ ___

ONEX ___ ___ ___ ___

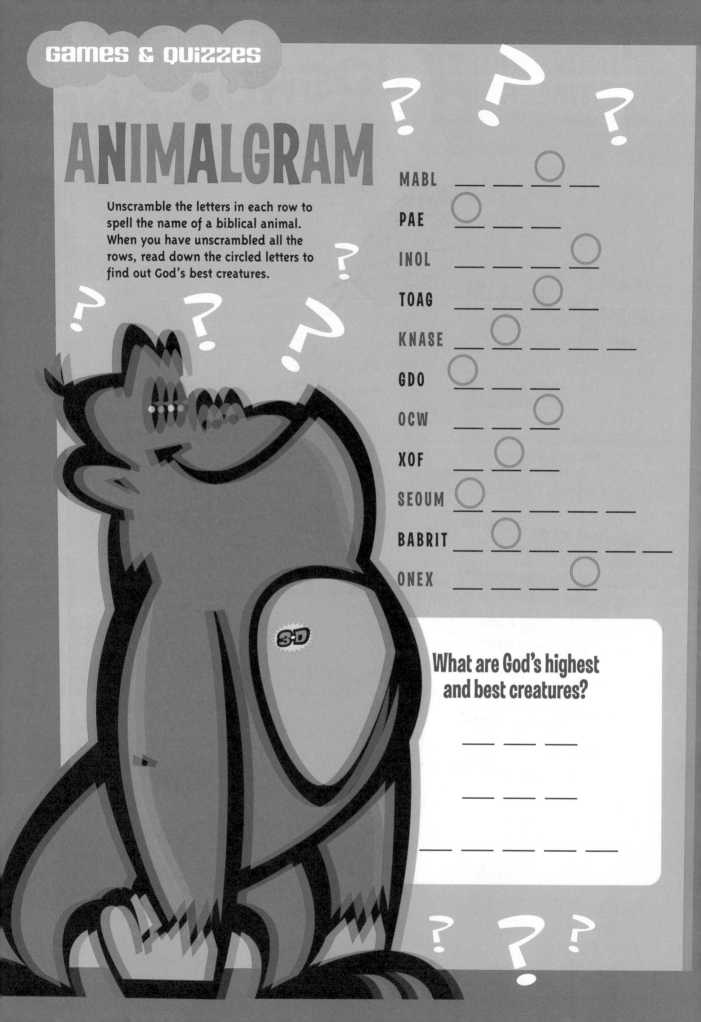

3-D

What are God's highest and best creatures?

___ ___ ___

___ ___ ___

___ ___ ___ ___

"They said to Joshua, 'The Lord surely has given us all of the land. All the people in that land are terribly afraid of us.'" *Joshua 2:24*

them, "Go into the hills. The king's men will not find you there. Hide there for three days. After the king's men return, you may go on your way."

¹⁷The men said to her, "You must do as we say. If not, we cannot be responsible for keeping our promise. ¹⁸You are using a red rope to help us escape. When we return to this land, you must tie it in the window through which you let us down. Bring your father, mother, brothers and all your family into your house. ¹⁹We can keep everyone safe who stays in this house. If anyone in your house is hurt, we will be responsible. If anyone goes out of your house and is killed, it is his own fault. We cannot be responsible for him. ²⁰But you must not tell anyone about this agreement. If you do, we are free from it."

²¹Rahab answered, "I agree to this." So she sent them away, and they left. Then she tied the red rope in the window.

²²The men left and went into the hills. There they stayed for three days. The king's men looked for them all along the road. But after three days, the king's men returned to the city without finding them. ²³Then the two men started back to Joshua. They left the hills and crossed the river. They went to Joshua son of Nun and told him everything that had happened to them. ²⁴They said to Joshua, "The Lord surely has given us all of the land. All the people in that land are terribly afraid of us."

Israelites enter the Promised Land

JOSHUA 3:1-17; 5:1-12

CROSSING THE JORDAN

3 Early the next morning Joshua and all the people of Israel left Acacia. They traveled to the Jordan River and camped there before crossing it. ²After three days the officers went through the camp. ³They gave orders to the people. They said, "You will see the priests and Levites carrying the Box^d of the Agreement with the Lord your God. Then you should leave where you are and follow it. ⁴That way you will know which way to go. You have never traveled this way before. But do not follow too closely. Stay about a thousand yards behind the Box of the Agreement."

⁵Then Joshua told the people, "Make yourselves holy for the Lord. Tomorrow the Lord will do amazing things among you."

⁶Joshua said to the priests, "Take the Box of the Agreement. Cross over the river ahead of the people." So the priests lifted the Holy Box and carried it ahead of the people.

⁷Then the Lord said to Joshua, "Today I will begin to make you a great man to all the Israelites. So the people will know I am with you just as I was with Moses. ⁸The priests will carry the Box of the Agreement. Tell them this: 'Go to the edge of the Jordan River and stand in the water.'"

⁹Then Joshua said to the people of Israel, "Come here. Listen to the words of the Lord your God. ¹⁰Here is proof that the living God is with you. Here is proof that he will drive out the Canaanites, Hittites, Hivites, Perizzites, Girgashites, Amorites and the Jebusites. ¹¹This is the proof: The Box of the Agreement will go ahead of you into the

The Box of the Agreement with the Lord, also known as the Ark of the Covenant, was a unique piece of furniture that the Israelites used for worship in the holiest part of the Temple. Several other furniture pieces that resemble it have been discovered in both ancient Egypt and Palestine, though the original box containing the manna, the tablets, and Aaron's rod has not been found.

LONG BEFORE PEOPLE LEARNED HOW TO WRITE OR EVEN make pots from clay, they discovered that flint, a kind of stone, could be split into smaller sharp and more usable pieces. A variety of tools were created using flint, including knives, scrapers (for removing flesh from hides), and sickles. Israelites also used it to circumcise infant boys.

LIVIN' IT!

NOW OR NEVER
JOSHUA 3:1-17

They had wandered in the desert together for 40 years. They had seen God's hand lead them across the river and deliver enemy nations into their hand with barely a fight. They were at last beginning to feel the blessing of God's beloved Promised Land. But with the blessing came a challenge from Joshua, "You must choose for yourselves today. You must decide whom you will serve."

What about you? We all live in a world that worships false gods—whether it's money, or beauty, or power, or other religions. Will you decide today to stand guard against anything that would make it harder to follow God? Ask God to search your heart and life to see if there is anything you need to get rid of or confess, and commit your way to the Lord right now.

Jordan River. It is the Agreement with the Lord of the whole world. [12]Now choose 12 men from among you. Choose 1 from each of the 12 tribes[d] of Israel. [13]The priests will carry the Holy Box of the Lord, the Master of the whole world. They will carry it into the Jordan ahead of you. When they enter the water, the river will stop flowing. The water will be stopped. It will stand up in a heap as if a dam were there."

[14]So the priests carried the Box of the Agreement. And the people left the place where they had camped. Then they started across the Jordan River. [15]During harvest the Jordan is flooded. So the river was at its fullest. The priests who were carrying the Holy Box came to the edge of the river. And they stepped into the water. [16]Just at that moment, the water stopped flowing. It stood up in a heap a great distance away at Adam. This is a town near Zarethan. The water flowing down to the Sea of Arabah (the Dead Sea[d]) was completely cut off. So the people crossed the river near Jericho. [17]The ground there became dry. The priests carried the Box of the Agreement with the Lord to the middle of the river and stopped. They waited there while all the people of Israel walked across. They crossed the Jordan River on dry land.

5 So the Lord dried up the Jordan River until the Israelites had crossed it. Now all the kings of the Amorites west of the Jordan heard about it. And the Canaanite kings living by the Mediterranean Sea heard about it. They were very scared. After that they were too afraid to face the Israelites.

REAL SUPER HEROES

RAHAB

She had been watching. She had heard about the mighty wonders Israel's God had performed: how he had freed them, fed them, and killed their enemies. So when Israel came knocking on her door, Rahab, the evil prostitute, had become a believer.

Even though her own people would have killed her if they had found out, Rahab risked her life to help Israel's spies get into Jericho. In return for the favor, they spared her life and the lives of her family. She was then able to become a part of the Israelite family.

No matter how big you think your sin is, God's love and forgiveness is even bigger. When we believe in him, he gladly invites us to join his family. God showers us with his protection and good gifts for the rest of our lives.

THE ISRAELITES ARE CIRCUMCISED

²At that time the Lord spoke to Joshua. He said, "Make knives from flint stones. Circumcise[d] the Israelites again." ³So Joshua made knives from flint stones. Then he circumcised the Israelites at Gibeath Haaraloth.

⁴This is why Joshua circumcised the men: After the Israelites left Egypt, all the men old enough to serve in the army died. They died in the desert on the way out of Egypt. ⁵The men who had come out of Egypt had been circumcised. But many were born in the desert on the trip from Egypt. They had not been circumcised.

⁶The Israelites had moved about in the desert for 40 years. During that time all the fighting men who had left Egypt had died. This was because they had not obeyed the Lord. So the Lord swore they would not see the land. This was the land he had promised their ancestors to give them. It was a land where much food grows. ⁷So their sons took their places. But none of the sons born on the trip from Egypt had been circumcised. So Joshua circumcised them. ⁸After all the Israelites had been circumcised, they stayed in camp until they were healed.

⁹Then the Lord said to Joshua, "As slaves in Egypt you were ashamed. But today I have removed that shame." So Joshua named that place Gilgal. And it is still named Gilgal today.

¹⁰The people of Israel were still camped at Gilgal on the plains of Jericho. It was there, on the evening of the fourteenth day of the month, they celebrated the Passover[d] Feast. ¹¹The next day after the Passover, the people ate some of the food grown on that land: bread made without yeast and roasted grain. ¹²The day they ate this food, the manna[d] stopped coming. The Israelites no longer got the manna from heaven. They ate the food grown in the land of Canaan that year.

Bible Critters — CRYING WOLF

Often when prophets warned about upcoming judgment, they compared the situation to when wolves tear up their prey—which is not a pretty sight. On their own, **WOLVES** look kind of like large, gray dogs. They grow to about four-and-a-half feet long and weigh around 80 pounds. They are known for their howl, which they use to call other wolves to begin or end a hunt, to tell the pack a wolf is lost, to warn the others, or just for fun. What makes them scary is simply the fact that they never travel alone. Wolves run in packs, and when grouped together, they are capable of killing and eating almost anything. But take heart. Wolves almost never attack people.

INCREDIBLE EDIBLES

ISRAELITES ENTER THE PROMISED LAND

INGREDIENTS

3 graham crackers

instant pudding mix

milk

measuring cup

plastic rectangular dish

HERE'S THE SCOOP:

God's power is so awesome and amazing! Read the story of the Israelites crossing the Jordan River in Joshua 3–4. Can you imagine being an Israelite? First God parted the Red Sea, making a way for them to escape slavery in Egypt. Next God stopped the Jordan River, and the Israelites walked through on dry ground.

We sometimes forget how awesome God's power and miracles are. God knows this about us. That is why he commanded the Israelites, "Tell the men to get 12 large rocks from the middle of the river. . . . They will be a sign among you. In the future your children will ask you, 'What do these rocks mean?' Tell them the Lord stopped the water from flowing in the Jordan" (Joshua 4:3, 6-7).

Tonight make this dessert for your family's meal. When your family asks why the graham crackers are standing up, tell them the story of how God stopped the water from flowing in the Jordan River.

TWELVE STANDING STONES RECIPE

1. Follow the directions on the instant pudding box to make pudding.

2. Pour the pudding into a rectangular container.

3. Break each graham cracker into 4 rectangular pieces.

4. Once pudding has set, stand the 12 graham crackers in pudding like standing stones.

The Fall of jeRicho

JOSHUA 6:1-27

LiViN' iT!

STRANGE STRATEGIES
JOSHUA 6:1-27

Can't you just see the look of shock that must have been on Joshua's face when God told him how he planned to conquer Jericho? Without a weapon, the Israelites simply marched one time around the city, six days in a row. Then on the seventh day, they marched seven times around it and BOOM! Down went the walls, and Jericho belonged to Israel.

One of the biggest things you'll notice about God as you read the Old Testament is that he does not do things we would consider "normal." His ways are not our ways, and we can't even begin to think like he does. That's why faith is so important. We must trust his goodness and that he knows what he's doing, even if it looks a little silly. We'll see God do amazing things in incredible ways through our lives, too, if we will listen to him and trust him.

THE FALL OF JERICHO

6 Now the people of Jericho were afraid because the Israelites were near. So they closed the city gates and guarded them. No one went into the city. And no one came out.

²Then the Lord spoke to Joshua. He said, "Look, I have given you Jericho, its king and all its fighting men. ³March around the city with your army one time every day. Do this for six days. ⁴Have seven priests carry trumpets made from horns of male sheep. Tell them to march in front of the Holy Box.ᵈ On the seventh day march around the city seven times. On that day tell the priests to blow the trumpets as they march. ⁵They will make one long blast on the trumpets. When you hear that sound, have all the people give a loud shout. Then the walls of the city will fall. And the people will go straight into the city."

⁶So Joshua son of Nun called the priests together. He said to them, "Carry the Box of the Agreement with the Lord. Tell seven priests to carry trumpets and march in front of it." ⁷Then Joshua ordered the people, "Now go! March around the city. The soldiers with weapons should march in front of the Box of the Agreement with the Lord."

⁸So Joshua finished speaking to the people. Then the seven priests began marching before the Lord. They carried the seven trumpets and blew them as they marched. The priests carrying the Box of the Agreement with the Lord followed them. ⁹The soldiers with weapons marched in front of the priests. And armed men walked behind the Holy Box. They were blowing their

> **"March around the city with your army one time every day. Do this for six days."**
>
> Joshua 6:3

GET CONNECTED

RELATIONSHIPS WITH FAMILY

Team Effort Even if Joshua had wanted to do it, he couldn't have conquered Jericho alone. God told him that all of the people had to do the marching. They had to work together, obeying God, to see him deliver their enemies into their hands.

God still wants his people to work together to build his kingdom. We were never meant to work alone. That's part of the reason God gave us families. It's also why we are part of God's family. What are some ways you can help unite your family to serve God better? Start by praying for them and then *with* them. Share with them what God is teaching you, and ask them about their own relationship with God. As you group together, you will be better prepared to face whatever lies ahead in your day.

3-D

trumpets. [10]But Joshua had told the people not to give a war cry. He said, "Don't shout. Don't say a word until the day I tell you. Then shout!" [11]So Joshua had the Holy Box of the Lord carried around the city one time. Then they went back to camp for the night.

[12]Early the next morning Joshua got up. And the priests carried the Holy Box of the Lord again. [13]The seven priests carried the seven trumpets. They marched in front of the Holy Box of the Lord, blowing their trumpets. The soldiers with weapons marched in front of them. Other soldiers walked behind the Holy Box of the Lord. All this time the priests were blowing their trumpets. [14]So on the second day they marched around the city one time. Then they went back to camp. They did this every day for six days.

[15]On the seventh day they got up at dawn. They marched around the city seven times. They marched just as they had on the days before. But on that day they marched around the city seven times. [16]The seventh time around the priests blew their trumpets. Then Joshua gave the command: "Now, shout! The Lord has given you this city! [17]The city and everything in it are to be destroyed as an offering to the Lord. Only Rahab the prostitute[d] and everyone in her house should remain alive. They must not be killed. This is because Rahab hid the

BLAST FROM THE PAST

THE FALL OF JERICHO MIGHT NOT SEEM SO INCREDIBLE until you understand a little about ancient architecture. Often cities like Jericho protected themselves from enemies by building a huge wall around the city. Not only was it high, but it was thick enough to be like a double wall with rooms inside. Then dirt was piled up on the outer part of the walls making a slope so that invaders would have to attack uphill.

Ways to Bowl

1. With your eyes shut
2. With the wrong hand
3. Underhanded
4. Backwards
5. With your family or friends
6. Using gutter guards
7. Teaming up with others
8. Eating cheese and nachos
9. Playing video games between sets
10. With empty soda cans and a ball—at home

you yourselves will be destroyed. You will also bring trouble to all of Israel. ¹⁹All the silver and gold and

out her father, mother, brothers and all those with her. They put all of her family in a safe place outside the camp of Israel.

"So the Lord was with Joshua. And Joshua became famous through all the land."

Joshua 6:27

things made from bronze and iron belong to the Lord. They must be saved for him."

²⁰When the priests blew the trumpets, the people shouted. At the sound of the trumpets and the people's shout, the walls fell. And everyone ran straight into the city. So the Israelites defeated that city. ²¹They completely destroyed every living thing in the city. They killed men and women, young and old. They killed cattle, sheep and donkeys.

²²Joshua spoke to the two men who had spied out the land. Joshua said, "Go into the prostitute's house. Bring her out. And bring out all the people who are with her. Do this because of the promise you made to her." ²³So the two men went into the house and brought out Rahab. They also brought

²⁴Then Israel burned the whole city and everything in it. But they did not burn the things made from silver, gold, bronze and iron. These were saved for the Lord. ²⁵Joshua saved Rahab the prostitute, her family and all who were with her. He let them live. This was because Rahab had helped the men he had sent to spy out Jericho. Rahab still lives among the Israelites today.

²⁶Then Joshua made this important promise. He said:
"Anyone who tries to rebuild
    this city of Jericho
will be punished by a curse
    from the Lord.
The man who lays the
    foundation of this city
will lose his oldest son.
The man who sets up the gates
    will lose his youngest son."
²⁷So the Lord was with Joshua. And Joshua became famous through all the land.

two spies we sent out. ¹⁸Don't take any of the things that are to be destroyed as an offering to the Lord. If you take them and bring them into our camp, then

FIT FOR THE FIGHT

Joshua and the Israelites were ready for Jericho. So are you ready for this puzzle? Read Joshua 6 to find the words that fill in the pieces to this spectacular fight—God's style!

ACROSS:

1. The name of the doomed city.

2. The number of days they marched around the city.

3. The instruments used to signal the people.

4. What the people were to do when they heard the instruments.

5. The special piece that traveled in front of the people.

DOWN:

1. How the people of Jericho felt.

2. Musical instruments made from male sheep.

3. The Israelites who led worship.

4. The only woman and her family who would be saved.

5. What Israel did around Jericho.

6. What fell on the last day.

JUDGES

DeBorah, the womAn judge
JUDGES 4:1—5:31

DEBORAH, THE WOMAN JUDGE

4 After Ehud died, the people of Israel again did what the Lord said was wrong. ²So he let Jabin, a king of Canaan, defeat Israel. Jabin ruled in the city of Hazor. Sisera was the commander of Jabin's army. Sisera lived in Harosheth Haggoyim. ³He had 900 iron chariots and was very cruel to the people of Israel for 20 years. So they cried to the Lord for help.

⁴There was a prophetess*ᵈ* named Deborah. She was the wife of Lappidoth. She was judge of Israel at that time. ⁵Deborah would sit under the Palm Tree of Deborah. This was between the cities of Ramah and Bethel, in the mountains of Ephraim. And the people of Israel would come to her to settle their arguments.

⁶Deborah sent a message to a man named Barak. He was the son of Abinoam. Barak lived in the city of Kedesh, which is in the area of Naphtali. Deborah said to Barak, "The Lord, the God of Israel, commands you: 'Go and

LiViN' iT!

WISE WOMEN
JUDGES 4:1-24

Deborah knew what had to be done. Sisera and his army had to be defeated. Deborah called on Barak to carry out the attack, but he was afraid to go alone. Confident in God's command, Deborah went with Barak to lead the Israelites to victory. Jael, another woman in the story, closes the deal when she pretended to be friends with Sisera. Once he was asleep, she nailed his head to the ground!

It's a very graphic story, but it is also one of strength. Whether you are young or old, guy or girl, you can act with authority when you know that what you are doing is in obedience to the Lord. Like Deborah and Jael, you can be a wise warrior of God by standing up for what is right. Most likely other Christians who are weak in their faith will be encouraged by your actions and will be challenged to do the same.

BiBLe BasicS

WHat is a PrOPHet?

A prophet is a messenger who speaks for someone else. God chose certain men and women (called prophetesses) to carry his message to his own people and the surrounding nations. Often God used prophets to warn people about judgment or punishment that was going to happen if the people didn't repent of their sins. Because their messages always sounded bad, not many people really liked to hear what the prophets had to say.

gather 10,000 men of Naphtali and Zebulun. Lead them to Mount Tabor. [7]I will make Sisera, the commander of Jabin's army, come to you. Sisera, his chariots and his army will meet you at the Kishon River. I will help you to defeat Sisera there.'"

[8]Then Barak said to Deborah, "I will go if you will go with me. But if you will not go with me, I won't go."

[9]"Of course I will go with you," Deborah answered. "But you will not get credit for the victory. The Lord will let a woman defeat Sisera." So Deborah went with Barak to Kedesh.

[10]At Kedesh, Barak called the people of Zebulun and Naphtali together. From them, he gathered 10,000 men to follow him. Deborah went with Barak also.

[11]Now Heber the Kenite had left the other Kenite people. (The Kenites were descendants[d] of Hobab, Moses' brother-in-law.) Heber had put up his tent by the great tree in Zaanannim. This is near Kedesh.

[12]Then Sisera was told that Barak son of Abinoam had gone up to Mount Tabor. [13]So Sisera gathered his 900 iron chariots and all the men with him. They went from Harosheth Haggoyim to the Kishon River.

[14]Then Deborah said to Barak, "Get up! Today is the day the Lord will help you defeat Sisera. You know the Lord has already cleared the way for you." So Barak led 10,000 men down from Mount Tabor. [15]He and his men attacked Sisera and his men. During the battle the Lord

REAL SUPER HEROES

DEBORAH

You have to understand that times were different back then. In ancient history, women were not highly valued. Though not in all cases, they were often treated more like servants than wives, and they rarely held important offices. Until Deborah.

Deborah didn't let her culture define her identity. Instead, she just followed God. As a prophetess (a messenger who spoke God's message), she listened to what God said—and spoke it to the people. She knew she was one of his own, and her role in God's family gave her the courage to use the gifts God had given her. So the people came to her. Men and women, soldiers and families of Israel came to her for advice and counsel, and she became the judge of Israel. Out of obedience to God, it was Deborah who instructed Barak to attack Sisera. And even though God promised victory, Barak would only attack if Deborah came with him. Israel won the battle, but the credit went to God and Deborah.

Deborah's confidence in God reminds us that God can do anything through us when we put our lives in his hands!

MAY COURAGE

1
Call someone from your class who needs a friend.

2

3
What are you most afraid of? Ask God for help to face your fear.

4

5
National Day of Prayer:
Pray for our leaders to fear God and make good decisions.

6

7
Write a letter to our servicemen and women, and thank them for their hard work and sacrifice for your freedom.

8
Hide-It-in-Your-Heart:
Remember that I commanded you to be strong and brave. So don't be afraid. The Lord your God will be with you everywhere you go (Joshua 1:9).

9

10
See if you can touch your tongue to your nose and show a friend.

11

12
Take a walk at the zoo, and feed the fish.

13

14
Invite the class bully home for dinner.

15

16
Start a memory verse club with your brothers and sisters.

17
Make homemade bubbles, and see how big you can make them.

18

19
Prayer Pointer: Ask God to give the President courage to do what is right, even when others want him to do what is wrong.

20
Try a new sport you've never played before.

21
Armed Forces Day:
Ask God to protect our military and their families.

22

23
Find a grassy hill, lie down, and count the clouds.

24

25
Visit a retirement center, and sing them your favorite Bible songs.

26
Hide-It-in-Your-Heart:
Have courage. May the Lord be with those who do what is right (2 Chronicles 19:11).

27

28

29
Hang red, white, and blue streamers from your front porch to celebrate Memorial Day.

30

31

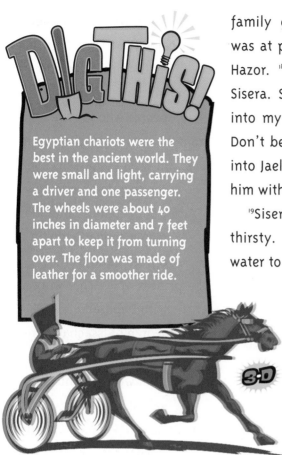

Egyptian chariots were the best in the ancient world. They were small and light, carrying a driver and one passenger. The wheels were about 40 inches in diameter and 7 feet apart to keep it from turning over. The floor was made of leather for a smoother ride.

confused Sisera and his army and chariots. So Barak and his men used their swords to defeat Sisera's army. But Sisera left his chariot and ran away on foot. [16]Barak and his men chased Sisera's chariots and army to Harosheth Haggoyim. They used their swords to kill all of Sisera's men. Not one of them was left alive.

[17]But Sisera himself ran away. He came to the tent where Jael lived. She was the wife of Heber, one of the Kenite family groups. Heber's family was at peace with Jabin king of Hazor. [18]Jael went out to meet Sisera. She said to him, "Come into my tent, master! Come in. Don't be afraid." So Sisera went into Jael's tent, and she covered him with a rug.

[19]Sisera said to Jael, "I am thirsty. Please give me some water to drink." So she opened a leather bag in which she kept milk and gave him a drink. Then she covered him up.

[20]Then Sisera said to Jael, "Go stand at the entrance to the tent. If anyone comes and asks you, 'Is anyone here?' say, 'No.'"

[21]But Jael, the wife of Heber, took a tent peg and a hammer. She quietly went to Sisera. Since he was very tired, he was sleeping. She hammered the tent peg through the side of Sisera's head and into the ground! And so Sisera died.

[22]Then Barak came by Jael's tent, chasing Sisera. Jael went out to meet him and said, "Come. I will show you the man you are looking for." So Barak entered her tent. There Sisera lay dead, with the tent peg in his head.

[23]On that day God defeated Jabin king of Canaan in the sight of Israel.

[24]Israel became stronger and stronger against Jabin king of Canaan. Finally, they destroyed him.

THE SONG OF DEBORAH

5 On that day Deborah and Barak son of Abinoam sang this song:

[2]"The leaders led Israel.
  The people volunteered to go
    to battle.
  Praise the Lord!
[3]Listen, kings.
  Pay attention, rulers!
I myself will sing to the Lord.

"i myself will sing to the Lord. i will make music to the Lord, the God of israel." *Judges 5:3*

I will make music to the Lord,
  the God of Israel.

[4]"Lord, in the past you came
  from Edom.

You marched from the land
of Edom,
and the earth shook.
The skies rained,
and the clouds dropped water.
⁵The mountains shook before the
Lord, the God of Mount
Sinai.
They shook before the Lord,
the God of Israel!

⁶"In the days of Shamgar son of
Anath,
in the days of Jael, the main
roads were empty.
Travelers went on the back
roads.
⁷There were no warriors in Israel
until I, Deborah, arose.
I arose to be a mother to Israel.
⁸At that time they chose to follow
new gods.
Because of this, enemies fought
us at our city gates.
No one could find a shield or a
spear
among the 40,000 men of Israel.
⁹My heart is with the commanders

of Israel.
They volunteered freely from
among the people.
Praise the Lord!

¹⁰"You who ride on white donkeys
and sit on saddle blankets,
listen!
And you who walk along the
road, listen!
¹¹Listen to the sound of the singers

**"So there was peace in the
land for 40 years."** *Judges 5:31*

at the watering holes.
There they tell about the victories
of the Lord.
They tell about the victories of
the Lord's warriors in
Israel.
Then the Lord's people went
down to the city gates.

¹²"Wake up, wake up, Deborah!
Wake up, wake up, sing a song!
Get up, Barak!
Go capture your enemies, son
of Abinoam!

¹³"Then the men who were left
came down to the
important leaders.
The Lord's people came down

to me with strong men.
¹⁴They came from Ephraim in the
mountains of Amalek.
Benjamin was among the
people who followed you.
From the family group of Makir
in West Manasseh, the
commanders came down.
And from Zebulun came those
men who lead with an
officer's staff.
¹⁵The princes of Issachar were
with Deborah.
The people of Issachar were
loyal to Barak.
They followed him into the
valley.
The Reubenites thought hard
about what they would do.
¹⁶Why did you stay by the
sheepfold?
Was it to hear the music
played for your sheep?
The Reubenites thought hard
about what they would do.
¹⁷The people of Gilead stayed
east of the Jordan River.
People of Dan, why did you
stay by the ships?
The people of Asher stayed at
the seashore.
They stayed at their safe
harbors.
¹⁸But the people of Zebulun
risked their lives.

So did the people of Naphtali
on the battlefield.

19"The kings came, and they
fought.
At that time the kings of
Canaan fought
at Taanach, by the waters of
Megiddo.
But they took away no silver
or possessions of Israel.
20The stars fought from heaven.
From their paths, they fought
Sisera.
21The Kishon River swept Sisera's
men away,
that old river, the Kishon River.
March on, my soul, with strength!
22Then the horses' hoofs beat the
ground.
Galloping, galloping go Sisera's
mighty horses.
23'May the town of Meroz be
cursed,' said the angel
of the Lord.
'Bitterly curse its people,
because they did not come to
help the Lord.
They did not fight the strong
enemy.'

24"May Jael, the wife of Heber
the Kenite,
be blessed above all women
who live in tents.

25Sisera asked for water,
but Jael gave him milk.
In a bowl fit for a ruler,
she brought him cream.
26Jael reached out and took the
tent peg.
Her right hand reached for
the workman's hammer.
And she hit Sisera! She smashed
his head!
She crushed and pierced the
side of his head!
27At Jael's feet he sank.
He fell, and he lay there.
At her feet he sank. He fell.
Where Sisera sank, there he
fell, dead!

28"Sisera's mother looked out
through the window.
She looked through the curtains.
She asked, 'Why is Sisera's
chariot so late in coming?
Why are sounds of his chariots'
horses delayed?'

29The wisest of her servant ladies
answer her.
And Sisera's mother says to
herself,
30'Surely they are taking the
possessions of the people
they defeated!
Surely they are dividing those
things among themselves!
A girl or two is being given to
each soldier.
Maybe Sisera is taking pieces
of dyed cloth.
Maybe they are even taking
pieces of dyed, embroidered
cloth for the necks of the
victors!'

31"Let all your enemies die this
way, Lord!
But let all the people who
love you
be powerful like the rising sun!"
So there was peace in the
land for 40 years.

History Highlights

➚ 1813–1760 B.C.
The Mari tablets were written.

7000 5000 3000 1000 0 1000 NOW

Gideon, the Mighty Warrior

JUDGES 6:1-2, 7-8, 11-24; 7:1-24; 8:28

THE MIDIANITES ATTACK ISRAEL

6 Again the people of Israel did what the Lord said was wrong. So for seven years the Lord let the people of Midian rule Israel. [2]The Midianites were very powerful and were cruel to the Israelites. So the Israelites made hiding places in the mountains. They also hid in caves and safe places.

• • •

[7]The Israelites cried out to the Lord for help against the Midianites. [8]So the Lord sent a prophet[d] to them.

• • •

THE ANGEL OF THE LORD VISITS GIDEON

[11]The angel of the Lord came and sat down under an oak tree at Ophrah. The oak tree belonged to Joash, who was one of the Abiezrite people. Joash was the father of Gideon. Gideon was separating some wheat from the chaff[d] in a winepress.[d] Gideon did this to keep the wheat from the Midianites. [12]The angel of the Lord appeared to Gideon and said, "The Lord is with you, mighty warrior!"

[13]Then Gideon said, "Pardon me, sir. If the Lord is with us, why are we having so many troubles? Our ancestors told us he did miracles.[d] They told us the Lord brought them out of Egypt. But now he has left us. He has allowed the Midianites to defeat us."

[14]The Lord turned to Gideon and said, "You have the strength to save the people of Israel. Go and save them from the Midianites. I am the one who is sending you."

[15]But Gideon answered, "Pardon me, Lord. How can I save Israel? My family group is the weakest in Manasseh. And I am the least important member of my family."

[16]The Lord answered him, "I will be with you. It will seem as if you are fighting only one man."

[17]Then Gideon said to the Lord, "If you are pleased with me, give me proof. Show me that it is really you talking with me. [18]Please

GET CONNECTED

RELATIONSHIPS WITH GOD

What's Wooly Right? Gideon didn't know what to do. Should he go to war or not? Would they win? He had important issues on his mind. So he used a piece of sheepskin to figure out God's will.

Do you wonder what God wants to do with your life? How can you know you're following his plan? We don't have to use a sheepskin, but God does give us other tools to find out his thoughts. First, we can pray for wisdom. Then we can search his Word for direction. If the Bible doesn't talk about it specifically, God can guide us through our parents. The Bible says that whatever we do, we need to keep God in mind as we do it.

Follow the sign!

What did Gideon use to find out what God was telling him to do? Color in the blocks according to the chart below to find out. (Also read Judges 6:39-40.)

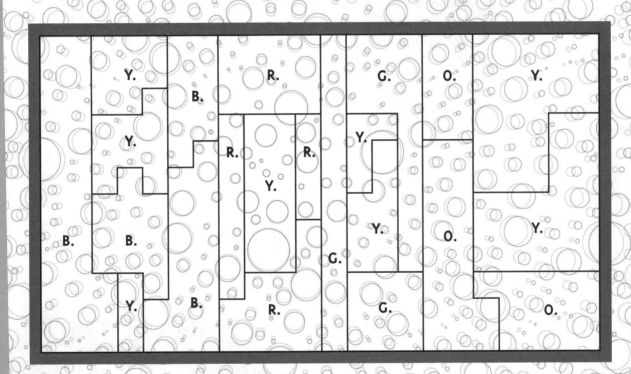

B — Black
Y — Yellow
R — Red
G — Green
O — Orange

3-D

wait here. Do not go away until I come back to you. Let me bring my offering and set it in front of you."

And the Lord said, "I will wait until you come back."

[19]So Gideon went in and cooked a young goat. He also took about 20 quarts of flour and made bread without yeast. Then he put the meat into a basket. And he put the broth from the boiled meat into a pot. He brought out the meat, the broth and the bread without yeast. He brought the food to the angel of the Lord. Gideon gave it to him under the oak tree.

[20]The angel of God said to Gideon, "Put the meat and the bread without yeast on that rock over there. Then pour the broth on them." And Gideon did as he was told. [21]The angel of the Lord had a stick in his hand. He touched the meat and the bread with the end of the stick. Then fire jumped up from the rock! The meat and the bread were completely burned up! And the angel of the Lord disappeared! [22]Then Gideon understood he had been talking to the angel of the Lord. So Gideon cried, "Lord God! I have seen the angel of the Lord face to face!"

[23]But the Lord said to Gideon, "Calm down! Don't be afraid! You will not die!"

[24]So Gideon built an altar there to worship the Lord. Gideon named the altar The Lord Is Peace. It still stands at Ophrah, where the Abiezrites live.

• • •

7 Early in the morning Jerub-Baal and all his men set up their camp at the spring of Harod. (Jerub-Baal is also called Gideon.) The Midianites were camped north of them. The Midianites were camped in the valley at the bottom of the hill called Moreh. [2]Then the Lord said to Gideon, "You have too many men

> **"So Gideon built an altar there to worship the Lord. Gideon named the altar The Lord is Peace."**
>
> *Judges 6:24*

REAL SUPER HEROES

GiDEON

After Deborah, God chose a godly man to serve as judge of Israel. In those days, God actually appeared to Gideon as an angel, and called him to duty. He instructed Gideon to tear down the false idols his own father had erected to worship. Gideon obeyed God, even though it made his dad and a bunch of Israelites really angry. But he knew he was doing the right thing, and he encouraged everyone else to do the same.

When God then told him to attack the Midianites, Gideon wanted to make certain he was hearing God clearly. He laid out a fleece (sheepskin), and asked God to make it wet and the ground dry. Then he reversed the test. God's answer was loud and clear, so Gideon gathered a small army of God's choosing and defeated the Midianites.

As we go through each day, we need to remember to talk to God, just like Gideon did. God still leads us, but we must take the time to ask him for guidance and listen for his wisdom.

to defeat the Midianites. I don't want the Israelites to brag that they saved themselves. ³So now, announce to the people, 'Anyone who is afraid may leave Mount Gilead. He may go back home.'" And 22,000 men went back home. But 10,000 remained.

their mouths. They lapped it as a dog does. All the rest got down on their knees to drink.

⁷Then the Lord said to Gideon, "I will save you, using the 300 men who lapped the water. And I will allow you to defeat Midian. Let all the other men go to their

GIDEON IS ENCOURAGED

So Gideon and his servant Purah went down to the edge of the enemy camp. ¹²The Midianites, the Amalekites and all the peoples from the east were camped in that valley. There were so many of them they

WHAT'S THE BIG DEAL ABOUT BAAL? Ancient people from Syria, Mesopotamia, and Egypt wrote about and drew pictures of this false god, dating from the middle of the third millennium to the last century B.C. Baal ("lord" in Hebrew) was the title given to the storm god Hadad. People thought Baal brought rain and the crops that thrived from the rain.

⁴Then the Lord said to Gideon, "There are still too many men. Take the men down to the water, and I will test them for you there. If I say, 'This man will go with you,' he will go. But if I say, 'That one will not go with you,' he will not go."

⁵So Gideon led the men down to the water. There the Lord said to him, "Separate them. Those who drink water by lapping it up like a dog will be in one group. Those who bend down to drink will be in the other group." ⁶There were 300 men who used their hands to bring water to

homes." ⁸So Gideon sent the rest of Israel to their homes. But he kept 300 men. He took the jars and the trumpets of those who went home.

Now the camp of Midian was in the valley below Gideon. ⁹That night the Lord spoke to Gideon. He said, "Get up. Go down and attack the camp of the Midianites. I will allow you to defeat them. ¹⁰But if you are afraid to go down, take your servant Purah with you. ¹¹When you come to the camp of Midian, you will hear what they are saying. Then you will not be afraid to attack the camp."

seemed like locusts.ᵈ They had so many camels no one could count them. There were as many as there are grains of sand on the seashore!

¹³When Gideon came to the enemy camp, he heard a man talking. That man was telling his friend about a dream. He was saying, "Listen, I dreamed that a loaf of barley bread rolled into the camp of Midian. It hit the tent so hard that the tent turned over and fell flat!"

¹⁴The man's friend said, "Your dream is about the sword of Gideon son of Joash, a man of

INCREDIBLE EDIBLES

GIDEON

INGREDIENTS

peanuts in shells
bowl

HERE'S THE SCOOP:

The story of how God calls and uses Gideon is amazing. Focus on the very first part of the story, "Gideon was separating some wheat from the chaff . . ." (Judges 6:11). Wheat, which we use to make bread, is a plant. To harvest the kernel (the food part of the wheat) it needs to be separated from the chaff.

God talks about separating the wheat from the chaff in the Bible over and over. As you live for Christ, God will continue to make your life more usable for his kingdom (the wheat) and help show you what sins you need to get rid of (the chaff). There are few opportunities for us today to physically separate wheat from chaff. So as you separate the peanut shells from the peanuts, think about the work God is doing in and through your life.

SHELLED PEANUTS RECIPE

1. To crack open a peanut shell, put the shell between your thumb and index finger with your thumb on the seam of the shell.

2. Squeeze your thumb and index finger together to crack the shell.

3. Put the shells in the bowl, and eat the peanuts!

3-D

Dig This!

It's no wonder that Gideon wanted to make sure he was doing what God wanted. He had a lot of ground to cover. The Angel of the Lord appeared at Ophrah, telling him how to gather his army. Then, with only 300 men, he left Harod and made the surprise attack on the sleeping Midianites just north of Mt. Moreh. His army chased the remaining Midianites through Succoth and Peniel, all the way to Karkor where their kings were captured and killed.

will blow our trumpets. When we blow our trumpets, you blow your trumpets, too. Then shout, 'For the Lord and for Gideon!'"

Israel. God will let Gideon defeat Midian and the whole army!"

¹⁵When Gideon heard about the dream and what it meant, he worshiped God. Then Gideon went back to the camp of Israel. He called out to them, "Get up! The Lord has defeated the army of Midian for you!" ¹⁶Then Gideon divided the 300 men into three groups. He gave each man a trumpet and an empty jar. A burning torch was inside each jar.

¹⁷Gideon told the men, "Watch me and do what I do. When I get to the edge of the camp, do what I do. ¹⁸Surround the enemy camp. I and everyone with me

MIDIAN IS DEFEATED

¹⁹So Gideon and the 100 men with him came to the edge of the enemy camp. They came just after the enemy had changed guards. It was during the middle watch of the night. Then Gideon and his men blew their trumpets and smashed their jars. ²⁰All three groups of Gideon's men blew their trumpets and smashed their jars. They held the torches in their left hands and the trumpets in their right hands. Then they shouted, "A sword for the Lord and for Gideon!" ²¹Each of Gideon's men stayed in his place around the

camp. But inside the camp, the men of Midian began shouting and running away.

²²When Gideon's 300 men blew their trumpets, the Lord caused all the men of Midian to fight each other with their swords! The enemy army ran away to the city of Beth Shittah. It is toward Zererah. They ran as far as the border of the city of Abel Meholah. It is near the city of Tabbath. ²³Then men of Israel from Naphtali, Asher and all of Manasseh were called out to chase the Midianites. ²⁴Gideon sent messengers through all the mountains of Ephraim. They said, "Come down and attack the Midianites. Take control of the Jordan River as far as Beth Barah. Do this before the Midianites can get to the river and cross it."

So they called out all the men of Ephraim. They took control of the Jordan River as far as Beth Barah.

• • •

8 So Midian was forced to be under the rule of Israel. Midian did not cause trouble anymore. And the land had peace for 40 years, as long as Gideon was alive.

Samson, the Philistines, & Delilah

JUDGES 13:1–14:9; 15:1-15; 16:1-30

THE BIRTH OF SAMSON

13 Again the people of Israel did what the Lord said was wrong. So he let the Philistines rule over them for 40 years.

²There was a man named Manoah from the city of Zorah. Manoah was from the tribe*ᵈ* of Dan. He had a wife, but she could not have children. ³The angel of the Lord appeared to Manoah's wife. He said, "You have not been able to have children. But you will become pregnant and have a son! ⁴Don't drink wine or beer. Don't eat anything that is unclean.*ᵈ* ⁵You will become pregnant and have a son. You must never cut his hair because he will be a Nazirite.*ᵈ* He will be given to God from birth. He will begin the work of saving Israel from the power of the Philistines."

⁶Then Manoah's wife went to him and told him what had happened. She said, "A man from God came to me. He looked like an angel from God. His appearance was frightening. I didn't ask him where he was from. And he didn't tell me his name. ⁷But he said to me, 'You will be pregnant and will have a son. Don't drink wine or beer. Don't eat anything that is unclean. The reason is that the boy will be a Nazirite to God. He will be that from his birth until the day of his death.'"

⁸Then Manoah said a prayer to the Lord: "Lord, I beg you to let the man of God come to us again. Let him teach us what we should do for the boy who will be born to us."

⁹God heard Manoah's prayer. The angel of God came to Manoah's wife again. This was while she was sitting in a field.

But her husband Manoah was not with her. ¹⁰So she ran to tell him, "He is here! The man who appeared to me the other day is here!"

¹¹Manoah got up and followed his wife. When he came to the man, he said, "Are you the man who spoke to my wife?"

The man said, "I am."

¹²So Manoah asked, "When

LIVIN' IT!

SHORTSIGHTED SAMSON
JUDGES 14:1-3

He had everything going for him! Samson was strong, good-looking, and he knew God's hand was upon him. So where did he go wrong?

God had already made it clear that Jews were only supposed to marry Jews. But Samson took one look at Delilah—an enemy Philistine—and decided she was too beautiful to pass up. Delilah ends up tricking Samson so that he lost his strength, his eyesight, and his freedom.

Like Samson, we are tempted to look at the beautiful things and people in this life and think we've got to have them for ourselves to be happy. But God warns us: Looks are deceiving. We need to look for inside beauty that shows the love of God when we are looking for close friends.

what you say happens, what kind of life should the boy live? What should he do?"

[13]The angel of the Lord said, "Your wife must do everything I told her to do. [14]She must not eat anything that grows on a grapevine. She must not drink any wine or beer. She must not eat anything that is unclean. She must do everything I have commanded her to do."

[15]Manoah said to the angel of the Lord, "We would like you to

"The Spirit of the Lord began to work in Samson."

Judges 13:25

stay awhile. We want to cook a young goat for you."

[16]The angel of the Lord answered, "Even if I stay awhile, I would not eat your food. But if you want to prepare something, offer a burnt offering to the Lord." (Manoah did not understand that the man was really the angel of the Lord.)

[17]Then Manoah asked the angel of the Lord, "What is your name? We want to know. Then we may honor you when what you have said really happens."

[18]The angel of the Lord said, "Why do you ask my name? It is

too wonderful for you to understand." [19]Then Manoah sacrificed a young goat on a rock. He also offered some grain as a gift to the Lord. The Lord did an amazing thing. Manoah and his wife watched what happened. [20]The flames went up to the sky from the altar. As the fire burned, the angel of the Lord went up to heaven in the fire! When Manoah and his wife saw that, they bowed facedown on the ground. [21]The angel of the Lord did not appear to them again. Then Manoah understood that the man was really the angel of the Lord. [22]Manoah said, "We have seen God! Surely we will die because of this!"

[23]But his wife said to him, "The Lord does not want to kill us. If he wanted to kill us, he would not have accepted our burnt offering or grain offering. He would not have shown us all these things. And he would not have told us all this."

[24]So the woman gave birth to a boy. She named him Samson. Samson grew, and the Lord blessed him. [25]The Spirit[d] of the Lord began to work in Samson. This was while he was in the city of Mahaneh Dan. It is between the cities of Zorah and Eshtaol.

SAMSON'S MARRIAGE

14 Samson went down to the city of Timnah. There he saw a young Philistine woman. [2]When he returned home, he said to his father and mother, "I saw a Philistine woman in Timnah. I want you to get her for me. I want to marry her."

[3]His father and mother answered, "Surely there is a woman from Israel you can marry. Do you have to marry a woman from the Philistines? The Philistines are not even circumcised."[d]

But Samson said, "Get that woman for me! She is the one I want!" [4](Samson's parents did not know that the Lord wanted this to happen. He was looking for a way to start a fight with the Philistines. They were ruling over Israel at this time.) [5]Samson went down with his father and mother to Timnah. They went as far as the vineyard near there. Suddenly, a young lion came roaring toward Samson! [6]The Spirit[d] of the Lord entered Samson with great power. Samson tore the lion apart with his bare hands. For him it was as easy as tearing apart a young goat. But Samson did not tell his father or mother what he had done. 7Then he went down to the city. There he talked to the Philistine woman, and he liked her.

8Several days later Samson went back to marry her. On his way he went over to look at the body of the dead lion. He found a swarm of bees in it. They had made some honey. 9Samson got some of the honey with his hands. He walked along eating it. When he came to his parents, he gave some to them. They ate it, too. But Samson did not tell them he had taken the honey from the body of the dead lion.

• • •

SAMSON TROUBLES THE PHILISTINES

15 At the time of the wheat harvest, Samson went to visit his wife. He took a young goat with him. He said, "I'm going to my wife's room." But her father would not let Samson go in.

2He said to Samson, "I thought you really hated your wife. So I gave her to the best man from the wedding. Her younger sister is more beautiful. Take her."

3But Samson said to him, "Now I have a good reason to hurt you Philistines. No one will blame me!" 4So

Samson went out and caught 300 foxes. He took 2 foxes at a time and tied their tails together. Then he tied a torch to the tails of each pair of foxes. 5Samson lit the torches. Then he let the foxes loose in the grainfields of the Philistines. In this way he burned up their standing grain and the piles of grain. He also burned up their vineyards and their olive trees.

6The Philistines asked, "Who did this?"

Someone told them, "Samson, the son-in-law of the man from Timnah, did. He did this because his father-in-law gave his wife to his best man."

REAL SUPER HEROES

SAMSON

He was called to service, even before he was born. An angel had appeared to Samson's parents, instructing them how to raise this special son who would help the Israelites.

Samson was also given specific instructions. As a Nazirite (one who makes a special promise to God), he was not allowed to drink alcohol, eat anything unclean, or cut his hair. These outward symbols showed that God had set him apart from others and intended to use him in mighty ways. As long as he kept his vow, God gave Samson extraordinary strength.

Samson used his gift to bring much trouble on the Philistines, a group of people who hated the Jews. He destroyed their crops, vineyards, and olive trees by burning them down. He killed 1,000 men with the jawbone of a donkey. But his deeds weren't all for good. He lost focus on God and instead desired the beauty and friendship of a Philistine woman. He told Delila the secret of his strength, and she had men come cut his hair. With all his strength gone, he was imprisoned, and his eyes were put out. It was in his despair that he remembered God and repented. God heard him, and as his hair grew back, so did his strength. In the end, Samson destroyed their Temple and all the people in it—including himself.

Samson teaches us how important it is to stand strong and keep doing good. We need to listen daily to God through his Word and stay in contact with him through prayer, so that we remain strong in Christ throughout all of our lives.

CRAFTS

SAMSON

- construction paper
- scissors
- markers
- stickers
- school picture
- clear packing tape

ALL ABOUT IT:

God made Samson for a special purpose. But Samson did not focus on God, and he did not listen to his God-fearing family and friends. Samson listened to his friend Delilah, who did not believe in God. She did not want the best for Samson. Eventually, Samson told Delilah his secret—the source of his power. Delilah cut Samson's hair when he was asleep. "In this way she began to make him weak. And Samson's strength left him" (Judges 16:19). We should choose friends who will help to make us better people and build us up, instead of tearing us down.

God makes each of us unique and special. God has made promises to you. You are important to God, and he wants you to be his special child. Make the bookmark, and use it to keep your place as you read about God's promises he has for you in the Bible.

BOOKMARK INSTRUCTIONS

1. Cut a bookmark size strip out of construction paper.

2. Decorate the bookmark on the front and back with markers and stickers.

3. Tape your school picture on the bookmark.

4. Using clear packing tape, seal your bookmark so it will last a long time.

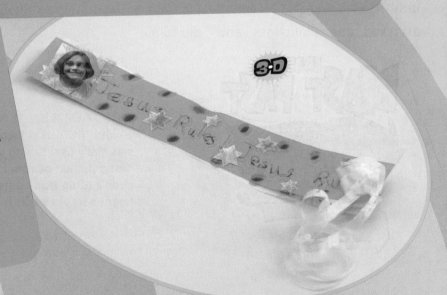

> "The ropes on him became weak like strings that had been burned. They fell off his hands!"
>
> *Judges 15:14*

So the Philistines burned Samson's wife and her father to death. [7]Then Samson said to the Philistines, "Since you did this, I will hurt you, too! I won't stop until I pay you back!" [8]Samson attacked the Philistines and killed many of them. Then he went down and stayed in a cave. It was in the rock of Etam.

[9]Then the Philistines went up and camped in the land of Judah. They stopped near a place named Lehi. [10]The men of Judah asked them, "Why have you come here to fight us?"

They answered, "We have come to make Samson our prisoner. We want to pay him back for what he did to our people."

[11]Then 3,000 men of Judah went to the cave in the rock of Etam. They said to Samson, "What have you done to us? Don't you know that the Philistines rule over us?"

Samson answered, "I only paid them back for what they did to me!"

[12]Then they said to him, "We have come to tie you up. We will give you to the Philistines."

Samson said to them, "Promise me you will not hurt me yourselves."

[13]The men from Judah said, "We agree. We will just tie you up and give you to the Philistines. We will not kill you." So they tied Samson with two new ropes. Then they led him up from the cave in the rock. [14]When Samson came to the place named Lehi, the Philistines came to meet him. They were shouting for joy. Then the Spirit[d] of the Lord entered Samson and gave him great power. The ropes on him became weak like strings that had been burned. They fell off his hands! [15]Samson found a jawbone of a donkey that had just died. He took it and killed 1,000 men with it!

BLAST FROM THE PAST

IN BIBLE TIMES, NAMES WERE MORE THAN JUST a word. The names themselves shed light on what that person was really like. Calling someone by name showed real closeness with that person. Likewise, God revealed himself to his people using many different names, each one showing a different part of who he is.

SAMSON GOES TO THE CITY OF GAZA

16 One day Samson went to Gaza. He saw a prostitute[d] there. He went in to spend the night with her. [2]Someone told the people of Gaza, "Samson has come here!" So they surrounded the place and hid and waited for him. Remaining very quiet, they stayed near the city gate all night. They said to each other, "When dawn comes, we will kill Samson!"

[3]But Samson only stayed with the prostitute until midnight. Then he got up and took hold of the doors and the two posts of the city gate. He tore them loose, along with the bar. Then he put them on his shoulders. And he carried them to the top of the hill that faces the city of Hebron!

SAMSON AND DELILAH

[4]After this, Samson fell in love with a woman named Delilah. She lived in the Valley of Sorek. [5]The kings of the Philistines went to Delilah. They said, "Try to find out what makes Samson so strong. Try to trick him into telling you. Find out how we could capture him and tie him up. Then we will be able to control him. If you do this, each one of us will give you 28 pounds of silver."

[6]So Delilah said to Samson, "Tell me why you are so strong. How could someone tie you up and take control of you?"

[7]Samson answered, "Someone would have to tie me up. He would have to use seven new bowstrings that have not been dried. If he did that, I would be as weak as any other man."

[8]Then the kings of the Philistines brought seven new bowstrings to Delilah. They had not been dried. She tied Samson with them. [9]Some men were hiding in another room. Delilah said to Samson, "Samson, the Philistines are about to capture you!" But Samson easily broke the bowstrings. They broke like pieces of string burned in a fire. So the Philistines did not find out the secret of Samson's strength.

[10]Then Delilah said to Samson, "You've made me look foolish. You lied to me. Please tell me. How could someone tie you up?"

[11]Samson said, "They would have to tie me with new ropes that have not been used before. Then I would become as weak as any other man."

WILD WORLD FACTS

Judges 14:1-9

A SWEET STOMACH

Did you know that honey bees have two stomachs? One is for regular food, and the other acts as a special storage place for nectar—the main ingredient they get from flowers and use to make honey. It takes anywhere from 100 to 1,500 flowers to fill their honey stomachs. Then they fly back to the hive where other worker bees suck the nectar out of their stomachs. These worker bees chew on the nectar for half an hour, breaking it down into simple sugars (a process that helps ward off bacteria). Then they line the honeycomb with the sugar paste and fan it with their wings to help it dry faster. As it dries, it becomes thicker—the substance we call honey.

A bee colony eats 120 to 200 pounds of honey a year. We don't know how much Samson ate, but we do know he wasn't supposed to get it from the carcass of a lion.

[Science Theater, pa.msu.edu]

HAIR TODAY, GONE TOMORROW

Samson was a strong man of God. How strong are you at remembering his story? Check out this puzzle and see!

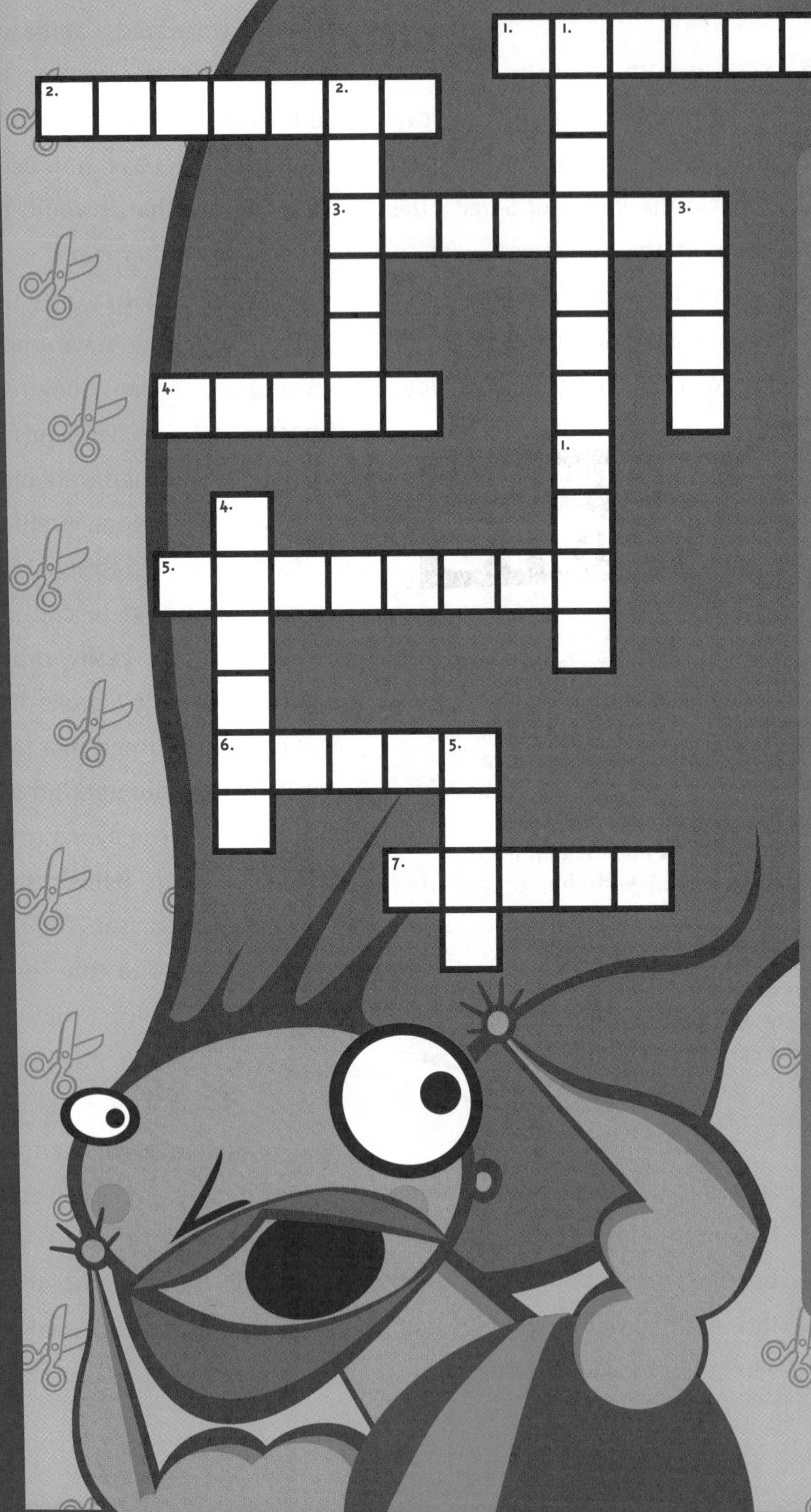

ACROSS:

1. The true source of Samson's strength
2. What Samson toppled to kill himself and the Philistines
3. The Philistine woman who betrayed him
4. The answer to Samson's riddle
5. The type of vow Samson took
6. Who told Samson's parents about Samson
7. The animals Samson used to set fields on fire

DOWN:

1. The group of people Samson fought
2. The kind of puzzle Samson enjoyed
3. What he could not cut
4. The name of Samson's dad
5. The animal Samson killed and where he later found honey

ANSWER KEY: Across: 1. Spirit; 2. pillars; 3. Delilah; 4. honey; 5. Nazirite; 6. angel; 7. foxes Down: 1. Philistines; 2. riddle; 3. hair; 4. Manoah; 5. lion

[12]So Delilah took new ropes and tied Samson. Some men were hiding in another room. Then she called out to him, "Samson, the Philistines are about to capture you!" But he broke the ropes as easily as if they were threads.

[13]Then Delilah said to Samson, "Until now, you have made me look foolish. You have lied to me. Tell me how someone could tie you up."

He said, "Use the loom.* Weave the seven braids of my hair into the cloth. Tighten it with a pin. Then I will become as weak as any other man."

Then Samson went to sleep. So Delilah wove the seven braids of his hair into the cloth. [14]Then she fastened it with a pin.

Again she called out to him, "Samson, the Philistines are about to capture you!" Samson woke up and pulled up the pin and the loom with the cloth.

[15]Then Delilah said to him, "How can you say, 'I love you,' when you don't even trust me? This is the third time you have made me look foolish. You haven't told me the secret of your great strength." [16]She kept bothering Samson about his secret day after day. He became so tired of it he felt he was going to die!

[17]So he told her everything. He said, "I have never had my hair cut. I have been set apart to God as a Nazirite[d] since I was born. If someone shaved my head, then I would lose my strength. I would become as weak as any other man."

[18]Delilah saw that he had told her everything sincerely. So she sent a message to the kings of the Philistines. She said, "Come back one more time. He has told me everything." So the kings of the Philistines came back to Delilah. They brought the silver they had promised to give her. [19]Delilah got Samson to go to sleep. He was lying in her lap. Then she called in a man to shave off the seven braids of Samson's hair. In this way she began to make him weak. And Samson's strength left him.

[20]Then she called out to him, "Samson, the Philistines are about to capture you!"

He woke up and thought, "I'll get loose as I did before and shake myself free." But he did not know that the Lord had left him.

[21]Then the Philistines captured Samson. They tore out his eyes. And they took him down to Gaza. They put bronze chains on

COOLSVILLE →

GET CONNECTED

RELATIONSHIPS WITH FRIENDS

Totally Cool When he was obedient, Samson had a certain look about him. He was strong and sober, and had long, flowing hair. God had given him some physical characteristics that showed the spiritual strength he had inside. But when he disobeyed and his hair was cut, he looked like everyone else—and lost his strength.

It's so tempting to want to be like everyone else. We want to act cool and look cool so that our friends actually think we're cool. And that's cool—if it honors God. But when we think we have to be disrespectful or unkind or disobedient to gain people's favor, we need to ask God to change our hearts. We need to care much more about what God thinks is cool than what anyone around us says.

16:13 **loom** A machine for making cloth from thread.

him. They put him in prison and made him grind grain. [22]But his hair began to grow again.

SAMSON DIES

[23]The kings of the Philistines gathered to celebrate. They were going to offer a great sacrifice to their god Dagon.[d] They said, "Our god has given us Samson

"Lord God, remember me. God, please give me strength one more time."

Judges 16:28

our enemy." [24]When they saw him, they praised their god. They said,

"This man destroyed our
country.
He killed many of us!
But our god helped us
capture our enemy."

[25]The people were having a good time at the celebration. They said, "Bring Samson out to perform for us." So they brought Samson from the prison. He performed for them. They made him stand between the pillars of the temple of Dagon. [26]A servant was holding his hand. Samson said to him, "Let me feel the pillars that hold up the temple. I want to lean against them." [27]Now the temple was full of men and women. All the kings of the Philistines were there. There were about 3,000 men and women on the roof.[n] They watched Samson perform. [28]Then Samson

prayed to the Lord. He said, "Lord God, remember me. God, please give me strength one more time. Let me pay these Philistines back for putting out my two eyes!" [29]Then Samson held the two center pillars of the temple. These two pillars supported the whole temple. He braced himself between the two pillars. His right hand was on one, and his left hand was on the other. [30]Samson said, "Let me die with these Philistines!" Then he pushed as hard as he could. And the temple fell on the kings and all the people in it. So Samson killed more of the Philistines when he died than when he was alive.

16:27 **roof** In Bible times houses were built with flat roofs. The roof was used for drying things such as flax and fruit. And it was used as an extra room, as a place for worship and as a place to sleep in the summer.

SAFE JOURNEY

The word "shalom" in the Bible is a Hebrew word that is often used in place of the words "hello," "goodbye," "God's blessing on you," or "Have a safe journey." Color the pieces of the stained glass window below that have a /•/ in them to reveal the literal meaning of this word.

STORIES FROM RUTH

Ruth

RUTH 1:1–4:22

THE STORY OF A GIRL FROM MOAB

1 Long ago the judges[n] ruled Israel. During their rule, there was a time in the land when there was not enough food to eat. A man named Elimelech left Bethlehem in Judah and moved to the country of Moab. He took his wife and his two sons with him. His wife was named Naomi, and his two sons were named Mahlon and Kilion. These people were from the Ephrathah district around Bethlehem in Judah. The family traveled to Moab and lived there.

³Later, Naomi's husband, Elimelech, died. So only Naomi and her two sons were left. ⁴These sons married women from Moab. The name of one wife was Orpah. The name of the other wife was Ruth. Naomi and her sons lived in Moab about ten years. ⁵Then Mahlon and Kilion also died. So Naomi was left alone without her husband or her two sons.

⁶While Naomi was in Moab, she heard that the Lord had taken care of his people. He had given food to them in Judah. So Naomi got ready to leave Moab and go back home. The wives of Naomi's sons also got ready to go with her. ⁷So they left the place where they had lived. And they started back on the way to the land of Judah. ⁸But Naomi said to her two daughters-in-law, "Go back home. Each of you go to your own mother's house.

> **"While Naomi was in Moab, she heard that the Lord had taken care of his people. He had given food to them in Judah."** *Ruth 1:6*

1:1–2 judges They were not judges in courts of law, but leaders of the people in times of emergency.

LIVIN' IT!

A STICKY SITUATION
RUTH 1:1—4:22

Naomi's husband had died, as well as her two sons. Ruth was Naomi's daughter-in-law. Normally, Ruth would have left when her husband died and returned to her homeland of Moab to find another husband. But she didn't. She stuck to Naomi and promised to be with her no matter what. Ruth had come to love the true God, and she was willing to give up the life she knew to follow what she now knew to be the truth.

In the end, Ruth was greatly rewarded for her obedience. God provided a husband and made her a part of the royal line of Christ. Like Ruth, we need to find what is true and right in this life. Then we need to make a commitment to the Lord to follow him wherever he leads us. As with Ruth, commitment to God always leads to abundant spiritual blessings.

You have been very kind to me and to my sons who are now dead. I hope the Lord will also be kind to you in the same way. ⁹I hope the Lord will give you another home and a new husband."

Then Naomi kissed the women. And they began to cry out loud. ¹⁰Her daughters-in-law said to her, "No. We will go with you to your people."

¹¹But Naomi said, "My daughters, go back to your own homes. Why do you want to go with me? I cannot give birth to more sons to give you new husbands. ¹²So go back to your own homes. I am too old to have another husband. But even if I had another husband tonight and if I had more sons, it wouldn't help! ¹³Would you wait until the babies were grown into men? Would you live for so many years without husbands? Don't do this thing. My life is much too sad for you to share. This is because the Lord is against me!"

¹⁴The women cried together again. Then Orpah kissed Naomi good-bye, but Ruth held on to her.

¹⁵Naomi said, "Look, your sister-in-law is going back to her own people and her own gods. Go back with her."

RUTH STAYS WITH NAOMI

¹⁶But Ruth said, "Don't ask me to leave you! Don't beg me not to follow you! Every place you go, I will go. Every place you live, I will live. Your people will be my people. Your God will be my God. ¹⁷And where you die, I will die. And there I will be buried. I ask the Lord to punish me terribly if I do not keep this promise: Only death will separate us."

¹⁸Naomi saw that Ruth had made up her mind to go with her. So Naomi stopped arguing with her. ¹⁹Naomi and Ruth went on until they came to the town of Bethlehem. When the two women entered Bethlehem, all the people became very excited. The women of the town said, "Is this Naomi?"

²⁰But Naomi told the people, "Don't call me Naomi.ⁿ Call me Mara,ⁿ because God All-Powerful has made my life very sad. ²¹When I left, I had all I wanted. But now, the Lord has brought me home with nothing. So why should you call me Naomi when the Lord has spoken against me?

1:20 Naomi This name means "happy" or "pleasant." **1:20 Mara** This name means "bitter" or "sad."

Ruth and Naomi fell on really hard times and had to make their way back to Naomi's home. But by trusting God, they encountered bountiful blessings. Straighten out these twisted words that tell part of their story.

1. OAPRH _____

2. AUGDHTRE-NI-WLA _____

3. BANDHSU _____

4. OAMB _____

5. FDIESL _____

6. ZABO _____

7. GNRIA _____

8. SHINTHREG OLOFR _____

9. TIVEREAL _____

10. ODEB _____

3-D

BLAST FROM THE PAST

God All-Powerful has given me much trouble."

²²So Naomi and her daughter-in-law Ruth, the woman from Moab, came back from Moab. They came to Bethlehem at the beginning of the barley harvest.

RUTH MEETS BOAZ

2 Now there was a rich man living in Bethlehem whose name was Boaz. Boaz was one of Naomi's close relatives from Elimelech's family.

²One day Ruth, the woman from Moab, said to Naomi, "Let me go to the fields. Maybe someone will be kind and let me gather the grain he leaves in his field."

Naomi said, "Go, my daughter."

³So Ruth went to the fields. She followed the workers who were cutting the grain. And she gathered the grain that they had left. It just so happened that the field belonged to Boaz. He was a close relative from Elimelech's family.

⁴When Boaz came from Bethlehem, he spoke to his workers: "The Lord be with you!"

And the workers answered, "May the Lord bless you!"

⁵Then Boaz spoke to his servant who was in charge of the workers. He asked, "Whose girl is that?"

⁶The servant answered, "She is the Moabite woman who came with Naomi from the country of Moab. ⁷She said, 'Please let me follow the workers and gather the grain that they leave on the ground.' She came and has remained here. From morning until just now, she has stopped only a few moments to rest in the shelter."

⁸Then Boaz said to Ruth, "Listen, my daughter. Stay here in my field to gather grain for yourself. Do not go to any other person's field. Continue following behind my women workers. ⁹Watch to see which fields they go to and follow them. I have warned the young men not to bother you. When you are thirsty, you may go and drink. Take water from the water jugs that the servants have filled."

¹⁰Then Ruth bowed low with her face to the ground. She said to Boaz, "I am a stranger. Why have you been so kind to notice me?"

"Boaz answered her, 'I know about all the help you have given to Naomi, your mother-in-law.'" *Ruth 2:11*

> **"Then Ruth said, 'You are very kind to me, sir. You have said kind words to me, your servant.'"**
>
> *Ruth 2:13*

[11]Boaz answered her, "I know about all the help you have given to Naomi, your mother-in-law. You helped her even after your husband died. You left your father and mother and your own country. You came to this nation where you did not know anyone. [12]The Lord will reward you for all you have done. You will be paid in full by the Lord, the God of Israel. You have come to him as a little bird finds shelter under the wings of its mother."

[13]Then Ruth said, "You are very kind to me, sir. You have said kind words to me, your servant. You have given me hope. And I am not even good enough to be one of your servants."

[14]At mealtime Boaz told Ruth, "Come here! Eat some of our bread. Here, dip your bread in our vinegar."

So Ruth sat down with the workers. Boaz gave her some roasted grain. Ruth ate until she was full, and there was some food left over. [15]Ruth rose and went back to work. Then Boaz told his servants, "Let her gather even around the bundles of grain. Don't tell her to go away. [16]Drop some full heads of grain for her. Let her gather that grain, and don't tell her to stop."

[17]So Ruth gathered grain in the field until evening. Then she separated the grain from the chaff.[d] There was about one-half bushel of barley. [18]Ruth carried the grain into town. And her mother-in-law saw what she had gathered. Ruth also gave her the food that was left over from lunch.

GET CONNECTED

RELATIONSHIPS WITH FAMILY

Fight for Peace There's no doubt it's hard. At times, it seems absolutely impossible to love your brother or sister. After all, don't all siblings fight? Isn't that just the way it is?

It's not the way God wants it to be. He wants us to have peaceful homes. He wants us to show love like he describes in Ruth, where we stick by each other's side, no matter what. Like the kind of love Jesus shows us. So how can you love your little sister when she calls you a name? Or when your older brother locks you in your room? Pray! Ask God for help. Ask him to give you his love and to help you remember the good things about your siblings. Then answer them the way God wants you to—no matter what they say back.

CRAFTS

RUTH

construction paper

ALL ABOUT IT:

When Ruth's husband died, she could have gone back to her home in Moab. But Ruth said to her mother-in-law Naomi, "Don't ask me to leave you! Don't beg me not to follow you! Every place you go, I will go. Every place you live, I will live. Your people will be my people. Your God will be my God" (Ruth 1:16). Ruth desired to live with Naomi and her God.

Ruth showed her faithfulness to God by staying with Naomi to take care of her every day. God rewarded her faithfulness with a new husband Boaz and baby Obed. We show our faithfulness to God when we read the Bible, attend church, and live our lives to serve God. Faithfully reading your Bible on a regular basis is an offering to God. It shows him that you desire to know him better. Make Bible faithfulness cards as a gift from you to God.

BIBLE FAITHFULNESS CARDS INSTRUCTIONS

Fold a piece of construction paper to make 8 boxes:

1. Fold it in half lengthwise.

2. Open it up, and fold it in half widthwise.

3. Then fold it in half again widthwise.

Each time you read the Bible, write the date in a box, and record what you think God was telling you through that Bible story. When you fill up a card, reread all the boxes, and give thanks to God for his plan for your life.

3-D

[19]Naomi asked her, "Where did you gather all this grain today? Where did you work? Blessed be the man who noticed you!"

tinue working. He said, 'Keep close by my servants until they have finished the harvest.'"

[22]Then Naomi said to her

continued working closely with the women servants of Boaz. She gathered grain until the barley harvest was finished. She also worked there through the end of the wheat harvest. And Ruth continued to live with Naomi, her mother-in-law.

GET CONNECTED

RELATIONSHIPS WITH FAMILY

All in the Family Boaz was a total success. He had land; he had money; and after he met Ruth, he realized he also had a duty. Ruth was a distant part of his family, and her husband had died. According to Jewish Law, it was his job to make sure she and her mother-in-law were treated well. So he married Ruth and took care of her and Naomi.

God wants us to take care of our family members, too. Do you have an elderly relative who needs a visit from you? Could your mom and dad use some help? Do your siblings have a need? Become aware of the needs around you, starting with your own family. Ask God to give you a heart for helping others and for strength to keep on serving your family.

NAOMI'S PLAN

3 Then Naomi, Ruth's mother-in-law, said to her, "My daughter, I must find a suitable home for you. That would be good for you. [2]Now Boaz is our close relative.[n] You worked with his women servants. Tonight he will be working at the threshing[d] floor. [3]Go wash yourself and put on perfume. Change your clothes, and go down to the threshing floor. But don't let him see you until he has finished eating and drinking. [4]Then he will lie down. Watch him so you will know the place where he lies down. Go there and lift the cover off his feet[n] and lie down. He will tell you what you should do."

[5]Then Ruth answered, "I will do everything you say."

[6]So Ruth went down to the threshing floor. She did all her mother-in-law told her to do. [7]After eating and drinking, Boaz

Ruth told her about whose field she had worked in. She said, "The man I worked with today is named Boaz."

[20]Naomi told her daughter-in-law, "The Lord bless him! The Lord still continues to be kind to all people—the living and the dead!" Then Naomi told Ruth, "Boaz is one of our close relatives,[n] one who will take care of us."

[21]Then Ruth said, "Boaz also told me to come back and con-

daughter-in-law Ruth, "It is good for you to continue working with his women servants. If you work in another field, someone might hurt you." [23]So Ruth

2:20; 3:2 close relatives In Bible times the closest relative could marry a widow without children so she could have children. He would care for this family, but they and their property would not belong to him. They would belong to the dead husband. **3:4 lift . . . feet** This showed Ruth was asking him to be her husband.

194

was feeling good. He went to lie down beside the pile of grain. Then Ruth went to him quietly. She lifted the cover from his feet and lay down.

[8]About midnight Boaz woke up suddenly and rolled over. He was startled! There was a woman lying near his feet! [9]Boaz asked, "Who are you?"

She said, "I am Ruth, your servant girl. Spread your cover over me because you are the one who is to take care of me."

[10]Then Boaz said, "The Lord bless you, my daughter. Your kindness to me is greater than the kindness you showed to Naomi in the beginning. You didn't look for a young man to marry, either rich or poor. [11]Now, my daughter, don't be afraid. I will do everything you ask. All the people in our town know you are a very good woman. [12]And it is true, I am a relative who is to take care of you. But there is a man who is a closer relative to you than I. [13]But stay here tonight. In the morning we will see if he will take care of you. If he decides to take care of you, that is fine. If he refuses to take care of you, I myself will marry you. Then I will buy back Elimelech's land for you. As surely as the Lord lives, I promise to do this. So lie here until morning."

[14]So Ruth lay near his feet until the morning. She rose while it was still too dark to be recognized. Boaz said to his servants, "Don't tell anyone that the woman came here to the

> "Your kindness to me is greater than the kindness you showed to Naomi in the beginning."
>
> *Ruth 3:10*

REAL SUPER HEROES

RUTH

Ruth had tasted the good life. But it wasn't riches or fame that made her cling to Naomi's side after her husband had died. Ruth vowed loyalty to her mother-in-law because she had come to love the God of Israel. Ruth was from Moab, a culture that served false gods. Through her husband—Naomi's son—Ruth had learned the truth about God. She was willing to give up her life as she knew it to stay close to God and the people who worshiped him.

Ruth's loyalty paid off in many ways. God provided a man (called a kinsman-redeemer) from Naomi's own family who would marry Ruth and provide for them both. Ruth and Boaz had a son named Obed, who was the father of Jesse, who became the father of David. Ruth had become a part of the bloodline of the promised Messiah, and she enjoyed blessing in this life and the next.

We live in a culture today much like the one Ruth experienced in Moab. Most folks don't know the truth about God. We need to learn the truth and develop friendships with others who know God in the same way. As we gain strength from God and his family, we are better equipped to show the way to the rest of the lost world.

BIBLE COUPLES

The Bible tells us the stories of many famous couples. In the puzzle below, first unscramble the names of the four men and four women. Then mark or color over the line that matches each man and each woman as husband and wife.

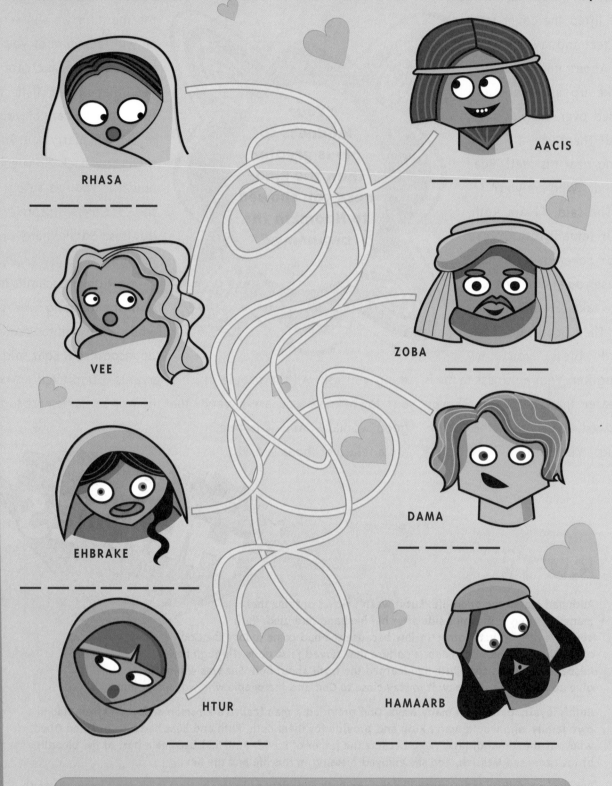

RHASA

_ _ _ _ _

AACIS

_ _ _ _ _

VEE

_ _ _

ZOBA

_ _ _ _ _

EHBRAKE

_ _ _ _ _ _ _

DAMA

_ _ _ _

HTUR

_ _ _ _

HAMAARB

_ _ _ _ _ _ _

WORD BANK Abraham Adam Boaz Eve Isaac Rebekah Ruth Sarah

GET CONNECTED

RELATIONSHIPS WITH AUTHORITY

Blessed Obedience She had trusted her enough to leave her home country and go to a land she didn't know. Ruth trusted Naomi, her mother-in-law, and had become like her own daughter. So when Naomi told her exactly how to win the affection of Boaz, Ruth followed her instructions exactly. Her obedience blessed Boaz, Naomi, and Ruth, too, who was included in the bloodline of Christ.

What keeps you from obeying your parents? Do you think they are holding out on you? Do you think your way is better? Ruth shows us that when we humble ourselves and trust God's leading through our parents, he is able to bless us more than we can imagine. Thank God today for your parents, and ask him to help you obey with your actions and your heart.

threshing[d] floor." [15]Then Boaz said to Ruth, "Bring me your shawl. Now, hold it open."

So Ruth held her shawl open, and Boaz poured six portions of barley into it. Boaz then put it on her back, and she went to the city.

[16]Ruth went to the home of her mother-in-law. And Naomi asked, "How did you do, my daughter?"

So Ruth told Naomi everything that Boaz did for her. [17]She said, "Boaz gave me these six portions of barley. He said, 'You must not go home without a gift for your mother-in-law.'"

[18]Naomi answered, "Ruth, my daughter, wait until you hear what happens. Boaz will not rest until he has finished doing what he should do this day."

BOAZ MARRIES RUTH

4 Boaz went to the city gate. He sat there until the close relative he had mentioned passed by. Boaz called to him,

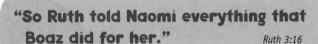

> "So Ruth told Naomi everything that Boaz did for her."
>
> *Ruth 3:16*

"Come here, friend! Sit down here!" So the man came over and sat down. [2]Boaz gathered ten of the old men who were leaders of the city. He told them, "Sit down here!" So they sat down.

[3]Then Boaz spoke to the close relative. He said, "Naomi has come back from the country of Moab. She wants to sell the piece of land that belonged to our relative Elimelech. [4]So I decided to say this to you: If you want to buy back the land, then buy it! Buy it in front of the people who live here and in front of the elders of my people. If you don't want to buy it, tell me. I am the only person after you who can buy back the land. If you don't buy it back, I will."

And the close relative said, "I will buy back the land."

[5]Then Boaz said, "When you buy the land from Naomi, you must marry Ruth, the dead man's wife. She is the woman from Moab. That way, the land will stay in her dead husband's family."

[6]The close relative answered, "Then I can't buy back the land.

BLAST FROM THE PAST

GENEALOGY WAS EXTREMELY IMPORTANT TO THE JEWS. If a husband died without any children to inherit his possessions, his brother would take over the family and help the widow raise a family for him. This law was written to help protect family names and their inheritances.

If I did, I might lose what I can pass on to my own sons. I cannot buy the land back. So you buy it yourself."

⁷Long ago in Israel when people traded or bought back something, one person took off his sandal and gave it to the other person. This was their proof of purchase.

⁸So the close relative said, "Buy the land yourself." And then he took off his sandal.

⁹Then Boaz spoke to the elders and to all the people. He said, "You are witnesses today of what I am buying from Naomi. I am buying everything that belonged to Elimelech and Kilion and Mahlon. ¹⁰I am also taking Ruth as my wife. She is the Moabite who was the wife of Mahlon. I am doing this so her dead husband's property will stay with his family. This way, his name will not be separated from his family and his land. You are witnesses this day."

"So all the people and elders who were at the city gate said, "We are witnesses. This woman will be coming into your home. We hope the Lord will make her like Rachel and Leah. They had many children. So the people of Israel grew in number. May you become powerful in the district of Ephrathah. May you become famous in Bethlehem! ¹²Tamar gave birth to Judah's son Perez." In the same way, may the Lord give you many children through Ruth. And may your family be great like his."

¹³So Boaz took Ruth and married her. The Lord let her become pregnant, and she gave birth to a son. ¹⁴The women told Naomi, "Praise

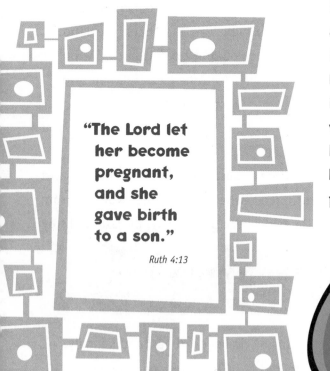

> **"The Lord let her become pregnant, and she gave birth to a son."**
>
> *Ruth 4:13*

the Lord who gave you this grandson. And may he become famous in Israel. ¹⁵He will give you new life. And he will take

seven sons. She has given birth to your grandson."

¹⁶Naomi took the boy, held him in her arms and cared for him.

Obed was Jesse's father. And Jesse was the father of David.

¹⁸This is the family history of Perez. Perez was the father of Hezron. ¹⁹Hezron was the father of Ram. Ram was the father of Amminadab. ²⁰Amminadab was the father of Nahshon. Nahshon was the father of Salmon. ²¹Salmon was the father of Boaz. Boaz was the father of Obed. ²²Obed was the father of Jesse, and Jesse was the father of David.

"The neighbors named him Obed. Obed was Jesse's father. And Jesse was the father of David."

Ruth 4:17

care of you in your old age. This happened because of your daughter-in-law. She loves you. And she is better for you than

¹⁷The neighbors gave the boy his name. These women said, "This boy was born for Naomi." The neighbors named him Obed.

1 SAMUEL

HanNah and Samuel

1 SAMUEL 1:1-28;
2:18-21; 3:1-21

SAMUEL'S BIRTH

1 There was a man named Elkanah son of Jeroham. He was from Ramathaim in the mountains of Ephraim. Elkanah was from the family of Zuph. (Jeroham was Elihu's son. Elihu was Tohu's son. And Tohu was the son of Zuph from the family group of Ephraim.) ²Elkanah had two wives. One was named Hannah, and the other was named Peninnah. Peninnah had children, but Hannah had none.

³Every year Elkanah left his town Ramah and went up to Shiloh. There he worshiped the Lord of heaven's armies and offered sacrifices to him. Shiloh was where Hophni and Phinehas served as priests of the Lord. They were the sons of Eli. ⁴When Elkanah offered sacrifices, he always gave a share of the meat to his wife Peninnah. He also gave shares of the meat to her sons and daughters. ⁵But Elkanah always gave a special share of the meat to Hannah. He did this because he loved Hannah and because the Lord had made Hannah unable to have children. ⁶Peninnah would upset Hannah and make her feel bad. She did this because the Lord had made Hannah unable to have children. ⁷This happened every year when they went up to the Tent[d] of the Lord at Shiloh. Peninnah would upset Hannah until Hannah would cry and not eat anything. ⁸Her husband Elkanah would say to her, "Hannah, why are you crying? Why won't you eat? Why are you sad? Don't I mean more to you than ten sons?"

⁹Once, after they had eaten their meal

> **"Why are you sad? Don't i mean more to you than ten sons?"**
>
> 1 Samuel 1:8

INCREDIBLE EDIBLES

SAMUEL
AND THE VOICE IN THE NIGHT

INGREDIENTS

- peanuts
- raisins
- small pretzels
- M&M's® (or other coated candies)
- Cheerios®
- 10 film containers

HERE'S THE SCOOP:

The prophets in the Old Testament heard God talking to them like we talk to each other—in an audible voice. Today we hear God talk to us through the words in the Bible. It is the Holy Spirit living within us that helps us hear God's voice telling us the right thing to do.

When God spoke to Samuel, Samuel was very quiet. You will need to be very quiet to match the food in the shakers. When you are finished, open the shakers and enjoy a fun snack.

SNACK INSTRUCTIONS

1. Fill the film containers like this: 2 with peanuts, 2 with raisins, 2 with pretzels, 2 with M&M's®, and 2 with Cheerios®.

2. Put the filled containers in a bowl, and mix them up.

3. Choose two containers. Shake them to see if they match.

4. When you have all the containers matched together, open them and enjoy your snack!

3-D

GET CONNECTED

RELATIONSHIPS WITH GOD

Are You Listening? Would you freak out if you were lying in bed at night and God called your name? It took several tries before Samuel realized that God was trying to get his attention. But when he finally figured it out, he responded with a heart of obedience and respect.

We might not get to hear a voice out loud like Samuel did, but God still tries to get our attention today. He uses his Word, other people, and the events of our day to direct our focus toward him. God loves to reveal himself to his children. But we have to grow hearts that listen and know when he is talking to us. Ask God to help your spirit to recognize his voice and to give you an obedient and respectful heart that listens.

Hellooo!

in Shiloh, Hannah got up. Now Eli the priest was sitting on a chair near the entrance to the Lord's Holy Tent. ¹⁰Hannah was very sad. She cried much and prayed to the Lord. ¹¹She made a promise. She said, "Lord of heaven's armies, see how bad I feel. Remember me! Don't forget me. If you will give me a son, I will give him back to you all his life. And no one will ever use a razor to cut his hair."[n]

¹²While Hannah kept praying, Eli watched her mouth. ¹³She was praying in her heart. Her lips moved, but her voice was not heard. So Eli thought she was drunk. ¹⁴He said to her, "Stop getting drunk! Throw away your wine!"

¹⁵Hannah answered, "No, master, I have not drunk any wine or beer. I am a woman who is deeply troubled. I was telling the Lord about all my problems. ¹⁶Don't think of me as an evil woman. I have been praying because of my many troubles and much sadness."

¹⁷Eli answered, "Go in peace. May the God of Israel give you what you asked of him."

1:11 And . . . hair People who made special promises not to cut their hair or to drink wine or beer were called Nazirites. These people gave their lives to the Lord. See Numbers 6:1-5.

REAL SUPER HEROES

SAMUEL

It might seem like Samuel had no choice. After all, before he was even conceived, his mother Hannah had promised to dedicate him to Temple service. At a very young age, his parents took him back to the Temple in order to keep her promise.

But Samuel could have rebelled. He could have rejected his calling and not listened to Eli, the high priest and his teacher. Eli's own sons had rejected his counsel, so why not Samuel? Because God had Samuel's heart. God himself called to Samuel in a voice loud enough to hear. He spoke his words of truth to him, and Samuel was hooked on God for life. Though others faded away from the Lord, Samuel kept his ears open and his heart attentive. He was the one who anointed Saul as king when the Lord said to do so. He was the one who witnessed God's selection of David, and he anointed David's head with oil. His life reached so many people it took two books of the Bible to record it.

Was Samuel spectacular? Not in the ordinary sense. But he was devoted to God, and God performed powerful miracles through him. We gain courage from Samuel as we see God's hand in his life. The same God calls to us and longs to have a lifelong relationship with us, too.

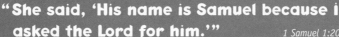

> **"She said, 'His name is Samuel because i asked the Lord for him.'"**
> *1 Samuel 1:20*

[18]Hannah said, "I want to be pleasing to you always." Then she left and ate something. She was not sad anymore.

[19]Early the next morning Elkanah's family got up and worshiped the Lord. Then they went back home to Ramah. Elkanah had sexual relations with his wife Hannah. And the Lord remembered her. [20]So Hannah became pregnant, and in time she gave birth to a son. She named him Samuel.[n] She said, "His name is Samuel because I asked the Lord for him."

HANNAH GIVES SAMUEL TO GOD

[21]Every year Elkanah went to Shiloh to offer sacrifices. He went to keep the promise he had made to God. He brought his whole family with him. So once again he went up to Shiloh. [22]But Hannah did not go with him. She told him, "When the boy is old enough to eat solid food, I will take him to Shiloh. Then I will give him to the Lord. He will become a Nazirite.[d] He will always live

there at Shiloh."

[23]Elkanah, Hannah's husband, said to her, "Do what you think is best. You may stay home until the boy is old enough to eat. May the Lord do what you have said." So Hannah stayed at home to nurse her son until he was old enough to eat.

[24]When Samuel was old enough to eat, Hannah took him to the Tent[d] of the Lord at Shiloh. She also took a three-

year-old bull, one-half bushel of flour and a leather bag filled with wine. [25]They killed the bull for the sacrifice. Then Hannah brought Samuel to Eli. [26]She said to Eli, "As surely as you live, my master, I am the same woman

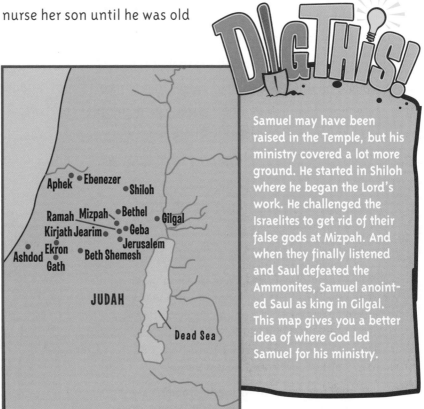

Samuel may have been raised in the Temple, but his ministry covered a lot more ground. He started in Shiloh where he began the Lord's work. He challenged the Israelites to get rid of their false gods at Mizpah. And when they finally listened and Saul defeated the Ammonites, Samuel anointed Saul as king in Gilgal. This map gives you a better idea of where God led Samuel for his ministry.

who stood near you praying to the Lord. [27]I prayed for this child. The Lord answered my prayer and gave him to me. [28]Now I give him back to the

---

 1:20 Samuel This name sounds like the Hebrew word for "God heard."

Lord. He will belong to the Lord all his life." And he worshiped the Lord there.

• • •

SAMUEL GROWS UP

2 But Samuel obeyed the Lord. He wore a linen holy vest.*d* ¹⁹Every year Samuel's mother would make a little coat for him. She would take it to him when she went to Shiloh. She went there with her husband for the sacrifice. ²⁰Eli would bless Elkanah and his wife. Eli would say, "May the Lord repay you with children through Hannah. They will take

the place of the boy Hannah prayed for and gave back to the Lord." Then Elkanah and Hannah would go home. ²¹The Lord was kind to Hannah. She became the mother of three sons and two daughters. And the boy Samuel grew up serving the Lord.

• • •

GOD CALLS SAMUEL

3 The boy Samuel served the Lord under Eli. In those days the Lord did not speak directly to people very often. There were very few visions.

²Eli's eyes were so weak he

GET CONNECTED

RELATIONSHIPS WITH GOD

A Heart's Cry Eli thought she had had too much wine. Hannah wasn't talking out loud, but she was crying out to God in her heart, and her lips were mouthing the words. No one in the world knew her pain and her deep longing. No one understood—except God. God heard the silent cry of her heart, and he answered.

Do you ever feel alone or misunderstood? Do you have hurt in your heart that you can't explain to others? Whatever you're feeling, God already knows all about it. He knows you better than you do. Don't be afraid to bring it to him in prayer. Be honest about what's going on inside you. Like Hannah, trust him to bring healing to your hurt in his way and time. He always hears, and he always answers with love.

LIVIN' IT!

GIVE AND TAKE
1 SAMUEL 1:1-28

Have you ever asked God for something—something you really, really wanted—and then God gave it to you? How did that make you feel? Now imagine having to give it back. Would you be able to do it?

Hannah was in the same situation. She had begged God for a child. She even promised to let him become a priest—which meant leaving him at the Temple when he was still a small child—if God would only grant her request. God answered, and Hannah kept her promise.

We need to remember that God's gifts to us are precious, but they are only gifts. We cannot close our hands around them and demand that they stay ours. We need to be so content with our relationship with God that we are willing to give up whatever he asks of us. This kind of attitude doesn't happen naturally. Ask God today to change your heart and make you love him more than anything else in life.

was almost blind. One night he was lying in bed. ³Samuel was also in bed in the Lord's Holy Tent.*d* The Box*d* of the Agreement was in the Holy Tent. God's lamp was still burning.

CRAFTS

HANNAH'S PRAYER

My Prayer journal

3-D

SUPPLIES

- notebook
- glitter glue pens
- cut papers
- stickers

GLUE

INSTRUCTIONS

1. Find a notebook you no longer use.

2. Decorate the cover with paper, stickers, and glitter glue. Make it really special.

3. On one sheet of paper, list the blessings God has given you through prayer.

4. On another sheet, list the blessings you are still asking God for.

Use your notebook on a regular basis, seeking God for your needs and praising him for his answers!

ALL ABOUT IT:

"Hannah was very sad. She cried much and prayed to the Lord" (1 Samuel 1:10). Hannah asked God for a blessing. A blessing is a gift of divine favor, not something you can buy from the store. Hannah asked for a gift only God could give—the gift of a baby.

When we pray, we ask God for blessings for ourselves and for our families. Can you think of a time when you really wanted something? How did you feel when you finally got that something? Just like God heard Hannah's prayer, God also hears your prayers.

Recording our prayers and God's answers is a powerful reminder that God hears and answers our prayers. Enjoy making your prayer journal today, and read it often.

⁴Then the Lord called Samuel. Samuel answered, "I am here!" ⁵He ran to Eli and said, "I am here. You called me."

But Eli said, "I didn't call you. Go back to bed." So Samuel went back to bed.

⁶The Lord called again, "Samuel!"

Samuel again went to Eli and said, "I am here. You called me."

Again Eli said, "I didn't call you. Go back to bed."

⁷Samuel did not yet know the Lord. The Lord had not spoken directly to him yet.

⁸The Lord called Samuel for the third time. Samuel got up and went to Eli. He said, "I am here. You called me."

Then Eli realized the Lord was calling the boy. ⁹So he told Samuel, "Go to bed. If he calls you again, say, 'Speak, Lord. I am your servant, and I am lis-tening.'" So Samuel went and lay down in bed.

¹⁰The Lord came and stood there. He called as he had before. He said, "Samuel, Samuel!"

Samuel said, "Speak, Lord. I am your servant, and I am listening."

¹¹The Lord said to Samuel, "See, I am going to do something in Israel. It will shock those who hear about it. ¹²At that time I will do to Eli and his family everything I promised. I will not stop until I have finished. ¹³I told Eli I would punish his family forever. I will do it because Eli knew his sons were evil. They spoke against me, but he did not control them. ¹⁴So here is what I promised Eli's family: 'Your guilt will never be removed by sacrifice or offering.'"

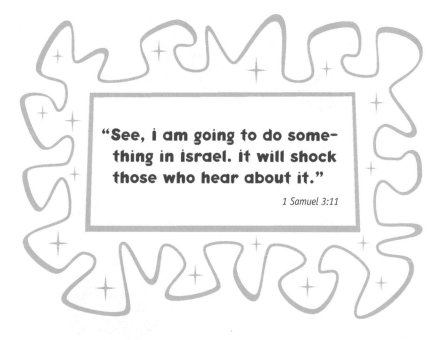

> "See, i am going to do something in israel. it will shock those who hear about it."
>
> 1 Samuel 3:11

ATTENTION! IF GOD WERE CALLING YOUR NAME, what would you say? In ancient times, a normal response to a boss or a higher-ranking soldier would be, "Here I am!" When Samuel responded first to Eli and then to God in this way, he was showing respect and obedience, just like a soldier coming to attention and returning a salute.

[15]Samuel lay down until morning. Then he opened the doors of the Tent[d] of the Lord. He was afraid to tell Eli about the vision. [16]But Eli said to him, "Samuel, my son!"

Samuel answered, "I am here."

[17]Eli asked, "What did the Lord say to you? Don't hide it from me. May God punish you terribly if you hide from me anything he said to you." [18]So Samuel told Eli everything. He did not hide anything from him. Then Eli said, "He is the Lord. Let him do what he thinks is best."

[19]The Lord was with Samuel as he grew up. He did not let any of Samuel's messages fail to come true. [20]Then all Israel, from Dan to Beersheba,[n] knew Samuel was a prophet[d] of the Lord. [21]And the Lord continued to show himself to Samuel at Shiloh. He also showed himself to Samuel through his word.

> **"He is the Lord. Let him do what he thinks is best."**
>
> *1 Samuel 3:18*

3:20 **Dan to Beersheba** Dan was the city farthest north in Israel. Beersheba was the city farthest south. So this means all the people of Israel.

Saul, the First King

I SAMUEL 9:14-17, 22, 25-27; 10:1-27; 15:1-35

SAUL MEETS SAMUEL

9 Saul and the servant went up to the town. Just as they entered the town, they saw Samuel. He was on his way up to the place of worship. So he was coming out of the city toward them.

¹⁵The day before Saul came, the Lord had told Samuel: ¹⁶"About this time tomorrow I will send you a man. He will be from Benjamin. You must appoint him as leader over my people Israel. He will save my people from the Philistines. I have seen the suffering of my people. I have listened to their cry."

¹⁷When Samuel first saw Saul, the Lord spoke to Samuel. He said, "This is the man I told you about. He will rule my people."

• • •

²²Then Samuel took Saul and his servant into a large room. He gave them a chief place at the table. About 30 guests were there.

• • •

²⁵After they finished eating, they came down from the place of worship. They went to the town. Then Samuel talked with Saul on the roofⁿ of his house. ²⁶At dawn they got up, and Samuel called to Saul on the roof. He said, "Get up, and I will send you on your way." So Saul got up. He went out of the house with Samuel. ²⁷Saul, his servant and Samuel were getting near the edge of the city. Samuel said to Saul, "Tell the servant to go on ahead of us. I have a message from God for you."

> **"This is the man I told you about. He will rule my people."** *1 Samuel 9:17*

SAMUEL APPOINTS SAUL

10 Samuel took a jar of olive oil. He poured the oil on Saul's head. He kissed

LIVIN' IT!

FALSE START
1 SAMUEL 19:14-27

Have you ever known someone who said they were a Christian, but later on decided they weren't going to live like one? While we can never know what's going on in someone's heart, Saul seemed to lack staying power. He had tasted God's goodness when God chose him to be king, but the pattern of bad and disobedient choices he made eventually cost him his kingship and his relationship with God.

How do you know you belong to God? Ask yourself, "Do I trust in Jesus alone to save me from my sins? Am I willing to obey God and accept him as being in charge over my life?" If you can answer yes to these, you can know that God's Spirit is in you. But life is often long and hard. Ask God to give you staying power. Pray for perseverance to always believe and trust in the Lord.

 9:25 roof In Bible times houses were built with flat roofs. The roof was used for drying things such as flax and fruit. And it was used as an extra room, as a place for worship and as a place to sleep in the summer.

Saul and said, "The Lord has appointed you to be leader of his people Israel. You will rule over the people of the Lord. You will save them from their enemies all around. This will be the sign that the Lord has appointed you as leader of his people. ²After you leave me today, you will meet two men. They will be near Rachel's tomb on the border of Benjamin at Zelzah. They will say to you, 'The donkeys you were looking for have been found. But now your father has stopped thinking about his donkeys. He is worrying about you. He is asking, "What will I do about my son?"'

³"Then you will go on until you reach the great tree at Tabor. There three men will meet you. They will be on their way to worship God at Bethel. One man will be carrying three young goats. The second man will be carrying three loaves of bread. And the third one will have a leather bag full of wine. ⁴They will greet you and offer you two loaves of bread. You

will accept the bread from them. ⁵Then you will go to Gibeah of God. There is a Philistine camp there. When you

3-D

"The Spirit of the Lord will enter you with power. You will prophesy with these prophets."

1 Samuel 10:6

come near this town, a group of prophets*d* will come out. They will be coming from the place of worship. And they will be playing harps, tambourines,*d* flutes and lyres.*d* And they will be prophesying. ⁶The Spirit*d* of the Lord will enter you with power. You will prophesy with these prophets. You will be changed into a different man. ⁷After these signs happen, do whatever you find to do. God will help you.

⁸"Go ahead of me to Gilgal. I

will come down to you. Then I will offer whole burnt offerings and fellowship offerings. But you must wait seven days. Then I will come and tell you what to do."

SAUL MADE KING

⁹When Saul turned to leave Samuel, God changed Saul's heart. All these signs came true that day. ¹⁰When Saul and his servant arrived at Gibeah, Saul met a group of prophets.*d* The Spirit*d* of God entered him. And he prophesied with the prophets. ¹¹People who had known Saul before saw him prophesying with the prophets. They asked each other, "What has happened to Kish's son? Is even Saul one of the prophets?"

¹²A man who lived there said, "Who is the father of these prophets?" This became a famous saying: "Is even Saul one of the prophets?" ¹³When Saul finished prophesying, he went to the place of worship.

¹⁴Saul's uncle asked him and his servant, "Where have you been?"

Saul said, "We were looking for the donkeys. When we couldn't find them, we went to talk to Samuel."

[15]Saul's uncle asked, "Please tell me. What did Samuel say to you?"

the Lord, the God of Israel, says: 'I led Israel out of Egypt. I saved you from Egypt's control. And I saved you from other kingdoms that were troubling you.' [19]But now you have rejected your God. He saves you from all your

[21]Samuel had them pass by in family groups, and Matri's family was chosen. Then he had each man of Matri's family pass by. And Saul son of Kish was chosen. But when they looked for Saul, they could not find him. [22]Then they asked the Lord, "Has Saul come here yet?"

The Lord said, "Yes. He's hiding behind the baggage."

[23]So they ran and brought him out. When Saul stood among the people, he was a head taller than anyone else. [24]Then Samuel said to the people, "See the man the Lord has chosen. There is no one like him among all the people."

Then the people shouted, "Long live the king!"

[25]Samuel explained the rights and duties of the king. He wrote the rules in a book and put the book before the Lord. Then he told the people to go to their homes.

[26]Saul also went to his home in Gibeah. God touched the

GET CONNECTED

RELATIONSHIPS WITH AUTHORITY

Checkmate God had been their leader from the beginning. But the Israelites decided they wanted to be like everyone else with an earthly kind of king. So God gave them what they asked for—a handsome, tall, kingly-lookin' guy. The problem, though, was that he didn't have much character, and his bad decisions led the people away from God.

Who do you think is cool? Is it a favorite ball player or singer or movie star? Think about who you admire, and then think about the kind of character they show. Do you really want to be *just* like them? Should you be just like them? If we want to be like people who don't know God, we need to ask ourselves why. Don't be like the Israelites who wanted to be like the rest of the world. Instead, value the kind of character in others that God says is important.

[16]Saul answered, "He told us the donkeys had already been found." But Saul did not tell his uncle what Samuel had said about his becoming king.

[17]Samuel called all the people of Israel to meet with the Lord at Mizpah. [18]He said, "This is what

troubles and problems. But you said, 'No! We want a king to rule over us.' Now come, stand before the Lord in your tribes[d] and family groups."

[20]Samuel brought all the tribes of Israel near. And the tribe of Benjamin was chosen.

> "See the man the Lord has chosen. There is no one like him among the people."
>
> *1 Samuel 10:24*

LIVIN' IT!

A BAD COVER-UP
1 SAMUEL 15:22-23

No mercy. God wanted all of the Amalekites—and everything that belonged to them— to be killed. It was Saul's mission to accomplish the task, which he partly obeyed. He killed most of them and destroyed some of the loot. But he kept the king alive, and his soldiers kept some of the property. Worst of all, Saul tried to offer a sacrifice to God to make him happy, even though he wasn't obeying.

God responded. He didn't want an outward show of devotion. He wanted Saul to have a heart that obeyed. A heart that truly loved him. So Saul was rejected. We need to keep a close watch on our hearts, too. Why do we do the things we do? Do we do it just because it looks good, or because we are obeying God? God won't be fooled. We need to be completely honest with him and ask him to help us love him with all of our hearts.

hearts of certain brave men who went along with him. ²⁷But some troublemakers said, "How can this man save us?" They hated Saul and refused to bring gifts to him. But Saul kept quiet.

• • •

SAUL REJECTED AS KING

15 Samuel said to Saul, "The Lord sent me to appoint you king over Israel. Now listen to his message. ²This is what the Lord of heaven's armies says: 'The Israelites came out of Egypt. But the Amalekites tried to stop them from going to Canaan. I saw what they did. ³Now go, attack the Amalekites. Destroy everything that belongs to them as an offering to the Lord. Don't let anything live. Put to death men and women, children and small babies. Kill the cattle and sheep, camels and donkeys.'"

⁴So Saul called the army together at Telaim. There were 200,000 soldiers and 10,000 men from Judah. ⁵Then Saul went to the city of Amalek and set up an ambush in the ravine. ⁶He said to the Kenites, "Go away. Leave the Amalekites so that I won't destroy you with them. You showed kindness to the Israelites when they came out of Egypt." So the Kenites moved away from the Amalekites.

⁷Then Saul defeated the Amalekites. He fought them all the way from Havilah to Shur, at the border of Egypt. ⁸He took Agag king of the Amalekites alive. But he killed all of Agag's army with the sword. ⁹But Saul and the army let Agag live. They also let the best sheep, fat cattle and lambs live. They let every good animal live. They did not want to destroy them. But when they found an animal that was weak or useless, they killed it.

¹⁰Then the Lord spoke his word to Samuel: ¹¹"Saul has stopped following me. And I am sorry I made him king. He has not obeyed my commands." Samuel was upset, and he cried out to the Lord all night long.

¹²Early the next morning Samuel got up and went to meet Saul. But the people told Samuel, "Saul has gone to Carmel. He has put up a monument in his own honor. Now he has gone down to Gilgal."

> **"Then the Lord spoke his word to Samuel: 'Saul has stopped following me. And I am sorry I made him king.'"**
>
> *1 Samuel 15:10-11*

¹³Then Samuel came to Saul. And Saul said, "May the Lord bless you! I have obeyed the Lord's commands."

¹⁴But Samuel said, "Then why do I hear cattle mooing and sheep bleating?"

¹⁵Saul answered, "The soldiers took them from the Amalekites. They saved the best sheep and cattle to offer as sacrifices to the Lord your God. But we destroyed all the other animals."

¹⁶Samuel said to Saul, "Stop! Let ime tell you what the Lord said to me last night."

Saul answered, "Tell me."

¹⁷Samuel said, "Once you didn't think much of yourself. But now you have become the leader of the tribes^d of Israel. The Lord appointed you to be king over Israel. ¹⁸And he told you to do something. He said, 'Go and destroy those evil people, the Amalekites. Make war on them until all of them are dead.' ¹⁹Why didn't you obey the Lord? Why did you take the best things? Why did you do what the Lord said was wrong?"

²⁰Saul said, "But I did obey the Lord. I did what the Lord told me to do. I destroyed all the Amalekites. And I brought back Agag their king. ²¹The soldiers took the best sheep and cattle to sacrifice to the Lord your God at Gilgal."

²²But Samuel answered,
"What pleases the Lord more:
    burnt offerings and
        sacrifices or obedience?
It is better to obey God
        than to offer a sacrifice.
    It is better to listen to God
        than to offer the fat of
        male sheep.
²³Refusing to obey is as bad as
        the sin of sorcery.^d
    Being stubborn is as bad as
        the sin of worshiping idols.
You have rejected the Lord's
        command.
    For this reason, he
        now rejects
        you as king."

²⁴Then Saul said to Samuel, "I have sinned. I didn't obey the Lord's commands. I didn't do what you told me. I was afraid of the people, and I did what they said. ²⁵Now I beg you, forgive my sin. Come back with me so I may worship the Lord."

²⁶But Samuel said to Saul, "I won't go back with you. You refused the Lord's command. And now he rejects you as king of Israel."

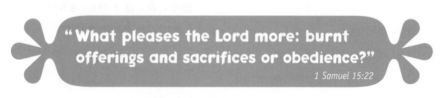

"What pleases the Lord more: burnt offerings and sacrifices or obedience?"
1 Samuel 15:22

TOP TEN

Ways to Go to Sleep

1. By watching a movie
2. By reading a book
3. Snuggled up with your mom
4. With a warm, fuzzy blanket
5. In a sleeping bag under the stars
6. On a beach chair in the breeze
7. To the sound of ocean waves
8. By watching football with your dad
9. By listening to the radio
10. While talking to God

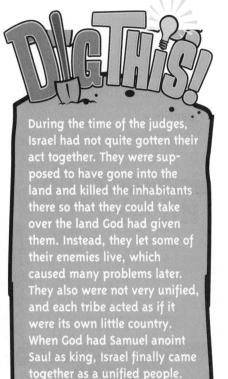

During the time of the judges, Israel had not quite gotten their act together. They were supposed to have gone into the land and killed the inhabitants there so that they could take over the land God had given them. Instead, they let some of their enemies live, which caused many problems later. They also were not very unified, and each tribe acted as if it were its own little country. When God had Samuel anoint Saul as king, Israel finally came together as a unified people.

²⁷As Samuel turned to leave, Saul caught his robe, and it tore. ²⁸Samuel said to him, "The Lord has torn the kingdom of Israel from you today. He has given it to one of your neighbors. He has given it to one better than you. ²⁹The Lord is the Eternal One of Israel. He does not lie or change his mind. He is not a man. So he does not change his mind as men do."

³⁰Saul answered, "I have sinned. But please honor me in front of my people's elders. Please honor me in front of the Israelites. Come back with me so that I may worship the Lord your God." ³¹So Samuel went back with Saul, and Saul worshiped the Lord.

³²Then Samuel said, "Bring me Agag king of the Amalekites."

Agag came to Samuel in chains. Yet Agag thought, "Surely the threat of death has passed."

³³Samuel said to him, "Your sword caused mothers to be without their children. Now your mother will have no children." And Samuel cut Agag to pieces before the Lord at Gilgal.

³⁴Then Samuel left and went to Ramah. But Saul went up to his home in Gibeah. ³⁵And Samuel never saw Saul again all the rest of his life. But he was sorry for Saul. And the Lord was very sorry he had made Saul king of Israel.

David Is Chosen

1 SAMUEL 16:1-13

SAMUEL GOES TO BETHLEHEM

16 The Lord said to Samuel, "How long will you continue to feel sorry for Saul? I have rejected him as king of Israel. Fill your container with olive oil and go. I am sending you to Jesse who lives in Bethlehem. I have chosen one of his sons to be king."

²But Samuel said, "If I go, Saul will hear the news. And he will try to kill me."

The Lord said, "Take a young calf with you. Say, 'I have come to offer a sacrifice to the Lord.'

³Invite Jesse to the sacrifice. Then I will show you what to do. You must appoint the one I show you."

⁴Samuel did what the Lord told him to do. When he arrived at Bethlehem, the elders of Bethlehem shook with fear. They met him and asked, "Are you coming in peace?"

⁵Samuel answered, "Yes, I come in peace. I have come to make a sacrifice to the Lord. Make yourselves holy for the Lord and come to the sacrifice with me." Then he made Jesse and his sons holy for the Lord. And he invited them to come to the sacrifice.

⁶When they arrived, Samuel saw Eliab. Samuel thought, "Surely the Lord has appointed this person standing here before him."

⁷But the Lord said to Samuel, "Don't look at how handsome Eliab is. Don't look at how tall he is. I have not chosen him. God does not see the same way people see. People look at the outside of a person, but the Lord looks at the heart."

⁸Then Jesse called Abinadab and told him to pass by Samuel. But Samuel said, "The Lord has not chosen

History Highlights

➜ **1625 B.C.**
Chariots were used by the Hittites.

7000 5000 3000 1000 0 1000 NOW

LIVIN' IT!

MORE THAN SKIN DEEP
1 SAMUEL 16:7

The time had come to crown a new king. Samuel was called to task, but he was clueless about God's choice. Like most of us, Samuel thought the biggest and best-looking boy ought to be chosen. But God thought differently.

God is not concerned about outward appearances. After all, beauty on the outside doesn't last long at all. What God does care about is the character inside our hearts. He says that humble, obedient hearts are truly beautiful. Even though David wasn't the biggest or oldest, he was chosen as king because he loved God. Next time you look in the mirror to make sure your hair is right or your clothes look good, remember David's story. Ask God to make your heart as beautiful as his.

What Really Matters

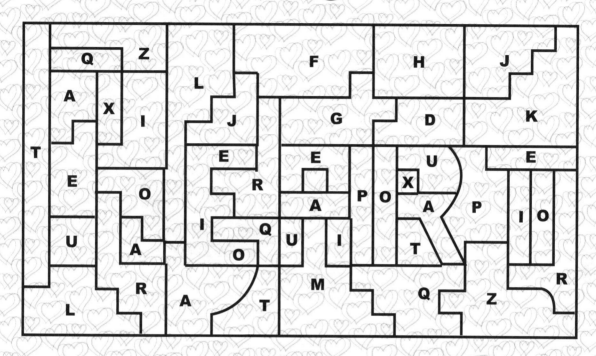

Color in only the vowels to discover what really matters to God! Write the verse on the lines below.

3-D

_____

_____

_____

_____

_____

_____

1 Samuel 16:7

this man either." ⁹Then Jesse had Shammah pass by. But Samuel said, "No, the Lord has not chosen this one." ¹⁰Jesse had seven of his sons pass by Samuel. But Samuel said to him, "The Lord has not chosen any of these."

¹¹Then he asked Jesse, "Are these all the sons you have?"

Jesse answered, "I still have the youngest son. He is out taking care of the sheep."

Samuel said, "Send for him. We will not sit down to eat until he arrives."

¹²So Jesse sent and had his youngest son brought in. He was a fine boy, tanned and handsome.

The Lord said to Samuel, "Go! Appoint him. He is the one."

¹³So Samuel took the container of olive oil. Then he poured oil on Jesse's youngest son to appoint him in front of his brothers. From that day on, the Lord's Spirit[d] entered David with power. Samuel then went back to Ramah.

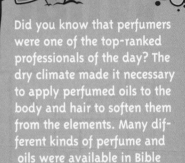

Smelly nelly perfume

Dig This!

Did you know that perfumers were one of the top-ranked professionals of the day? The dry climate made it necessary to apply perfumed oils to the body and hair to soften them from the elements. Many different kinds of perfume and oils were available in Bible times, and many were brought in from distant lands on ships or through caravans. Sometimes, perfumes were even used as medicine!

JUNE RESPECT

1
PRAYER POINTER: Ask God to help you understand what it means to respect your parents and then to help you do it.

2

3
Hide-It-in-Your-Heart: Don't envy sinners. But always respect the Lord (Proverbs 23:17).

4

5

6
Obey your parents the very first time they ask—all day long.

7

8
Go swimming, and see how long you can hold your breath underwater.

9
Surprise your dad by cleaning out the garage.

10

11
Help your mom return the shopping cart to the right place.

12

13
Spend a Saturday with friends picking up trash around the neighborhood.

14
Flag Day

15

16
See how tall of an ice-cream cone you can make, and share it with your family.

17
PRAYER POINTER: Pray for your siblings and friends to grow in respect toward those in authority over you.

18

19
Invite the neighborhood friends over for a cookout.

20
Write a thank-you note for your postal worker, and tape it to the front of the mailbox.

21

22
Make a list of all the things you love about summer.

23

24

25
Hide-It-in-Your-Heart: Honor your father and your mother. Then you will live a long time in the land (Exodus 20:12).

26

27
Build a campfire in the backyard (with your parents!), and make S'mores.

28
Bake a batch of cookies for the garbage collectors to give them when they reach your house.

29

30
Cut out paper butterflies. Attach them to strings, and tape them to your ceiling.

BIBLE CRITTERS

3-D

EWE OUGHT TO KNOW

It took more than just watching a bunch of **SHEEP.** A shepherd had to know their habits. Know what they ate. Understand their weaknesses. Above all, he had to protect and care for them. So what are sheep like? Actually, there are many different kinds, some looking like deer or goats and others looking more like the wooly kind you might see on a farm. In general, sheep—like cows—chew cud (they spit up old food and chew it again). In fact, they have four different parts to their stomach to help them digest their food, which consists of grass, flowers, young plants, and leaves. The males are called rams, and the females are ewes.

David and Goliath

I SAMUEL 17:1-58

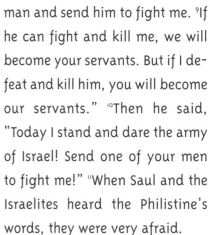

DAVID AND GOLIATH

17 The Philistines gathered their armies for war. They met at Socoh in Judah. Their camp was at Ephes Dammim between Socoh and Azekah. ²Saul and the Israelites gathered in the Valley of Elah. And they camped there. They took their positions to fight the Philistines. ³The Philistines controlled one hill. The Israelites controlled another. The valley was between them.

⁴The Philistines had a champion fighter named Goliath. He was from Gath. He was about nine feet four inches tall. He came out of the Philistine camp. ⁵He had a bronze helmet on his head. And he wore a coat of scale armor. It was made of bronze and weighed about 125 pounds. ⁶He wore bronze protectors on his legs. And he had a small spear of bronze tied on his back. ⁷The wooden part of his larger spear was like a weaver's rod. And its blade weighed about 15 pounds. The officer who carried his shield walked in front of him.

⁸Goliath stood and shouted to the Israelite soldiers, "Why have you taken positions for battle? I am a Philistine, and you are Saul's servants! Choose a man and send him to fight me. ⁹If he can fight and kill me, we will become your servants. But if I defeat and kill him, you will become our servants." ¹⁰Then he said, "Today I stand and dare the army of Israel! Send one of your men to fight me!" ¹¹When Saul and the Israelites heard the Philistine's words, they were very afraid.

¹²Now David was the son of Jesse, an Ephrathite. Jesse was from Bethlehem in Judah. He had eight sons. In Saul's time Jesse was an old man. ¹³His three oldest sons followed Saul to the war. The first son was Eliab. The second son was Abinadab. And the

1 Samuel 17:1-11
A GIANT TRUTH

WILD WORLD FACTS

No one wanted to mess with Goliath. The Bible says that he was about 9 feet 4 inches tall! (And not too nice, to boot). The Bible talks about other people in the Bible (referred to as Nephilim) who were also very large people.

According to the *Guinness Book of World Records,* the tallest man ever known in recent history was named Robert Pershing Wadlow. He was born at a normal 8 pounds 6 ounces, but by the time he was 8 years old, he was already 6 feet 2 inches and weighed 195 pounds! As an adult, Robert reached a height of 8 feet 11 inches and weighed 490 pounds.

God makes some people big and some people small, but it is never the outside of a person that is important. God cares about our hearts, and he loves us and wants to use us just like we are.

[hazardkentucky.com/wadlow.htm]

third son was Shammah. [14]David was the youngest son. Jesse's three oldest sons followed Saul. [15]But David went back and forth from Saul to Bethlehem. There he took care of his father's sheep.

[16]The Philistine Goliath came out every morning and evening. He stood before the Israelite army. This continued for 40 days.

[17]Now Jesse said to his son David, "Take this half bushel of cooked grain. And take ten loaves of bread. Take them to your brothers in the camp. [18]Also take ten pieces of cheese. Give them to the commander of your brothers' group of 1,000 soldiers. See how your brothers are. Bring back something to show me they are all right. [19]Your brothers are with Saul and the army in the Valley of Elah. They are fighting against the Philistines."

[20]Early in the morning David left the sheep with another shepherd. He took the food and left as Jesse had told him. When David arrived at the camp, the army was leaving. They were going out to their battle positions. The soldiers were shouting their war cry. [21]The Israelites and Philistines were lining up their men to face each other in battle.

[22]David left the food with the man who kept the supplies. Then he ran to the battle line and talked to his brothers. [23]While he was talking with them, Goliath came out. He was the Philistine champion from Gath. He shouted things against Israel as usual, and David heard it. [24]When the Israelites saw Goliath, they were very much afraid and ran away.

[25]They said, "Look at this man Goliath. He keeps coming out to speak against Israel. The king will give much money to the man who kills Goliath. He will also give his daughter in marriage to whoever kills him. And his father's family will not have to pay taxes in Israel."

[26]David asked the men who stood near him, "What will be done to reward the man who kills this Philistine? What will be done for whoever takes away the shame from Israel? Goliath

SMALL WONDERS
1 SAMUEL 17:1-58

His brothers tried to send him away. As older siblings often do, they thought their younger brother was just getting in the way. But what they thought didn't matter to David. What the king thought didn't even matter. Even though he was only a young boy, David knew it was wrong for Goliath to make fun of God. So he did something about it.

You might be tempted to think that you are too young to serve the Lord. Maybe you think it's something you can do someday, when people listen to you. But God wants your attention right now. It doesn't matter how young you are, or how smart, or how popular. What matters is that you belong to God. When you obey him, he gives you power from heaven to do all the amazing works he has asked you to do.

> **"Look at this man Goliath. He keeps coming out to speak against Israel."**
>
> *1 Samuel 17:25*

DAVID & GOLIATH

SUPPLIES

branch
large rubber band
quarter size bouncy balls

INSTRUCTIONS

1. Find a fallen branch that looks like a Y. With your parent's help, trim the branch so that the top two branches of the Y are about 4 inches long and the bottom 5-6 inches long.

2. Tie the rubber band to the top two branches of the Y.

3. Launch the bouncy balls using your homemade sling shot!

(Best to use this outside. And don't ever sling hard objects or aim the sling toward people, critters, or breakable things like windows!)

3-D

ALL ABOUT IT:

Goliath was a lot bigger than David, but David knew his God was A LOT bigger than Goliath. David had faith in God to protect him, so David approached Goliath with confidence: "You come to me using a sword, a large spear and a small spear. But I come to you in the name of the Lord of heaven's armies. He's the God of the armies of Israel! You have spoken out against him" (1 Samuel 17:45).

Saul's armor was too big and too heavy for David. God used David to defeat Goliath with a sling and a few rocks. Imagine such a weapon against a huge giant. You don't have to have special things or clothes for God to use you. He can use you just as you are.

is a Philistine. He is not circumcised. [d] Why does he think he can speak against the armies of the living God?"

27 The Israelites told David what they had been saying. They said, "This is what will be done for the man who kills Goliath."

28 David's oldest brother Eliab heard David talking with the soldiers. He became angry with David. He asked David, "Why did you come here? Who's taking care of those few sheep of yours in the desert? I know you are proud. Your attitude is very bad. You came down here just to watch the battle!"

29 David asked, "Now what have I done wrong? Can't I even talk?" 30 He then turned to other people and asked the same questions. And they gave him the same answer as before. 31 Some men heard what David said and told Saul. Then Saul ordered David to be sent to him.

32 David said to Saul, "Don't let anyone be discouraged. I, your servant, will go and fight this Philistine!"

33 Saul answered, "You can't go out against this Philistine and fight him. You're only a boy. Goliath has been a warrior since he was a young man."

34 But David said to Saul, "I, your servant, have been keeping my father's sheep.

When a lion or bear came and took a sheep from the flock, 35 I would chase it. I would attack it and save the sheep from its mouth. When it attacked me, I caught it by its fur. I would hit it and kill it. 36 I, your servant, have killed both a lion and a bear! Goliath, the Philistine who is not circumcised, will be like

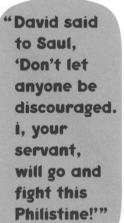

"David said to Saul, 'Don't let anyone be discouraged. i, your servant, will go and fight this Philistine!'"

1 Samuel 17:32

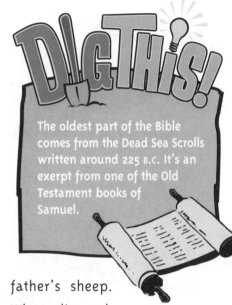

The oldest part of the Bible comes from the Dead Sea Scrolls written around 225 B.C. It's an exerpt from one of the Old Testament books of Samuel.

DAVID

When no one else would believe, David did. Goliath made fun of Israel and their God, and David would not stand for it—even though he was just a young boy. His faith was strong and his God even stronger, so he defeated the great giant—armed with a slingshot, stones, and the God of the universe.

The rest of David's life was just as spectacular. He eventually became king over Israel, ruling with wisdom and leading the people in peace. But he wasn't perfect. David committed some of the worst sins you can imagine. But he always repented and became remembered as "the man after God's own heart."

Like David, you can do incredible things if you have God on your side. And yes, you'll make mistakes, too. But remember to repent and trust in God's forgiveness. Become a child after God's own heart.

JUST SLINGIN' IT!

Nobody thought David was ready for the big giant—but are you? Test your Bible knowledge to see just how much you know about this incredible story from Scripture.

1 WHO WERE THE IS-RAELITES FIGHTING?
A The Amalekites
B The Moabites
C The Philistines
D The Assyrians

2 HOW TALL WAS GOLIATH?
A 6 ft. 2 in.
B 8 ft. 8 in.
C 14 ft. 2 in.
D 9 ft. 4 in.

3 GOLIATH'S ARMOR WEIGHED 125 POUNDS AND WAS MADE OUT OF:
A gold
B bronze
C steel
D iron

4 WHY DID DAVID GO TO THE BATTLE IN THE FIRST PLACE?
A He wanted to see what was going on.
B He always wanted to be a soldier.
C He was spying on his brothers.
D He was obeying his dad and taking food to his brothers.

5 WHAT REWARD DID THE KING OFFER TO THE ONE WHO KILLED GOLIATH?
A a lot of money
B his daughter's hand in marriage
C relief from taxes
D all of the above

6 HOW DID DAVID'S BROTH-ERS RESPOND TO DAVID WHEN THEY SAW HIM?
A They hugged him and said they were glad he came.
B They pretended like they didn't know him.
C They got angry and accused him of having a bad attitude.
D None of the above.

7 WHAT TWO ANIMALS HAD DAVID KILLED WHILE PRO-TECTING HIS SHEEP?
A a badger and an ocelot
B a bear and a panther
C a hippo and a lion
D a lion and a bear

8 HOW MANY STONES DID DAVID CARRY WITH HIM FOR HIS SLING?
A 5   B 2
C 4   D 1

9 WHY WASN'T DAVID AFRAID OF GOLIATH?
A He knew he was a good shot.
B He wanted the prize money.
C He trusted God to win it for him.
D He was trying to impress his brothers.

10 AFTER THE BATTLE, WHAT DID DAVID GIVE TO SAUL?
A Goliath's spear
B Goliath's armor
C Goliath's ring
D Goliath's head

Score 9-10: Bullseye.
Score 7-8: You're a sharp-shooter—just give it a little more effort.
Score 5-6: Amateur—but not out of your league. Sharpen your skills!
Score 4 or below: Time to get some more stones. Read 1 Samuel 17 more closely!

Answer: 1. c; 2. d; 3. b; 4. d; 5. d; 6. c; 7. d; 8. a; 9. c; 10. d

the lion or bear I killed. He will die because he has stood against the armies of the living God. [37]The Lord saved me from a lion and a bear. He will also save me from this Philistine."

Saul said to David, "Go, and may the Lord be with you." [38]Saul put his own clothes on David. He put a bronze helmet on David's head and armor on his body. [39]David put on Saul's sword and tried to walk around.

> **"You come to me using a sword, a large spear and a small spear. But i come to you in the name of the Lord of heaven's armies."**
>
> *1 Samuel 17:45*

3-D

But he was not used to all the armor Saul had put on him. He said to Saul, "I can't go in this. I'm not used to it." Then David took it all off. [40]He took

GET CONNECTED

RELATIONSHIPS WITH FAMILY

R-E-S-P-E-C-T "Oh, no! Here he comes again," they muttered to themselves. His brothers saw their youngest brother David talking to the soldiers about Goliath. Eliab, his oldest brother, accused him of just wanting to watch the battle. He told him to go back to his sheep.

Imagine if David had listened to him! Israel's entire history would be changed. Fortunately, David understood that God had a special plan for him, regardless of what his brothers thought.

Are you an older brother or sister? Do you tend to look down on your younger siblings? God says that we need to treat others as better than ourselves. We are all created in God's image. Out of respect for God, we should show kindness and respect—even to the youngest in the family. When we do, we get to share in God's work in their lives and ours.

his stick in his hand. And he chose five smooth stones from a stream. He put them in his pouch and held his sling in his hand. Then he went to meet Goliath.

[41]At the same time, the Philistine was coming closer to David. The man who held his shield walked in front of him. [42]Goliath looked at David. He saw that David was only a boy, tanned and handsome. He looked down at David with disgust. [43]He said, "Do you think I am a dog, that you come at me with a stick?" He used his gods' names to curse David. [44]He said to David, "Come here. I'll feed your body to the birds of the air and the wild animals!"

[45]But David said to him, "You come to me using a sword, a large spear and a small spear. But I come to you in the name of the Lord of heaven's armies. He's the God of the armies of Israel! You have spoken out against him. [46]Today the Lord will give you to me. I'll kill you, and I'll cut off your head. Today I'll feed the bodies of the Philistine soldiers to the birds of the air and the wild animals. Then all the

world will know there is a God in Israel! ⁴⁷Everyone gathered here will know the Lord does not need swords or spears to save people. The battle belongs to him! And he will help us defeat all of you."

⁴⁸As Goliath came near to attack him, David ran quickly to meet him. ⁴⁹He took a stone from his pouch. He put it into his sling and slung it. The stone hit the Philistine on his forehead and sank into it. Goliath fell face-down on the ground.

⁵⁰So David defeated the Philistine with only a sling and a stone! He hit him and killed him. He did not even have a sword in his hand. ⁵¹David ran and stood beside the Philistine. He took Goliath's sword out of its holder and killed him. Then he cut off Goliath's head.

When the Philistines saw that their champion was dead, they turned and ran. ⁵²The men of Israel and Judah shouted and started chasing the Philistines. They chased them all the way to the entrance to the city of Gath. And they chased them to the gates of Ekron.

Many of the Philistines died. Their bodies lay on the Shaaraim road as far as Gath and Ekron. ⁵³The Israelites returned after chasing the Philistines. Then they took many things from the Philistine camp. ⁵⁴David took Goliath's head to Jerusalem. He also put Goliath's weapons in his own tent.

⁵⁵Saul had watched David go out to meet Goliath. Saul spoke to Abner, commander of the army. He said, "Abner, who is that young man's father?"

Abner answered, "As surely as you live, my king, I don't know."

⁵⁶The king said, "Find out whose son he is."

⁵⁷When David came back from killing Goliath, Abner brought him to Saul. David still held Goliath's head.

⁵⁸Saul asked him, "Young man, who is your father?"

David answered, "I am the son of your servant Jesse of Bethlehem."

BLAST FROM THE PAST

Y-NOT SLINGS? When we think of a sling, most of us picture the kind we can make out of a y-shaped twig with elastic connecting the branches. But David's sling was different. His was made out of leather and had two, long, thin straps with a pocket in the middle. To use it, the stone was placed in the pocket and the straps were held in the same hand and swung around in the air to gain speed. When one strap was released, the stone went flying out like a bullet.

David and Jonathan

1 SAMUEL 18:1-4;
19:1-10; 20:1-42

SAUL FEARS DAVID

18 When David finished talking with Saul, Jonathan felt very close to David. He loved David as much as he loved himself. ²Saul kept David with him from that day on. He did not let David go home to his father's house. ³Jonathan made an agreement with David. He did this because he loved David as much as himself. ⁴He took off his coat and gave it to David. He also gave David his uniform, including his sword, bow and belt.

• • •

SAUL PLANS TO KILL DAVID

19 Saul told his son Jonathan and all his servants to kill David. But Jonathan cared very much for David. ²So he warned David, "My father Saul is looking for a chance to kill you. Watch out in the morning. Hide in a secret place. ³I will go out

and stand with my father in the field where you are hiding. I'll talk to him about you. Then I'll let you know what I find out."

⁴Jonathan talked to Saul his father. He said good things about David. Jonathan said, "You are the king. Don't do wrong to your servant David. He did nothing wrong to you. What he did has helped you greatly. ⁵David risked his life when he killed Goliath the Philistine. The Lord won a great victory for all Israel. You saw it, and you were happy. Why would you do wrong against David? He's innocent. There's no reason to kill him!"

⁶Saul listened to Jonathan. Then he made this promise: "As surely as the Lord lives, David won't be put to death."

⁷So Jonathan called to David. He told David everything that had been said. And he brought David to Saul. So David was with Saul as before.

⁸When war broke out again, David went out to fight the Philistines. He defeated them, and they ran away from him.

LIVIN' IT!

LOVE TRIUMPHS
1 SAMUEL 18:1-4

You were supposed to be voted the class favorite. But instead, your best friend won the award. What did you do? How did you feel?

Most people would feel hurt and jealous. But not Jonathan. Jonathan trusted in the Lord, and he knew that God was in control. Even though he had to humbly give up his right to become king after Saul, he continued to love David—even though David took his throne.

When we understand that God decides every event in our lives, it makes it easier to handle disappointments. While we may still feel the loss, we understand that God is working out an even better plan for us, and we must simply trust his goodness. It also frees us to love other people with God's kind of love, no matter what happens to us.

⁹But once again an evil spirit from the Lord entered Saul. He was sitting in his house, and he had his spear in his hand. David was playing the harp. ¹⁰Saul tried to pin David to the wall with his spear. But David moved away from him. So Saul's spear went into the wall. And David ran away that night.

"Saul tried to pin David to the wall with his spear."

1 Samuel 19:10

• • •

DAVID AND JONATHAN

20 Then David ran away from Naioth in Ramah. He went to Jonathan and asked, "What have I done? What is my crime? How have I sinned against your father so that he's trying to kill me?"

²Jonathan answered, "No! You won't die! See, my father doesn't do anything without first telling me. It doesn't matter if it is very important or just a small thing. Why would he refuse to tell me he wants to kill you? No, it's not true!"

³But David took an oath. He said, "Your father knows very well that I'm your friend. He has said to himself, 'Jonathan must not know about it. If he knows, he will tell David.' But as surely as the Lord lives and as you live, I am very close to death!"

⁴Jonathan said to David, "I'll do anything you want me to do."

⁵So David said, "Look, tomorrow is the New Moon[d] festival. I am supposed to eat with the king. But let me hide in the field until the third evening. ⁶Your father may notice I am gone. If he does, tell him, 'David begged me to let him go to his hometown of Bethlehem. Every year at this time, his family group offers a sacrifice.' ⁷If your father says, 'Fine,' I am safe. But if he becomes angry, you can believe he wants to hurt me. ⁸Jonathan, be kind to me, your servant. You have made an agreement with me before the Lord. If I am guilty, you may kill me yourself! Why hand me over to your father?"

⁹Jonathan answered, "No, never! If I learn that my father plans to harm you, I will warn you!"

REAL SUPER HEROES

JONATHAN

If you want to know what it takes to be a true friend, take a look at Jonathan. Jonathan was Saul's oldest son, the guy who was supposed to become king after his father. He also had become best friends with David, the new kid on the block who had killed Goliath and was growing in popularity.

Most people would have felt threatened at David's success. Rumor had it that many Israelites wanted David as king. But Jonathan trusted God. He didn't see leadership as something to be taken by force, because he knew that God was the one who controlled such things. Instead of being jealous, Jonathan became even more committed to David. When he discovered that his father was trying to kill David, he risked his own life by trying to convince his father to come to his senses. When he saw his father's hardened heart, he went back to David to warn him to flee.

When we trust God like Jonathan did, we don't need to be threatened by other people's success. Instead, we can have grateful hearts for God's blessing in our lives and reach out to others with the love God shows us.

¹⁰David asked, "Who will let me know if your father answers you unkindly?"

¹¹Then Jonathan said, "Come, let's go out into the field." So Jonathan and David went together into the field.

¹²Jonathan said to David, "I promise this before the Lord, the God of Israel: At this same time day after tomorrow, I will find out how my father feels. If he feels good toward you, I'll send word to you. I'll let you know. ¹³But my father may mean to hurt you. If so, I will let you know and send you away safely. May the Lord punish me terribly if I don't do this. And may the Lord be with you as he has been with my father. ¹⁴But show me the kindness of the Lord as long as I live. Do this so that I may not die. ¹⁵You must not stop showing your kindness to my family. Don't do this, even when the Lord has destroyed all your enemies from the earth."

¹⁶So Jonathan made an agreement with David. He said, "May the Lord punish David's enemies." ¹⁷And Jonathan asked David to repeat his promise of love for him. He did this because he loved David as much as he loved himself.

¹⁸Jonathan said to David, "Tomorrow is the New Moon festival. Your seat will be empty. So my father will notice you're gone. ¹⁹On the third day go to the place where you hid when this trouble began. Wait by the rock Ezel. ²⁰On the third day I will shoot three arrows to the side of the rock. I will shoot as if I am shooting at a target. ²¹Then I will send a boy and tell him to go find the arrows. I may say to him, 'Look, the arrows are on this side of you. Bring them here.' If so, you may come out of hiding. You may do this as surely as the Lord lives because you are safe. There is no danger. ²²But I may say to the boy, 'Look, the arrows are beyond you.' If I do, you must go, because the Lord has sent you away. ²³Remember what we talked about. The Lord is a witness between you and me forever."

²⁴So David hid in the field. And

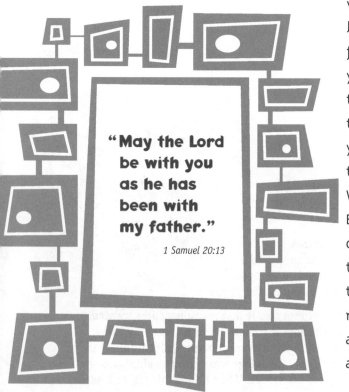

"May the Lord be with you as he has been with my father."

1 Samuel 20:13

DIG THIS!

It was the biggest game of hide and seek ever played—only David was playing for his life. How could he escape Saul so many times, when Saul had entire armies out looking for him? Similar to the scenes you may have watched on T.V. when American soldiers are searching for terrorists in the desert regions of the Middle East, David was also able to make use of the caves and rugged terrain for his benefit. It's also why David penned so many psalms about being dry and thirsty. He saw the spiritual connection with what he was physically experiencing.

INCREDIBLE EDIBLES

FRIENDSHIP COOKIES

INGREDIENTS

2 1/4 C. flour

1 tsp. baking soda

1 tsp. salt

2 sticks of butter (softened)

3/4 C. sugar

3/4 C packed brown sugar

1 tsp. vanilla

2 eggs

1 3/4 C. chocolate chips

HERE'S THE SCOOP:

Jonathan and David were best friends. After David killed Goliath, Jonathan's dad had David come to live with them. Jonathan and David formed a close friendship and treated each other as if they were brothers.

It's great to have friends who care about and look after you. Maybe you already have a best friend with whom you share your secrets. Maybe you're still looking for one such friend. Invite a friend over to make cookies. Give your friend half of the ingredients, and take turns following the recipe. When you're finished, enjoy your friend and your treat!

COOKIE RECIPE

1. Ask your parent to preheat the oven to 350 degrees.

2. Mix the flour, salt, and baking soda in a large bowl; set aside.

3. In a larger bowl mix the butter, eggs, vanilla, white sugar, and brown sugar.

4. One friend mixes the batter while the other one pours the flour mixture in slowly.

5. Stir in the chocolate chips last.

6. Drop spoonfuls of dough on ungreased cookie sheets (12 cookies per sheet).

7. Ask your mom to bake the cookies one sheet at a time for 9-11 minutes.

when the New Moon festival came, the king sat down to eat. [25]He sat where he always sat, near the wall. Jonathan sat across from him, and Abner sat next to him. But David's place was

> **"Go in peace. We have promised by the Lord that we will be friends."** *1 Samuel 20:42*

empty. [26]That day Saul said nothing. He thought, "Maybe something has happened to David so that he is unclean."[d] [27]But the next day was the second day of the month. And David's place was empty again. So Saul said to Jonathan, "Why hasn't the son of Jesse come to

the festival yesterday or today?" [28]Jonathan answered, "David begged me to let him go to Bethlehem. [29]He said, 'Let me go, because our family has a sacrifice in the town. And my brother has ordered me to be there. Now if I am your friend, please let me go and see my brothers.' That is why he has not come to the king's table."

[30]Then Saul became very angry with Jonathan. He said, "You son of an evil and disobedient woman! I know you are on the side of David son of Jesse! You bring shame on yourself and on your mother who gave birth to you. [31]As long as Jesse's son lives, you'll never be king or have a kingdom. Now send for David and bring him to me. He must die!"

[32]Jonathan asked his father, "Why should David be killed? What wrong has he done?" [33]Then Saul threw his spear at Jonathan, trying to kill him. So Jonathan knew that his father really wanted to kill David. [34]Jonathan was very angry and left the table. That second day of the month he refused to eat. He was upset about what his father wanted to do to David.

[35]The next morning Jonathan went out to the field. He went to meet David as they had agreed. He had a young boy with him. [36]Jonathan said to the boy, "Run and find the arrows I shoot." When he ran, Jonathan shot an arrow beyond him. [37]The boy ran to the place where Jonathan's arrow fell. But Jonathan called, "The arrow is beyond you!" [38]Then he shouted, "Hurry! Go quickly! Don't stop!" The boy picked up the arrow and brought it back to his master.

GET CONNECTED

RELATIONSHIPS WITH FRIENDS

Built to Last If you were going to build a house, would you carefully place brick on brick, or would you constantly destroy the work you've begun?

God says that our friendships are a lot like building a house. It takes time, love, and attention to build a friendship that will last. But if you say unkind things, even just to be funny, it can tear your friend and your friendship down. God wants us to be all about encouraging our friends to keep loving him and helping them to see how special they are to God and to us. Think of something encouraging you could say to each person in your life today, and begin the work of building up others.

WILD WORLD FACTS

1 Samuel 19:1-3

CRAViN' CAViN'

In Bible times, they were used as storage units, hiding places, and even burial grounds. Birthed by something as simple as rain or as complex as a tectonic shift from an earthquake, caves are amazing creations of God that scores of people around the world love to explore.

If you'd like to try your hand at spelunking (exploring caves), you can—and you don't even have to travel to Bible lands to do it. The top 10 caves in America are: Ape Cave, Washington; Moaning Cavern, California; Carlsbad Caverns, New Mexico; Jewel Cave, South Dakota; Niagara Cave, Minnesota; Meramec Caverns, Missouri; Caverns of Sonora, Texas; Polar Cave, New Hampshire; Luray Caverns, Virginia; and Mammoth Cave, Kentucky. Happy spelunking!

[Gorp.away.com]

³⁹(The boy knew nothing about what this meant. Only Jonathan and David knew.) ⁴⁰Then Jonathan gave his weapons to the boy. He told him, "Go back to town."

⁴¹When the boy left, David came out from the south side of the rock. He bowed facedown on the ground before Jonathan. He did this three times. Then David and Jonathan kissed each other. They cried together, but David cried the most.

⁴²Jonathan said to David, "Go in peace. We have promised by the Lord that we will be friends. We said, 'The Lord will be a witness between you and me, and between our descendants^d forever.'" Then David left, and Jonathan went back to town.

STORIES FROM 2 SAMUEL

Saul Dies and David Becomes King

David is King!

2 SAMUEL 1:1-16; 5:1-25

DAVID LEARNS ABOUT SAUL'S DEATH

1 Now Saul was dead. And after David had defeated the Amalekites, he returned to Ziklag. He stayed there two days.

²On the third day a young man came to Ziklag. He came from Saul's camp. To show his sadness his clothes were torn, and he had dirt on his head. He came and bowed facedown on the ground before David.

³David asked him, "Where did you come from?"

The man answered him, "I escaped from the Israelite camp."

⁴David asked him, "What happened? Please tell me!"

The man answered, "The people have run away from the battle. Many of them have fallen dead. Saul and his son Jonathan are dead also."

⁵David said to him, "How do you know Saul and his son Jonathan are dead?"

⁶The young man answered, "I happened to be on Mount Gilboa. There I saw Saul leaning on his spear. The Philistine chariots and the men riding in them were coming closer to Saul. ⁷When he looked back and saw me, he called to me. I answered him, 'Here I am!'

> "To show his sadness his clothes were torn, and he had dirt on his head."
> *2 Samuel 1:2*

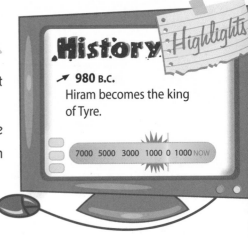

History Highlights

➤ **980 B.C.**
Hiram becomes the king of Tyre.

7000 5000 3000 1000 0 1000 NOW

LIVIN' IT!

SERIOUS SUBMISSION
2 SAMUEL 1:1-16

David knew the throne was his. Samuel had anointed him long ago. But God had not yet made the change take place. As long as Saul was still alive, David considered him God's appointed king. When Saul finally did die, David put the Amalekite to death who killed him, because David respected God's authority to the very end.

Like David, we should respect our authorities. Sometimes we have wonderful parents and teachers, and it's easy to obey. But sometimes it's not so easy. Sometimes we don't like them, or we just don't want to obey. But we need to remember that God himself gives us the parents and teachers who are over us. When we respect and obey them, we are respecting and obeying God.

SUBMIT

8"Then Saul asked me, 'Who are you?'

"I told him, 'I am an Amalekite.'

9"Then Saul said to me, 'Please come here and kill me. I am badly hurt and am almost dead already.'

10"'So I went over and killed him. He had been hurt so badly I knew he couldn't live. Then I took the crown from his head and the bracelet from his arm. I have brought them here to you, my master."

"Then David tore his clothes to show his sorrow. And all the men with him did also. 12They were very sad and cried. They did not eat until evening. They cried for Saul and his son Jonathan. And they cried for the Israelites who had been killed with swords.

DAVID ORDERS THE AMALEKITE KILLED

13David asked the young man who brought the report, "Where are you from?"

The young man answered, "I am the son of a foreigner. I am an Amalekite."

14David asked him, "Why were you not afraid to kill the Lord's appointed king?"

15Then David called one of his men. David told him, "Go! Kill the Amalekite!" So the Israelite killed the Amalekite. 16David had said to the Amalekite, "You are responsible for your own death. You have spoken against yourself! You said, 'I have killed the Lord's appointed king.'"

• • •

DAVID IS MADE KING OF ISRAEL

5 Then all the tribes[d] of Israel came to David at Hebron. They said to him, "Look, we are your own family. 2In the past Saul was king over us. But you were the one leading us in battle for Israel. The Lord said to you,

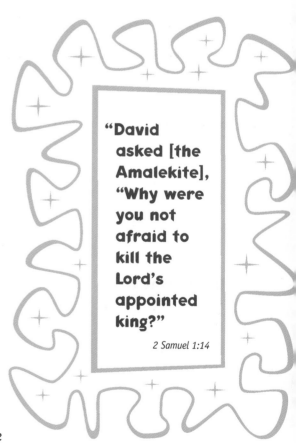

"David asked [the Amalekite], "Why were you not afraid to kill the Lord's appointed king?"

2 Samuel 1:14

'You will be like a shepherd for my people, the Israelites. You will become their ruler.'"

³All the elders of Israel came to King David at Hebron. Then he made an agreement with them in Hebron in front of the Lord. Then they poured oil on David to make him king over Israel.

⁴David was 30 years old when he became king. He ruled 40 years. ⁵He was king over Judah in Hebron for 7 years and 6 months. And he was king over all Israel and Judah in Jerusalem for 33 years.

⁶The king and his men went to Jerusalem to attack the Jebusites who lived there. The Jebusites said to David, "You can't come into our city. Even our people who are blind and crippled can stop you." They said this because they thought David could not enter their city. ⁷But David did take the city of Jerusalem with its strong walls. It became the City of David.

⁸That day David said to his men, "To defeat the Jebusites you must go through the water tunnel. Then you can reach those 'crippled' and 'blind' enemies. This is why people say, 'The blind and the crippled cannot enter the palace.'"

⁹So David lived in the city with its strong walls. He called it the City of David. David built more buildings around it. He began where the land was filled in on the east side of the city. He also built more buildings inside the city. ¹⁰He became stronger and stronger, because the Lord of heaven's armies was with him.

¹¹Hiram king of the city of Tyre

WILD WORLD FACTS

2 Samuel 1:1-4

MUMMY MAKE-OVER

Not everyone got the special treatment—and maybe they should have been glad. When kings died, their bodies were preserved, a practice called mummification. Normally, when people die, bacteria present in their body breaks down the soft tissues until there is nothing left but bone. In order to keep this from happening, embalmers (the folks who preserve the bodies) would remove all the organs and soak them in a chemical called Natron that destroyed the bacteria and then place the organs in a jar. They would fill the empty body cavity with Natron salt packing. Then they would rub the skin with special chemicals (using a combination of baking soda and salt) so the body could be preserved. The result would be a dried-out, shrunken body that they would then dress up in jewelry and clothes.

Embalming was an expensive process reserved for royalty. Most folks were simply wrapped with clothes containing spices such as myrrh. What the Egyptians failed to realize was that treatment of the body after death had no effect on the soul. God says we must belong to him in this life if we want to be a part of his kingdom in the next life.

[t3.preservice.org]

> **"David was 30 years old when he became king. He ruled 40 years."**
>
> 2 Samuel 5:4

> "David knew the Lord really had made him king of Israel. And he knew the Lord had made his kingdom very important." *2 Samuel 5:12*

sent messengers to David. He also sent cedar logs, carpenters and men to cut stone. They built a palace for David. ¹²Then David knew the Lord really had made him king of Israel. And he knew the Lord had made his kingdom very important. This was because the Lord loved his people, the Israelites.

¹³In Jerusalem David took for himself more slave women[d] and wives. This was after he moved there from Hebron. More sons and daughters were born to David. ¹⁴These are the names of the sons born to David in Jerusalem: Shammua, Shobab, Nathan, Solomon, ¹⁵Ibhar, Elishua, Nepheg, Japhia, ¹⁶Elishama, Eliada and Eliphelet.

DAVID DEFEATS THE PHILISTINES

¹⁷Now the Philistines heard that David had been made king over Israel. So all the Philistines went to look for him. But when David heard the news, he went down to a safe place. ¹⁸So the Philistines came and camped in the Valley of Rephaim. David asked the Lord, "Should I attack the Philistines? Will you help me defeat them?"

¹⁹The Lord said to David, "Go! I will certainly help you defeat them."

²⁰So David went to Baal Perazim and defeated the Philistines

10 TOP TEN

Ways to Witness to Your Neighbors

1. Invite them to go to church with you.
2. Become their friend.
3. Have them over to play and eat.
4. Offer to cut their grass.
5. Ask how you can pray for them.
6. Ask them what they believe.
7. Tell them how you became a Christian.
8. Send them an encouraging note.
9. Tell them you appreciate them.
10. Make them a meal when they are in need.

DIG THIS!

How did David conquer the Jebusites? Even though it seemed as if their city was perfectly protected since it sat on the top of a steep hill, David discovered its greatest strength and weakness: their water shaft. The Jebusites had dug a shaft down into the spring below their city which kept them supplied with water. David came up the shaft into the city, where he defeated them. The water shaft is still visible today.

> "He became stronger and stronger because the Lord of heaven's armies was with him." *2 Samuel 5:10*

there. David said, "Like a flood of water, the Lord has broken through my enemies." So David named the place Baal Perazim." [21]The Philistines left their idols behind at Baal Perazim. And David and his men carried these idols away.

[22]Once again the Philistines came and camped at the Valley of Rephaim. [23]David prayed to the Lord. This time the Lord told David, "Don't attack the Philistines from the front. Instead, go around them. Attack them opposite the balsam trees. [24]You will hear the sound of marching in the tops of the balsam trees. Then you must act quickly. I, the Lord, will have gone ahead of you and defeated the Philistine army." [25]So David did what the Lord commanded. He defeated the Philistines and chased them all the way from Gibeon to Gezer.

> "i, the Lord, will have gone ahead of you and defeated the Philistine army."
>
> *2 Samuel 5:24*

5:20 Baal Perazim This name means "the Lord breaks through."

JULY PURITY

Hide-It-in-Your-Heart: 1
How can a young person live a pure life? He can do it by obeying your word (Psalm 119:9).

2
Write your own song about why you're thankful for our country.

3

Independence Day! 4
Invite friends over to eat watermelon and watch the fireworks.

5

Prayer Pointer: 6
Ask God to help you guard your heart against the sin in the world.

7

8
Sit on your front lawn at night, and listen to the crickets.

9

10
Make a peanut-butter-covered pine cone, and hang it by a string in your yard to feed the squirrels.

11

12

13
Surprise your friends with homemade gifts, and tell them it's Christmas in July.

14

15

16
Go the whole day without turning on the T.V.

Hide-It-in-Your-Heart: 17
Even a child is known by his behavior. His actions show if he is innocent and good (Proverbs 20:11).

18

19
Make up a bedtime story for your younger siblings.

20

21

22
Swim five laps in the pool.

23

24
Prayer Pointer: Ask God to show you if there are any T.V. programs, video games, music, or anything else that keeps you from thinking pure thoughts, then repent of your sin.

25
Take a tent to camp on the beach under the stars.

26

27
Collect a jar of sand, and remember that God's thoughts toward you outnumber the grains in your jar and the whole earth!

28

29

30
Sell something your family made together and give the profits to your church.

31

David and Bathsheba

2 SAMUEL 11:1–12:25

DAVID AND BATHSHEBA

11 In the spring the kings would go out to war. So in the spring David sent out Joab, his servants and all the Israelites. They destroyed the Ammonites and attacked the city of Rabbah. But David stayed in

> **"That woman is Bathsheba daughter of Eliam. She is the wife of Uriah the Hittite."**
>
> *2 Samuel 11:3*

Jerusalem. [2]One evening David got up from his bed. He walked around on the roof[n] of his palace. While he was on the roof, he saw a woman bathing. She was very beautiful. [3]So David sent his servants to find out who she was. A servant answered, "That woman is Bathsheba daughter of Eliam. She is the wife of Uriah the Hittite." [4]David sent messengers to bring Bathsheba to him.

When she came to him, he had sexual relations with her. (Now Bathsheba had purified herself from her monthly period.) Then she went back to her house. [5]But Bathsheba became pregnant. She sent word to David, saying, "I am pregnant."

[6]So David sent this message to Joab: "Send Uriah the Hittite to me." So Joab sent Uriah to David. [7]Uriah came to David. And David asked him how Joab was, how the soldiers were and how the war was going. [8]Then David said to Uriah, "Go home and rest."

So Uriah left the palace. The king also sent a gift to him. [9]But Uriah did not go home. He slept outside the door of the palace. He slept there as all the king's officers did.

[10]The officers told David, "Uriah did not go home."

Then David said to Uriah, "You came from a long trip. Why didn't you go home?"

[11]Uriah said to him, "The Holy Box[d] and the soldiers of Israel and Judah are staying in tents. My master Joab and his officers are camping out in the fields. It

LIVIN' IT!

BE CAREFUL, LITTLE EYES . . .
2 SAMUEL 11:1-27

He was known as a man after God's own heart. He wrote songs of praise and had loved God from his youth. So what happened to make David commit some of the worst sins possible?

At the time, David was not where he was supposed to be. He should have been at war, but instead he was wandering around his palace. Then he was looking at what he shouldn't have seen—the wife of another man. Then he caved. He took what didn't belong to him, and tried to cover it up by having her husband killed.

David wasn't any different from us. Even the most devoted Christian will fall into sin if we don't carefully watch over what we let our minds think and our eyes see. God warns us that Satan is always looking for a way to trick and destroy us, and the sin in our own hearts makes it all the more easy to fall prey. Ask God to protect you from sin and to help you make wise choices that will lead you away from temptation.

11:2 roof In Bible times houses were built with flat roofs. The roof was used for drying things such as flax and fruit. And it was used as an extra room, as a place for worship and as a place to sleep in the summer.

CRAFTS

BUBBLE BATH

INGREDIENTS

1/4 C. shampoo

1/2 C. water

ALL ABOUT IT:

David saw a beautiful woman taking a bath, then he sinned. This story is a great example of the difference between temptation and sin. When David *saw* Bathsheba, he was tempted. When he *sent* for her, he sinned.

When our parents discipline us they are teaching us to avoid turning a temptation into the act of sinning against God. Make this bubble bath for your mom and yourself. While enjoying your bubble bath, thank God that he washes away our sins when we ask him for forgiveness.

Give your mom her bubble-bath gift, and thank her for disciplining you and teaching you how to avoid sinning when tempted.

BUBBLE BATH INSTRUCTIONS

1. Mix the shampoo and water in a plastic bowl.

2. As you start to run the water for your bath, pour the bubble-bath mixture into the running water.

3. Enjoy your long bubble bath!

3-D

isn't right for me to go home to eat and drink and have sexual relations with my wife!"

[12]David said to Uriah, "Stay here today. Tomorrow I'll send you back to the battle." So Uriah stayed in Jerusalem that day and the next. [13]Then David called Uriah to come to see him. Uriah ate and drank with David. David made Uriah drunk, but he still did not go home. That evening Uriah went to sleep with the king's officers outside the king's door.

[14]The next morning David wrote a letter to Joab and sent it by Uriah. [15]In the letter David wrote, "Put Uriah on the front lines where the fighting is worst.

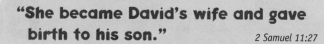

> "She became David's wife and gave birth to his son."
>
> 2 Samuel 11:27

Then leave him there alone. Let him be killed in battle."

[16]Joab watched the city and saw where its strongest defenders were. He put Uriah there. [17]The men of the city came out to fight against Joab. Some of David's men were killed. And Uriah the Hittite was one of them.

[18]Then Joab sent a report to David about everything that had happened in the war. [19]Joab told the messenger, "Tell King David what happened in

the war. [20]After you finish, the king may become angry. He may ask you, 'Why did you go so near the city to fight? Didn't you know they would shoot arrows from the city wall? [21]Do you remember who killed Abimelech son of Jerub-Besheth?" It was a woman on the city wall. She threw a large stone for grinding grain on Abimelech. She killed him there in Thebez. Why did you go so near the wall?' If King David asks that, you must answer, 'Your servant Uriah the Hittite also died.'"

[22]The messenger went in and told David everything Joab had told him to say. [23]The messenger told David, "The men of Ammon were winning. They came out and attacked us in the field. But we fought them back to the city gate. [24]The men on the city wall shot arrows at your servants. Some of your men were killed. Your servant

GET CONNECTED

RELATIONSHIPS WITH FRIENDS

Tough Love They had been friends. Both loved the Lord. So it couldn't have been easy for Nathan to confront David about his sin, but he did. He presented the truth in a creative way that would help David see the seriousness of his sin. And Nathan's words were well received by David.

God wants us to speak honestly with one another, as well. If a friend talks to you about a sin in your life, don't be mean to them. Don't even try to defend yourself. Just listen, and then ask God to show you if what they are saying is true, so that you can repent. Likewise, if God asks you to confront a friend about their sin, make sure that you do it in humility and love—knowing that you are capable of doing the same kind of wrong. Pray that you will keep your friendship and help your friend to avoid the dangers of sin.

11:21 Jerub-Besheth Another name for Gideon.

LIVIN' IT!

FORGIVEN
2 SAMUEL 12:1-25

David was crushed. Nathan the prophet had exposed David's darkest sin, and the light of truth shined on his heart. He had wronged God in the worst possible way. He had hurt the relationship that he treasured most deeply. So what would he do?

He did the only thing he could do—and what we all should do when we fall on our face—he repented and asked God for forgiveness. So God wiped his slate clean.

David did have to experience the consequences of his sin. His first child with Bathsheba died. But his relationship with God was restored, and he was still known for being a man after God's heart.

When you realize you're in sin, don't try to hide. Don't pretend that it will go away. Instead, go straight to God and ask for forgiveness. You will find a forgiving father and a strengthened friendship with him every time.

Uriah the Hittite also died."

²⁵David said to the messenger, "Say this to Joab: 'Don't be upset about this. The sword kills everyone the same. Make a stronger attack against the city and capture it.' Encourage Joab with these words."

²⁶When Bathsheba heard that her husband was dead, she cried for him. ²⁷After she finished her time of sadness, David sent servants to bring her to his house. She became David's wife and gave birth to his son. But the Lord did not like what David had done.

DAVID'S SON DIES

12 The Lord sent Nathan to David. When Nathan came to David, Nathan said, "There were two men in a city. One man was rich, but the other was poor. ²The rich man had very many sheep and cattle. ³But the poor man had nothing except one little female lamb he had bought. The poor man fed the lamb. It grew up with him and his children. It shared his food and drank from his cup. It slept in his arms. The lamb was like a daughter to him.

⁴"Then a traveler stopped to visit the rich man. The rich man wanted to give food to the traveler. But he didn't want to take one of his own sheep or cattle to feed the traveler. Instead, he took the lamb from the poor man. The rich man killed the lamb and cooked it for his visitor."

⁵David became very angry at the rich man. He said to Nathan, "As surely as the Lord lives, the man who did this should die! ⁶He must pay for the lamb four times for doing such a thing. He had no mercy!"

⁷Then Nathan said to David, "You are the man! This is what the Lord, the God of Israel, says: 'I appointed you king of Israel. I saved you from Saul. ⁸I gave you his

"As surely as the Lord lives, the man who did this should die!"

2 Samuel 12:5

241

David's Prayer

David sinned against God by taking another man's wife and having her husband killed. David eventually admitted his sin and asked God to forgive him. Use the secret vowel code below to complete David's prayer of confession from Psalm 51.

G_D, B_ M_RC_F_L T_ M_ B_C__S_ Y__ _R_ L_V_NG.

B_C__S_ Y__ _R_ _LW_YS R__DY T_ B_ M_RC_F_L,

W_P_ __T _LL MY WR_NGS. W_SH _W_Y _LL MY

G__LT _ND M_K_ M_ CL__N _G__N.   PSALM 51:1-2

Secret Vowel Code:

🍎 = A   🌼 = E

💕 = I   🔔 = O   ☘ = U

3-D *Wear your 3-D glasses as you write the answers.*

MOONTHLY CALENDAR

Do you have a hard time keeping track of what day it is? Be glad, then, that you're not a Jewish kid living in Bible times. The Jewish calendar is different from the kind used by most westerners (called a Gregorian calendar). Instead, the Jewish calendar is lunar (based on the moon) and is determined by the beginning of the new moon. In ancient times, this meant that people had to watch the moon to determine the months. When the first sliver of moon appeared after a dark moon, two eyewitnesses would run to the Sanhedrin (the Jewish leaders) and tell them. Then they would declare a new month.

Because the Jewish calendar is based on the moon, the dates of holidays do not change as they do with the Gregorian calendar. The problem with lunar calendars is that they do not match up with solar years (the time of the earth's orbit around the sun). So in the fourth century, a man named Hillel devised a new calendar based on math and astronomy, which added a couple of months to the Jewish calendar to make up the difference. Some Jews today still follow Hillel's model.

[Jewfaq.org]

2 SAMUEL 12:9-17

kingdom and his wives. And I made you king of Israel and Judah. And if that had not been enough, I would have given you even more. ⁹So why did you ignore the Lord's command? Why did you do what he says is wrong? You killed Uriah the Hittite with the sword of the Am-monites! And you took his wife to become your wife! ¹⁰So there will always be people in your family who will be killed by a sword. This is because you showed that you did not respect me! And you took the wife of Uriah the Hittite!'

¹¹"This is what the Lord says: 'I am bringing trouble to you from your own family. While you watch, I will take your wives from you. And I will give them to someone who is very close to you. He will have sexual relations with your wives, and everyone will know it. ¹²You had sexual relations with Bathsheba in secret. But I will do this so all the people of Israel can see it.'"

¹³Then David said to Nathan, "I have sinned against the Lord."

Nathan answered, "The Lord has taken away your sin. You will not die. ¹⁴But what you did caused the Lord's enemies to lose all respect for him. For this reason the son who was born to you will die."

¹⁵Then Nathan went home. And the Lord caused the son of David and Bathsheba, Uriah's widow, to become very sick. ¹⁶David prayed to God for the baby. David refused to eat or drink. He went into his house and stayed there. He lay on the ground all night. ¹⁷The elders of David's family came to him. They tried to pull him up from the ground. But he refused

"So why did you ignore the Lord's command? Why did you do what he says is wrong?"

2 Samuel 12:9

243

2 SAMUEL 12:18-25

GET CONNECTED

to get up. And he refused to eat food with them.

[18]On the seventh day the baby died. David's servants were afraid to tell him that the baby was dead. They said, "Look, we tried to talk to David while the baby was alive. But he refused to listen to us. If we tell him the baby is dead, he may harm himself."

[19]But David saw his servants whispering. Then he understood that the baby was dead. So he asked them, "Is the baby dead?"

They answered, "Yes, he is dead."

[20]Then David got up from the floor. He washed himself, put lotions on himself and changed his clothes. Then he went into the Lord's house to worship. After that, he went home and asked for something to eat. His servants gave him some food, and he ate.

[21]David's servants said to him, "Why are you doing this? When the baby was still alive, you refused to eat. You cried. But when the baby died, you got up and ate food."

[22]David said, "While the baby was still alive, I refused to eat, and I cried. I thought, 'Who knows? Maybe the Lord will feel sorry for me and let the baby live.' [23]But now the baby is dead. So why should I go without food? I can't bring him back to life. Some day I will go to him. But he cannot come back to me."

[24]Then David comforted Bathsheba his wife. He slept with her and had sexual relations with her. She became pregnant again and had another son. David named the boy Solomon. The Lord loved Solomon. [25]The Lord sent word through Nathan the prophet[d] to name the baby Jedidiah.[n] This was because the Lord loved the child.

> "The Lord has taken away your sin. You will not die."
>
> *2 Samuel 12:13*

 12:25 **Jedidiah** This name means "loved by the Lord."

244

Though he loved God, David made some major mistakes.

UNSCRAMBLE THE WORDS

that tell the story of sin and forgiveness.

1 _ _ _ _ _ _
PLAAEC

2 _ _ _ _ _ _ _ _ _ _ _
FEWI FO UHIRA

3 _ _ _ _ _ _ _
TTIHETI

4 _ _ _
RWA

5 _ _ _ _
BJOA

6 _ _ _ _ _ _
NTHNAA

7 _ _ _ _
LMAB

8 _ _ _ _ _ _
KLLEID

9 _ _ _ _ _ _ _ _ _
SHEBHTBAA

10 _ _ _ _ _ _ _ _
NOMOSLO

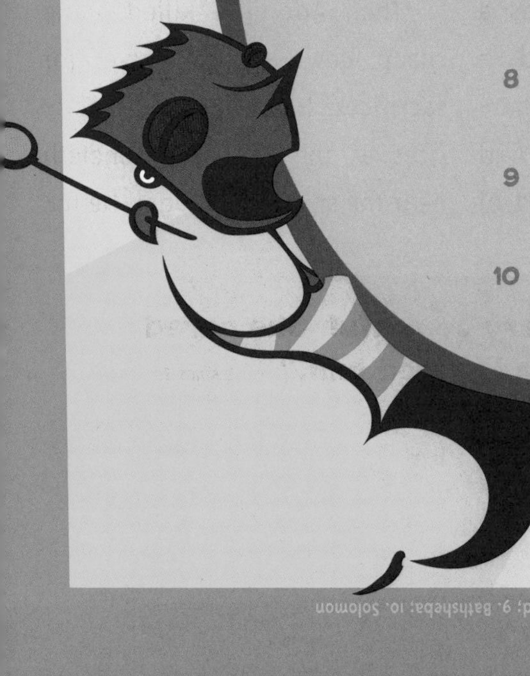

Answers: 1. palace; 2. wife of Uriah; 3. Hittite; 4. war; 5. Joab; 6. Nathan; 7. lamb; 8. killed; 9. Bathsheba; 10. Solomon

STORIES FROM 1 KINGS

Solomon Becomes King
1 KINGS 1:1—2:4

ADONIJAH TRIES TO BECOME KING

1 At this time King David was very old. His servants covered him with blankets, but he could not keep warm. ²So they said to him, "We will find a young woman to care for you. She will lie close to you and keep you warm." ³So the king's servants looked everywhere in Israel for a beautiful young woman. They found a girl named Abishag from the Shunammite people. They brought her to the king. ⁴The girl was very beautiful. She cared for the king and served him. But King David did not have sexual relations with her.

⁵⁻⁶Adonijah was King David and Haggith's son. He was born next after Absalom. He was a very handsome man. He said, "I will be the king." So he got chariots and horses for himself. And he got 50 men to run ahead of him. Now David had never interfered with him by questioning what he did.

⁷Adonijah talked with Joab son of Zeruiah. He also talked with Abiathar the priest. They told him they would help him. ⁸But several men did not join Adonijah. These men were Zadok the priest, Benaiah son of Jehoiada, Nathan the prophet,[d] Shimei, Rei and King David's special guard.

⁹Then Adonijah killed some sheep, cows and fat calves for sacrifices. He made these sacrifices at the Stone of Zoheleth near the spring, En Rogel. He in-

> "The girl was very beautiful. She cared for the king and served him." *1 Kings 1:4*

BiBLe Basics

WHat is an Heir?

No, it's not what grows on your head. An heir is a person who receives the belongings of someone else—usually a relative—after they die. While the Old Testament gives a lot of examples of wealth being passed down to children, the New Testament explains how we as God's children are coheirs with Christ. Because God has adopted us into his family, we will all share in the goodness and blessing God gives to Jesus.

vited all his brothers, the other sons of King David, to come. He invited all the rulers and leaders of Judah also. ¹⁰But Adonijah did not invite Nathan the prophet, Benaiah, his father's special guard or his brother Solomon.

¹¹When Nathan heard about this, he went to Bathsheba. She was the mother of Solomon. Nathan asked her, "Have you heard what Adonijah, Haggith's son, is doing? He has made himself king. And our real king, David, does not know it. ¹²Your life and the life of your son Solomon may be in danger. But I will tell you how to save yourselves. ¹³Go to King David and say to him, 'My master and king, you made a promise to me. You promised that my son Solomon would be the king after you. You said he would rule on your throne. So why has Adonijah become king?' ¹⁴While you are still talking to him, I will come in. I will tell the king that what you have said about Adonijah is true."

¹⁵So Bathsheba went in to see the king in his bedroom. He was now very old. Abishag, the girl from Shunam, was caring for him there. ¹⁶Bathsheba bowed down before the king.

He asked, "What do you want?"

¹⁷She answered, "My master, you made a promise to me in the name of the Lord your God. You said, 'Your son Solomon will become king after me. He will rule on my throne.' ¹⁸But now Adonijah has become king. And you did not know it. ¹⁹Adonijah has killed many cows, fat calves and sheep for sacrifices. And he has invited all your sons. He also has invited Abiathar the priest and Joab the commander of your

1 Kings 2:1-4
TAKE A DEEP BREATH

WILD WORLD FACTS

What are you doing right now (other than reading this article)? You probably didn't even notice it—but you're breathing! Why? Because you have to have oxygen to live. How? God designed your body in a very special way that allows you to breathe in the air, extract the oxygen, and carry it to all the cells in your body which need it to live.

Basically, your diaphragm is a muscle below your lungs that pulls down, creating a space in your chest for your lungs to expand (get bigger). As the lungs get bigger, air flows into them. When the diaphragm relaxes, the space gets smaller, and the lungs get pressed down, forcing the remaining air out of them. In the short time in between movement, your body is hard at work breaking down the air, channeling it to your blood, and sending it to your body. God says that every single breath we breathe comes from him. Every single moment of our lives—whether we realize it or not—is in God's hands.

[Yahooligans: Ask Earl]

army. But he did not invite Solomon, your son who serves you. ²⁰My master and king, all the people of Israel are watching you. They are waiting for you to decide who will be king after you. ²¹As soon as you die, Solomon and I will be treated as criminals."

²²While Bathsheba was still talking with the king, Nathan the prophet arrived. ²³The servants told the king, "Nathan the prophet is here." So Nathan went to the king and bowed facedown on the ground before him.

²⁴Then Nathan said, "My master and king, have you said that Adonijah will be the king after you? Have you decided he will rule on your throne after you? ²⁵Today he has sacrificed many cows, fat calves and sheep. And he has invited all your other sons, the commanders of the army and Abiathar the priest. Right now they are eating and drinking with him. They are saying, 'Long live King Adonijah!' ²⁶But he did not invite me, Zadok the priest, Benaiah son of Jehoiada or your son Solomon. ²⁷Did you do this? We are your servants. Why didn't you tell us whom you chose to be the king after you?"

DAVID MAKES SOLOMON KING

²⁸Then King David said, "Tell Bathsheba to come in!" So she came in and stood before the king.

²⁹Then the king said, "The Lord has saved me from all trouble. As surely as he lives, I make this promise to you. ³⁰Today I will do what I promised you in the past. I made that promise in the name of the Lord, the God of Israel. I promised that your son Solomon would be king after me. I promised he would rule on my throne after me."

³¹Then Bathsheba bowed facedown on the ground before the king. She said, "Long live my master King David!"

³²Then King David said, "Tell Zadok the priest, Nathan the prophet[d] and Benaiah son of Jehoiada to come in here." So they came before the king. ³³Then the king said to them, "Take my servants with you and put my son Solomon on my own mule. Take him down to the spring called Gihon. ³⁴There Zadok the priest and Nathan the prophet should pour olive oil on him and make him king over Israel. Blow the trumpet and shout, 'Long live King Solomon!' ³⁵Then come back here with him. He will sit on my

"The king said, 'The Lord has saved me from all trouble.'"

1 Kings 1:29

History Highlights

↗ 973 B.C.
Solomon and David Reign

7000 5000 3000 1000 0 1000 NOW

BiBLe CRiTTeRS

3-D

DEER ME

The Bible talks about deer, specifically **GAZELLES,** as a source for food, as well as a picture for how God helps his people rise above the worries of this world. Gazelles are beautiful creatures that can live well in the rocky and dry climate of the Middle East. Dorcas Gazelles are the smallest of the breed, but they also have the longest limbs that help them spring into the air. Kind of like us, they like to hang out in small groups, though when all the groups are together they can equal to more than 100 gazelles. Both males and females have horns, and they're mainly active around dusk and dawn.

10 TOP TEN

Ways to Spend Your Money

1. Tithe.

2. Give it to a mercy ministry.

3. Put it into a savings account.

4. Buy a gift for your mom.

5. Buy lunch for a friend.

6. Play Laser Tag.

7. Buy a Christian CD.

8. Go to the movies with friends.

9. Go bowling.

10. Buy some new clothes.

³⁸So Zadok the priest, Nathan the prophet and Benaiah son of Jehoiada went down. The Kerethites and Pelethites, the king's bodyguards, went with them. They put Solomon on King David's mule and went with him to the spring called Gihon. ³⁹Zadok the priest took with him the container of olive oil from the Holy Tent.ᵈ He poured the olive oil on Solomon's head to show he was the king. Then they blew the trumpet. And all the people shouted, "Long live King Solomon!" ⁴⁰All the people followed Solomon into the city. They were playing flutes and shouting for joy. They made so much noise the ground shook.

Jonathan son of Abiathar the priest arrived. Adonijah said, "Come in! You are an important man. So you must be bringing good news."

⁴³But Jonathan answered, "No! Our master King David has made Solomon the new king. ⁴⁴King David sent Zadok the priest, Nathan the prophet, Benaiah son of Jehoiada and all the king's bodyguards with him. They put Solomon on the king's own mule. ⁴⁵And Zadok the priest and Nathan the prophet poured olive oil on Solomon at Gihon to make him king. Then they went into the city, shouting with joy. Now the whole city is excited. That is the noise you hear. ⁴⁶Solomon has now become the king. ⁴⁷All the king's officers have come to tell King David that he has done

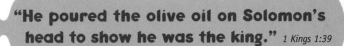

> **"He poured the olive oil on Solomon's head to show he was the king."** *1 Kings 1:39*

throne and rule in my place. I have chosen him to be the ruler over Israel and Judah."

³⁶Benaiah son of Jehoiada answered the king, "This is good! And may your God make it happen. ³⁷The Lord has always helped you, our king. Let the Lord also help Solomon. And let King Solomon be an even greater king than you."

⁴¹At this time Adonijah and all the guests with him were finishing their meal. They heard the sound from the trumpet. Joab asked, "What does all that noise from the city mean?"

⁴²While Joab was speaking,

a good thing. They are saying, 'May your God make Solomon even more famous than you. And may your God make Solomon an even greater king than you.'" Jonathan continued, "And King David bowed down on his bed to

iT'S THE DoGGoNE TRUTH. Dogs really are man's best friend, and they have been since the very beginning. Dogs were actually the first tamed animals to provide companionship for humans. However, in ancient times, they were often thought of in the same way pigs were. Both were scavengers and ran wild, if they were not controlled. Dogs actually held part in ancient religious ceremonies as a way to get rid of sin and disease. People believed they could get rid of their sicknesses by placing them on the animals.

worship God. ⁴⁸He said, 'Praise the Lord, the God of Israel. Today he has made one of my sons the king and allowed me to see it.'"

⁴⁹Then all of Adonijah's guests were afraid, and they left quickly. ⁵⁰Adonijah was also afraid of Solomon. So he went and took hold of the corners of the altar.ⁿ ⁵¹Then someone told Solomon, "Adonijah is afraid of you. He is at the altar, holding on to its corners. He says, 'Tell King Solomon to promise me today that he will not kill me.'"

⁵²So Solomon answered, "Adonijah must show that he is a man of honor. If he does, I promise that he will not lose even a hair from his head. But if he does anything wrong, he will die." ⁵³Then King Solomon sent some men to get Adonijah. They brought him to King Solomon. So Adonijah came before King Solomon and bowed down. Then Solomon said, "Go home."

THE DEATH OF DAVID

2 It was almost time for David to die. So he talked to Solomon and gave him his last commands. ²David said, "My time to die is near. Be a good and strong leader. ³Obey everything that the Lord commands. Follow the commands he has given us. Obey all his laws, and do what he told us. Obey what is written in the teachings of Moses. If you do these things, you will be successful in all you do and wherever you go. ⁴And if you obey the Lord, he will keep the promise he made to me. He promised: 'Your descendantsᵈ must live as I tell them. They must have complete faith in me. If they do this, then a man from your family will always be king over the people of Israel.'

1:50 corners of the altar If a person were innocent of a crime, he could run into the Holy Place. If he held on to the corners of the altar there, he would not be punished. The corners looked like horns.

Solomon's Wisdom and Kingdom

1 KINGS 3:4-15; 4:20-34

SOLOMON ASKS FOR WISDOM

3 King Solomon went to Gibeon to offer a sacrifice. He went there because it was the most important place of worship. He offered 1,000 burnt offerings on that altar. 5While he was at Gibeon, the Lord came to him in a dream during the night. God said, "Ask for anything you want. I will give it to you."

6Solomon answered, "You were very kind to your servant, my father David. He obeyed you. He was honest and lived right. And you showed great kindness to him when you allowed his son to be king after him. 7Lord my God, you have allowed me to be king in my father's place. But I am like a little child. I do not have the wisdom I

ask that you give me wisdom. Then I can rule the people in the right way. Then I will know the difference between right and wrong. Without wisdom, it is impossible to rule this great people of yours."

10The Lord was pleased that Solomon had asked him for this. 11So God said to him, "You did not ask for a long life. And you did not ask for riches for yourself. You did not ask for the death of your enemies. Since you asked for wisdom to make the right decisions, 12I will give you what you asked. I will give you wisdom and understanding.

> **"So i ask that you give me wisdom. Then i can rule the people in the right way."** *1 Kings 3:8*

need to do what I must do. 8I, your servant, am here among your chosen people. There are too many of them to count. 9So I

Your wisdom will be greater than anyone has had in the past. And there

will never be anyone in the future like you. 13Also, I will give you what you did not ask for. You will have riches and honor. During your life no other king will be as great as you. 14I ask you to follow me and obey my laws and commands. Do this as your father David did. If you do, I will also give you a long life."

LIVIN' IT!

THE REAL GENIE
1 KINGS 3:4-15

Have you ever seen Aladdin? In the story, a young Arab boy discovers a bottle. When he rubs it, a genie pops out and promises to grant whatever the boy wishes. What would you wish?

In a way, Solomon actually had a similar experience. In a dream, God offered to grant whatever wish he had. But instead of asking for fame or money, Solomon wanted wisdom. God was more than happy to answer, making Solomon the wisest man in the world.

Do you want to be wise like Solomon? We don't have to wait for a genie to pop out of a bottle. God promises to give us wisdom whenever we ask him for it. Remember that God values wisdom because it helps us know him better. As you go through your day, remember to turn to God and ask him for wisdom to walk in his ways.

Bible Critters

HUNGRY, HUNGRY HOPPERS

Did you know that **LOCUST** plagues are not just a part of the past? There are actually control centers monitoring the situation now, particularly in the northern parts of Africa. For thousands of years, locusts have been known as highly destructive pests. A type of grasshopper, locusts travel together in groups called swarms that can devour all the vegetation in sight. Desert locust swarms have been known to spread out over an area of 29 million square kilometers, extending into 60 different countries (more than 20% of the earth's total land surface). During these times, locusts have the potential to damage the livelihood of more than a tenth of the world's population.

For more info on this small but devastating creature, go online and check out the Desert Locust Information Service of the Migratory Pests Group.

3-D

[15] Then Solomon woke up. He knew that God had talked to him in the dream. Then he went to Jerusalem and stood before the Box[d] of the Agreement with the Lord. There he gave burnt offerings and fellowship offerings to the Lord. After that, he gave a feast for all of his leaders and officers.

• • •

SOLOMON'S KINGDOM

4 There were many people in Judah and Israel. There were as many people as there were grains of sand on the seashore. The people ate, drank and were happy. [21] Solomon ruled over all the kingdoms from the Euphrates River to the land of the Philistine people. His kingdom went as far as the border of Egypt. These countries brought Solomon the payments he demanded. And they obeyed him all his life.

[22] Solomon needed much food each day to feed himself and all the people who ate at his table. It took 185 bushels of fine flour and 375 bushels of meal. [23] It also took 10 cows that were fed good grain, 20 cows that were raised in the fields and 100 sheep. And it took 3 different kinds of deer and fat birds.

[24] Solomon ruled over all the countries west of the Euphrates River. This was the land from Tiphsah to Gaza. And Solomon had peace on all sides of his kingdom. [25] During Solomon's life Judah and Israel, from Dan to Beersheba,[n] lived in peace. Each man was able to sit under his own fig trees and grapevines.

[26] Solomon had 4,000 stalls for his chariot horses. And he had 12,000 chariot soldiers. [27] Each month one of the district governors gave King Solomon all the food he needed. This was

> **"Solomon ruled over all the countries west of the Euphrates River....And Solomon had peace on all sides of his kingdom."**
>
> 1 Kings 4:24

 4:25 **Dan to Beersheba** Dan was the city farthest north in Israel. Beersheba was the city farthest south. So this means all the people of Israel.

CRAFTS

SOLOMON'S WISDOM

SUPPLIES

sand
squirt bottle with water
sand toys

SAND CASTLE INSTRUCTIONS

Fill a sandbox or a plastic tub with sand, and have fun building sand castles. Can you count the grains of sand that you are playing with? Of course not, but God can! Think about how big God is and how special you are to him.

ALL ABOUT IT:

Sometimes God uses sand to describe things that are so big in number we cannot understand them. Solomon's "wisdom was as hard to measure as the sand on the seashore" (1 Kings 4:29). "There were as many people as there were grains of sand on the seashore" (1 Kings 4:20) in Solomon's kingdom.

Yet the God of the universe knows your name, how you feel, and what you desire. How cool is that!

3-D

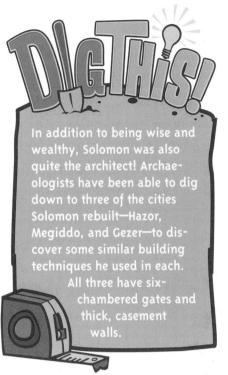

DIG THIS!

In addition to being wise and wealthy, Solomon was also quite the architect! Archaeologists have been able to dig down to three of the cities Solomon rebuilt—Hazor, Megiddo, and Gezer—to discover some similar building techniques he used in each. All three have six-chambered gates and thick, casement walls.

enough for every person who ate at the king's table. The governors made sure he had everything he needed. ²⁸They also gave the king enough barley and straw for the chariot and work horses. Each person brought this grain to the required places.

SOLOMON'S WISDOM

²⁹God gave great wisdom to Solomon. Solomon could understand many things. His wisdom was as hard to measure as the sand on the seashore. ³⁰His wisdom was greater than the wisdom of all the men in the East. And his wisdom was greater than all the wisdom of the men in Egypt. ³¹He was wiser than any other man on earth. He was even wiser than Ethan the Ezrahite. He was wiser than Heman, Calcol and Darda. They were the sons of Mahol. King Solomon became famous in all the countries around Israel and Judah. ³²During his life King Solomon spoke 3,000 wise teachings. He also knew 1,005 songs. ³³He taught about many different kinds of plants. He taught about everything from the great cedar trees of Lebanon to the hyssop that grows out of the walls. He also taught about animals, birds, crawling things and fish. ³⁴People from all nations came to listen to King Solomon's wisdom. The kings of all nations sent them to listen to him. These kings had heard of Solomon's wisdom.

TOP TEN

Ways to Make Mondays Special

1. Commit it to God in prayer.
2. Think good thoughts about it.
3. Talk to a new person on purpose.
4. Learn a new vocabulary word.
5. Memorize a new verse.
6. Spend Monday afternoons hanging out with mom.
7. Make a fun dessert.
8. Plan the rest of your week.
9. Watch football with your dad.
10. Get ahead in your homework.

Solomon Builds the Temple

1 KINGS
5:1-12;
6:1, 11-14

SOLOMON PREPARES TO BUILD THE TEMPLE

5 Now King Hiram was the king of Tyre. He had always been a friend of David. Hiram heard that Solomon had been made king in David's place. So he sent his messengers to Solomon. ²Then Solomon sent this message back to King Hiram: ³"You remember that my father David had to fight many wars with the countries around him. So he was never able to build a temple for worship to the Lord his God. David was waiting until the Lord allowed him to defeat all his enemies. ⁴But now the Lord my God has given me peace. There is peace on all sides of my country. I have no enemies now. My people are in no danger.

⁵"The Lord made a promise to my father David. The Lord said, 'I will make your son king after you. And he will build a temple for worship to me.' Now, I plan to build that temple for worship to the Lord my God. ⁶And so I ask for your help. Send your men to cut down cedar trees for me from Lebanon. My servants will work with yours. I will pay your servants whatever wages you decide. We don't have anyone who can cut down trees as well as the people of Sidon can."

⁷When Hiram heard what Solomon asked, he was very happy. He said, "I thank the Lord today! He has given David a wise son to rule over this great nation!" ⁸Then

BIBLE BASICS

WHAT IS A TITHE?

The word *tithe* actually means "tenth." God commanded his people to give a tithe, or a tenth, of whatever they earned (whether money or possessions) back to God. This money was used to keep the Temple services working, as well as to help the needy. In addition to tithes, people were also able to bring offerings—special gifts that they wanted to give to show their thankfulness to God. The New Testament tells us that Christians need to continue to give offerings as God has prospered and blessed us to continue the work God is doing in the world.

BLAST FROM THE PAST

CHERUBS OF ANCIENT TIMES were not the cute little babies with wings we find on stationery or art today. Ancient Middle-Eastern art show cherubs as part human and part animal creatures with large wings. They're the same kind of creatures mentioned in 1 Kings 6 that Solomon used to decorate the Temple.

SOLOMON BUILDS THE TEMPLE

CRAFTS

SUPPLIES

Legos®
friends
masking tape

ruler with
centimeter
markings

ALL ABOUT IT:

God gave Solomon instructions to build a Temple "90 feet long . . . 30 feet wide . . . 45 feet high" (1 Kings 6:2). It is hard for us to imagine how big the Temple was. Remember Solomon didn't have CAT machines to move the stones and wood he needed to make God's Temple!

Invite your friends to come over for a temple-making party. Ask them to bring their Legos® building blocks. Before time for the party, measure and tape off a 90 centimeter by 30 centimeter rectangle on the floor. That will be where you start your walls. When the walls are 45 centimeters high, your Temple will be complete.

If you and your friends have the time, make the inside rooms of your temple! When you're done, take a picture of the temple and the builders who made it!

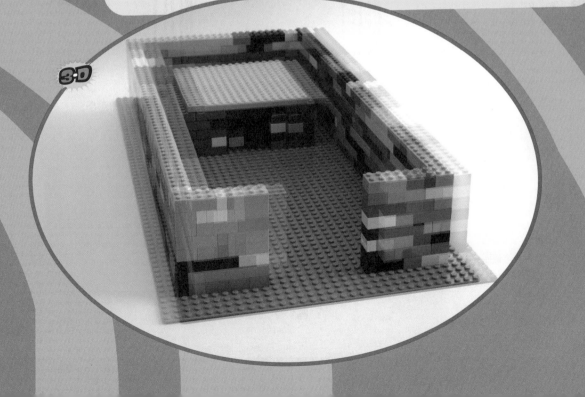

CONNECT THE D•TS

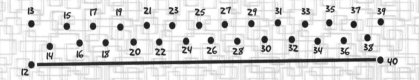

God had kept his promise to David.
Now Solomon rejoiced to keep his father's
promise to God. Connect the dots and write in
the verse that reveals God's special work built
in and through his servant Solomon.

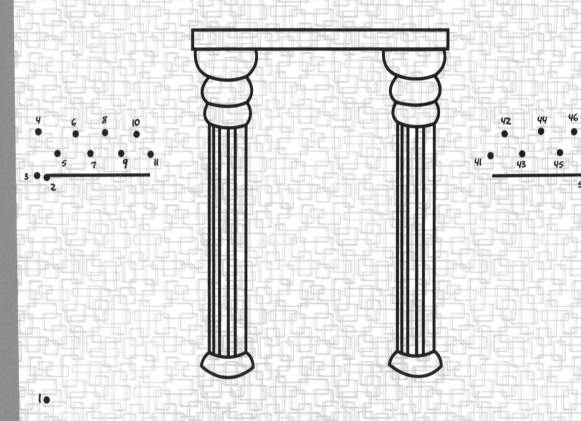

_____

_____

_____

1 KINGS 5:5

3·D

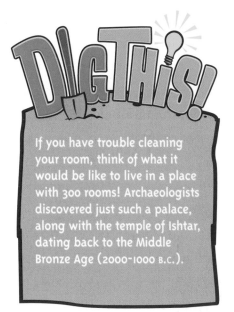

Hiram sent back this message to Solomon: "I received the message you sent. I will give you all the cedar and pine trees you want. ⁹My servants will bring them down from Lebanon to the sea. There I will tie them together. Then I will float them down the shore to the place you choose. There I will separate the logs, and you can take them away. In return you will give food to all those who live with me." ¹⁰So Hiram gave Solomon as much cedar and pine as he wanted. ¹¹And Solomon gave Hiram about 125,000 bushels of wheat each year. It was to feed all those who lived with Hiram. And Solomon gave him about 115,000 gallons of pure olive oil every year.

¹²The Lord gave wisdom to Solomon as he had promised. And there was peace between Hiram and Solomon. These two kings made a treaty between themselves.

• • •

SOLOMON BUILDS THE TEMPLE

6 So Solomon began to build the Temple.ᵈ This was 480 years after the people of Israel had left Egypt. (This was the fourth year of King Solomon's rule over Israel.) It was the second month, the month of Ziv.

• • •

¹¹The Lord spoke his word to Solomon: ¹²"Obey all my laws and commands. If you do, I will do for you what I promised your father David. ¹³And I will live among the children of Israel in this Temple you are building. I will never leave the people of Israel."

¹⁴So Solomon finished building the Temple.

1 Kings 6:1-14
IT MAKES SCENTS

WILD WORLD FACTS

Incense was an important part of the worship offered in the tabernacle that God had Israel build. But Israel was not alone in the use of incense. Many religions used it with the hope that its pleasing scent would keep their gods happy. In fact, it is still widely used today in a large number of religious ceremonies.

Incense is simply a preparation of plant parts which are ground into a powder. Essential oils taken from various plants and/or animals are added to make the mixture smell even better. Incense can be thrown in powder form onto a fire to be burned, or it can be shaped into a stick or cone that can be slowly burned. The fire releases the chemicals in the powder that produce a powerfully fragrant smell.

God says that our prayers are like incense to him. When we call out to him in need and depend on him for help, we become a fragrant aroma to him.

[Thefreedictionary.com]

The Queen of Sheba and Solomon's Wealth

1 KINGS 10:1—11:6

BLAST FROM THE PAST

FASHION IS NOTHING NEW. In fact, from the beginning, clothes have been a way for people around the world to show how important someone was or what kind of occupation they had. Prophets in biblical days stood out not only because of their message, but also because of their clothes. Unlike the society around them, prophets wore very simple garments with leather belts to show that they were concerned about God's kingdom, not earthly wealth.

THE QUEEN OF SHEBA VISITS SOLOMON

10 Now the queen of Sheba heard about Solomon's fame. So she came to test him with hard questions. ²She traveled to Jerusalem with a very large group of servants. There were many camels carrying spices, jewels and much gold. She came to Solomon and talked with him about all that she had in mind. ³Solomon answered all her questions. Nothing was too hard for him to explain to her. ⁴The queen of Sheba learned that Solomon was very wise. She saw the palace he had built. ⁵She saw his many officers and the food on his table. She saw the palace servants and their good clothes. She was shown the servants who served him at feasts. And she was shown the whole burnt offerings he made in the Temple[d] of the Lord. All these things amazed her.

⁶So she said to King Solomon, "I heard in my own country about your achievements and wisdom. And all of it is true. ⁷I could not believe it then. But now I have come and seen it with my own eyes. I was not told even half of it! Your wisdom and wealth are much greater than I had heard. ⁸Your men and officers are very lucky! In always serving you, they are able to hear your wisdom! ⁹Praise the Lord your God! He was pleased to make you king of Israel. The Lord has constant love for Israel. So he made you king to keep justice and to rule fairly."

¹⁰Then the queen of Sheba gave the king

> **"Your wisdom and wealth are much greater than I had heard."** 1 Kings 10:7

History Highlights

➤ **800 B.C.**
Earliest reference to hardening steel by quenching is given.

7000 5000 3000 1000 0 1000 NOW

AUGUST mercy

1

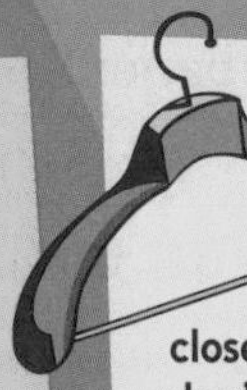

2 Go through your closet, and give what you don't use to charity.

3

4 Help your siblings gather their school supplies.

5 Prayer Pointer: Pray that God would awaken the church to meet the growing needs of others around them.

6

7 Call your grandparents, and ask them if they have any prayer requests.

8 Hide-It-in-Your-Heart: Evil people should stop being evil. They should stop thinking bad thoughts. They should return to the Lord, and he will have mercy on them. They should come to our God, because he will freely forgive them (Isaiah 55:7).

9

10

11 Vacuum the house for your mom.

12

13 Pick the person who is normally picked last to be first on your team.

14 Stroll your baby sister or brother around the block.

15 SUMMER WAS TAST-AY!

16 Make a list of all the things you want to do this school year, and tape it to your mirror.

17

18 Write a creative story about all your summer adventures, and tell it to your class.

19

20

21 Play outside until it gets dark.

22

23 Prayer Pointer: Pray for missionaries in third-world countries to meet the physical and spiritual needs of those around them.

24

25 See how many fireflies you can collect in a jar.

26 Write a missionary family to let them know you're praying for them.

27

28

29 Tell your neighborhood friends why you believe in Jesus, and invite them to do the same.

30

31 Hide-It-in-Your-Heart: I want faithful love more than I want animal sacrifices. I want people to know me more than I want burnt offerings (Hosea 6:6).

about 9,000 pounds of gold. She also gave him many spices and jewels. No one since that time has brought more spices into Israel than the queen of Sheba gave King Solomon.

> **"Every year King Solomon received about 50,000 pounds of gold."** *1 Kings 10:14*

¹¹(Hiram's ships brought gold from Ophir. They also brought from there very much juniper wood and jewels. ¹²Solomon used the juniper wood to build supports for the Temple of the Lord and the palace. He also used it to make harps and lyres[d] for the musicians. Such fine juniper wood has not been brought in or seen since that time.)

¹³King Solomon gave the queen of Sheba many gifts. He gave her gifts that a king would give to another ruler. Then he gave her whatever else she wanted and asked for. After this, she and her servants went back to her own country.

SOLOMON'S WEALTH

¹⁴Every year King Solomon received about 50,000 pounds of gold. ¹⁵Besides that he also received gold from the traders and merchants. And he received gold from the kings of Arabia and governors of the land.

¹⁶King Solomon made 200 large shields of hammered gold. Each shield contained about seven and one-half pounds of gold. ¹⁷He also made 300 smaller shields of hammered gold. They each contained about three and three-fourths pounds of gold. The king put them in the Palace of the Forest of Lebanon.

¹⁸Then King Solomon built a large throne of ivory. And he covered it with pure gold. ¹⁹There were six steps leading up to the throne. The back of the throne was round at the top. There were armrests on both sides of the chair. And beside each armrest was a statue of a lion. ²⁰Twelve lions stood on the six steps. There was one lion at each end of each step. Nothing like this had ever been made for any other kingdom. ²¹All of Solomon's

WILD WORLD FACTS

1 Kings 10:1-29

GO FOR THE GOLD

In ancient history, people didn't use paper bills or coins as money. Instead, they used gold and silver as items of value which could be traded for food or services. It's one of the reasons the Israelites loaded up on their way out of Egypt, leaving the Egyptians stripped of all their bulky, golden jewelry.

Even though we use currency today, gold is still a valuable commodity. In fact, a one-ounce gold nugget is worth $2,000 – $4,000 today! Lots of people in America actually enjoy mining for gold here in our own country as an adventurous sort of vacation. In addition to California, a streak of gold mines and potential gold sites lie stretching from Alabama to Washington, D.C. You can even purchase maps that will help lead you to the best potential sites to dig. And just in case you were wondering, the largest gold nugget ever uncovered weighed 45 pounds.

While it is fun to go on a treasure hunt, the Bible warns us to keep our eyes focused on heavenly treasures which, unlike gold, last forever.

[Goldmaps.com]

Ways to Surprise Your Friend

1. Write them a kind note.

2. Make them cookies with their initials on them.

3. Put your picture in their locker.

4. Invite their whole family over for dinner.

5. Ask them something you've never asked before.

6. Take time to play with their younger siblings.

7. Ask their parents a thoughtful question.

8. Get permission first, and roll their room.

9. Write a verse on a card, and slip it in their backpack.

10. Suggest a game that they like (but you don't).

the ships returned. They brought back gold, silver, ivory, apes and baboons.

²³So Solomon had more riches and wisdom than all the other kings on earth. ²⁴People everywhere wanted to see King Solomon. They wanted to hear the wisdom God had given him. ²⁵Every year everyone who came brought a gift. They brought things made of gold and silver, along with clothes, weapons, spices, horses and mules.

²⁶So Solomon had many chariots and horses. He had 1,400 chariots and 12,000 chariot soldiers. He kept some in special cities for the chariots. And he kept some with him in Jerusalem. ²⁷In Jerusalem silver was as common as stones while Solomon was king. Cedar trees were as common as the fig trees growing on the mountain slopes. ²⁸Solomon brought in horses from Egypt and Kue. His traders bought them in Kue and brought them to Israel. ²⁹A chariot from Egypt cost about 15 pounds of silver. And a horse cost about 3³/₄ pounds of silver.

drinking cups were made of gold. All of the dishes in the Palace of the Forest of Lebanon were pure gold. Nothing was made from silver. In Solomon's time people did not think silver was valuable.

²²King Solomon also had many trading ships at sea, along with Hiram's ships. Every three years

The traders also sold horses and chariots to the kings of the Hittites and the Arameans.

SOLOMON'S MANY WIVES

11 But King Solomon loved many women who were not from Israel. He loved the daughter of the king of Egypt. He also loved women of the Moabites, Ammonites, Edomites, Sidonians and Hittites. ²The Lord had told the Israelites, "You must not marry people of other nations. If you do, they will cause you to follow their gods." But Solomon fell in

> **"People everywhere wanted to see King Solomon. They wanted to hear the wisdom God had given him."**
>
> *1 Kings 10:24*

CRAFTS

SOLOMON'S WEALTH

SUPPLIES

aluminum foil

ALL ABOUT IT:

It was impossible to measure Solomon's wealth. Even with all the wealth he already had, people would still bring him more gifts of gold and silver when they visited him. The same is true for our king—God—today. He created and owns all that is in the world. Yet we still bring him our offerings on Sunday so that his will is done on earth through our churches.

If you had lived in Solomon's day, what gift would you have taken to the king? Using aluminum foil, create a gift for Solomon. You could make a crown, a ring, or a piece of furniture to be put in Solomon's Temple. Have fun, and make as many treasures as you wish!

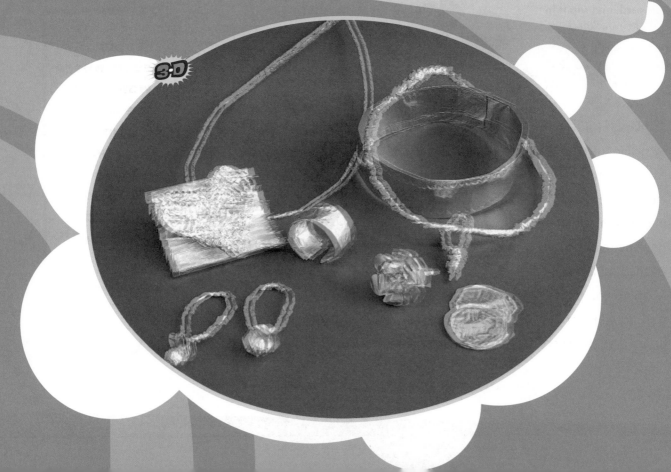

3-D

love with these women. ³He had 700 wives who were from royal families. He also had 300 slave women*d* who gave birth to his children. His wives caused him to turn away from God. ⁴As Solomon grew old, his wives caused him to follow other gods. He did not follow the Lord completely as his father David had done. ⁵Solomon worshiped Ashtoreth,*d* the goddess of the people of Sidon. And he worshiped Molech,*d* the hated god of the Ammonites. ⁶So Solomon did what the Lord said was wrong. He did not follow the Lord completely as his father David had done.

LIVIN' IT!

WEAKEST LINK
1 KINGS 11:1-4

Solomon was the wisest man in the world, but he had one big weakness—women. He liked women so much that he married hundreds, in fact. Many of his wives did not believe in God, and they worshiped idols. Even though Solomon loved God, his faith became weak because he spent so much time with others who hurt his belief in God.

We will never have to worry about marrying a hundred people. But we do need to watch very carefully who we allow to become our closest friends. God made us all in a way where we need each other to encourage us to stay strong in God's Word. When we forget to fellowship with other believers, we begin to listen to the lies of the world around us, and that can shake our faith. Who are your friends? If you need to find someone with a stronger faith to encourage you, talk to your parents. And ask God to help you find friends who will build you up.

2 KINGS

Elijah and the Whirlwind

2 KINGS 2:1-17

GET CONNECTED

RELATIONSHIPS WITH FRIENDS

The Mentor Mantle Elisha had watched carefully. Elijah had a particularly difficult task from God. Years were spent exposing sin and calling God's people to repent. Elisha had even witnessed incredible miracles that God performed through Elijah. When Elijah's work on earth was done, he was ready to pass his mantle—something like a cloak or a cape that symbolized God's call for him—on to Elisha. And Elisha was more than ready to take his place.

God gives us older, more experienced Christians in our lives to help shape and develop us, too. He instructs the older ones to teach and the younger ones to listen. Do you have a mentor—someone older than you who can help you grow closer to God? If not, talk to your parents about it, and ask God to give you your own "Elijah" so you can learn God's ways and grow to become a leader for others one day.

ELIJAH IS TAKEN TO HEAVEN

2 It was near the time for the Lord to take Elijah. He was going to take him by a whirlwind up into heaven. Elijah and Elisha were at Gilgal. ²Elijah said to Elisha, "Please stay here. The Lord has told me to go to Bethel."

But Elisha said, "As the Lord lives, and as you live, I won't leave you." So they went down to Bethel. ³A group of the prophets[d] at Bethel came to Elisha. They said to him, "Do you know the Lord will take your master away from you today?"

Elisha said, "Yes, I know. But don't talk about it."

DIG THIS!

Why would the men of Jericho bother Elisha about their spring? It was the main source of water and life for the entire region! Jericho has the lowest elevation of any city on earth (840 feet below sea level) and rarely gets rain in its dry climate. This spring—today called "Elisha's Spring"—still gushes 1,000 gallons of water per minute. Elisha healed the water, and the city was saved.

Bible Critters
THE BEAR FACTS

Even in Bible times, **BEARS** were a menace. Like lions, they were a known source of danger for travelers. Today there are more than eight different kinds of bears—American black bears, Asiatic black bears, brown bears (grizzlies), giant pandas, polar bears, sloth bears, spectacled bears, and sun bears. All bears are omnivorous, meaning they eat meat and plants—except for the polar bear that only eats meat (a carnivore). Because food is hard to find in the cold months, bears go into a kind of hibernation—a state where their body temperature drops, their breathing slows way down, and they don't have to eat or eliminate their food. But be careful! Bears aren't true hibernators, and they can be woken up in the winter, too.

3-D

[4] Elijah said to him, "Stay here, because the Lord has sent me to Jericho."

But Elisha said, "As the Lord lives, and as you live, I won't leave you."

So they went to Jericho. [5] A group of the prophets at Jericho came to Elisha. They said, "Do you know that the Lord will take your master away from you today?"

Elisha answered, "Yes, I know. But don't talk about it."

[6] Elijah said to Elisha, "Stay here. The Lord has sent me to the Jordan River."

Elisha answered, "As the Lord lives, and as you live, I won't leave you."

So the two of them went on. [7] Fifty men from a group of the prophets came. They stood far from where Elijah and Elisha were by the Jordan. [8] Elijah took off his coat. Then he rolled it up and hit the water. The water divided to the right and to the left. Then Elijah and Elisha crossed over on dry ground.

[9] After they had crossed over, Elijah said to Elisha, "What can I do for you before I am taken from you?"

Elisha said, "Leave me a double share of your spirit."[n]

[10] Elijah said, "You have asked

2:9 "Leave . . . spirit." By law, the first son in a family would inherit a double share of his father's possessions. Elisha is asking to inherit a share of his master's power. He is not asking for twice as much power as Elijah had.

REAL SUPER HEROES

ELIJAH

Israel had grown evil. They worshiped idols instead of God and sinned in many ways. But Elijah was different. He belonged to God and served as God's prophet to a people who didn't want to hear his message. To prove his God was real, he challenged the followers of Baal to a test. Their god failed, but Elijah's God showed up loud and clear. Then the Baal worshipers were killed.

God worked many other miracles through Elijah to help remind Israel who the true God really was. Elijah spent his entire life trying to help turn Israel back to the truth.

It's never easy when you choose to stand up for God's truth. Even if everyone else is doing the wrong thing, we need to be different. We must pray that God would turn their hearts to him and remain firm in the truth we know.

LIVIN' IT!

WHAT A RIDE!
2 KINGS 2:1-12

Elisha knew the time had come. All the prophets were saying it. God was about to take Elijah home. But Elisha was so sad he didn't want to talk about it.

Have you ever lost a loved one? We are almost never ready for the people we love to die, even if we know they are going to heaven. The loss just hurts our hearts, and God knows all about it. But the truth is, we all do have a time when our work on earth is done. We might not get picked up in a fiery chariot like Elijah was, but all those who belong to Jesus will just as certainly be taken directly from this life to be with Jesus.

It's okay to be sad when someone dies, but we should not lose hope. This life is only a breath—it wasn't meant to last long. That's why we spend the time we do have here living for the eternal life we get to have with God in heaven. Make the most of every moment you have here on earth so that you will be ready when the time comes to meet your Savior in heaven.

a hard thing. But if you see me when I am taken from you, it will be yours. If you don't, it won't happen."

"Elijah and Elisha were still walking and talking. Then a chariot and horses of fire appeared. The chariot and horses of fire separated Elijah from Elisha. Then Elijah went up to heaven in a whirlwind. ¹²Elisha saw it and shouted, "My father! My father! The chariots of Israel and their horsemen!" Elisha did not see him anymore. Elisha grabbed his own clothes and tore them to show how sad he was.

¹³He picked up Elijah's coat that had fallen from him. Then Elisha returned and stood on the bank of the Jordan. ¹⁴Elisha hit the

had." They came to meet him. And they bowed down to the ground before him. ¹⁶They said to him, "There are 50 strong men with us! Please let them go and look for your master. Maybe the Spirit^d of the Lord has taken Elijah up and set him down. He may be on some mountain or in some valley."

WILD WORLD FACTS

2 Kings 2:11-12
WILD WIND

It would have been wild enough to have just seen the chariots . . . or the angels. But all of it happening in the fury of a whirlwind must have taken Elisha's breath away.

Whirlwinds, tornadoes, and even the furious wind of a thunderstorm give us a glimpse of God's mighty power. But his incredible creativity can be found in the simplest breeze.

So how does God make the wind blow? It actually has a lot to do with temperature. The air around us is made up of tiny particles called molecules that are always pushing against one another and us. When these molecules are warmed, they expand outward and the air becomes lighter and pushes less (called low pressure). Cold molecules press tightly together, weigh more, and push harder (called high pressure). High pressure air always pushes toward lower levels of pressure, which moves the molecules and causes wind.

[Science Theater; pa.msu.edu]

water with Elijah's coat. He said, "Where is the Lord, the God of Elijah?" When he hit the water, it divided to the right and to the left. Then Elisha crossed over.

¹⁵A group of the prophets at Jericho were watching. They said, "Elisha now has the spirit Elijah

But Elisha answered, "No. Don't send them."

¹⁷The group of prophets begged Elisha until he hated to refuse them anymore. Then he said, "Send them." So they sent 50 men who looked for three days. But they could not find Elijah.

CRAFTS

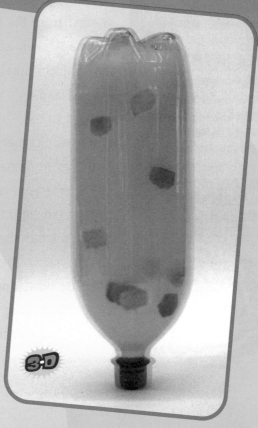

ELIJAH AND THE WHIRLWIND

SUPPLIES

plastic jar with a lid
Monopoly® houses
three drops of liquid
dishwashing detergent

ALL ABOUT IT:

Elijah was taken to heaven in a whirlwind. Today tornadoes and hurricanes are the closest things that resemble whirl-winds. Both are destructive and bring fear and heartache. God used the whirlwind in the Old Testament to take Elijah to heaven. God's ways are not our ways. Think about God's awesome power and how he can use all things for good as you make your own tornado.

INSTRUCTIONS

1. Fill your jar 3/4 full with water.

2. Put three drops of liquid soap and a few Monopoly® houses in the jar.

3. Screw the lid on tight.

4. Shake the jar 15 times, then twist the jar in your hand.

5. Watch the tornado take shape in the bottle.

3-D

Elisha and Naaman the Leper

2 KINGS 5:1-27

LIVIN' IT!

THE MOUTH OF BABES
2 KINGS 5:1-14

Ever been in a room full of adults when one of them asks you a question? Some kids seem just fine with the attention, but most get quiet and scared. We think that we really don't have anything to offer, and we just want to be left alone.

Naaman, a very important military man, had a very young maid serving in his home. It would have been very easy for her to blend in the background and be quiet. But she didn't. She knew her master needed the truth, and she was willing to tell it, no matter what happened. Her bravery ended up saving his life.

All around you, people are living lives without knowing Jesus. You can choose to be shy and quiet, or you can pray for strength and look for the chance to share God's truth with them to help save their spiritual lives. Ask God to help you to be bold and courageous like Naaman's young maid, and speak up with God's gospel of hope.

NAAMAN IS HEALED

5 Naaman was commander of the army of the king of Aram. He was a great man to his master. He had much honor because the Lord had used him to give victory to Aram. He was a mighty and brave man. But he had a harmful skin disease.

[2] The Arameans had gone out to steal from the Israelites. And they had taken a little girl as a captive from Israel. This little girl served Naaman's wife. [3] She said to her mistress, "I wish that my master would meet the prophet[d] who lives in Samaria. He would heal Naaman of his disease."

[4] Naaman went to the king. He told him what the girl from Israel had said. [5] The king of Aram said, "Go now. And I will send a letter to the king of Israel." So Naaman left and took about 750 pounds of silver. He also took about 150 pounds of gold and ten changes of clothes with him. [6] He brought the letter to the king of Israel. It read, "I am sending my servant Naaman to you. I'm sending him so you can heal him of his skin disease."

[7] The king of Israel read the letter. Then he tore his clothes to show how upset he was. He said, "I'm not God! I can't kill and make alive again! Why does this man send someone with a harmful skin disease for me to heal? You can see that the king of

> **"Go wash in the Jordan River seven times. Then your skin will be healed, and you will be clean."**
> *2 Kings 5:10*

Aram is trying to start trouble with me!"

[8] Elisha, the man of God, heard that the king of Israel had torn his clothes. So he sent a message to the king. It said, "Why have you become so upset that you tore your clothes? Let Naaman come to me. Then he will know there is a prophet in Israel!" [9] So Naaman went with his horses and chariots to Elisha's house. And he stood outside the door.

[10] Elisha sent a messenger to

WILD WORLD FACTS

2 Kings 5:1-14

A LITTLE GOES A LONG WAY

Leprosy has been around for a long time. The first official case was recorded in 600 B.C., but the disease has been known to affect people from many different cultures around the world from ancient times all the way into the present day.

The good news is that now there is a cure for this disease. Leprosy is caused by a bacteria that is transmitted in fluid from the nose and mouth. It causes damage to the skin, limbs, eyes, and nerves. A treatment was discovered in the 1940s, then enhanced in the 1960s, that has helped to greatly reduce the number of leprosy victims in the world. Over the past 20 years, more than 12 million leprosy patients have been cured.

The best way that we can help the countries that still battle this disease—and many others—is to provide money for the medical missionaries that serve them. Ask your pastor what your church is doing to help the sick and needy around the world—and see how you can help!

[WorldHealthOrganization.com]

Naaman. The messenger said, "Go and wash in the Jordan River seven times. Then your skin will be healed, and you will be clean."

"Naaman became angry and left. He said, "I thought Elisha would surely come out and stand before me. I thought he would call on the name of the Lord his God. I thought he would wave his hand over the place and heal the disease! ¹²Abana and Pharpar, the rivers of Damascus, are better than all the waters of Israel! Why can't I wash in them and become clean?" So Naaman went away very angry.

¹³But Naaman's servants came near and talked to him. They said, "My father, if the prophet had told you to do some great thing, wouldn't you have done it? Doesn't it make more sense just to do it? After all, he only told you, 'Wash, and you will be clean.'" ¹⁴So Naaman

REAL SUPER HEROES

ELISHA

Elisha had big shoes to fill. Elijah, his mentor, had been taken to heaven in a whirlwind, following a life dedicated to God and filled with great acts of faith. Now it was Elisha's turn. Elijah had actually left behind his coat—a symbol that he was passing God's holy calling on to Elisha.

God confirmed Elisha as the new prophet of the Lord when he parted the waters of the Jordan River. Others who stood by and watched realized he now had the powers of Elijah. From that moment on, Elisha's life was filled with miracles, and God used him in many ways. Through Elisha God made poisoned water pure. He had bears attack and kill Elisha's enemies. He gave him wisdom in ways to secure Israel and defeat her enemies. He provided for the widow's needs through never-ending oil. Later, he raised her son from the dead. Through Elisha God multiplied bread, made poisoned stew good, healed Naaman of his leprosy, and made an axe-head float. Elisha obeyed the Lord in every area, and God accomplished amazing work through his surrendered heart.

Even more important than the miracles was Elisha's message. He urged his people to remain true to God and stay away from false idols. His life gave proof of the almighty power of God. Thousands of years later, his testimony still holds true. We serve the same powerful God, and the same spirit that was in Elijah and Elisha lives in us, too.

THE CURIOUS CURE

Naaman didn't know of any doctors who could help him. Lepers were usually a hopeless cause. But one little girl knew what to do. How about you? How would you do if you were in her shoes? Check out this quiz to find out!

1 WHO WAS NAAMAN?
A a donkey
B a prophet
C the king of Aram
D commander of the army

2 WHY DID NAAMAN HAVE AN ISRAELITE GIRL IN HIS HOME?
A She was friends with his daughter.
B She had gotten lost, and he had taken her in.
C She was an orphan.
D She had been taken captive and made a servant.

3 WHAT DID THE LITTLE GIRL TELL NAAMAN TO DO?
A "Go to a prophet for healing."
B "Ask the village doctor for help."
C "Bathe in the Jordan River."
D "Pray to God."

4 WHAT DID NAAMAN DO?
A He rebuked the girl.
B He laughed and said she was crazy.
C He listened and asked his king for help.
D He went back to bed.

5 WHY DID THE KING OF ISRAEL TEAR HIS ROBES WHEN HE GOT THE LETTER FROM ARAM'S KING?
A He didn't like the outfit anyway.
B He didn't know what to do.
C He was afraid of Aram's king.
D Both b and c.

6 WHAT DID ELISHA TELL NAAMAN TO DO TO BE HEALED?
A "Close your eyes, and count to ten."
B "Beg God for mercy."
C "Go wash in the Jordan River seven times."
D "Rub mud all over your disease."

7 HOW DID NAAMAN RESPOND TO ELISHA'S DIRECTIONS?
A He was thrilled and immediately obeyed.
B He got angry, felt insulted, and refused at first.
C He asked him why.
D He went back home.

8 WHO MADE NAAMAN CHANGE HIS MIND?
A the king of Israel
B the king of Aram
C the little girl
D his own servants

9 WHAT HAPPENED WHEN HE OBEYED?
A His skin became clean.
B His arm fell off.
C His leprosy got worse.
D Everybody danced.

10 WHAT HAPPENED TO GEHAZI, ELISHA'S SERVANT?
A He got rich.
B He performed a miracle.
C He got Naaman's disease.
D He got fired.

Score 9-10: You have the miracle cure!
Score 7-8: Recovery is slow but sure.
Score 5-6: Read the medicine label one more time!
Score 4 or below: You've taken a turn for the worse! Call the ambulance!

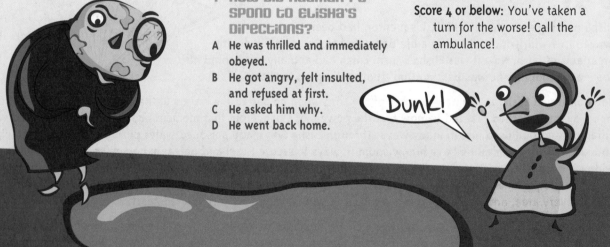

Dunk!

GET CONNECTED

RELATIONSHIPS WITH AUTHORITY

Treat Your Teachers Have you ever thought about what life would be like without your teachers? No church, no Sunday school, no education at all. What would you do?

We take our teachers for granted because they are always right where we need them to be. But like God's other good gifts, we need to see just how valuable and special our teachers are—particularly those who help us know God better.

Teachers hold a special place in God's heart, too. He says we should share all good things with those who teach us. So, today, tell your teachers you appreciate them. Let them know that God is using them to teach you how to be a better person. And remember to lift them up in prayer, as well.

went down and dipped in the Jordan seven times. He did just as Elisha had said. Then Naaman's skin became new again. It was like the skin of a little boy. And Naaman was clean!

[15]Naaman and all his group came back to Elisha. He stood before Elisha and said, "Look. I now know there is no God in all the earth except in Israel! Now please accept a gift from me."

[16]But Elisha said, "I serve the Lord. As surely as the Lord lives, I won't accept anything." Naaman urged him to take the gift, but he refused.

[17]Then Naaman said, "If you won't take the gift, then please give me some dirt. Give me as much as two of my mules can carry. From now on I'll not offer any burnt offering or sacrifice to any other

gods. I'll only offer sacrifices to the Lord. [18]But let the Lord pardon me for this: My master goes into the temple of Rimmon[n] to worship. When he goes, he will lean on my arm. Then I must bow in that temple. May the Lord pardon me when I do that."

[19]Elisha said to him, "Go in peace."

Naaman left Elisha and went a short way. [20]Gehazi was the servant of Elisha the man of God. Gehazi thought, "My master has not accepted what Naaman the Aramean brought. As surely as the Lord lives, I'll run after him. I'll get something from him." [21]So he went after him.

Naaman saw someone running after him. So he got off the

⭐ **5:18 temple of Rimmon** The place where the Aramean people worshiped the false god Rimmon.

REAL SUPER HEROES

NAAMAN'S MAID

She was only a little Jewish girl, a slave in a strange land. We don't even know her name. But because of Naaman's maid's courage to speak the truth, she led her master—the captain of the Syrian army—to God.

Naaman had a bad skin disease that had no cure. It wasn't normal for a servant to tell anything to the master, especially a child servant, but she told him anyway about the prophet Elisha who could heal him. Naaman listened, went, and was healed. He realized that Israel's God was the only true God, and he worshiped him with thanksgiving.

Don't let people scare you because they are older than you. Remember that God is on your side. And just like Naaman's maid, you can help them by telling them about God.

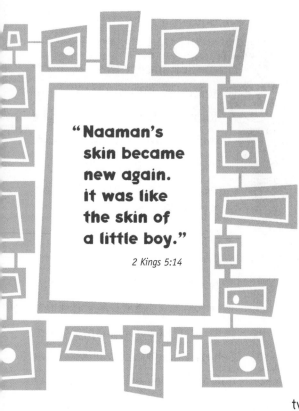

> "Naaman's skin became new again. it was like the skin of a little boy."
>
> *2 Kings 5:14*

chariot to meet Gehazi. He said, "Is everything all right?"

²²Gehazi said, "Everything is all right. My master has sent me. He said, 'Two young men just came to me. They are from the group of the prophets in the mountains of Ephraim. Please give them 75 pounds of silver and two changes of clothes.'"

²³Naaman said, "Please take 150 pounds." He urged Gehazi to take it. He tied 150 pounds of silver in two bags with two changes of clothes. Then he gave them to two of his servants. They carried them for Gehazi. ²⁴When they came to the hill, Gehazi took these things from Naaman's servants. And he put them in the house. He let Naaman's servants go, and they left.

²⁵Then he came in and stood before his master. Elisha said to him, "Where have you been, Gehazi?"

Gehazi said, "I didn't go anywhere."

²⁶But Elisha said to him, "My spirit was with you. I knew when the man turned from his chariot to meet you. This isn't a time to receive money, clothes, olives and grapes. It isn't a time to receive sheep, oxen, male servants and female servants. ²⁷Naaman's skin disease will come on you and your children forever." When Gehazi left Elisha, he had the disease. He was as white as snow.

CRAFTS

ELISHA AND NAAMAN
THE LEPER

SUPPLIES

freezer bag
white glue
liquid starch

ALL ABOUT IT:

Naaman did not want to dip himself in the Jordan River seven times. He thought Elisha's instructions for healing were too ordinary. But we must remember that God can do amazing things with ordinary people and ordinary actions. God is interested in our hearts and our desire to serve him. When we have a humble spirit, God can use us in his plans.

Mix these ordinary things together to see something extraordinary!

INSTRUCTIONS

1. Measure out and pour two tablespoons of white glue in a freezer zipper bag.

2. Stir in one tablespoon of liquid starch.

3. Knead the mixture in the bag, and see what happens.

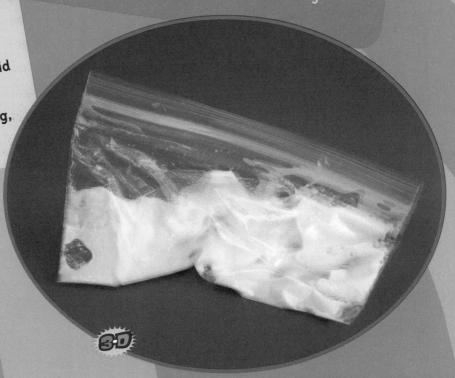

3-D

Joash, the Boy King

2 KINGS 11:1—12:2

ATHALIAH AND JOASH

11 Now Ahaziah's mother, Athaliah, saw that her son was dead. Then she killed all the royal family. ²But Jehosheba took Joash, Ahaziah's son. She stole him from among the other sons of the king who were about to be murdered. (Jehosheba was King Jehoram's daughter and Ahaziah's sister.) She put Joash and his nurse in a bedroom. She hid Joash from Athaliah. So he was not killed. ³He was hidden with her in the Temple[d] of the Lord for six years. During that time Athaliah ruled the land.

From around 840 B.C., Israel was divided into two separate nations: the Northern Kingdom of Israel, and the Southern Kingdom of Judah. Both groups had their own line of kings—most of which disobeyed God, served false gods, and worked hard to kill anyone who got in the way of their power. When Athaliah seized power in Judah, she tried to have all of her grandsons killed. If she had succeeded, there would not have been any descendants from Judah through which the promised Messiah was to come.

⁴In the seventh year Jehoiada sent for the commanders of groups of 100 men. He sent for guards and the Carites, the royal bodyguards. He brought them together in the Temple of the Lord. Then he made an agreement with them. There, in the Temple of the Lord, he made them promise loyalty. Then he showed them the king's son. ⁵He commanded them, "This is what you must do. A third of you who come in on the Sabbath[d] will guard the king's palace. ⁶Another third of you will be at the Sur Gate. And another third will be at the gate behind the guard.

This way you will guard the Temple. ⁷Two groups will go off duty on the Sabbath. They must protect the Temple of the Lord for the king. ⁸All of you must stand around the king. Each man must have his weapon in his hand. If anyone comes near, kill him. Stay close to the king when he goes out and when he comes in."

⁹The commanders over 100 men obeyed everything Jehoia-

> **"She hid Joash from Athaliah. So he was not killed."** *2 Kings 11:2*

da the priest had commanded. Each one took his men who were beginning their Sabbath duty. Each one also took those who were ending their Sabbath duty. Both groups came to Jehoiada the priest. ¹⁰And he gave spears and shields to the commanders. They used to belong to King David. They were kept in the Temple of the Lord.

JOASH BECOMES KING

¹¹Then each of the guards took his place. Each man had his weapon in his hand. There were guards from the south side of the Temple[d] to the north side.

GET CONNECTED

RELATIONSHIPS WITH AUTHORITY

Brace Yourself God has given us families to help protect and develop us. And he decides who your parents are. But some parents may not yet belong to Jesus. Because of the sin in their hearts, they may choose to make very bad decisions that could hurt you either physically or spiritually.

If you are a child of parents who don't love God, you need to find support somewhere else. Talk to your Sunday school teacher or maybe the parent of a friend who is a Christian. Get others to pray for you and your parents, and ask God to change their hearts. In the meantime, continue to show them respect and love out of obedience to God. It may be your attitude that allows them to see the work of God in you and that draws them to Christ.

They stood by the altar and the Temple and around the king. ¹²Jehoiada brought out the king's son. He put the crown on Joash. Then he gave Joash a copy of the Agreement with the Lord. They appointed him king and poured olive oil on him. They clapped their hands and said, "Long live the king!"

¹³Athaliah heard the noise of the guards and the people. So she came to the people at the Temple of the Lord. ¹⁴She looked, and there was the king. He was standing by the pillar, as the custom was. The officers and trumpeters were standing beside him. All the people of the land were very happy and were blowing trumpets. Then Athaliah tore her clothes to show how upset she was. She screamed, "Traitors! Traitors!"

¹⁵Jehoiada the priest gave orders to the commanders of 100 men who led the army. He said, "Surround her with soldiers. Kill with a sword anyone who follows her." He said this because he had said, "Don't put Athaliah to death in the Temple of the Lord." ¹⁶So they caught her when she came to where the horses enter the palace grounds.

WILD WORLD FACTS

2 Kings 11:17-18

THAT WAS THEN—AND NOW

It wasn't just a part of the Jewish culture. Almost all of the nations around Israel that didn't know God also offered sacrifices. But because they didn't know the truth about the real God and his love, they believed they had to offer up everything—even their own kids—to keep the gods happy.

As horrible as it sounds, some cultures today still practice ritual sacrifices. Mostly the reports come from India and a few countries in Africa. People in this world today are dying to know that they can be forgiven and accepted by the God of this universe. But they still don't know the truth. We must pray that God will raise up workers who will bring the good news of the gospel to these dark lands and that he will turn their hearts to him.

[Wikipedia: Sacrifice]

Ways to Watch the Stars

1. On a blanket
2. Sitting on the hood of your car
3. With a friend
4. With a map of the constellations
5. With a telescope
6. Talking to God with your eyes open
7. With a pizza and soda
8. In a sleeping bag
9. From a boat
10. In a field in the country

There she was put to death.

17Then Jehoiada made an agreement. It was between the Lord and the king and the people. They agreed to be the Lord's special people. He also made an agreement between the king and the people. 18All the people of the land went to the temple of Baal[d] and tore it down. They smashed the altars and idols into small pieces. And they killed Mattan, the priest of Baal, in front of the altars.

Then Jehoiada the priest placed guards at the Temple of the Lord. 19He took with him the commanders of 100 men and the Carites, the royal bodyguards. He took the guards and all the people of the land. Together they took the king out of the Temple of the Lord. They went into the palace through the gate of the guards. Then the king sat on the royal throne. 20So all the people of Judah were very happy. And Jerusalem had peace because Athaliah had been put to death with the sword at the palace.

21Joash was seven years old when he became king.

12 Joash became king of Judah in Jehu's seventh year as king of Israel. Joash ruled for 40 years in Jerusalem. His mother's name was Zibiah. She was from Beersheba. 2Joash did what the Lord said was right all the time Jehoiada the priest taught him.

LIVIN' IT!

GOOD ADVICE
2 KINGS 12:1-2

Imagine what it would be like to become king at only seven years of age! Would it mean endless Playstation® games and piles of candy, or would you get down to business as you sat on your throne?

Becoming king at age seven, Joash knew he was in over his head. He had not yet gained the knowledge he needed to rule the land of Judah. So he asked for help from a wise man that he trusted—an older man who followed God and would be able to help him rule.

At your age, you too have a lot to learn. The idea of being in charge may sound fun, but it also means a lot of responsibility. God wants you to take this time in your life to learn as much as you can about him. He provides his Word, Christian parents, teachers, and friends to help you make the best decisions. As you obey godly advice, you grow in understanding. Eventually you will become an adult who can also help others walk in wisdom.

CRAFTS

JOASH, THE BOY KING

three cans with lids
construction paper
markers
tape and scissors

BANK

TOY S
ON SALE
BIG SALE!

3-D

INSTRUCTIONS

1. Cut a construction paper band to fit around each can.

2. Decorate one band to look like your church.

3. Decorate another band to look like a bank.

4. Decorate the last band to look like a store.

5. Tape the bands on the cans, and put the lids on top.

ALL ABOUT IT:

What do you do with your allowance or the money that you earn? Do you spend it right away? Or save it? Joash collected the people's money for rebuilding the Temple in one box and their money for the priests separately. When the money was divided, there was enough for the Temple repairs and the priests.

Make these cans to help you divide your money into three groups. Put money in one can to give to the church. Save money in another can to buy bigger things you want in the future. Use the money in the last can to spend on something you want. When you are given money or earn money, divide it into the three cans right away.

Hezekiah, King of Judah

2 KINGS 18:1—19:37

HEZEKIAH KING OF JUDAH

18 Hezekiah son of Ahaz king of Judah became king. This was during the third year Hoshea son of Elah was king of Israel. ²Hezekiah was 25 years old when he became king. And he ruled 29 years in Jerusalem. His mother's name was Abijah daughter of Zechariah. ³Hezekiah did what the Lord said was right. He did just as his ancestor David had done. ⁴He removed the places where false gods were worshiped. He broke the stone pillars they worshiped. He cut down the Asherah*ᵈ* idols. Also the Israelites had been burning incense*ᵈ* to the bronze snake made by Moses. (It was called Nehushtan.) But Hezekiah broke it into pieces.

⁵Hezekiah trusted in the Lord, the God of Israel. There was no one like him among all the kings of Judah. There was no king like him, before him or after him. ⁶Hezekiah was loyal to the Lord. He did not stop following the Lord. He obeyed the commands the Lord had given Moses. ⁷And the Lord was with Hezekiah. He had success in everything he did. He turned against the king of Assyria and stopped serving him. ⁸Hezekiah defeated the Philistines all the way to Gaza and its borders. He defeated them everywhere, from the watchtower to the strong, walled city.

> **"Hezekiah trusted in the Lord, the God of Israel. There was no one like him among all the kings of Judah."** *2 Kings 18:5*

THE ASSYRIANS CAPTURE SAMARIA

⁹Shalmaneser king of Assyria surrounded Samaria and attacked it. This was in the fourth year Hezekiah was king. And it was the seventh year Hoshea son of Elah was king of Israel. ¹⁰After three years the Assyrians captured Samaria. This was in the sixth year Hezekiah was king. And it was Hoshea's ninth year as king of Israel. ¹¹The king of Assyria took the Israelites away to Assyria. He put them in Halah and in Gozan on the Habor River. He also put them in the cities of the Medes. ¹²This happened because they did not obey the Lord

GET CONNECTED

RELATIONSHIPS WITH FAMILY

Secret Support Being a grown-up, especially a parent, is really hard work—so hard that they even need your help.

When you look at your parents, they probably seem like they have everything under control. But really, they are kids like you who have just grown older. They still need wisdom, and protection, and guidance—but now they need to get it directly from God instead of their parents. They need you to pray for them that they will raise you in God's wisdom and that they will honor God in all their decisions. Make it a daily habit to pray for your parents and their relationship with God, starting right now.

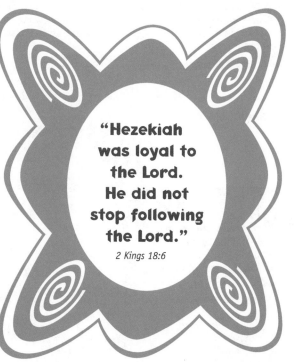

DIG THIS!

The Bible doesn't need any backup, but the Mari letters do help prove that the people and events talked about in the Bible really did exist. Archaeologists discovered the Mari letters—some 20,000 clay tablets that date from the time of Hammurabi (1750 B.C.)—that give information about the Hebrew people and mention many of the same people, places, and events that occur in Bible texts.

their God. They broke his agreement. They did not obey all that Moses, the Lord's servant, had commanded. They would not listen to the commands or do them.

ASSYRIA ATTACKS JUDAH

¹³During Hezekiah's fourteenth year as king, Sennacherib king of Assyria attacked Judah. He attacked all the strong, walled cities of Judah and defeated them. ¹⁴Then Hezekiah king of Judah sent a message to the king of Assyria at Lachish.

He said, "I have done wrong. Leave me alone. Then I will pay anything you demand of me." So the king of Assyria told Hezekiah how much to pay. It was about 22,000 pounds of silver and 2,000 pounds of gold. ¹⁵Hezekiah gave him all the silver that was in the Temple^d of the Lord. And he gave him all the silver in the palace treasuries. ¹⁶Hezekiah cut off all the gold that covered the doors of the Temple of the Lord. He also removed the gold from the doorposts. Hezekiah had put gold on these doors himself. He gave it all to the king of Assyria.

"Hezekiah was loyal to the Lord. He did not stop following the Lord."
2 Kings 18:6

ASSYRIA TROUBLES HEZEKIAH

¹⁷The king of Assyria sent out his supreme commander, his chief officer and his field commander. They went with a large army from Lachish to King Hezekiah in Jerusalem. When they came near the waterway from the upper pool, they stopped. The upper pool is on the road to the Washerman's Field. ¹⁸They called for the king. So Eliakim, Shebna and Joah went out to meet them. Eliakim son of Hilkiah was the palace manager. Shebna was the royal assistant. And Joah son of Asaph was the recorder.

¹⁹The field commander said to them, "Tell Hezekiah this:

"'The great king, the king of Assyria, says: You have nothing to trust in to help you. ²⁰You say you have battle plans and power for war. But your words mean nothing. Whom are you trusting for help so that you turn against me? ²¹Look, you are depending on Egypt to help you. Egypt is like a splintered walking stick. If you lean on it for help, it will stab you

SEPTEMBER — FAITH

1 Go on a nature walk, and look for God's hand in the details of creation.

2

3 Set a goal for how often you want to walk or run this month, then achieve it.

4

5 Prayer Pointer: Ask God, who gives us the gift of faith, to increase your faith in his promises.

6

7 Hide-It-in-Your-Heart: See, the nation that is evil and trusts in itself will fail. But those who do right because they trust in God will live (Habakkuk 2:4).

8

9

10 Wake up early, and make breakfast for your parents.

11

12

13 Write a poem or prayer about why you believe in Jesus.

14 Go to a football game with your friends, and see who can cheer the loudest.

15

16

17

18 Bring bags of candy corn to your teachers, and tell them that you appreciate them.

19

20 Prayer Pointer: Pray for wisdom for your church pastor that he will know how to lead the church into deeper faith and trust in Christ.

21

22 First Day of Fall

23 Swing on a swing with your eyes closed.

24

25

26 Hide-It-in-Your-Heart: Abram believed the Lord. And the Lord accepted Abram's faith, and that faith made him right with God (Genesis 15:6).

27

28

29 Think of three good things about your brothers and sisters, then tell them.

30

and hurt you. The king of Egypt will hurt those who depend on him. [22]You might say, "We are depending on the Lord our God." But Hezekiah destroyed the Lord's altars and the places of worship. Hezekiah told Judah and Jerusalem, "You must worship only at this one altar in Jerusalem."

[23]"'Now make an agreement with my master, the king of Assyria: I will give you 2,000 horses if you can find enough men to ride them. [24]You cannot defeat one of my master's least important officers. So why do you depend on Egypt to give you chariots and horsemen? [25]I have not come to attack and destroy this place without an order from the Lord. The Lord himself told me to come to this country and destroy it.'"

[26]Then Eliakim son of Hilkiah, Shebna and Joah spoke to the field commander. They said, "Please speak to us in the Aramaic language. We understand

it. Don't speak to us in Hebrew because the people on the city wall can hear you."

[27]But the commander said, "No. My master did not send me to tell these things only to you and your king. My master sent me to tell them also to those people sitting on the wall. They will have to eat their own dung and drink their own urine like you."

[28]Then the commander stood and shouted loudly in the Hebrew language. He said, "Listen to the word from the great king, the king of Assyria! [29]The king says you should not let Hezekiah fool you. Hezekiah can't save you from my power. [30]Don't let Hezekiah talk you into trusting the Lord. Hezekiah says, 'The Lord will surely save us. This city won't be given over to the king of Assyria.'

[31]"Don't listen to Hezekiah. The king of

> **"Hezekiah says, 'The Lord will surely save us. This city won't be given over to the king of Assyria.'"**
>
> *2 Kings 18:30*

Assyria says, 'Make peace with me. Come out of the city to me. Then everyone will be free to eat the fruit from his own grapevine and fig tree. Everyone will be free to drink water from his own well. [32]Then I will come and take you to a land like your own. It is a land with grain and new wine. It has bread and vineyards. It is a land of olives and honey. Then you can choose to live and not to die!'

"Don't listen to Hezekiah. He is fooling you when he says, 'The Lord will save us.' [33]The god of any other nation has not saved his people from the power of the king of Assyria. [34]Where are the gods of Hamath and Arpad? Where are the gods of Sepharvaim, Hena and Ivvah? They did not save Samaria from my power. [35]Not one of all the gods of these countries has saved his people

History Highlights

↗ **605 B.C.**
Nebuchadnezzar attacks Jerusalem and takes captives, including Daniel.

7000 5000 3000 1000 0 1000 NOW

WHAT DO YOU DO WHEN YOU'RE SAD?
People in ancient times cried, too—but they also showed their distress in some really weird ways. Often they would tear their clothes (which were hand-sewn and not easy to get), or they would put ashes on their head—something they thought of as dirt. Doing this showed how deeply upset they were.

from me. Then the Lord cannot save Jerusalem from my power."

³⁶The people were silent. They didn't answer the commander at all. This was because King

> **"When King Hezekiah heard the message, he tore his clothes."**
>
> *2 Kings 19:1*

Hezekiah had ordered, "Don't answer him."

³⁷Then Eliakim, Shebna and Joah tore their clothes to show how upset they were. (Eliakim son of Hilkiah was the palace manager. Shebna was the royal assistant. And Joah son of Asaph was the recorder.) The three men went to Hezekiah and told him what the field commander had said.

JERUSALEM WILL BE SAVED

19 When King Hezekiah heard the message, he tore his clothes. And he put on rough cloth to show how sad he was. Then he went into the Temple*d* of the Lord. ²Hezekiah sent Eliakim, Shebna and the older priests to Isaiah. Eliakim was the palace manager, and Shebna was the royal assistant. The men were all wearing the rough cloth when they came to Isaiah. He was a prophet,*d* the son of Amoz. ³These men told Isaiah, "This is what Hezekiah says: Today is a day of sorrow and punishment and disgrace. It is sad, as when a child should be born, but the mother is not strong enough to give birth to it. ⁴The king of Assyria sent his field commander to make fun of the living God. Maybe the Lord your God will hear what the commander said. Maybe the Lord your God will punish him for what he said. So pray for the

> **"Don't be frightened by the words the servants of the king of Assyria said against me."** *2 Kings 19:5*

LIVIN' IT!

**POTENT PRAYERS
2 KINGS 19:1-37**

Hezekiah had a problem. The king of Assyria had sent him a letter telling him that the Jews were going to be destroyed. So what did he do? He told God. He took the letter and laid it before God, then prayed for help. God, his father, answered his prayer by killing 185,000 Assyrians in their sleep.

Just like Hezekiah, we serve a mighty God whose power is far greater than we can imagine! Whenever we face hard times, or mean people, or sin—or whatever comes into our lives—we can go straight to God in prayer. God loves to hear from us, and he will always answer in the way that is the very best for us. So never lose heart. Nothing in this world should shake you, because you have the God of all creation on your side. Just remember to bring everything before him in prayer, then wait for him to act.

few people of Israel who are left alive."

⁵When Hezekiah's officers came to Isaiah, ⁶he said to them, "Tell your master this: The Lord says, 'Don't be afraid of what you have heard. Don't be frightened by the words the servants of the king of Assyria

said against me. ⁷Listen! I am going to put a spirit in the king of Assyria. He will hear a report that will make him return to his own country. And I will cause him to die by the sword there.'"

⁸The field commander heard that the king of Assyria had left Lachish. So the commander left and found the king fighting against the city of Libnah.

⁹The king received a report that Tirhakah was coming to attack him. Tirhakah was the Cushite king of Egypt. When the king of Assyria heard this, he sent messengers to Hezekiah. The king said: ¹⁰"Say this to Hezekiah king of Judah: Don't be fooled by the god you trust. Don't believe him when he says Jerusalem will not be defeated by the king of Assyria. ¹¹You have heard what the kings of Assyria have done. They have completely defeated every country. Do not think you will be saved. ¹²The gods of those people did not save them.

My ancestors destroyed them. My ancestors defeated the cities of Gozan, Haran and Rezeph. They defeated the people of Eden living in Tel Assar. ¹³Where are the kings of Hamath and Arpad? Where is the king of the city of Sepharvaim? Where are the kings of Hena and Ivvah?"

> **"Lord, God of israel... Only you are God of all the kingdoms of the earth."**
>
> *2 Kings 19:15*

HEZEKIAH PRAYS TO THE LORD

¹⁴Hezekiah received the letter from the messengers and read it. Then he went up to the Templeᵈ of the Lord. Hezekiah spread the letter out before the Lord. ¹⁵And he prayed to the Lord: "Lord, God of Israel, your throne is between the gold creatures with wings! Only you are God of all the kingdoms of the earth. You made the heavens and the earth. ¹⁶Hear, Lord, and listen. Open your eyes, Lord, and see. Listen

to the word Sennacherib has said to insult the living God. [17]It is true, Lord. The kings of Assyria have destroyed these countries and their lands. [18]These kings have thrown the gods of these nations into the fire. But they were only wood and rock statues that men made. So the kings have destroyed them. [19]Now, Lord our God, save us from the king's power. Then all the kingdoms of the earth will know that you, Lord, are the only God."

GOD ANSWERS HEZEKIAH

[20]Then Isaiah son of Amoz sent a message to Hezekiah. Isaiah said, "The Lord, the God of Israel, says this: I have heard your prayer to me about Sennacherib king of Assyria. [21]So this is what the Lord has said against Sennacherib:

[22]You have insulted me and
    spoken against me.
You have raised your voice
    against me.
You have a proud look on
    your face.

> **"King of Assyria, surely you have heard. Long ago i, the Lord, planned these things."**
>
> *2 Kings 19:25*

You disobey me, the Holy
    One of Israel!
[23]You have used your
    messengers to insult
    the Lord.
You have said, "I have
    many chariots.
With them I have gone to

pine trees.
I have reached its farthest
    places.
I have gone to its best
    forests.
[24]I have dug wells in foreign
    countries.
I have drunk water there.
By the soles of my feet,
    I have dried up all the
    rivers of Egypt."

[25]"King of Assyria, surely you
    have heard.
Long ago I, the Lord,
    planned these things.
Long ago I planned them.
    Now I have made them
    happen.
I allowed you to turn those
    strong, walled cities
    into piles of rocks.
[26]The people living in those
    cities were weak.

> **"The Lord, the God of Israel, says this: I have heard your prayer to me about Sennacherib king of Assyria."** *2 Kings 19:20*

'The people of Jerusalem
    hate you and make fun
    of you.
The people of Jerusalem
    laugh at you as you
    run away.

the tops of the mountains.
I have climbed the highest
    mountains of Lebanon.
I have cut down its tallest
    cedars.
I have cut down its best

They were frightened and
    put to shame.
They were like grass in
    the field.
They were like tender,
    young grass.

HEZEKIAH'S PRAYER

Hidden in the message below is the prayer that Hezekiah prayed to the Lord when Jerusalem was threatened to be defeated by the Assyrians. Each word in the message is written backwards. To complete the prayer, write each word—from beginning to end—on the blank lines. The first word is done for you.

YLNO UOY ERA DOG

FO LLA EHT SMODGNIK FO EHT HTRAE.

RAEH, DROL, DNA NETSIL.

NEPO RUOY SEYE, DROL, DNA EES.

2 Kings 19:15-16

ONLY ___ ___ ___

__ ___ ___ _____ __ ___ _____.

____, ____, ___ _____.

____ ____ ____, ____, ___ ___.

3-D

They were like grass that
grows on the housetop.
It is burned by the wind
before it can grow.

27"'I know when you rest and
when you come and go.
I know how you speak
against me.
28You speak strongly
against me.
And I have heard your
proud words.
So I will put my hook in
your nose.
And I will put my bit in
your mouth.
Then I will force you to leave
my country
the same way that you
came.'
29"Then the Lord said, 'Hezekiah, I will give you this sign:
This year you will eat the
grain that grows wild.
And the second year you
will eat what grows wild
from that.
But in the third year, plant
grain and harvest it.

Plant vineyards and eat
their fruit.
30Some of the people in the
family of Judah
will be saved.
Like plants that take root,
they will grow strong and
have many children.
31A few people will come out
of Jerusalem alive.
There will be a few from
Mount Zion^d who will live.
The strong love of the Lord
of heaven's armies
will cause this to happen.'

32"So this is what
the Lord says about
the king of Assyria:
'He will not
enter this city.
He will not even
shoot an
arrow here.
He will not fight
against it
with shields.
He will not build a
ramp to attack
the city walls.

33He will return to his country
the same way he came.
He will not enter this city,'
says the Lord.
34The Lord says, 'I will defend
and save this city.
I will do this for myself
and for David, my
servant.'"

35That night the angel of the
Lord went out. He killed 185,000
men in the Assyrian camp. The
people got up early the next
morning. And they saw all the
dead bodies! 36So Sennacherib

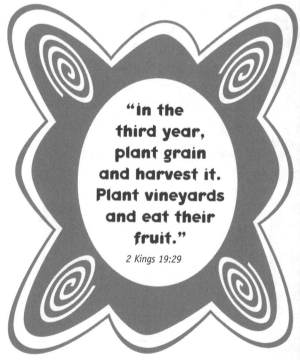

"in the third year, plant grain and harvest it. Plant vineyards and eat their fruit."
2 Kings 19:29

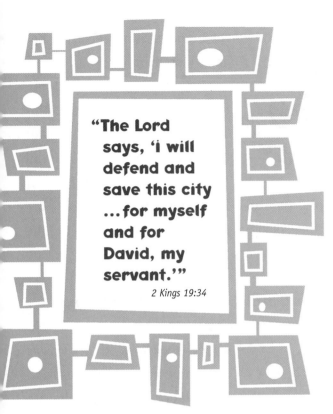

"The Lord says, 'i will defend and save this city ...for myself and for David, my servant.'"

2 Kings 19:34

king of Assyria left. He went back to Nineveh and stayed there.

³⁷One day Sennacherib was worshiping in the temple of his god Nisroch. While he was there, his sons Adrammelech and Sharezer killed him with a sword. Then they escaped to the land of Ararat. So Sennacherib's son Esarhaddon became king of Assyria.

the Fall of Jerusalem

2 KINGS 24:1—25:30

24 While Jehoiakim was king, Nebuchadnezzar king of Babylon attacked the land of Judah. So Jehoiakim became Nebuchadnezzar's servant for three years. Then Jehoiakim turned against Nebuchadnezzar. And he broke away from his rule. [2]The Lord sent men from Babylon, Aram, Moab and Ammon against Jehoiakim. He sent them to destroy Judah. This happened the way the Lord had said it would through his servants the prophets.[d]

[3]The Lord commanded this to happen to the people of Judah. He did it to remove them from his presence. This was because of all the sins Manasseh had done. [4]He had killed many innocent people. He had filled Jerusalem with their blood. And the Lord would not forgive these sins.

[5]The other things that happened while Jehoiakim was king

> **"Jehoiachin was 18 years old when he became king."** 2 Kings 24:8

and all he did are written down. They are in the book of the history of the kings of Judah. [6]Jehoiakim died, and his son Jehoiachin became king in his place.

[7]The king of Egypt did not come out of his land again. This was because of the king of Babylon. He had captured all that belonged to the king of Egypt. He took all the land from the brook of Egypt to the Euphrates River.

JEHOIACHIN KING OF JUDAH

[8]Jehoiachin was 18 years old when he became king. He was king three months in Jerusalem. His mother's name was Nehushta daughter of Elnathan. She was from Jerusalem. [9]Jehoiachin did what the Lord said was wrong, just as his father had done.

LIVIN' IT!

FALLEN BUT NOT FORGOTTEN
2 KINGS 24:1-20

Jerusalem was defeated. Judah was taken captive. After a long series of evil kings who hated God, God brought a long-deserved punishment. For the Israelites, it seemed as if life was over. Maybe even as if God had left them for dead as they left their homes to become slaves in Babylon.

Even though the people didn't deserve it, God still held out hope. Yes, there were definite consequences to their sin. But God would prove to be faithful, even though the people weren't. His love for his people continued, and it eventually nailed his own son, Jesus, to the cross so that they might be saved.

God promises to never leave us. Even though we may face hard times and may experience God's discipline, we can know that he allows it as a good father would. He is still with us, and his love is just as sure.

Top Ten

Ways to Study for a Test

1. With a group of friends
2. By rewriting your notes
3. By reading the text
4. By meeting with your teacher
5. By writing an outline
6. By making a sample test
7. By quizzing your friends and vice versa
8. By memorizing notes
9. By praying for help
10. Alone in your room

[10]At that time the officers of Nebuchadnezzar king of Babylon came up to Jerusalem. They surrounded the city and attacked it. [11]Nebuchadnezzar himself came to the city while his officers were attacking it. [12]Jehoiachin king of Judah surrendered to the king of Babylon. Jehoiachin's mother, servants, elders and officers also surrendered. Then the king of Babylon made Jehoiachin a prisoner. This was in the eighth year Nebuchadnezzar was king. [13]Nebuchadnezzar took all the treasures from the Temple[d] of the Lord. He also removed the treasures from the palace. He took all the gold objects Solomon king of Israel had made for the Temple. This happened as the Lord had said it would. [14]Nebuchadnezzar took away all the people of Jerusalem. This included all the leaders and all the wealthy people. He also took all the craftsmen and metal workers. There were 10,000 prisoners in all. Only the poorest people in the land were left. [15]Nebuchadnezzar carried away Jehoiachin to Babylon. He took the king's mother and his wives. He also took the officers and leading men of the land. They were taken captive from Jerusalem to Babylon. [16]The king of Babylon also took all 7,000 soldiers. These men were all strong and able to fight in war. And 1,000 craftsmen and metal workers were taken, too. Nebuchadnezzar took them as prisoners to Babylon. [17]He made Mattaniah king in Jehoiachin's place. Mattaniah was Jehoiachin's uncle. He also changed Mattaniah's name to Zedekiah.

ZEDEKIAH KING OF JUDAH

[18]Zedekiah was 21 years old when he became king. And he was king in Jerusalem for 11 years. His mother's name was Hamutal daughter of Jeremiah.[n] She was from Libnah. [19]Zedekiah did what the Lord said was wrong, just as Jehoiakim had done. [20]All this happened in Jerusalem and Judah because the Lord was angry with them. Finally, he threw them out of his presence.

> **"Nebuchadnezzar took all the treasures from the Temple of the Lord. He also removed the treasures from the palace."**
>
> 2 Kings 24:13

24:18 Jeremiah This is not the prophet Jeremiah but a different man with the same name.

> "Nebuzaradan set fire to the Temple of the Lord and the palace. He also set fire to all the houses of Jerusalem."
>
> *2 Kings 25:9*

THE FALL OF JERUSALEM

Zedekiah turned against the king of Babylon.

25 Then Nebuchadnezzar king of Babylon marched against Jerusalem with his whole army. This happened during Zedekiah's ninth year, tenth month and tenth day as king. He made a camp around the city. Then he built devices all around the city walls to attack it. ²The city was under attack until Zedekiah's eleventh year as king. ³By the ninth day of the fourth month, the hunger was terrible in the city. There was no food for the people to eat. ⁴Then the city wall was broken through. And the whole army ran away at night. They went through the gate between the two walls by the king's garden. The Babylonians were still surrounding the city. Zedekiah and his men ran toward the Jordan Valley. ⁵But the Babylonian army chased King Zedekiah. They caught up with him in the plains of Jericho. All of his army was scattered from him. ⁶So they captured Zedekiah and took him to the king of Babylon at Riblah. There he passed sentence on Zedekiah. ⁷They killed Zedekiah's sons as he watched. Then they put out his eyes. They put bronze chains on him and took him to Babylon.

⁸Nebuzaradan was the commander of the king's special guards. This officer of the king of Babylon came to Jerusalem. This was on the seventh day of the fifth month. This was in Nebuchadnezzar's nineteenth year as king of Babylon. ⁹Nebuzaradan set fire to the Temple[d] of the Lord and the palace. He

GET CONNECTED

RELATIONSHIPS WITH FAMILY

Fight for Families How many families do you know around you that have divorced parents? How about families with kids who don't obey or respect their parents? Even families that seemed strong at the beginning can begin to fall apart. Why?

Just like Israel, we can forget about God. If we stop obeying and forget to read and listen to his Word, we will fall away from the truth. Forgetting God tears families apart. Destroying families is Satan's number one strategy to disrupt God's work and break God's heart. God wants us to stay strong as individuals, as families, and as his children. Pray right now that God would protect your parents and family, and ask for wisdom to see any sin in your lives that would destroy your relationships with each other.

OLD testament tie-ins

Many people in the Bible are associated with a certain item that was important
in some way in their life as it is recorded in the Scripture. With a pencil,
connect the item with the correct Bible character by going through the maze.

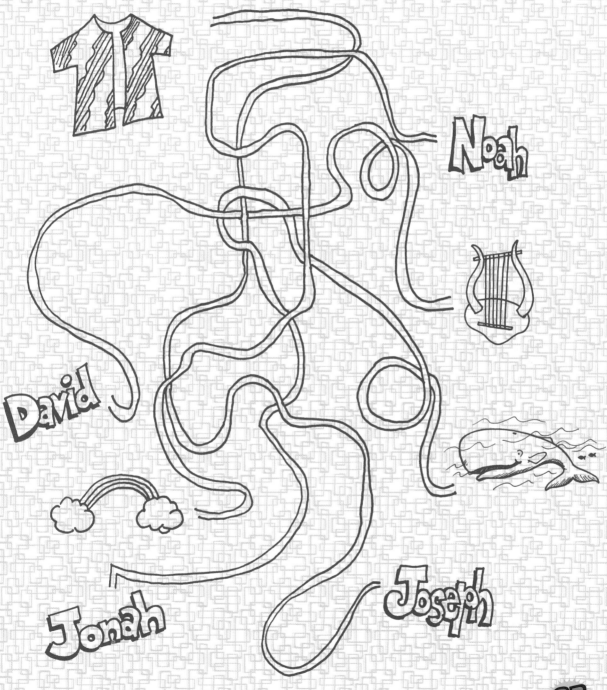

also set fire to all the houses of Jerusalem. Every important building was burned.

[10]The whole Babylonian army broke down the walls around Jerusalem. That army was led by the commander of the king's special guards. [11]Nebuzaradan, the commander of the guards, took captive the people left in

the people were also taken away. [12]But the commander left behind some of the poorest people of the land. They were to take care of the vineyards and fields.

[13]The Babylonians broke up the bronze pillars, the bronze stands and the large bronze bowl, which was called the Sea. These were in the Temple of the

> **"The whole Babylonian army broke down the walls around Jerusalem."**
>
> *2 Kings 25:10*

trimmers, dishes and all the bronze objects. These were used to serve in the Temple. [15]The commander of the king's special guards took away the pans for carrying hot coals. He also took the bowls and everything made of pure gold or silver. [16]There was so much bronze that it could not be weighed. There were two pillars and the large bronze bowl. There were also the movable stands which Solomon had made for the Temple of the Lord. [17]Each pillar was about 27 feet high. The bronze capital[d] on top of the pillar was about 4 1/2 feet high. It was decorated with a net design and bronze pomegranates[d] all around

GET CONNECTED

RELATIONSHIPS WITH AUTHORITY

Don't Follow That Leader King after king had taken the throne, each one seemingly more evil than the one before. It was no wonder that Israel had left their God, and no wonder that they ended up in captivity.

While God does place our authority figures over us, and while we should always be respectful, we don't always have to agree with them. In your lifetime you will encounter some people, maybe even some teachers, who will tell you the Bible is make-believe. That creation never happened. Maybe even that God doesn't exist.

Study God's Word for yourself so that you will be ready when anyone challenges your faith. Be prepared to give a reason for why you believe what you do. Then, even if it is an adult who tries to lead you astray, you can stand firm on the truth of God's Word and help your friends stay on track, as well.

Jerusalem. And he took captive those who had surrendered to the king of Babylon. The rest of

Lord. Then they carried the bronze to Babylon. [14]They also took the pots, shovels, wick

> **"The Babylonians broke up the bronze pillars, the bronze stands and the large bronze bowl, which was called the Sea."** *2 Kings 25:13*

BIBLE BASICS

WHO ARE THE BABYLONIANS?

The Babylonians, also known as Chaldeans, were a people who lived to the east of Israel. Babylon was the largest city in Babylonia. Because the people of Babylon worshiped foreign gods, Babylonians and Israelites were not friends. When Nebuchadnezzar became king, he conquered the Israelite land and forced the people of Judah to go to Babylonia as slaves.

it. The other pillar also had a net design. It was like the first pillar.

JUDAH IS TAKEN PRISONER

¹⁸The commander of the guards took some prisoners. He took Seraiah the chief priest, Zephaniah the priest next in rank, and the three doorkeepers. ¹⁹The commander also took other people who were still in the city. He took the officer in charge of the fighting men. He also took five people who advised the king. And he took the royal assistant who selected people for the army. And he took 60 other men who were in the city. ²⁰Nebuzaradan, the

commander, took all these people. And he brought them to the king of Babylon at Riblah. ²¹There at Riblah, in the land of Hamath, the king had them killed. So the people of Judah were led away from their country as captives.

GEDALIAH BECOMES GOVERNOR

²²Nebuchadnezzar king of Babylon left some people in the land of Judah. He appointed Gedaliah son of Ahikam as governor. (Ahikam was the son of Shaphan.)

²³The army captains and their men heard that the king of Babylon had made Gedaliah governor. So they all came to Gedaliah at Mizpah. They were Ishmael son of Nethaniah and Johanan son of Kareah. Also there were Seraiah son of Tanhumeth the Netophathite, Jaazaniah son of the Maacathite and their men. ²⁴Then Gedaliah made promises to these army captains and their men. He said, "Don't be afraid of the Babylonian officers. Live in the land and serve the king of Babylon. Then everything will go well for you."

²⁵Ishmael was the son of Nethaniah. Nethaniah was the son of Elishama from the king's family. In the seventh month Ishmael came with ten men and killed Gedaliah. They also killed the men of Judah and Babylon who were with Gedaliah at Mizpah. ²⁶Then all the people, from the least important to the most important, ran away to Egypt. The army leaders also went. This was because they were afraid of the Babylonians.

JEHOIACHIN IS SET FREE

²⁷Jehoiachin king of Judah was held in Babylon for 37 years. In the thirty-seventh year Evil-Merodach became king of Babylon. He let Jehoiachin out of prison on the twenty-seventh day of the twelfth month. ²⁸Evil-Merodach spoke kindly to Jehoiachin. He gave Jehoiachin a seat of honor. It was above the seats of the other kings who were with him in Babylon. ²⁹So Jehoiachin put away his prison clothes. For the rest of his life, he ate at the king's table. ³⁰Every day the king gave Jehoiachin an allowance. This lasted as long as he lived.

STORIES FROM

NEHEMIAH

Nehemiah
Rebuilds the Wall

NEHEMIAH 1:1—3:1;
4:1-23; 6:1, 9-16

NEHEMIAH'S PRAYER

1 These are the words of Nehemiah son of Hacaliah.

I, Nehemiah, was in the capital city of Susa. It was in the month of Kislev. This was in the twentieth year.[n] ²One of my brothers named Hanani came from Judah. Some other men were with him. I asked them about the Jews who lived through the captivity. And I also asked about Jerusalem.

³They answered, "Nehemiah, those who are left from the captivity are back in the area of Judah. But they are in much trouble and are full of shame. The wall around Jerusalem is broken down. And its gates have been burned."

⁴When I heard these things, I sat down and cried for several days. I was sad and did not eat food. I prayed to the God of heaven. ⁵I said, "Lord, God of heaven, you are the great God who is to be respected. You keep your agreement of love with those who love you and obey your commands. ⁶Listen carefully. Look at me. Hear the prayer

> **"Lord, God of heaven, you are the great God who is to be respected."** *Nehemiah 1:5*

During the Babylonian exile, many Jews traveled to Elephantine, an island in the Nile River in the northern part of Egypt. They built colonies there and left behind a huge collection of papyri (the kind of paper they used for writing) and pieces of pottery with inscriptions on them. Much of the information we have today on fifth-century B.C. Jews comes from these artifacts.

 1:1 **twentieth year** This is probably referring to the twentieth year King Artaxerxes I ruled Persia.

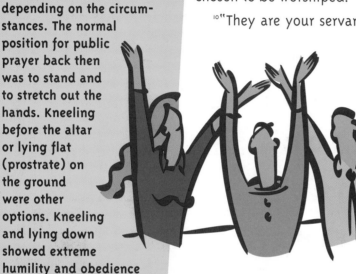

JUST LIKE TODAY, people in Bible days prayed in different positions depending on the circumstances. The normal position for public prayer back then was to stand and to stretch out the hands. Kneeling before the altar or lying flat (prostrate) on the ground were other options. Kneeling and lying down showed extreme humility and obedience to God.

you are unfaithful, I will scatter you among the nations. ⁹But if you come back to me and obey my commands, I will gather your people. I will gather them from the far ends of the earth. And I will bring them from captivity to where I have chosen to be worshiped.'

¹⁰"They are your servants and your people. You have saved them with your great strength and power. ¹¹Lord, listen carefully to my prayer. I am your servant. And listen to the prayers of your servants who love to honor you. Give me, your servant, success today. Allow this king to show kindness to me."

I was the one who served wine to the king.

your servant is praying to you day and night. I am praying for your servants, the people of Israel. I confess the sins we Israelites have done against you. My father's family and I have sinned against you. ⁷We have been wicked toward you. We have not obeyed the commands, rules and laws you gave your servant Moses.

⁸"Remember what you taught your servant Moses. You said, 'If

NEHEMIAH IS SENT TO JERUSALEM

2 It was the month of Nisan. It was in the twentieth year King Artaxerxes was king. He wanted some wine. So I took some and gave it to the king. I had not been sad in his presence before. ²So the king said, "Why does your face look sad? You are not sick. Your heart must be sad."

Then I was very afraid. ³I said to the king, "May the king live forever! My face is sad because the city where my ancestors are buried lies in ruins. And its gates have been destroyed by fire."

⁴Then the king said to me, "What do you want?"

First I prayed to the God of heaven. ⁵Then I answered the

> **"Why does your face look sad? You are not sick. Your heart must be sad."**
>
> *Nehemiah 2:2*

GOOD FOOD

Unscramble the label on each container to discover what kind of food is inside.
All of these foods are mentioned in the Bible.

R O L U F _ _ _ _ _

O N Y H E _ _ _ _ _

N R O C _ _ _ _

S T R U i F _ _ _ _ _

S F i H _ _ _ _

3-D

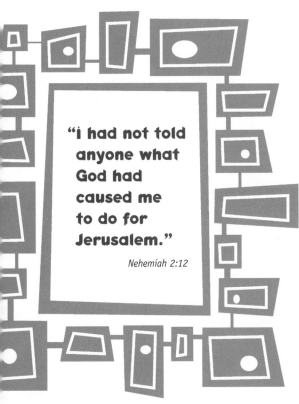

"i had not told anyone what God had caused me to do for Jerusalem."

Nehemiah 2:12

king, "Send me to the city in Judah where my ancestors are buried. I will rebuild it. Do this if you are willing and if I have pleased you."

⁶The queen was sitting next to the king. He asked me, "How long will your trip take? When will you get back?" It pleased the king to send me. So I set a time.

⁷I also said to him, "If you are willing, give me letters for the governors west of the Euphrates River. Tell them to let me pass safely through their lands on my way to Judah. ⁸And may I have a letter for Asaph? He is the keeper of the king's forest. Tell him to give me timber. I will need it to make boards for the gates of the palace. It is by the Temple.ᵈ The wood is also for the city wall and the house I will live in." So the king gave me the letters. This was because God was showing kindness to me.

⁹So I went to the governors west of the Euphrates River. I gave them the king's letters. The king had also sent army officers and soldiers on horses with me.

¹⁰Sanballat the Horonite and Tobiah the Ammonite leader heard about this. They were upset that someone had come to help the Israelites.

NEHEMIAH INSPECTS JERUSALEM

¹¹I went to Jerusalem and stayed there three days. ¹²Then at night I started out with a few men. I had not told anyone what God had caused me to do for Jerusalem. There were no animals with me except the one I was riding.

REAL SUPER HEROES

NEHEMIAH

Nehemiah shares his story much like a grandfather remembering the past. As his story unfolds, you find not only facts, but also the heart behind this man who truly loved God and his people. His story happened in the time when the Israelites had returned to Judah after having been held captive for many years. His desire was to rebuild the broken-down walls surrounding Jerusalem and restore the hope of community his people had once enjoyed.

Rebuilding a lost kingdom would not be easy. Many of the surrounding nations didn't want the Jews to become strong again. They threatened Nehemiah and tried many times to stop his efforts. But Nehemiah was a man of prayer. Instead of fearing man, he immediately turned to God for help. His prayers reveal an honest heart—one not afraid to admit weakness or need. They were prayers that trusted God to do the work. And God answered.

Nehemiah reminds us that our strength lies not in our determination or our ability, but in God who causes all things to work according to his will.

¹³It was night. I went out through the Valley Gate. I rode toward the Dragon Well and the Trash Gate. I was inspecting the walls of Jerusalem. They had been broken down. And the gates had been destroyed by fire. ¹⁴Then I rode on toward the Fountain Gate

GET CONNECTED

RELATIONSHIPS WITH FAMILY

The Family Fortress Nehemiah knew that Jerusalem needed protection from enemies. That's why he prayed and worked so hard to rebuild the walls of Jerusalem. They needed a fortress so the city could become strong again.

Our families need protection, just like Jerusalem. We need to build walls around us, too—though not the brick and mortar kind. We need to protect ourselves from the sneaky ways Satan tries to come in and break up our families. Do you have a sibling who has wronged you? Talk with them about it, and forgive him. Were you disrespectful to your mom? Apologize. Work hard to make sure that no bitterness or bad feelings grow in your heart toward anyone in your family. Pray even harder that God will be the fortress around your family, to protect you and shower you with grace and peace.

and the King's Pool. But there was not enough room for the animal I was riding to get through. ¹⁵So I went up the valley at night. I was inspecting the wall. Finally, I turned and went back in through the Valley Gate. ¹⁶The officers did not know where I had gone or what I was doing. I had not yet said anything to the Jews, the priests, the important men or the officers. I had not said anything to any of the others who would do the work.

¹⁷Then I said to them, "You can see the trouble we have here. Jerusalem is a pile of ruins. And its gates have been burned. Come, let's rebuild the wall of Jerusalem. Then we won't be full of shame any longer." ¹⁸I also told them how God had been kind to me. And I told them what the king had said to me.

Then they answered, "Let's start rebuilding." So they began to work hard.

¹⁹But Sanballat the Horonite, Tobiah the Ammonite leader and Geshem the Arab heard about it. They made fun of us and laughed at us. They said, "What are you doing? Are you turning against the king?"

²⁰But I answered them, "The God of heaven will give us success. We are God's servants. We will start rebuilding. But you have no share in Jerusalem. You have no claim or past right to it."

BUILDERS OF THE WALL

3 Eliashib the high priest and his fellow priests went to work. They rebuilt the Sheep Gate. They gave it to the Lord's service and set its doors in place. They worked as far as the Tower of the Hundred, and they gave it to the Lord's service. Then they went on to the Tower of Hananel.

• • •

THOSE AGAINST THE REBUILDING

4 Sanballat heard we were rebuilding the wall. He was very angry, even furious. He made fun of the Jews. ²He said to his friends and the army of Samaria, "What are these weak

> **"Don't be afraid of them. Remember the Lord. He is great and others are afraid of him."** *Nehemiah 4:14*

Jews doing? They think they can rebuild the wall. They think they will offer sacrifices. Maybe they think they can finish rebuilding it in only one day. They can't bring stones back to life. These are piles of trash and ashes."

³Tobiah the Ammonite was next to Sanballat. Tobiah said, "A fox could climb up on what they are building. Even it could break down their stone wall."

⁴I prayed, "Hear us, our God. We are hated. Turn the insults of Sanballat and Tobiah back on their own heads. Let them be captured and taken away like valuables that are stolen. ⁵Do not hide their guilt. Do not take away their sins so you can't see them. The builders have seen them make you angry."

⁶So we rebuilt the wall until all of it went halfway up. The people were willing to work hard.

⁷But Sanballat, Tobiah, the Arabs, the Ammonites and the men from Ashdod were very

angry. They heard that the repairs to Jerusalem's walls were continuing. And they heard that the holes in the wall were being closed. ⁸So they all made plans

> **"A fox could climb up on what they are building. Even it could break down their stone wall."** *Nehemiah 4:3*

against Jerusalem. They planned to come and fight and stir up trouble. ⁹But we prayed to our God. And we appointed guards to watch for them day and night.

¹⁰The people of Judah said, "The workers are getting tired. There is too much dirt and trash. We cannot rebuild the wall."

"And our enemies said, "The Jews won't know it or see us. But we will come among them and kill them. We will stop the work."

¹²Then the Jews who lived near our enemies came. They told us ten times, "Everywhere you turn, the enemy will attack us." ¹³So I put some of the people behind the lowest places along the wall. And I put some at the open places. I put families together with their swords, spears and bows. ¹⁴Then I looked around. I stood up and spoke to the important men, the leaders and the rest of the people. I said, "Don't be afraid of them. Remember the Lord. He is great and others are afraid of him. And fight for your brothers, your sons and daughters, your

wives and your homes."

[15]Then our enemies heard that we knew about their plans. God had ruined their plans. So we all went back to the wall. Each person went back to his own work.

[16]From that day on, half my men worked on the wall. The other half was ready with spears, shields, bows and armor. The officers stood in back of the people of Judah [17]who were building the wall. Those who carried materials did their work with one hand. They carried a weapon in the other hand. [18]Each builder wore his sword at his side as he worked. The man who blew the trumpet to warn the people stayed next to me.

[19]Then I spoke to the important men, the leaders and the rest of the people. I said, "This is a very big job. We are spreading out along the wall. We are far apart. [20]So wherever you hear the sound of the trumpet, assemble there. Our God will fight for us."

[21]So we continued to work. Half the men held spears. We worked from sunrise till the stars came out. [22]At that time I also said to the people, "Let every man and his helper stay inside Jerusalem at night. They can be our guards at night. And they can be workmen during the day." [23]Neither I, my brothers, my men nor the guards with me ever took off our clothes. Each person carried his weapon even when he went for water.

• • •

MORE PROBLEMS FOR NEHEMIAH

6 Then Sanballat, Tobiah, Geshem the Arab and our other enemies heard that I had rebuilt the wall. There was not one gap in it. But I had not yet set the doors in the gates.

• • •

[9]Our enemies were trying to scare us. They were thinking, "They will get too weak to work. Then the wall will not be finished."

LIVIN' IT!

A MIGHTY FORTRESS NEHEMIAH 6:1, 9-16

Nehemiah had more than one enemy. Several of the surrounding nations were upset that he had successfully rebuilt Jerusalem's wall. All that was left were the doors and gates. So his enemies plotted together. They hired prophets to tell Nehemiah lies to make him sin. They worked hard to try to kill him, but they couldn't. Nehemiah never listened to them. He obeyed only God.

Like Nehemiah, we have an enemy after our souls. Satan and his followers want to trick us into sin so that we won't follow God. We need to remember Nehemiah. We must stay on guard and keep close to God through prayer. God says that he is a mighty fortress, and Satan can never win against him. That's why we're always safe when we're obeying God.

But I prayed, "God, make me strong."

[10]One day I went to the house of Shemaiah son of Delaiah. Delaiah was the son of Mehetabel. Shemaiah had to stay at home.

> **"Wherever you hear the sound of the trumpet, assemble there. Our God will fight for us."**
>
> *Nehemiah 5:20*

CRAFTS

NEHEMIAH REBUILDS THE WALL

3-D

SUPPLIES

sugar cubes
glue
food coloring
small paper plate

INSTRUCTIONS

1. On a small paper plate, squeeze out a line of glue and place one row of sugar cubes on the glue.

2. To make a rainbow wall, use food coloring. Place one to two drops of coloring on each sugar cube.

3. Cover the top of the sugar cubes with glue, and lay down a second row.

4. Repeat coloring, glue, and sugar cubes until your wall is done.

ALL ABOUT IT:

Before Nehemiah asked the king to let him go rebuild the city wall, he prayed to God: "Lord, listen carefully to my prayer. I am your servant. . . . Give me, your servant, success today. Allow this king to show kindness to me" (Nehemiah 1:11). When we pray before we do things, we allow God to use us.

Not only did the king allow Nehemiah to rebuild the city wall, but he also sent people to help him rebuild it. Prayer is powerful!

Think about the wall you want God to tear down and rebuild in your life. As you see your wall this week, ask God to help you build walls of faithfulness and belief.

He said, "Nehemiah, let's meet in the Temple[d] of God. Let's go inside the Temple and close the doors. Men are coming at night to kill you."

[11]But I said, "Should a man like me run away? Should I run into the Temple to save my life? I will not go." [12]I knew that God had not sent him. Tobiah and Sanballat had paid him to prophesy against me. [13]They paid him to frighten me so I would do this and sin. Then they could give me a bad name to shame me.

[14]I prayed, "Remember Tobiah and Sanballat, my God. Remember what they have done. Also remember the prophetess Noadiah and the other prophets who have been trying to frighten me."

THE WALL IS FINISHED

[15]So the wall of Jerusalem was completed. It was on the twenty-fifth day of the month of Elul. It took 52 days to rebuild. [16]Then all our enemies heard about it. And all the nations around us saw it. So they were shamed. They understood that the work had been done with the help of our God.

"So the wall was completed....it took 52 days to rebuild....And all the nations around us saw it....They understood that the work had been done with the help of our God."

Nehemiah 6:15-16

NEHEMIAH REBUILDS THE WALL

Complete the story below by using the words in the word pool at the bottom of this page. You can read the entire story in Nehemiah 1-6.

Nehemiah was a _____ of the king of Persia. One day when he was _____ the king, the king said, "Why are you so _____?" Nehemiah answered, "The _____ where my ancestors are buried lies in _____. And its _____ have been destroyed by _____." The king asked, "What do you want?" First, Nehemiah _____ to the God of _____ and then said, "Send me to the city in _____. I will rebuild it." It pleased the king to send Nehemiah.

So Nehemiah went to _____ and stayed there _____ days. He went out at night to inspect the _____ of Jerusalem. Then he said to the people, "Come, let's _____ the wall of Jerusalem."

The people began to rebuild the gates and wall, even though some people made fun of them and _____ at them. When the wall was rebuilt about _____ up, _____, _____, the Arabs, and the Ammonites made plans to _____ Jerusalem. But the people of Judah prayed and appointed _____ to watch out for them while they continued to build. Nehemiah organized the people so that half of them built while the other half was ready with _____, _____, _____, and armor. Nehemiah told the people, "This is a very big _____, but our God will fight for us."

So the people continued to work, and the wall was _____ in 52 _____. When the enemies of the people of Israel heard what had been done, they were _____. They understood that the work had been done with the _____ of God.

Word Pool

bows   city   completed   days   fight
fire   gates   guards   halfway   heaven   help
Jerusalem   job   Judah   laughed   prayed   rebuild
ruins   sad   Sanballat   servant   serving   shamed
shields   spears   three   Tobiah   wall

ESTHER

QueEn Esther

ESTHER 1–5; 7–8

Vashti about the king's command. But she refused to come. Then the king became very angry. His anger was like a burning fire.

QUEEN VASHTI DISOBEYS THE KING

1 This is what happened during the time of King Xerxes. He was the king who ruled the 127 areas from India to Cush. ²In those days King Xerxes ruled from his capital city of Susa. ³In the third year of his rule, he gave a banquet. It was for all his important men and royal officers. The army leaders from the countries of Persia and Media were there. And the important men from all Xerxes' empire were there.

• • •

⁹Queen Vashti also gave a banquet. It was for the women in the royal palace of King Xerxes.

¹⁰On the seventh day of the banquet, King Xerxes was very happy because he had been drinking much wine. He gave a command to the seven eunuchs*d* who served him. They were Mehuman, Biztha, Harbona, Bigtha, Abagtha, Zethar and Carcas. ¹¹He commanded them to bring him Queen Vashti, wearing her royal crown. She was to come to show her beauty to the people and important men. She was very beautiful. ¹²The eunuchs told Queen

• • •

¹⁶Then Memucan spoke to the king and the other important men. He said, "Queen Vashti has not done wrong to the king alone. She has also done wrong to all the important men and all

History Highlights

486 B.C.
Xerxes I of Persia, also known as Ahaseurus, chooses Esther as queen.

7000 5000 3000 1000 0 1000 NOW

CRAFTS

QUEEN ESTHER

3-D

SUPPLIES

cereal box

scissors

construction paper

glitter glue

buttons, sequins,
   old costume jewelry

stapler

INSTRUCTIONS

1. Cut a four-inch band off the middle of a cereal box.

2. Cut peaks in the top of the band.

3. Cut and staple the "crown" to fit your head.

4. Glue construction paper on the crown to cover the cereal label.

5. Decorate your crown with glitter glue, sequins, buttons, and old costume jewelry.

ALL ABOUT IT:

Esther was afraid to talk to the king, but she knew that if she did, she would be able to help her family and friends. Esther's cousin Mordecai encouraged Esther when he said, "Who knows, you may have been chosen queen for just such a time as this" (Esther 4:14). Mordecai had faith that the Jews would be saved. However, he also saw that God had placed Esther in the right place at the right time.

Esther listened to her cousin's advice and was used by God to help save the Jews. When you accept Christ as your personal Savior, you become a child of God. You, too, are royalty! You are a prince or princess of the King. Just like Esther, there will be times in your life when you will be in just the right place at just the right time to be used by God to further his kingdom.

After you've made your crown, put it in your room where you will see it and remember your relationship with the King of heaven and earth.

the people in all the empire of King Xerxes. ¹⁷All the wives of the important men of Persia and Media will hear about the queen's actions. Then they will no longer honor their husbands. They will say, 'King Xerxes commanded Queen Vashti to be brought to him. But she refused to come.' ¹⁸Today the wives of the important men of Persia and Media have heard about the queen's actions. And they will speak in the same way to their husbands. And there will be no end to disrespect and anger.

¹⁹"So, our king, if it pleases you, give a royal order. And let it be written in the laws of Persia and Media, which cannot be changed. The law should say Vashti is never again to enter the presence of King Xerxes. Also let the king give her place as queen to someone who is better than she is. ²⁰And let the king's order be announced everywhere in his large kingdom. Then all the women will respect their husbands, from the greatest to the least important."

²¹The king and his important men were happy with this advice. So King Xerxes did as Memucan suggested.

• • •

ESTHER IS MADE QUEEN

2 Then the king's personal servants had a suggestion. They said, "Let a search be made for beautiful young virgins*d* for the king.

• • •

⁴Then let the girl who most pleases the king become queen in place of Vashti." The king liked this advice. So he did as they said.

⁵Now there was a Jewish man in the palace of Susa. His name was Mordecai son of Jair. Jair was the son of Shimei.

LiViN' iT!

THE GREAT ADVENTURE
ESTHER 4:14

If she could have written the story of her life, she couldn't have dreamed of such an amazing plot. First, Esther's parents had died. She was an orphan until her cousin Mordecai adopted her as his own. Both she and Mordecai had been taken captive under King Nebuchadnezzar's rule. Then, over all the other women in the kingdom, Esther was chosen to become the Queen of Persia. As queen, she was able to save her people and destroy her enemies.

Sometimes we think we know how we want our life to go. We decide what we think is normal— hair, clothes, friends, grades, whatever—and we just try to make our "normal" work out. But God isn't normal. He has incredible ideas for us beyond our wildest imaginations! We need to let go of our plans and ask him to work out his plans for us. Experiencing God's adventure is the only way to really live!

And Shimei was the son of Kish. Mordecai was from the tribe[d] of Benjamin. [6]Mordecai had been taken captive from Jerusalem by Nebuchadnezzar king of Babylon. Mordecai was part of the group taken into captivity with Jehoiachin king of Judah. [7]Mordecai had a cousin named Hadassah, who had no father or mother. So Mordecai took care of her. Hadassah was also called Esther, and she had a very pretty figure and face. Mordecai had adopted her as his own daughter when her father and mother died.

[8]The king's command and order had been heard. And many girls had been brought to the palace in Susa. They had been put under the care of Hegai. When this happened,

"The king was pleased with Esther more than with any of the other virgins."
Esther 2:17

Esther was also taken to the king's palace. She was put into the care of Hegai, who was in charge of the women. [9]Esther pleased Hegai, and he liked her. So Hegai quickly began giving Esther her beauty

treatments and special food. He gave her seven servant girls chosen from the king's palace. Then Hegai moved Esther and her seven servant girls to the best part of the women's quarters.

[10]Esther did not tell anyone about her family or who her people were. Mordecai had told her not to. [11]Every day Mordecai walked back and forth near the courtyard. This was where the king's women lived. He wanted to find out how Esther was and what was happening to her.

[12]Before a girl could take her turn with King Xerxes, she had to complete 12 months of beauty

REAL SUPER HEROES

ESTHER

Esther had it made. The king had chosen her—a beautiful Jewish woman— to be his queen. So when Mordecai told her that she needed to risk her life to help the Israelite people, she could have easily said no. But she didn't.

Esther loved God and her people more than she loved her own wonderful, royal life. She understood that God had allowed her to be queen just so that she could save her people. And she did. After a lot of prayer and fasting (going without food), Esther wisely showed the king Haman's evil plans to destroy the Jews. Esther and her people were spared, and Haman was hanged as a result.

God has a special plan for you, too. He has made you just the way you are so that you can serve him in your own unique way. Pray that he will show you what your gifts are and how you can use them for his glory.

treatments. These were ordered for the women. For 6 months she was treated with oil and myrrh.[d] And she spent 6 months with perfumes and cosmetics. [13]Then she was ready to go to the king. Anything she asked for was given to her. She could take it with her from the women's quarters to the king's palace. [14]In the evening she would go to the king's palace. And in the morning she would return to another part of the women's quarters. There she would be placed under the care of a man named Shaashgaz. Shaashgaz was the king's eunuch in charge of the slave women.[d] The girl would not go back to the king again unless he was pleased with her. Then he would call her by name to come back to him.

[15]Esther daughter of Abihail, Mordecai's uncle, had been adopted by Mordecai. The time came for Esther to go to the king. She asked for only what Hegai suggested she should take. (Hegai was the king's eunuch who was in charge of the women.) And everyone who saw Esther liked her. [16]So Esther was taken to King Xerxes in the royal palace. This happened in the tenth month, the month of Tebeth. It was in Xerxes' seventh year as king.

DIG THIS!

No matter what you call him, Mordecai was a hero. Under the name "Marduka," archaeologists have found mention of him in several different places—including an ancient Babylonian tablet dating back to the reign of King Xerxes I that was found in modern central Iraq. The same name has also been found in Aramaic papyri of the same century.

[17]And the king was pleased with Esther more than with any of the other virgins. And he liked her more than any of the others. So King Xerxes put a royal crown on Esther's head. And he made her queen in place of Vashti. [18]Then the king gave a great banquet for Esther. He invited all his important men and royal officers. He announced a holiday in all the empire. And he was generous and gave everyone a gift.

• • •

HAMAN PLANS TO DESTROY THE JEWS

3 After these things happened, King Xerxes honored Haman son of Hammedatha the Agagite. He gave Haman a new rank that was higher than all the important men. [2]And all the royal officers at the king's gate would bow down and kneel before Haman. This was what the king had ordered. But Mordecai would not bow down, and he did not kneel.

• • •

[5]Then Haman saw that Mordecai would not bow down to him or kneel before him. And he became very angry. [6]He had been

"He announced a holiday in all the empire. And he was generous and gave everyone a gift."

Esther 2:18

WHO RULES THE ROOST?

Esther was chosen as queen of Persia—but even then, she knew God was in control. How much do you know about her royal story of service? Take this quiz and see for yourself.

1 WHO WAS KING IN ESTHER'S DAY?

A Nebuchadnezzar
B Hiram
C Xerxes
D Tutankhamun

2 WHY WAS HE LOOKING FOR A QUEEN?

A His wife had died.
B He had never been married.
C His wife annoyed him, so he got rid of her.
D He wanted to please the people.

3 WHAT WAS HIS FIRST WIFE'S NAME?

A Ruth
B Deborah
C Delilah
D Vashti

4 WHO WERE ESTHER'S PARENTS?

A John and Mary
B Abihail, Mordecai's uncle
C Haman and Jezebel
D Elizabeth and Hezekiah

5 HOW LONG DID THE BEAUTY TREATMENTS LAST?

A a day
B a week
C a month
D a year

6 WHAT DID MORDECAI DISCOVER AFTER ESTHER BECAME QUEEN?

A Evil men were plotting to kill the king.
B Evil men were plotting to kill Esther.
C The king had a secret treasury.
D None of the above.

7 WHO DID HAMAN PLAN TO KILL?

A the Babylonians
B the Jews
C the Persians
D the king

8 HOW DID ESTHER TELL THE KING THE NEWS?

A She held several banquets.
B She sent him a letter.
C She gave the message through a servant.
D She hoped he'd figure it out.

9 WHAT DID HAMAN BUILD?

A a house for himself
B a bridge for the army
C a hanging platform to kill Mordecai
D a bow and arrow for the king

10 WHO DIED IN THE END?

A Mordecai
B Haman
C Esther
D the king

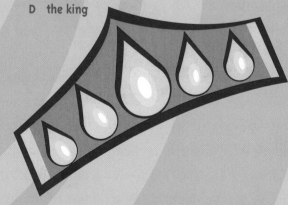

Score 9-10: Congratulations! You have the golden scepter. **Score 7-8:** Good—you're next in line.
Score 5-6: You're a servant in the court. **Score 4 or below:** Peasant status! Read up to become royalty!

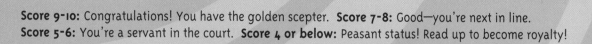

ANSWERS: 1: c; 2: c; 3: d; 4: b; 5: d; 6: a; 7: b; 8: a; 9: c; 10: b

LIVIN' IT!

STRENGTH IN NUMBERS
ESTHER 4:16

Here she was—queen of Persia. Esther could have become a snob. She could have pretended like she wasn't a part of the Jewish culture, which ranked low in the order of social importance. But she didn't. She remembered that, above all, she belonged to God and was a part of his family. When it came time to risk her position and life to save her people, she turned to the Jews for help. She asked them to fast (give up eating) and pray so that God would give her success.

God gives us other believers to encourage and help us, too. We should never feel alone in this world, not only because God is always with us, but also because he wants us to stay connected to his people. By going to church and having Christian friends, we are able to stay strong in our faith and receive help when we need it most.

told who the people of Mordecai were. And he thought of himself as too important to try to kill only Mordecai. So he looked for a way to destroy all of Mordecai's people, the Jews, in all of Xerxes' kingdom.

•••

⁸Then Haman said to King Xerxes, "There is a certain group of people in all the areas of your kingdom. They are scattered among the other people. They keep themselves separate. Their customs are different from those of all the other people. And they do not obey the king's laws. It is not right for you to allow them to continue living in your kingdom. ⁹If it pleases the king, let an order be given to destroy those people. Then I will pay 375 tons of silver to those who do the king's business. They will put it into the royal treasury."

¹⁰So the king took his signet ring off and gave it to Haman. Haman son of Hammedatha, the Agagite, was the enemy of the Jews. ¹¹Then the king said to Haman, "The money and the people are yours. Do with them as you please."

•••

¹³Letters were sent by messengers to all the king's empire. They stated the king's order to destroy, kill and completely wipe out all the Jews. That meant young and old, women and little children, too. The order said to kill all the Jews on a single day. That was to be the thirteenth day of the twelfth month, which was Adar. And it said to take all the things that belonged to the Jews. ¹⁴A copy of the order was to be given out as a law in every area. It was to be made known to all the people so that they would be ready for that day.

¹⁵The messengers set out, hurried by the king's command. At the same time the order was given in the palace at Susa. And the king and Haman sat down to drink. But the city of Susa was in confusion.

> "No man or woman may go to the king in the inner courtyard without being called."
>
> *Esther 4:11*

Dig This!

MORDECAI ASKS ESTHER TO HELP

4 Now Mordecai heard about all that had been done. To show how upset he was, he tore his clothes. Then he put on rough cloth and ashes. And he went out into the city crying loudly and very sadly.

. . .

⁴Esther's servant girls and eunuchs^d came to her and told her about Mordecai. Esther was very upset and afraid. She sent clothes for Mordecai to put on instead of the rough cloth. But he would not wear them. ⁵Then Esther called for Hathach. He was one of the king's eunuchs chosen by the king to serve her. Esther ordered him to find out what was bothering Mordecai and why.

⁶So Hathach went to Mordecai. Mordecai was in the city

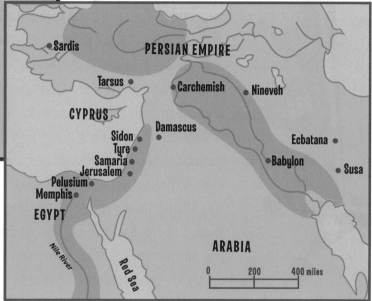

square in front of the king's gate. ⁷Then Mordecai told Hathach everything that had happened to him. And he told Hathach about the amount of money Haman had promised to pay into the king's treasury for the killing of the Jews. ⁸Mordecai also gave him a copy of the order to kill the Jews, which had been given in Susa. He wanted Hathach to show it to Esther and to tell her about it. And Mordecai told him to order Esther to go into the king's presence. He wanted her to beg for mercy and to plead with him for her people.

⁹Hathach went back and reported to Esther everything Mordecai had said. ¹⁰Then Esther told Hathach to say to Mordecai, ¹¹"All the royal officers and people of the royal areas know this: No man or woman may go to the king in the inner courtyard without being called. There is only one law about this. Anyone who enters must be put to death. But if the king holds out his gold scepter,^d that person may live. And I have not been called to go to the king for 30 days."

¹²And Esther's message was given to Mordecai. ¹³Then Mordecai gave orders to say to Esther: "Just because you live in the king's palace, don't think that out of all the Jews you alone

> **"Who knows, you may have been chosen queen for just such a time as this."**
> Esther 4:14

313

> "Then i will go
> to the king,
> even though
> it is against
> the law.
> And if i
> die, i die."
>
> *Esther 4:16*

will escape. ¹⁴You might keep quiet at this time. Then someone else will help and save the Jews. But you and your father's family will all die. And who knows, you may have been chosen queen for just such a time as this."

¹⁵Then Esther sent this answer to Mordecai: ¹⁶"Go and get all the Jews in Susa together. For my sake, give up eating. Do not eat or drink for three days, night and day. I and my servant girls will also give up eating. Then I will go to the king, even though it is against the law. And if I die, I die."

¹⁷So Mordecai went away. He did everything Esther had told him to do.

ESTHER SPEAKS TO THE KING

5 On the third day Esther put on her royal robes. Then she stood in the inner courtyard of the king's palace, facing the king's hall. The king was sitting on his royal throne in the hall, facing the doorway. ²The king saw Queen Esther standing in the courtyard. When he saw her, he was very pleased. He held out to her the gold scepter[d] that was in his hand. So Esther went up to him and touched the end of the scepter.

³Then the king asked, "What is it, Queen Esther? What do you want to ask me? I will give you as much as half of my kingdom."

⁴Esther answered, "My king, if it pleases you, come today with Haman to a banquet. I have prepared it for you."

• • •

HAMAN IS HANGED

7 So the king and Haman went in to eat with Queen Esther. ²They were drinking wine. And the king said to Esther on this second day also, "What are you asking for? I will give it to you. What is it you want? I will give you as much as half of my kingdom."

³Then Queen Esther answered, "My king, I hope you are pleased with me. If it pleases you, let me live. This is what I ask. And let my people live, too. This is what I want. ⁴I ask this because my people and I have been sold to be destroyed. We are to be killed and completely wiped out. If we had been sold as male and female slaves, I would have kept quiet. That would not be enough of a problem to bother the king."

GAMES & QUIZZES

ACROSS

1 To give up eating (4:16)
2 Mordecai's father (2:5)
4 King's house (1:5)
5 What Mordecai wore: Sackcloth (or rough cloth) and _____ (4:1)
6 Each drinking vessel was unique, different from the _____ vessels (1:7)
9 All the officials gave _____ to the Jews (9:3)
10 What Esther invited the king and Haman to attend (5:8)
11 King Xerxes' response to Harbona: "_____ Haman on it!" (7:9)
12 Goes with ashes: _____cloth (4:1)

DOWN

1 Another word for banquet or celebration with lots of food
2 Mordecai's nationality; he was a _____ (2:5)
3 King Xerxes' first queen (1:9)
4 Esther asked the king to spare her _____ (7:3)
7 Official documents were sealed with the king's _____ (8:8)
8 What Esther became (2:17)
10 The king called for a _____ to be read to him when he couldn't sleep (6:1)

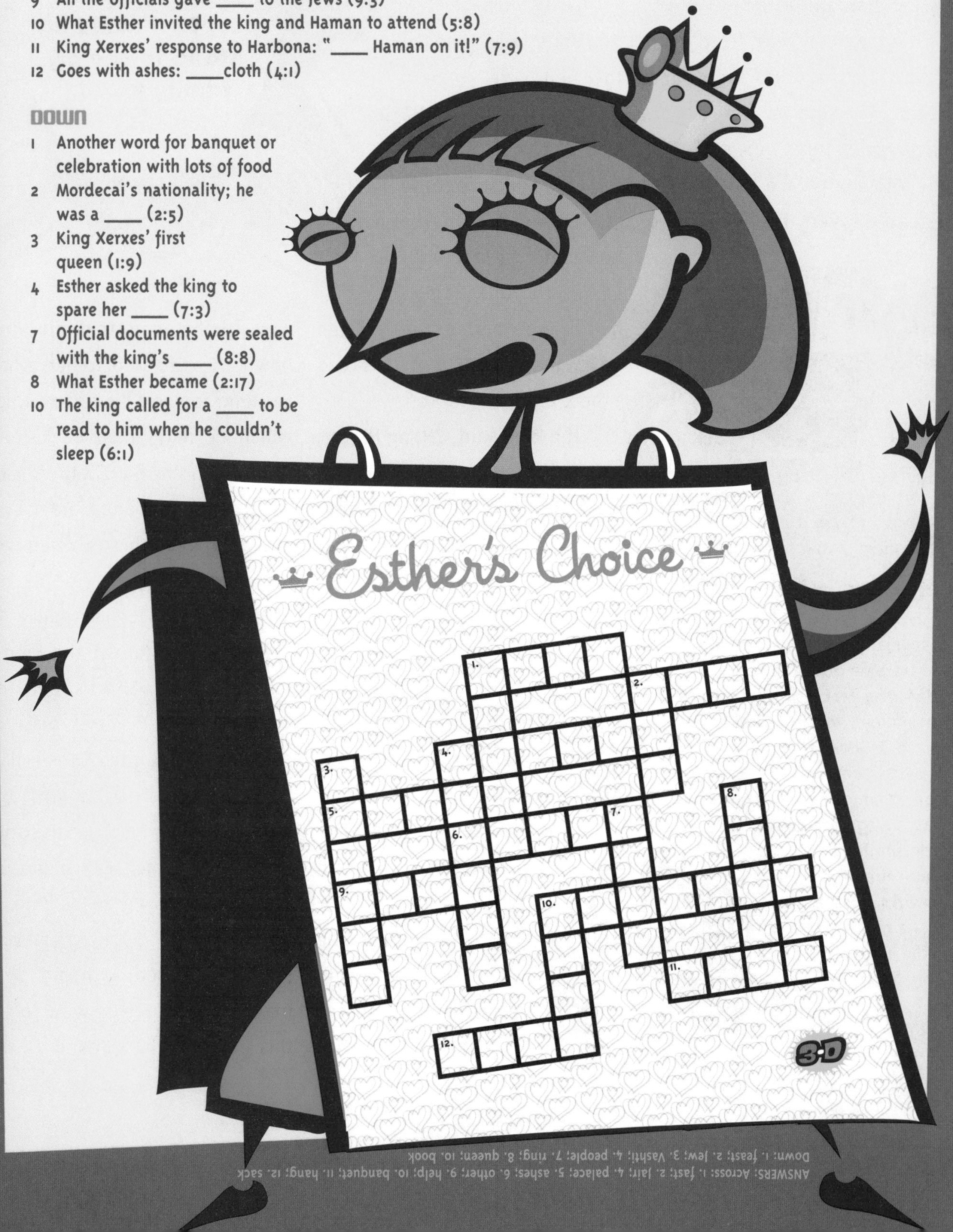

👑 After each clue, you will find the chapter and verse in the book of Esther where the answer may be found.

♛ ~ Esther's Choice ~ ♛

3-D

⁵Then King Xerxes asked Queen Esther, "Who is he? Where is he? Who has done such a thing?"

⁶Esther said, "A man who is against us! Our enemy is this wicked Haman!"

Then Haman was filled with terror before the king and queen. ⁷The king was very angry. He got up, left his wine and went out into the palace garden. But Haman stayed inside to beg Queen Esther to save his life. He could see that the king had already decided to kill him.

• • •

⁹Harbona was one of the eunuchs[d] there serving the king. He said, "Look, a platform for hanging people stands near Haman's house. It is 75 feet high. This is the one Haman had prepared for Mordecai, who gave the warning that saved the king."

The king said, "Hang Haman on it!" ¹⁰So they hanged Haman on the platform he had prepared for Mordecai. Then the king was not so angry anymore.

• • •

THE KING HELPS THE JEWS

8 That same day King Xerxes gave Queen Esther everything Haman had left when he died. Haman had been the enemy of the Jews. And Mordecai came in to see the king. He came because Esther had told the king how he was related to her. ²Then the king took off his signet[d] ring, which he had taken back from Haman. And he gave it to Mordecai. Then Esther put Mordecai in charge of everything Haman had left when he died.

³Once again Esther spoke to the king. She fell at the king's feet and cried. She begged the king to stop the evil plan of Haman the Agagite. Haman had thought up the plan against the Jews. ⁴The king held out the gold scepter[d] to Esther. Esther got up and stood in front of the king.

⁵She said, "My king, I hope you are pleased with me. And maybe it will please you to do this. You might think it is the

BLAST FROM THE PAST

IT AIN'T EASY BEING BEAUTIFUL— especially if you were trying to become queen in Esther's day. The process of becoming queen was long and hard. It took Esther four years to enter the palace, and then one full year of applying special lotions, perfumes, and makeup—the works—just to get one night with the emperor.

> "i could not stand to see that terrible thing happen to my people. i could not stand to see my family killed."
>
> Esther 8:6

right thing to do. And maybe you are happy with me. If so, let an order be written to cancel the letters Haman wrote. [6]I could not stand to see that terrible thing happen to my people. I could not stand to see my family killed."

[7]King Xerxes answered Queen Esther and Mordecai the Jew. He said, "Because Haman was against the Jews, I have given his things to Esther. And my soldiers have hanged him. [8]Now write another order in the king's name. Write it to the Jews as it seems best to you. Then seal the order with the king's signet[d] ring. No letter written in the king's name and sealed with his signet ring can be canceled."

"Because Haman was against the Jews, I have given his things to Esther." Esther 8:7

PSALMS

The Praise Book for God's People

PSALMS 1; 36; 42; 84

BIBLE BASICS

WHAT IS CHAFF?

Chaff is the outer part, or husk, of grain. During harvest time, the stalks of grain were cut down, and the upper portion crushed. The chaff was separated from the grain by tossing both up into the air. Since the chaff was much lighter than the grain, the wind would blow away the chaff, while the grain would fall back to the threshing floor where it was gathered. The Bible also speaks of unbelievers as being "chaff."

TWO WAYS TO LIVE

1 Happy is the person who doesn't listen to the wicked.
He doesn't go where sinners go.
He doesn't do what bad people do.
²He loves the Lord's teachings.
He thinks about those teachings day and night.
³He is strong, like a tree planted by a river.
It produces fruit in season.
Its leaves don't die.
Everything he does will succeed.

⁴But wicked people are not like that.
They are like useless chaff[d] that the wind blows away.
⁵So the wicked will not escape God's punishment.
Sinners will not worship God with good people.
⁶This is because the Lord protects good people.
But the wicked will be destroyed.

GET CONNECTED

RELATIONSHIPS WITH GOD

Grow Up Memorizing Scripture is like roots to a plant. Without roots, the plant dies. Without remembering God's truth, we'll forget who God really is. So we need to take time to grow our roots.

It's not as hard as it may seem. Just pick a verse or a chapter that you want to remember. Every day, read over it several times, and try to say it in your head. Then, throughout the day, remind yourself of it and even say it to someone else. Just think: If you learned just one verse a week, you'd know 52 verses by the end of the year!

WICKED MEN AND A GOOD GOD

For the director of music.
Of David, the servant of the Lord.

36 Sin speaks to the wicked man in his heart.
He has no fear of or respect for God.
² He thinks too much of himself.
He doesn't see his sin and hate it.
³ His words are wicked lies.
He is no longer wise or good.
⁴ At night he makes evil plans.
What he does leads to nothing good.
He doesn't refuse things that are evil.

⁵ Lord, your love reaches to the heavens.
Your loyalty goes to the skies.
⁶ Your goodness is as high as the mountains.
Your justice is as deep as the great ocean.
Lord, you protect both men and animals.
⁷ God, your love is so precious!
You protect people as a bird protects her young under her wings.
⁸ They eat the rich food in your house.
You let them drink from your river of pleasure.
⁹ You are the giver of life.
Your light lets us enjoy life.

¹⁰ Continue to love those who know you.
And continue to do good to those who are good.
¹¹ Don't let proud people attack me.
Don't let the wicked force me away.
¹² Those who do evil have been defeated.
They are overwhelmed; they cannot do evil any longer.

• • •

> "Your goodness is as high as the mountains. Your justice is as deep as the great ocean. Lord, you protect both men and animals."
>
> *Psalm 36:6*

LIVIN' IT!

THE COLOR OF JOY
PSALM 36:9

What makes life fun? Why do we enjoy the little pleasures like walks on the beach, time with friends, baking cookies, and more? God could have made life always very serious. Plain. Boring. But he didn't. If we'll notice, life can be vibrant, exciting, and fun!

What makes life fun? The Bible says that it is the light of God that brings us joy. When we are really experiencing a full relationship with God, his light shines into every moment. We see purpose behind every event. We see the smile of our Creator peeking through as we enjoy the very thing he created us to enjoy. In essence, when we enjoy God as the giver of life, we can drink deeply of the goodness and joy that comes from every moment spent with him.

WISHING TO BE NEAR GOD
For the director of music.
A maskil[d] of the sons of Korah.

42 A deer thirsts for a
   stream of water.
In the same way, I thirst
   for you, God.
[2]I thirst for the living God.
   When can I go to meet
   with him?
[3]Day and night, my tears
   have been my food.
People are always saying,
   "Where is your God?"
[4]When I remember these
   things,
   I speak with a broken heart.
I used to walk with the crowd.

I led the happy crowd to
   God's Temple,[d]
   with songs of praise.

[5]Why am I so sad?
   Why am I so upset?
I should put my hope in God.
   I should keep praising him,
   My Savior and [6]my God.

I am very sad.
   So I remember you while I
   am in the land where the
   Jordan River begins.
I will remember you while I
   am near the Hermon
   mountains

and on the mountain
   of Mizar.
[7]Troubles have come again
   and again.
   They sound like waterfalls.
Your waves are crashing
   all around me.
[8]The Lord shows his true
   love every day.
   At night I have a song,
   and I pray to my living
   God.
[9]I say to God, my Rock,[d]
   "Why have you forgotten
   me?
Why am I sad
   and troubled by my
   enemies?"
[10]My enemies' insults make
   me feel
   as if my bones were
   broken.
They are always saying,
   "Where is your God?"

[11]Why am I so sad?
   Why am I so upset?
I should put my hope
   in God.
   I should keep praising him,
   my Savior and my God.

> "A deer thirsts for a stream of water.
> in the same way, i thirst for you, God.
> i thirst for the living God." *Psalm 42:1-2*

"Why am i so sad? Why am i so upset? i should put my hope in God."

Psalm 42:11

• • •

WISHING TO BE IN THE TEMPLE
For the director of music. By the gittith.ᵈ
A song of the sons of Korah.

84 Lord of heaven's armies, how lovely is your Temple!ᵈ

²I want to be in
  the courtyards of the
    Lord's Temple.
My whole being wants
  to be with the living God.
³The sparrows have found a
    home.
  And the swallows have
    nests.
They raise their young near
    your altars,
  Lord of heaven's armies,
    my King and my God.
⁴Happy are the people who
    live at your Temple.
  They are always praising
    you.   *Selah*ᵈ

⁵Happy are those whose
    strength comes from you.
  They want to travel to
    Jerusalem.
⁶As they pass through the
    Valley of Baca,
  they make it like a spring.

The autumn rains fill it with
    pools of water.
⁷The people get stronger as
    they go.
  And everyone meets with
    God in Jerusalem.

"Lord of heaven's armies, how lovely is your Temple. i want to be in the courtyards of the Lord's Temple. My whole being wants to be with the living God."

Psalm 84:1-2

BLAST FROM THE **PAST**

CAN YOU iMAGiNE WHAT THE ANCIENT PEOPLE THOUGHT THE SUN WAS?
Many people believed it was a god, and they worshiped it. Egyptians named it Re, the sun god. In Mesopotamia, the sun was considered the god Shamash. Canaanite worshipers called it Shemesh, and worshiped it along with a host of other idols.

THE WAY OF THE RIGHTEOUS

Life can be tough. The best way to survive and be happy is to always look to the Lord. Read your Bible and learn from it. God's Word shows you how to be a good person! Work your way through this maze towards the Bible and the "tree planted by a river" (read Psalm 1). Make sure to avoid the pitfalls along the way!

STEALING

ANGER

CHEATING

LAZINESS

GOSSIP

LYING

⁸Lord God of heaven's armies,
    hear my prayer.
  God of Jacob, listen to
    me.   *Selah*
⁹God, look at our shield.
  Be kind to your appointed
    king.

¹⁰One day in the courtyards of
    your Temple is better
  than a thousand days
    anywhere else.
  I would rather be a
    doorkeeper in the
  Temple of my God

than live in the homes
    of the wicked.
¹¹The Lord God is like
    our sun and
    shield.
  The Lord gives us
    kindness and
    glory.
  He does not hold back
    anything good
  from those whose life
    is innocent.
¹²Lord of heaven's armies,
  happy are the people
    who trust you!

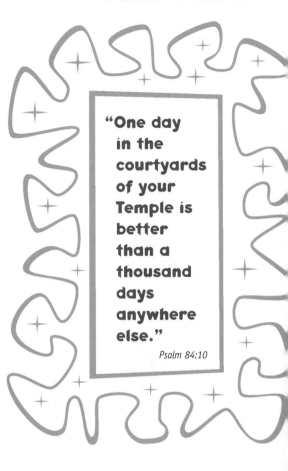

**"One day
in the
courtyards
of your
Temple is
better
than a
thousand
days
anywhere
else."**

Psalm 84:10

Songs of David

PSALMS 4; 8; 9; 23; 51; 63; 139; 145

AN EVENING PRAYER
For the director of music. With stringed instruments. A song of David.

4 Answer me when I pray to you,
my God who does what is right.
Lift the load that I carry.
Be kind to me and hear my prayer.

2 People, how long will you turn my honor into shame?
You love what is false, and you look for new lies.

Selah[d]

3 You know that the Lord has chosen for himself those who are loyal to him.
The Lord listens when I pray to him.

4 When you are angry, do not sin.
Think about these things quietly as you go to bed.   *Selah*

5 Do what is right as a sacrifice to the Lord.
And trust the Lord.

6 Many people ask,
"Who will give us anything good?
Lord, be kind to us."

7 But you have made me very happy.
I am happier than they are, even with all their grain and wine.

8 I go to bed and sleep in peace.
Lord, only you keep me safe.

. . .

"**You know that the Lord has chosen for himself those who are loyal to him. The Lord listens when i pray to him.**"

Psalm 4:3

GOD'S GREATNESS AND MAN'S WORTH
For the director of music. By the gittith.[d] A song of David.

8 Lord our Master,
your name is the most wonderful name in all the earth!
It brings you praise in heaven above.

2 You have taught children and babies to sing praises to you.
This is because of your enemies.
And so you silence your enemies and destroy those who try to get even.

3 I look at the heavens, which you made with your hands.
I see the moon and stars, which you created.

4 But why is man important to you?
Why do you take care of human beings?

5 You made man a little lower than the angels.
And you crowned him with glory and honor.

6 You put him in charge of everything you made.

You put all things under
his control:
⁷all the sheep, the cattle
and the wild animals,
⁸the birds in the sky,
the fish in the sea,
and everything that lives
under water.

⁹Lord our Master,
your name is the most
wonderful name in all
the earth!

• • •

> "Lord our
> Master,
> your name
> is the most
> wonderful
> name in all
> the earth!
> it brings
> you praise
> in heaven
> above."
>
> *Psalm 8:1*

THANKSGIVING FOR VICTORY
*For the director of music. To the tune of
"The Death of the Son." A song of David.*

9 I will praise you, Lord,
with all my heart.
I will tell all the miracles[d]
you have done.
²I will be happy because
of you.
God Most High, I will sing
praises to your name.

³My enemies turn back.
They are overwhelmed and
die because of you.
⁴You have heard what I
complained to you
about.
You sat on your throne
and judged by what
was right.
⁵You spoke strongly against
the foreign nations
and destroyed the wicked
people.
You wiped out their names
forever and ever.
⁶The enemy is gone forever.
You destroyed their
cities.
No one even remembers
them.

⁷But the Lord rules forever.
He sits on his throne
to judge.

LIVIN' IT!

A JOYFUL NOISE
PSALMS 4; 8; 9

Even when he was out in the
fields tending his sheep, David
was always busy praising the
Lord through song. In fact, it
was David's harp that often
soothed Saul's terrible temper
when David played for him in
his courts.

God has given us the gift of
music, too. Even if we can't
sing a lick, we can make what
David calls a joyful noise to
God. It just requires a grateful
heart that longs to tell God
how wonderful he is. Music
can help us fellowship with
God in deeper ways than
words alone ever could.

As you read some of David's
songs, think of ways you could
put his words to music. Then
sing them either out loud or in
your heart to God
throughout the day.

⁸The Lord will judge the
world by what is right.
He will decide what is fair
for the nations.
⁹The Lord defends those
who suffer.

He protects them in times
of trouble.

[10]Those who know the Lord
trust him.

He will not leave those who
come to him.

• • •

THE LORD THE SHEPHERD
A song of David.

23 The Lord is my
shepherd.

I have everything I need.

[2]He gives me rest in green
pastures.

He leads me to calm water.

[3]He gives me new strength.

For the good of his name,
he leads me on paths that
are right.

[4]Even if I walk
through a very dark valley,

I will not be afraid
because you are with me.

Your rod and your shepherd's
staff comfort me.

[5]You prepare a meal for me
in front of my enemies.

You pour oil of blessing on
my head. [n]

You give me more than I
can hold.

[6]Surely your goodness and
love will be with me
all my life.

And I will live in the house of
the Lord forever.

• • •

A PRAYER FOR FORGIVENESS
*For the director of music. A song of David
when the prophet[d] Nathan came to David
after David's sin with Bathsheba.*

51 God, be merciful to me
because you are
loving.

Because you are always ready
to be merciful,
wipe out all my wrongs.

[2]Wash away all my guilt
and make me clean again.

[3]I know about my wrongs.

I can't forget my sin.

[4]You are the one I have
sinned against.

I have done what you say is
wrong.

So you are right when
you speak.

You are fair when you
judge me.

WHILE MOST OF
THE PSALMS WERE
written for general wor-
ship, Psalm 51 takes a
special place in history.
This song of repentance
was written directly in
response to the sin
David committed with
Bathsheba by killing her
husband and taking her
as his wife. Despite the
seriousness of the sin,
David knew God was
faithful to forgive.

[5]I was brought into this world
in sin.

In sin my mother gave birth
to me.

[6]You want me to be
completely truthful.

> **"Surely your goodness and love will be with me all my life.
> And i will live in the house of the Lord forever."**
> *Psalm 23:6*

  23:5 pour oil . . . head This can mean that God gave him great wealth and blessed him.

SING AND
SHOUT!

Search the Psalms to find the answers—and shout for joy to the Lord when you're finished!

ACROSS

1 What the wicked man thinks about (Psalm 36).

2 Happy is the person who loves the Lord's _____ (Psalm 1).

3 What God does for us in times of trouble (Psalm 9).

4 What our souls and the deer have in common (Psalm 42).

5 One day here is better than a thousand elsewhere (Psalm 84).

6 God is the Lord of _____ armies (Psalm 84).

DOWN

1 God's _____ is better than life (Psalm 63).

2 What God takes away for us to be clean (Psalm 51).

3 We should grow strong roots like this (Psalm 1).

4 How the people who trust the Lord feel (Psalm 84).

5 The part of God that goes up to the skies (Psalm 36).

6 What we are to do when we are very sad (Psalm 42).

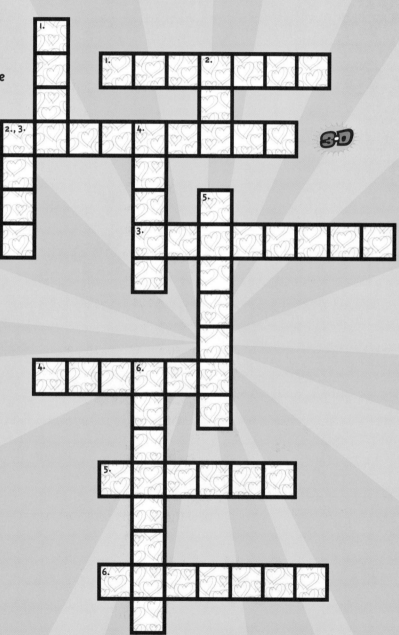

3-D

So teach me wisdom.

[7]Take away my sin, and I
will be clean.
Wash me, and I will be
whiter than snow.

[8]Make me hear sounds of
joy and gladness.
Let the bones you crushed
be happy again.

[9]Turn your face from my sins.
Wipe out all my guilt.

[10]Create in me a pure heart,
God.
Make my spirit right
again.

[11]Do not send me away
from you.
Do not take your Holy
Spirit[d] away from me.

"God, you will not reject a heart that is broken and sorry for its sin." *Psalm 51:17*

[12]Give me back the joy
that comes when you
save me.
Keep me strong by giving
me a willing spirit.

[13]Then I will teach your ways
to those who do wrong.
And sinners will turn back
to you.

[14]God, save me from the guilt
of murder.
God, you are the one who
saves me.
I will sing about your
goodness.

[15]Lord, let me speak
so I may praise you.

[16]You are not pleased by
sacrifices.
Otherwise, I would give
them.
You don't want burnt
offerings.

[17]The sacrifice God wants is a
willing spirit.
God, you will not reject
a heart that is broken and
sorry for its sin.

[18]Do whatever good you wish
for Jerusalem.
Rebuild the walls of
Jerusalem.

[19]Then you will be pleased
with right sacrifices and
whole burnt offerings.
And bulls will be offered on
your altar.

• • •

WISHING TO BE NEAR GOD
A song of David when he was in the desert of Judah.

63 God, you are my God.
I want to follow you.
My whole being
thirsts for you,
like a man in a dry,
empty land
where there is no water.

[2]I have seen you in the
Temple.[d]
I have seen your strength
and glory.

[3]Your love is better than life.
I will praise you.

[4]I will praise you as long as
I live.

"Take away my sin, and i will be clean. Wash me, and i will be whiter than snow."

Psalm 51:7

I will lift up my hands in
prayer to your name.
5 I will be content as if I had
eaten the best foods.
My lips will sing. My mouth
will praise you.

6 I remember you while I'm
lying in bed.
I think about you through
the night.
7 You are my help.
Because of your protection,
I sing.
8 I stay close to you.
You support me with your
right hand.

• • •

GOD KNOWS EVERYTHING
For the director of music. A song of David.

139
Lord, you have
examined me.
You know all about me.
2 You know when I sit down
and when I get up.
You know my thoughts
before I think them.
3 You know where I go and
where I lie down.
You know well everything
I do.

4 Lord, even before I say a
word,
you already know what I
am going to say.
5 You are all around me—

"**i praise you
because you
made me in an
amazing and
wonderful
way. What you
have done is
wonderful.**"

Psalm 139:14

in front and in back.
You have put your hand
on me.
6 Your knowledge is amazing
to me.
It is more than I can
understand.

7 Where can I go to get away
from your Spirit?d
Where can I run from you?
8 If I go up to the skies, you
are there.
If I lie down where the dead
are, you are there.

9 If I rise with the sun in
the east,
and settle in the west
beyond the sea,
10 even there you would
guide me.
With your right hand you
would hold me.

11 I could say, "The darkness
will hide me.
The light around me will
turn into night."
12 But even the darkness is not
dark to you.
The night is as light as the
day.
Darkness and light are the
same to you.

13 You made my whole being.
You formed me in my
mother's body.
14 I praise you because you
made me in an amazing
and wonderful way.
What you have done is
wonderful.
I know this very well.
15 You saw my bones being
formed

"**Your knowledge is amazing to me. it is
more than i can understand.**" *Psalm 139:6*

The Songs of David

David poured out his heart to God in the songs he wrote. We know the words he penned, but not the melody he used to sing the words to God. Creating your own song for God is easier than you think!

First, start with a tune like "Row, Row, Row Your Boat." Make up your own words for the song. Here is an example of my verse:

Jesus loves me, this I know is true.
And I thank him every day for all I get to do.

Now you try to write a verse to the tune of "Row, Row, Row Your Boat." As you get better, find longer songs and write your own words to them. Sing your praises to God, for he delights in hearing you sing!

Row, row, row, your boat gent – ly

(your words) _____

down the stream; mer – ri – ly,

(your words) _____

mer – ri – ly, mer – ri – ly, mer – ri – ly,

(your words) _____

life is but a dream.

(your words) _____

Ways to Sing a Song

1. Loudly in the shower
2. Riding in your car
3. As a duet with your friend
4. Making up new words
5. Pretending to be an opera singer
6. Whistling the tune
7. With a smile on your face
8. Acapella (without any instruments)
9. Praising the Lord
10. In your head

as I took shape in my
mother's body.
When I was put together
there,
16 you saw my body as it
was formed.
All the days planned for me
were written in your book
before I was one day old.

17God, your thoughts are
precious to me.
They are so many!
18If I could count them,
they would be more
than all the grains
of sand.
When I wake up,
I am still with you.

• • •

PRAISE TO GOD THE KING
A song of praise. Of David.

145 I praise your
greatness,
my God the King.
I will praise you forever
and ever.
2I will praise you every day.
I will praise you forever
and ever.

STORIES FROM

PROVERBS

Wise Words

PROVERBS 1–3; 10–11

WHY PROVERBS IS IMPORTANT

1 These are the wise words of Solomon son of David. Solomon was king of Israel.

²They teach wisdom and self-control.
They give understanding.
³They will teach you how to be wise and self-controlled.
They will teach you what is honest and fair and right.

⁴They give the ability to think to those with little knowledge.
They give knowledge and good sense to the young.
⁵Wise people should also listen to them and learn even more.
Even they will find wise advice in these words.
⁶Then they will be able to understand wise words and stories.

They will understand the words of wise men and their riddles.

⁷Knowledge begins with respect for the Lord.
But foolish people hate wisdom and discipline.

WARNINGS AGAINST EVIL

⁸My child, listen to your father's teaching.
And do not forget your mother's advice.
⁹Their teaching will beautify your life.
It will be like flowers in your hair or a chain around your neck.

> **"Knowledge begins with respect for the Lord. But foolish people hate wisdom and discipline."**
>
> *Proverbs 1:7*

LIVIN' iT!

¹⁰My child, sinners will try to
lead you into sin.
But do not follow them.
¹¹They might say, "Come
with us.
Let's ambush and kill
someone.
Let's attack some harmless
person just for fun.
¹²Let's swallow them alive,
as death does.
Let's swallow them whole,
as the grave does.
¹³We will take all kinds of
valuable things.

WALK IN WISDOM
PROVERBS 1:1-19

What better person to turn to for wisdom than the man famous
for being the wisest in the world? Solomon gives us thought
after thought to consider as we walk through life. He urges us
to look hard for true wisdom. We need to understand what is
really important in this life, and leave everything
else behind as we devote ourselves to it.

So what is really important, according to
Solomon? Gaining wisdom. How do we gain
wisdom? We can ask God for it—and we can
obey what we already know God has told us
to do. When we obey God, we begin to
think more like him. His Spirit is freed to use
us as he intends. We understand why we
were put here on this earth, and we are better
able to make future decisions that will strength-
en our relationship with God. Take time right
now to ask God for the desire to be wise,
and start obeying him.

> **"My child
> listen to your
> father's
> teaching.
> And do not
> forget your
> mother's
> advice.
> Their teach-
> ing will
> beautify
> your life."**
>
> *Proverbs 1:8-9*

> **"Greed takes away the life of
> the greedy person."** *Proverbs 1:19*

We will fill our houses
with what we steal.
¹⁴Come join us,
and we will share with you
what we steal."
¹⁵My child, do not go along
with them.
Do not do what
they do.
¹⁶They run to do evil.
They are quick to kill.

¹⁷It is useless to spread out a net
right where the birds can
see it!
¹⁸These men are setting their
own trap.
They will only catch
themselves!
¹⁹All greedy people end up
this way.
Greed takes away the life
of the greedy person.

> **"Trust the Lord with all your heart."**
>
> *Proverbs 3:5*

History *Highlights*

↗ **445 B.C.**
Athens and Sparta agree to 30 years of peace; Nehemiah's journey to Jerusalem begins.

7000 5000 3000 1000 0 1000 NOW

REWARDS OF WISDOM

2 My child, believe what
  I say.
  And remember what I
    command you.
²Listen to wisdom.
  Try with all your heart to
    gain understanding.
³Cry out for wisdom.
  Beg for understanding.
⁴Search for it as you would
    for silver.
  Hunt for it like hidden
    treasure.
⁵Then you will understand
    what it means to respect
    the Lord.
  Then you will begin to
    know God.

GET CONNECTED

RELATIONSHIPS WITH GOD

Solomon Says Turn on the T.V., and you'll find news people, talk-show hosts, and lots of other people telling others what to do. Open the newspaper, and you'll see special sections devoted to helping others figure out life. But the Bible gives us a better advice column than any T.V. show or newspaper.

Solomon, the wisest man on the earth, wrote the Book of Proverbs as a collection of tips on how to avoid sin, obey God, and become wise. God's Spirit told him what to write. If we want to become wise like Solomon, we need to get our guidance from God, not from the people of this world. Read through Proverbs, and underline the verses that help you to become wise. Memorize them, and ask God to help you apply them in your life.

blah blah

3 Don't ever stop being kind
    and truthful.
  Let kindness and truth
    show in all you do.
  Write them down in your
    mind as if on a tablet.
⁴Then you will be respected
    and pleasing to both
    God and men.

⁵Trust the Lord with all
    your heart.
  Don't depend on your
    own understanding.
⁶Remember the Lord in
    everything you do.
  And he will give you success.

⁷Don't depend on your
    own wisdom.
  Respect the Lord and refuse
    to do wrong.

BïBLe CRïtteRS

3-D

WAKE UP, SLEEPYHEAD

If you asked a **SLOTH**, he'd say being slothful isn't so bad. Sloths are very slow-moving mammals that spend their entire lives hanging upside down in trees. They eat fruit, leaves, and tender shoots. And they camouflage themselves with the algae that grows in their fur. While they are most active at night, sloths sleep for more than 15 hours a day. The harpy eagle and the jaguar are its two greatest enemies, but sloths stay well hidden among the leaves of trees.

Solomon warns people against "sloth"—not the animal, but the action. We should never be lazy, but instead be active and alert in obeying God's Word and doing what is right.

TOP TEN

Ways to Throw a Party

1. Invite your class to come home with you after school.
2. Have a theme where everyone dresses up.
3. At a farm with hayrides and bonfires.
4. At the ice-skating rink.
5. Invite neighborhood friends.
6. Go on a scavenger hunt.
7. Have a progressive dinner at each person's house.
8. Invite all the new kids at school.
9. Invite your Sunday school class.
10. Have relay races in the front yard.

"The Lord corrects those he loves, just as a father corrects the child that he likes."

Proverbs 3:12

⁸Then your body will be
    healthy.
  And your bones will
    be strong.

⁹Honor the Lord by giving
    him part of your wealth.
  Give him the firstfruits*d*
    from all your crops.
¹⁰Then your barns will be full.
  And your wine barrels will
    overflow with new wine.

¹¹My child, do not reject the
    Lord's discipline.
  And don't become angry
    when he corrects you.

¹²The Lord corrects those
    he loves,
  just as a father corrects
    the child that he
    likes.

• • •

10 A lazy person will
    end up poor.
  But a hard worker will
    become rich.

• • •

¹⁹If you talk a lot, you are
    sure to sin.
  If you are wise, you will
    keep quiet.

WILD WORLD FACTS

Proverbs 10:27

COUNTING THE DAYS

Ever noticed how long the folks in the Old Testament days lived? Can you imagine living over 900 years? Today the average life span (the amount of time people are expected to live) is much shorter, and it is very different from culture to culture. The average age span for a person living in Zambia is 37 years, while the life span for the average Japanese person is 85. Blue whales live from 40 to 80 years. Dogs live up to 25 years. Turtles live up to 150 years. In general, plants outlive animals and people. Some trees are known to be thousands of years old. And some corals can live for many thousands of years.

While we don't have any idea how many days on earth God has given us, God does. He wants us to use every moment to learn more about him, draw closer to him, and help others to know him. Then, when our bodies die, his children will be ready to live with him forever.

[Wikipedia: Lifespan]

---

²⁷Whoever respects the Lord
will have a long life.
But an evil person will have
his life cut short.

• • •

³²Good people say the right
thing.
But the wicked tell lies.

• • •

11 Pride leads only
to shame.
It is wise not to be proud.
³Good people will be guided
by honesty.
But dishonesty will destroy
those who are not
trustworthy.

ISAIAH

IsAiah's Prophecies about Jesus

ISAIAH 7:10-15;
9:6-7; 11:1-10

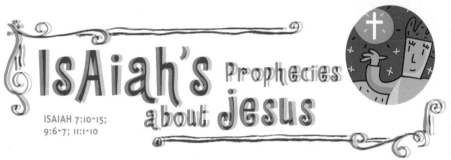

IMMANUEL—GOD IS WITH US

7 Then the Lord spoke to Ahaz again. [11]The Lord said, "Ask for a sign to prove to yourself that these things are true. It may be a sign from as deep as the place where the dead are or as high as the heavens."

[12]But Ahaz said, "I will not ask for a sign. I will not test the Lord."

[13]Then Isaiah said, "Ahaz, descendant[d] of David, listen very carefully! Isn't it bad enough that you wear out the patience of people? Do you have to wear out the patience of my God also? [14]But the Lord himself will give you a sign: The virgin[n] will be pregnant. She will have a son, and she will name him Immanuel.[n] [15]He will be eating milk curds and honey when he learns to reject what is evil and to choose what is good.

• • •

9 A child will be born to us. God will give a son to us.

ISAIAH LIVED IN JUDAH IN THE EIGHTH CENTURY B.C. and prophesied in Jerusalem, especially to kings Ahaz and Hezekiah. His message was that no human power could stand in the way of Assyria. Judah's only hope was faith in God's power to protect his chosen people.

7:14 virgin The Hebrew word means "a young woman." Often this meant a girl who was not married and had not yet had sexual relations with anyone.
7:14 Immanuel This name means "God is with us."

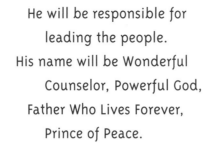

DIVINE APPOINTMENT
ISAIAH 7:14

If someone told you exactly what you would be 20 years from now, would you believe them? Probably not. We don't have the ability to see into the future, and we can only guess what God has in store for us in this life. But God does know, and has known, what the plan is for each of his children. In fact, he planned it out before he even made the world.

We get a glimpse of God's plan in Isaiah. Although written many hundreds of years before Jesus was born, it foretells exactly how the Savior would come to earth. Many passages in Isaiah give even more detail about the special Son of God who would come to live and die for God's people.

As God's kids, we can be full of joy because we know that nothing comes into our lives by mistake. God is close by us, and he is at work finishing the full picture of who he is as he changes us and makes us more like Jesus. Take a closer look at the events that happen today. Can you see the hand of God at work in you?

He will be responsible for leading the people.
His name will be Wonderful Counselor, Powerful God, Father Who Lives Forever, Prince of Peace.

"A child will be born to us. God will give a son to us. He will be responsible for leading the people."
Isaiah 9:6

7Power and peace will be in his kingdom.
It will continue to grow.
He will rule as king on David's throne
and over David's kingdom.
He will make it strong,
by ruling with goodness and fair judgment.
He will rule it forever and ever.
The Lord of heaven's armies will do this
because of his strong love for his people.

• • •

THE KING OF PEACE IS COMING

11 A branch will grow from a stump of a tree that was cut down.
So a new king will come from the family of Jesse.[n]

2The Spirit[d] of the Lord will rest upon that king.
The Spirit gives him wisdom, understanding, guidance and power.
And the Spirit teaches him to know and respect the Lord.
3This king will be glad to obey the Lord.
He will not judge by the way things look.
He will not judge by what people say.
4He will judge the poor honestly.
He will be fair in his decisions for the poor people of the land.
At his command evil people will be punished.
By his words the wicked will be put to death.
5Goodness and fairness will give him strength.
They will be like a belt around his waist.

6Then wolves will live in peace with lambs.

11:1 **Jesse** King David's father.

10 TOP TEN

Ways to Minister to the Elderly

1. Hold their hand.
2. Look them in their eyes and smile.
3. Ask them about their childhood.
4. Go to them for advice.
5. Bake them cookies.
6. Read the Bible to them.
7. Ask them to listen to your memory verse.
8. Visit with them regularly.
9. Mow their yard or rake the leaves.
10. Tell them you love them, and pray for them.

And leopards will lie down to rest with goats. Calves, lions and young bulls will eat together. And a little child will lead them. 7Cows and bears will eat together in peace. Their young will lie down together. Lions will eat hay as oxen do. 8A baby will be able to play near a cobra's hole. A child will be able to put his hand into the nest of a poisonous snake. 9They will not hurt or destroy each other on all my holy mountain. The earth will be full of the knowledge of the Lord, as the sea is full of water.

10At that time the new king from the family of Jesse will stand as a banner for the people. The nations will come together around him. And the place where he lives will be filled with glory.

OCTOBER PERSEVERANCE

1 Prayer Pointer: Ask God for strength to do the right thing.

2 Go for a morning jog, and see how long you can run.

3

4 Volunteer to rake your neighbor's yard. If more leaves fall, do it again.

5 Keep your room clean every day this month.

6 Make caramel apples for your family.

7

8 Hide-It-in-Your-Heart: But you should be strong. Don't give up, because you will get a reward for your good work (2 Chronicles 15:7).

9

10

11 Throw the football with your dad.

12

13 Take a nap.

14 Ask your mom how you can best help her today.

15

16

17

18

19 Prayer Pointer: Ask God to give you creative ways to encourage others to stay strong in their faith.

20

21

22 Make a thank-you card for your Sunday school teacher, and take it to her.

23

24 Read your favorite book in a hammock outside.

25

26

27 Hide-It-in-Your-Heart: The Lord gives strength to those who are tired. He gives more power to those who are weak (Isaiah 40:29).

28

29

30

31 Halloween: Pray for the salvation of every person who comes to your door.

JEREMIAH

Jeremiah, Chosen and Mistreated

JEREMIAH 1:4-19; 38:1-13

GOD CALLS JEREMIAH

1 The Lord spoke these words to me:

⁵"Before I made you in your mother's womb, I chose you.
Before you were born, I set you apart for a special work.
I appointed you as a prophet[d] to the nations."

⁶Then I said, "But Lord God, I don't know how to speak. I am only a boy."

⁷But the Lord said to me, "Don't say, 'I am only a boy.' You must go everywhere that I send you. You must say everything I tell you to say. ⁸Don't be afraid of anyone, because I am with you. I will protect you," says the Lord.

⁹Then the Lord reached out with his hand and touched my mouth. He said to me, "See, I am putting my words in your mouth. ¹⁰Today I have put you in charge of nations and kingdoms. You will pull up and tear down, destroy and overthrow. You will build up and plant."

TWO VISIONS

¹¹The Lord spoke this word to me: "Jeremiah, what do you see?"

I answered the Lord and said, "I see a stick of almond wood."

¹²The Lord said to me, "You have seen correctly! And I am watching to make sure my words come true."

¹³The Lord spoke his word to me again: "Jeremiah, what do you see?"

> **" 'You must say everything I tell you to say. Don't be afraid of anyone, because I am with you. I will protect you,' says the Lord."** *Jeremiah 1:7-8*

BLAST FROM THE PAST

IT MAY HAVE BEEN A LONG TIME AGO, but the way warriors fought wars was really pretty cool. Archers who rode in chariots could shoot their arrows without stopping. They often wore long-sleeved, knee-length leather shirts covered in 500 to 1,000 scales. Each whole suit weighed around 50 pounds. Archaeologists have found ancient Assyrian art that pictures the chariots, and many copper scales have been discovered, as well.

I answered the Lord and said, "I see a pot of boiling water. It is tipping over from the north!"

¹⁴The Lord said to me, "Disaster will come from the north. It will happen to all the people who live in this country. ¹⁵In a short time I will call all of the people in the northern kingdoms," said the Lord.

"Those kings will come and set up their thrones
near the entrance of the gates of Jerusalem.
They will attack the city walls around Jerusalem.
They will attack all the cities in Judah.
¹⁶And I will announce my judgments against my people.

I will do this because of their evil in turning away from me.
They offered sacrifices to other gods.
And they worshiped idols they had made with their own hands.

¹⁷"Jeremiah, get ready. Stand up and speak to the people. Tell them everything I tell you to say. Don't be afraid of the people. If you are afraid of them, I will give you good reason to be afraid of them. ¹⁸Today I am going to make you a strong city, an iron pillar, a bronze wall. You will be able to stand against everyone in the land: Judah's kings, officers, priests and the people of

REAL SUPER HEROES

JEREMIAH

He was only a boy when God called him to become a prophet. Think about it—at about your age, Jeremiah was told to go speak to nations about their attitude toward God! He was to confront them about their sin, their idolatry, and warn them about the punishment to come for their disobedience.

Jeremiah was afraid. After all, what can a young boy do? On his own, nothing. But God was the one who called him, and God would put the right words in his mouth. God himself promised to protect him.

Later in his life, when Jeremiah found himself at the bottom of a well—the place his angry audience had thrown him—he probably questioned God. Life didn't look as successful as he had expected. But even though times were hard, God was faithful. He caused the king to remember Jeremiah and to rescue him. Jeremiah realized an important lesson: Living an obedient life is never easy, but it is always right. And obedience leads to an even deeper relationship with our Lord.

CRAFTS

JEREMIAH IN THE WELL

SUPPLIES

- tin can with lid
- construction paper (cut to fit can)
- black marker
- crayons
- tape
- slips of paper

ALL ABOUT IT:

Jeremiah tried to deliver God's message to the people, but they didn't want to hear it. So they threw him in a well. God sometimes sends people to help us correct our thinking and turn to him and his ways.

Jeremiah was thrown into the well to keep him from speaking God's truth. Sometimes we put ourselves in a kind of well—maybe a timeout—when we don't obey. We need someone to help us out of the "well," and God uses the Bible and our parents to help guide us as we make choices growing up. Give thanks to God for the guidance your parents provide, and listen to their teaching.

HEART CRAFT INSTRUCTIONS

1. Use the marker and crayons to make bricks on the construction paper.

2. Tape the colored paper around the tin can.

3. Write the thoughts and actions that keep you from doing what God has said on the slips of paper.

4. On the back of each slip of paper, write the thought or action that will help you do what God has called you to do.

5. Fill your "well" with the slips of paper. When you've disobeyed in some way, pull out a slip of paper and read what you need to do to be obedient.

3-D

the land. [19]They will fight against you. But they will not defeat you. This is because I am with you, and I will save you!" says the Lord.

> **" 'But they will not defeat you. This is because i am with you, and i will save you!' says the Lord."** *Jeremiah 1:19*

JEREMIAH IS THROWN INTO A WELL

38 Some of the officers heard what Jeremiah was prophesying.[d] They were Shephatiah son of Mattan, Gedaliah son of Pashhur, Jehucal son of Shelemiah and Pashhur son of Malkijah. Jeremiah was telling all the people this message: [2]"This is what the Lord says: 'Everyone who stays in Jerusalem will die in war. Or he will die of hunger or terrible diseases. But everyone who surrenders to the Babylonian army will live. They will escape with their lives and live.' [3]And this is what the Lord says: 'This city of Jerusalem will surely be handed over to the army of the king of Babylon. He will capture this city!'"

[4]Then the officers said to the king, "Jeremiah must be put to death! He is making the soldiers who are still in the city become discouraged. He is discouraging everyone by the things he is saying. He does not want good to happen to us. He wants to ruin the people of Jerusalem."

WILD WORLD FACTS

Jeremiah 38:1-13

iT'S ALL WELL AND GOOD

You might not see it, but the water beneath your feet is one of the most important resources we have! Wells are simply the holes people dig into the earth's layers to reach water below. Back in Bible times, they dug with shovels and buckets. Today we have large drills that can quickly penetrate deep into the earth.

When it rains, water hits the earth's surface and slowly seeps into the ground. Below the surface are several layers of earth. Gravity moves the water toward the center of the earth, and it fills all the spaces in between the rocks. Deep underneath lies a layer of earth called bedrock, which is so firm that water cannot pass through it. Instead, it flows sideways until it eventually seeps into lakes or streams. Some wells tap into this sideways flowing water. Other kinds, like Artesian wells, use the pressure of the earth to shoot the water up from below.

[USGS.gov]

LIViN' iT!

CONSIDER THE COST
JEREMIAH 38:1-13

What do you think Jeremiah thought as he sat in the well, knee-deep in mud? He had been obedient. He told the people exactly what God wanted him to say. What he got in return was a lot of angry people who wanted him to be quiet. So they tried to kill him.

If you obey God, do you expect life to be perfect? Do you think that when bad times come God is punishing you? Learn from Jeremiah. God does allow trials in our lives, but they are not always punishment. Often, they are tools God uses to draw us closer to him. We need to understand that following God is not easy in a sinful world. Don't be surprised at the hard times. Instead, use them to cling even tighter to the truth. Trust God in the good and bad times. Perfection only comes in heaven.

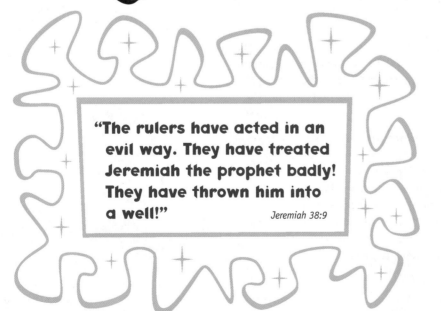

⁵King Zedekiah said to them, "Jeremiah is in your control. I cannot do anything to stop you!"

⁶So the officers took Jeremiah and put him into the well of Malkijah, the king's son. That well was in the courtyard of the guards. The officers used ropes to lower Jeremiah into the well. It did not have any water in it, only mud. And Jeremiah sank down into the mud.

⁷But Ebed-Melech heard that the officers had put Jeremiah into the well. Ebed-Melech was a Cushite, and he was a eunuch[d] in the palace. King Zedekiah was sitting at the Benjamin Gate. ⁸So Ebed-Melech left the palace and went to the king. Ebed-Melech said, ⁹"My master and king, the rulers have acted in an evil way. They have treated Jeremiah the prophet badly! They have thrown him into a well! They have left him there to die! When there is no more bread in the city, he will starve."

¹⁰Then King Zedekiah commanded Ebed-Melech the Cushite: "Ebed-Melech, take 30 men from the palace with you. Go and lift Jeremiah the prophet out of the well before he dies."

¹¹So Ebed-Melech took the men with him. And he went to a room under the storeroom in the palace. He took some old rags

> **"The rulers have acted in an evil way. They have treated Jeremiah the prophet badly! They have thrown him into a well!"**
> *Jeremiah 38:9*

and worn-out clothes from that room. Then he let those rags down with some ropes to Jeremiah in the well. [12]Ebed-Melech the Cushite said to Jeremiah, "Put not hide anything from me. But tell me everything honestly."

[15]Jeremiah said to Zedekiah, "If I give you an answer, you will probably kill me. And even if I your family will live. [18]You must not refuse to surrender to the officers of the king of Babylon. If you do, Jerusalem will be given to the Babylonian army.

> **"Obey the Lord by doing what i tell you. Then things will go well for you. And your life will be saved."** *Jeremiah 38:20*

these old rags and worn-out clothes under your arms. They will be pads for the ropes." So Jeremiah did as Ebed-Melech said. [13]The men pulled Jeremiah up with the ropes and lifted him out of the well. And Jeremiah stayed under guard in the courtyard.

ZEDEKIAH QUESTIONS JEREMIAH

[14]Then King Zedekiah sent someone to get Jeremiah the prophet.[d] He had Jeremiah brought to the third entrance to the Temple[d] of the Lord. Then the king said to Jeremiah, "I am going to ask you something. Do give you advice, you will not listen to me."

[16]But King Zedekiah made a secret promise to Jeremiah. He said, "As surely as the Lord lives who has given us breath and life, I will not kill you. And I promise not to give you to the officers who want to kill you."

[17]Then Jeremiah said to Zedekiah, "This is what the Lord God of heaven's armies, the God of Israel, says: 'You must surrender to the officers of the king of Babylon. Then your life will be saved. And Jerusalem will not be burned down. And you and They will burn Jerusalem down. And you will not escape from them.'"

[19]Then King Zedekiah said to Jeremiah, "I'm afraid of some of the Jews. They have already gone over to the side of the Babylonian army. I'm afraid the Babylonians may hand me over to them. And they will treat me badly."

[20]But Jeremiah answered, "The Babylonians will not hand you over to the Jews. Obey the Lord by doing what I tell you. Then things will go well for you. And your life will be saved.

EZEKIEL

Valley of Dry Bones
EZEKIEL 37:1-14

THE VISION OF DRY BONES

37 I felt the power of the Lord was on me. He brought me out by the Spirit[d] of the Lord. And he put me down in the middle of a valley. It was full of bones. [2]The Lord led me around among the bones. There were many bones on the bottom of the valley. I saw the bones were very dry. [3]Then he asked me, "Human being, can these bones live?"

I answered, "Lord God, only you know."

[4]The Lord said to me, "Prophesy[d] to these bones. Say to them, 'Dry bones, hear the word of the Lord. [5]This is what the Lord God says to the bones: I will cause breath to enter you.

LIVIN' iT!

SAVING SKELETONS
EZEKIEL 37:1-14

When Ezekiel had his vision, he could only see a valley of dry bones. No life to be found. It was the perfect picture of hopelessness. How could something so dead ever see life again? God told Ezekiel to preach to the bones—to tell all that was dead the secret to life. And when Ezekiel obeyed, the bones put on flesh and became alive again.

We live in a world full of people who don't know God. Just like the dry bones in the valley, people who don't know Jesus are dead in the spiritual sense. They are unable to respond to God or any spiritual thing. But as we speak God's truth, God is able to change their hearts and raise their spirits from the dead. He can work the miracle of life through us.

Do you know someone who needs to hear the hope of the gospel? Pray for God to give you the right words. Speak with boldness, knowing that you hold the key to life.

GET CONNECTED

RELATIONSHIPS WITH FRIENDS

Breath of Life Ezekiel was staring at the bleached, white bones when God asked him, "Can these bones live?" Ezekiel didn't know. It really didn't seem possible, and yet he knew that nothing is impossible with God.

God showed Ezekiel that by preaching the Word of God to the bones, they would indeed become alive again. Through Ezekiel's vision, God also encourages us. He lets us know that no person is too far from God to be brought back to him. God can change any heart, no matter how heartless they may seem. Remember Ezekiel when you come across the chance to share your faith with others. Remember that your job is to speak the truth in love. God is the one who will breathe new life into their souls.

come from the four winds. Breathe on these people who were killed so they can live again.'" ¹⁰So I prophesied as the Lord commanded me. And the breath came into them, and they came to life. They stood on their feet. They were a very large army.

"Then the Lord said to me: "Human being, these bones are like all the people of Israel. They say, 'Our bones are dried up, and our hope has gone. We are destroyed.' ¹²So, prophesy, and say to

Then you will live. ⁶I will put muscles on you. I will put flesh on you. I will cover you with skin. Then I will put breath in you, and you will live. Then you will know that I am the Lord.'"

⁷So I prophesied as I was commanded. While I prophesied, there was a noise and a rattling. The bones came together, bone to bone. ⁸I looked and saw muscles come on the bones. Flesh grew, and skin covered the bones. But there was no breath in them.

⁹Then the Lord said to me, "Prophesy to the wind." Prophesy, human being, and say to the wind: 'This is what the Lord God says: Wind,

History Highlights

437 B.C.
The final walls of Jerusalem are completed, according to Josephus (a famous historian).

7000 5000 3000 1000 0 1000 NOW

BLAST FROM THE PAST

EZEKIEL WAS MORE THAN JUST A PROPHET. He was also a priest. A close look at the words he used to describe the Temple and its services showed that God intended the ceremonies to become a picture for what Israel was facing at the moment and in the future.

37:9 wind This Hebrew word could also mean "breath" or "spirit."

Ezekiel had a really weird vision from God. Unscramble these words to find some clues to what God was telling him.

1. PRISIT FO ETH ROLD _____

2. LLEYAV _____

3. YRD SEBNO _____

4. YPROCPHE _____

5. SLMUEC _____

6. DNIW _____

7. THEBRAE _____

8. RALEIS _____

9. GRESAV _____

10. DROL _____

Answers: 1. Spirit of the Lord; 2. valley; 3. dry bones; 4. prophecy; 5. muscle; 6. wind; 7. breathe; 8. Israel; 9. graves; 10. Lord

Top Ten

Ways to Make Grocery Shopping Fun

1. Cut coupons with your mom.

2. Bring your friends along.

3. Plan a meal.

4. Pull the cart instead of pushing it.

5. Offer to help the bag boy.

6. Ask the butcher his name and why he likes meat.

7. Turn it into a scavenger hunt.

8. Eat a doughnut from the bakery.

9. Pretend your cart is a bus, and push your younger siblings.

10. Pick out groceries to give to a needy family.

them: 'This is what the Lord God says: My people, I will open your graves. And I will cause you to come up out of your graves. Then I will bring you into the land of Israel. ¹³This is how you, my people, will know that I am the Lord. I will open your graves and cause you to come up from them. ¹⁴And I will put my Spirit inside you. You will come to life. Then I will put you in your own land. And you will know that I, the Lord, have spoken and done it, says the Lord.'"

BLAST FROM THE PAST

WHY DID EZEKIEL DREAM ABOUT DRY BONES? The main reason is that God gave him a vision. But, in terms of history, what Ezekiel saw in his dream was a fairly common sight. Battles between armies often happened in valleys. As one army was beaten by the other, a large pile of bones would remain, drying in the sun. What wasn't normal was having the bones come back to life. Through this vision, Ezekiel understood that the defeated Israelites would become a nation again by the power of God.

STORIES FROM

DANIEL

Shadrach, Meshach, and Abednego
DANIEL 3:1-30

THE GOLD IDOL AND BLAZING FURNACE

3 Now King Nebuchadnezzar had a gold statue made. That statue was 90 feet high and 9 feet wide. He set up the statue on the plain of Dura in the area of Babylon. ²Then the king called the important leaders: the governors, assistant governors, captains of the soldiers, people who advised the king, keepers of the treasury, judges, rulers and all other officers in his kingdom. He wanted these men to come to the special service for the statue he had set up. ³So they all came for the special service. And they stood in front of the statue that King Nebuchadnezzar had set up. ⁴Then the man who made announcements for the king spoke in a loud voice. He said, "People, nations and men of every language, this is what you are commanded to do: ⁵You will hear the sound of the horns, flutes, lyres,^{d} zithers,^{n} harps, pipes and all the other musical instruments. When this happens, you must bow down and worship the gold statue. This is the one King Nebuchadnezzar has set up. ⁶Everyone must bow down and worship this gold statue. Anyone who doesn't will be quickly thrown into a blazing furnace."

⁷Now people, nations and men who spoke every language were there. And they heard the

> **"Everyone must bow down and worship this gold statue. Anyone who doesn't will be quickly thrown into a blazing furnace."**
>
> *Daniel 3:6*

sound of the horns, flutes, lyres, zithers, pipes and all the other musical instruments. So they bowed down and worshiped the gold statue that King Nebuchadnezzar had set up.

⭐ **3:5 zithers** Musical instruments with 30 to 40 strings.

THE TRUE TEST

It was hard to stand alone, but even harder to walk into a fiery furnace because of your faith in God. Take this test to see how well you remember the trial that tested the faith of three brave men from Israel. Score 9-10: You're on fire (in a good way)! Score 7-8: Warm enough. Score 5-6: Down to the embers. You need some stoking. Score 4 or below: Who threw the water? Time to regather the sticks and start again!

1. HOW TALL WAS THE STATUE THAT NEBUCHADNEZZAR MADE?
A. 10 feet
B. 20 feet
C. 40 feet
D. 90 feet

2. HOW DID THE PEOPLE KNOW WHEN TO BOW DOWN?
A. The king shouted out orders.
B. Archers shot arrows in the air.
C. Musicians played instruments.
D. All the people yelled.

3. WHAT WOULD HAPPEN IF YOU DIDN'T OBEY?
A. The king would yell at you.
B. All the people would attack you.
C. They'd put you in jail.
D. You'd be thrown into a fire.

4. WHO DISOBEYED THE KING?
A. Jobab, Nehu, and Eliezar
B. Shadrach, Meshach, and Abednego
C. No one
D. Daniel, Joash, and Abraham

5. WHY DID THEY DISOBEY?
A. They were rebellious.
B. They served the true God of Israel.
C. They didn't like Nebuchadnezzar.
D. They wanted to see what would happen.

6. WHAT WERE THE THREE MEN WEARING WHEN THEY WERE PUT IN THE FIERY FURNACE?
A. Nothing
B. Special flame-resistant body suits
C. All of their normal clothes and turbans
D. Black robes

7. WHO WAS KILLED BY THE FIRE?
A. The three brave Israelites
B. The soldiers who threw them in
C. The king
D. No one

8. HOW MANY PEOPLE DID THE KING SEE WALKING AROUND INSIDE THE FURNACE?
A. 3
B. 1
C. 2
D. 4

9. WHAT DID THE PEOPLE NOTICE WHEN THE MEN CAME OUT?
A. They didn't smell like smoke.
B. Their robes weren't burned.
C. Their hair and bodies weren't touched by fire.
D. All of the above.

10. WHAT WAS THE KING'S REACTION?
A. He ordered soldiers to make the furnace even hotter.
B. He knocked over his own statue.
C. He had a temper tantrum.
D. He praised Israel's God and began to believe in him.

⁸Then some Babylonians came up to the king. They began speaking against the men of Judah. ⁹They said to King Nebuchadnezzar, "Our king, live forever! ¹⁰Our king, you gave a command. You said that everyone would hear the horns, lyres, zithers, harps, pipes and all the other musical instruments. Then they would have to bow down and worship the gold statue. ¹¹Anyone who wouldn't do this was to be thrown into a blazing furnace. ¹²Our king, there are some men of Judah who did not pay attention to your order. You made them important officers in the area of Babylon. Their names are Shadrach, Meshach and Abednego. They do not serve your gods. And they do not worship the gold statue you have set up."

¹³Nebuchadnezzar became very angry. He called for Shadrach, Meshach and Abednego. So those men were brought to the king. ¹⁴And Nebuchadnezzar said, "Shadrach, Meshach and Abednego, is it true that you do not serve my gods? And is it true that you did not worship the gold statue I have set up? ¹⁵Now, you will hear the sound of the horns, flutes, lyres, zithers, harps, pipes and all the other musical instruments. And you must be ready to bow down and worship the statue I made. That will be good. But if you do not worship it, you will be thrown quickly into the blazing furnace. Then no god will be able to save you from my power!"

¹⁶Shadrach, Meshach and Abednego answered the king. They said, "Nebuchadnezzar, we do not need to defend ourselves to you. ¹⁷You can throw us into the blazing furnace. The God we serve is able to save us from the furnace and your power. If he does this, it is good. ¹⁸But even if God does not save us, we want

> **"We will not serve your gods. We will not worship the gold statue you have set up."**
>
> Daniel 3:18

SHADRACH, MESHACH, ABEDNEGO

It was not only expected; it was required. King Nebuchadnezzar had established the law: Bow down to the 90-foot golden statue he had erected, or you would die!

Shadrach, Meshach, and Abednego knew the rules. But they knew the true Ruler of the world. Obeying God was so important that they were willing to die for their faith. The king became angry because he didn't believe in their God. So he threw them into a furnace that was so hot it burned and killed the men who tied them up and threw them into the furnace—and they were standing outside of it.

God rewarded Shadrach, Meshach, and Abednego's obedience and spared them from the fire. They were able to walk around the furnace, alongside an angel of God, and come out unharmed. King Nebuchadnezzar was so amazed that he became a believer in God, too! When we trust in God—regardless of what the world around us says—we experience his love and protection in amazing ways, and we can have a lasting impact on the world around us.

BLAST FROM THE PAST

iT MiGHT SEEM SURPRISING, but the Bible has a lot to say about slavery. In ancient times, some people were born into slavery, but many others lost their freedom as a result of war. In this way, even the rich and powerful could become slaves, as well as the poor. King Nebuchadnezzar chose slaves for his palace who were physically fit, wealthy, and smart. He gave them new names that showed they were his servants.

you, our king, to know this: We will not serve your gods. We will not worship the gold statue you have set up."

[19]Then Nebuchadnezzar was furious with Shadrach, Meshach and Abednego. He ordered the furnace to be heated seven times hotter than usual. [20]Then he commanded some of the strongest soldiers in his army to tie up Shadrach, Meshach and Abednego. The king told the soldiers to throw them into the blazing furnace.

[21]So Shadrach, Meshach and Abednego were tied up and thrown into the blazing furnace.

They were still wearing their robes, trousers, turbans and other clothes. [22]The king was very angry when he gave the command. And the furnace was made very hot. The fire was so hot that the flames killed the strong soldiers who took Shadrach, Meshach and Abednego there. [23]Firmly tied, Sha-

drach, Meshach and Abednego fell into the blazing furnace.

[24]Then King Nebuchadnezzar was very surprised and jumped to his feet. He asked the men who advised him, "Didn't we tie up only three men? Didn't we throw them into the fire?"

They answered, "Yes, our king."

GET CONNECTED

RELATIONSHIPS WITH FRIENDS

Three's Company The Bible makes it sound so cut and dried, but it couldn't have been easy. Refusing to obey the king in order to obey God meant certain death. But Shadrach, Meshach, and Abednego had their faith in God, and they had each other.

We should never underestimate the importance of surrounding ourselves with friends who love and fear the Lord. As you go about your day at school, church, or in your neighborhood, pay attention to what your friends are saying and doing. Do any of them talk about God? Do they have a desire to serve him? If so, work hard to strengthen that friendship, and ask God to bring others into your life who can help you fight the good fight and finish the race being faithful to God.

CRAFTS

THE FIERY FURNACE

SUPPLIES

old birthday hat

white construction paper

cotton balls, lace, white fabric, netting

glue

glitter

styrofoam ball

yarn

wire hanger

ALL ABOUT IT:

Shadrach, Meshach, and Abednego would not pray to another god even when threatened with being thrown into a fiery furnace. They stood firm in their faith and ended up being thrown in the fire. The king said, "Look! I see four men. They are walking around in the fire. They are not tied up, and they are not burned. The fourth man looks like a son of the gods" (Daniel 3:25).

God sent his angel to be with Shadrach, Meshach, and Abednego. Angels are heavenly beings that can sometimes look like people. God used an angel to tell Mary she would give birth to Jesus. God used angels to tell the shepherds not to be afraid to go find Jesus when he was born. The angel in this story protected Shadrach, Meshach, and Abednego from harm.

There are no real pictures of angels. What do you think they look like? Have fun creating your own angel as you thank God for real angels who protect us day and night.

INSTRUCTIONS

1. Use the birthday hat as the body and the styrofoam ball as the head.

2. Twist a wire hanger to make wings, and have a parent help you cut off the rest of the hanger.

3. Use your imagination to decorate your angel.

LIVIN' IT!

STANDING TALL
DANIEL 3:1-30

Everyone else was doing it. When the music started, everyone bowed down to worship the idol that Nebuchadnezzar had commanded the entire kingdom to worship. Everyone, that is, except Shadrach, Meshach, and Abednego. They refused to obey the king because they wanted to obey God more. In the end, God saved them even in a fiery furnace, and he used their faith to help change the king's heart.

Chances are you won't face any fiery furnaces in your life. But you will face many times when the kids around you are choosing to do things that God would not allow. We need to remember that the culture around us—just like the culture around Shadrach, Meshach, and Abednego—doesn't know or serve God. Our lives should look different from their lives. We should still love them, but we need to stand strong on the truth of God's Word and not be moved. Pray today for strength, desire, and wisdom to obey what's right.

[25]The king said, "Look! I see four men. They are walking around in the fire. They are not tied up, and they are not burned. The fourth man looks like a son of the gods."

[26]Then Nebuchadnezzar went to the opening of the blazing furnace. He shouted, "Shadrach, Meshach and Abednego, come out! Servants of the Most High God, come here!"

So Shadrach, Meshach and Abednego came out of the fire. [27]When they came out, the princes, assistant governors, governors and royal advisers crowded around them. They saw that the fire had not harmed their bodies. Their hair was not burned. Their robes were not burned. And they didn't even smell like smoke.

[28]Then Nebuchadnezzar said, "Praise the God of Shadrach, Meshach and Abednego. Their God has sent his angel and saved his servants from the fire! These three men trusted their God. They refused to obey my command. And they were willing to die rather than serve or worship any god other than their own. [29]So I now make this law: The people of any nation or language must not say anything against the God of Shadrach, Meshach and Abednego. Anyone who does will be torn apart. And his house will be turned into a pile of stones. No other god can save his people like this." [30]Then the king promoted Shadrach, Meshach and Abednego in the area of Babylon.

Daniel Explains the King's Dream

DANIEL 4:1-37

NEBUCHADNEZZAR'S DREAM OF A TREE

4 King Nebuchadnezzar sent a letter. It went to the people, nations and those who speak every language in all the world. The letter said:

I wish you great wealth!

[2]The Most High God has done miracles[d] and wonderful things for me. I am happy to tell you about these things.

[3]The things he has done are great.
His miracles are mighty.
His kingdom continues forever.
His rule will continue for all time.

[4]I, Nebuchadnezzar, was at my palace. I was happy and successful. [5]I had a dream that made me afraid. As I was lying on my bed, I saw pictures and visions in my mind. Those things

made me very afraid. [6]So I gave an order. All the wise men of Babylon were to be brought to me. I wanted them to tell me what my dream meant. [7]The fortune-tellers, magicians and wise men came. I told them about the dream. But those men could not tell me what it meant.

[8]Finally, Daniel came to me. (I called him Belteshazzar to honor my god. The spirit of the holy gods is in him.) I told my dream to Daniel. [9]I said, "Belteshazzar, you are the most important of all the fortune-tellers. I know that the spirit of the holy gods is in you. I know there is no secret that is too hard for you to understand. This was what I dreamed.

> **"i had a dream that made me afraid. As i was lying on my bed, i saw pictures and visions in my mind. Those things made me very afraid."**
>
> *Daniel 4:5*

Tell me what it means. [10]These are the visions I saw while I was lying in my bed: I looked, and there in front of me was a tree. It was standing in the middle of the earth. The tree was very tall.

BLAST FROM THE PAST

WHAT DO WE KNOW ABOUT NEBUCHADNEZZAR? He was the second king to hold that name and ruled from 605-562 B.C. He was an important king because he defeated the Egyptians at Carchemish. He was also known for great building projects, including Babylon's summer palace, fortification of the city, the ziggurat (which some think may have been the Tower of Babel), and the royal hanging gardens. He is also recorded in other Greek, Latin, and Jewish writings.

BiBLE BASiCS

WHAT ARE ANGELS?

Angels are a group of beings that God created to live with him in heaven before the world was made. Archangel Lucifer and one-third of all the other angels disobeyed God and were thrown out of heaven. They are now invisible demons who try to keep people from accepting Jesus as their Savior. The good angels serve God by serving and helping his children. They protect Christians, fight against evil, and help carry out God's will on earth. Even though we can't see any of this going on around us, the Bible says that we are in a war for our souls, and angels are all around us.

"The tree grew large and strong. The top of the tree touched the sky. It could be seen from anywhere on earth. ¹²The leaves of the tree were beautiful. It had plenty of good fruit on it. On the tree was food for everyone. The wild animals found shelter under the tree. And the birds lived in its branches. Every animal ate from it.

¹³"I was looking at those things in the vision while lying on my bed. And then I saw a holy angel coming down from heaven. ¹⁴He spoke very loudly. He said, 'Cut down the tree, and cut off its branches. Strip off its leaves. Scatter its fruit around. Let the animals that are under the tree run away. Let the birds that were in its branches fly away. ¹⁵But let the stump and its roots stay in the ground. Put a band of iron and bronze around it. Let it stay in the field with the grass around it.

"'Let the man become wet with dew. Let him live among the animals and plants of the earth. ¹⁶Let him not think like a man any longer. Let him have the mind of an animal for seven years.

¹⁷"'Messengers gave this command. The holy ones declared the sentence. This is so all the people may know that the Most High God rules over the kingdoms of men. God gives those kingdoms to anyone he wants. And he chooses people to rule them who are not proud.'

¹⁸"That is what I, King Nebuchadnezzar, dreamed. Now Daniel, called Belteshazzar, tell me what the dream means. None of the wise men in my kingdom can explain it to me. But you can, because the spirit of the holy gods is in you."

> "None of the wise men in my kingdom can explain it to me. But you can, because the spirit of the holy gods is in you."
>
> *Daniel 4:18*

DANIEL 4:19-25

DANIEL EXPLAINS THE DREAM

[19] Then Daniel (also called Belteshazzar) was very quiet for a while. His thoughts made him afraid. So the king said, "Belteshazzar, do not let the dream or its meaning make you afraid."

Then Daniel, called Belteshazzar, answered the king. He said, "My master, I wish the dream were about your enemies. And I wish its meaning were for those who are against you! [20] You saw a tree in your dream. The tree grew large and strong. Its top touched the sky. It could be seen from all over the earth. [21] Its leaves were beautiful, and it had plenty of fruit. The fruit gave food for everyone. It was a home for the wild animals. And its branches were nesting places for the birds. That is the tree you saw. [22] My king, you are that tree! You have become great and powerful. You are like the tall tree that touched the sky. And your power reaches to the far parts of the earth.

[23] "My king, you saw a holy angel coming down from heaven. He said, 'Cut down the tree and destroy it. But leave the stump and its roots in the ground. Put a band of iron and bronze around it. Leave it in the field with the grass. Let him become wet with dew. He will live like a wild animal for seven years.'

[24] "This is the meaning of the dream, my king. The Most High God has commanded these things to happen to my master the king: [25] You will be forced away from people. You will live among the wild animals. People will feed you grass like an ox. And dew from the sky will make you wet. Seven years will pass, and then you will learn this lesson: The Most High God is ruler over the

> ### "The Most High God is ruler over the kingdoms of men."
> *Daniel 4:25*

10 TOP TEN

Ways to Make Your Siblings Smile

1. Give them a big hug.
2. Let them have the biggest piece.
3. Tell them something nice you like about them.
4. Help them with their homework.
5. Ask them to join you and your friends.
6. Let them go first.
7. Pray for them.
8. Tell them you love them.
9. Watch a movie with them.
10. Make their bed.

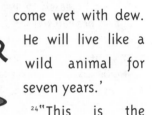

History Highlights

↗ **336 B.C.**
Darius III is the last Persian king.

7000 5000 3000 1000 0 1000 NOW

kingdoms of men. And the Most High God gives those kingdoms to anyone he wants.

²⁶"The stump of the tree and its roots were to be left in the ground. This means your kingdom will be given back to you. This will happen when you learn that heaven rules your kingdom. ²⁷So, my king, please accept my advice. I advise you to stop sinning and do what is right. Stop doing wicked things and be kind to poor people. Then you might continue to be successful."

THE KING'S DREAM COMES TRUE

²⁸All these things happened to King Nebuchadnezzar. ²⁹Twelve months after the dream, King Nebuchadnezzar was walking on the roof*ⁿ* of his palace in Babylon. ³⁰And he said, "Look at Babylon. I built this great city. It is my palace. I built this great place by my power to show how great I am."

³¹The words were still in his mouth when a voice came from heaven. The voice said, "King Nebuchadnezzar, these things will happen to you: Your royal power has been taken away from you. ³²You will be forced away from people. You will live with the wild animals. You will be fed grass like an ox. Seven years will pass before you learn this lesson: The Most High God rules over the kingdoms of men. And the Most High God gives those kingdoms to anyone he wants."

³³Those things happened quickly. Nebuchadnezzar was forced to go away from people. He began eating grass like an ox. He became wet from dew. His hair grew long like the feathers

Awake

of an eagle. And his nails grew long like the claws of a bird.

³⁴Then at the end of that time, I, Nebuchadnezzar, looked up toward heaven. And I could think correctly again. Then I gave praise to the Most High God. I gave honor and glory to him who lives forever.

God's rule is forever.
His kingdom continues for all time.

STOP

"So, my king, please accept my advice. I advise you to stop sinning and do what is right. Stop doing wicked things and be kind to poor people. Then you might continue to be successful."

Daniel 4:27

4:29 *roof* In Bible times houses were built with flat roofs. The roof was used for drying things such as flax and fruit. And it was used as an extra room, as a place for worship and as a place to sleep in the summer.

november contentment

1 All Saints Day

2 First thing every morning this month, write down one of God's blessings in your life.

3 Share your favorite game or toy with your siblings.

4

5 Visit a pumpkin patch, and help your mom make pumpkin pie.

6 Prayer Pointer: Ask God to forgive you for complaining and to give you a heart of gratitude.

7

8 Make a list of all the reasons why you love your mom then show it to her.

9

Pie me

10 Make a scarecrow for your porch with a sign that says, "Happy Thanksgiving."

11 Veterans Day: Remember to pray for our military.

12 Hide-It-in-Your-Heart: Give thanks to the Lord and pray to him. Tell the nations what he has done (1 Chronicles 16:8).

13

14 Start a canned-food drive at your school.

15 Take your younger siblings on a wagon ride around the block.

16

17

18 Hide-It-in-Your-Heart: Come into his city with songs of thanksgiving. Come into his courtyards with songs of praise. Thank him, and praise his name (Psalm 100:4).

19

20

21 As a family, take food for Thanksgiving to a needy family.

22

23 Write to missionaries you know, and ask them what their greatest need is.

24

25 Invite a widow or single parent over for Thanksgiving dinner.

26

27

28 Pop some popcorn, and watch football with your dad.

29 Prayer Pointer: Ask God to help you and all his children to recognize God's goodness in your life.

30

³⁵People on earth
    are not truly important.
God does what he wants
    with the powers of heaven
    and the people on earth.
No one can stop his powerful
    hand.
    No one can question the
    things he does.

³⁶So, at that time I could think correctly again. And God gave back my great honor and power as king. The people who advise me and the royal family came to me for help again. I became king again. And I became even greater and more powerful than before. ³⁷Now I, Nebuchadnezzar, give praise and honor and glory to the King of heaven. Everything he does is right. He is always fair. And he is able to make proud people humble.

"**He is always fair. And he is able to make proud people humble.**" *Daniel 4:37*

Daniel in the Lions' Den

DANIEL 6:1-28

GET CONNECTED

RELATIONSHIPS WITH FRIENDS

Bearing Burdens It was King Darius's fault that Daniel was in the predicament anyway. He just wasn't thinking when he made a law for everyone to pray only to him. He had forgotten that Daniel prayed to God. And now Daniel, his favorite servant, was in the lions' den. Darius was so upset that he couldn't eat or sleep. At the crack of dawn, he got up to check on Daniel and set him free.

When you know of another Christian who is in trouble, how do you respond? Do you go on with your day thinking, *Well, that's too bad for him*? Or do you stop what you're doing to pray? God wants us to bear one another's burdens. When another believer is hurting, we should hurt, too. We should also look for ways to lighten one another's load.

DANIEL AND THE LIONS

6 Darius thought it would be a good idea to choose 120 governors. They would rule through all of his kingdom. ²And he chose three men as supervisors over those 120 governors. Daniel was one of these three supervisors. The king set up these men so that he would not be cheated. ³Daniel showed that he could do the work better than the other supervisors and the governors. Because of this, the king planned to put Daniel in charge of the whole kingdom.

> **"Daniel was trustworthy. He was not lazy and did not cheat the king."** *Daniel 6:4*

⁴So the other supervisors and the governors tried to find reasons to accuse Daniel. But he went on doing the business of the government. And they could not find anything wrong with him. So they could not accuse him of doing anything wrong. Daniel was trustworthy. He was not lazy and did not cheat the king. ⁵Finally these men said, "We will never find any reason to accuse Daniel. But we must find something to complain about. It will have to be about the law of his God."

⁶So the supervisors and the governors went as a group to the king. They said: "King Darius, live forever! ⁷The supervisors, assistant governors, governors, the people who advise you and the captains of the soldiers have all agreed on something. We think the king should make this law that everyone would have to obey: No one should pray to any god or man except to you, our king. This should be done for the next 30 days. Anyone who doesn't obey will be thrown into the

LiViN' iT!

LIVING OUT LOUD
DANIEL 6:1-28

Even though Daniel was well aware that it might mean death by lions, he still continued to pray to God, despite the king's order that no one pray to anyone other than him. Not only did Daniel keep praying to God—he did it three times a day in front of the window of his home where everyone could see! Daniel wanted the world to know that he served the only true God, and would not stop just to please an earthly king.

Do you sometimes want to hide your relationship with Jesus? Do you feel like your friends might laugh if they find out you go to church and pray? Are you afraid to speak about your faith at school because of what the teachers might say? Remember Daniel. He was bold about his actions because he knew they were right. You, too, can be confident in your faith, knowing that it is better to please God than men. Don't be afraid of what others think. Just like he did for Daniel, God can deliver you and work to change the hearts of the same people who don't understand his ways.

lions' den. ⁸Now, our king, make the law. Write it down so it cannot be changed. The laws of the Medes and Persians cannot be canceled." ⁹So King

Darius made the law and had it written.

¹⁰When Daniel heard that the new law had been written, he went to his house. He went to his upstairs room. The windows of that room opened toward Jerusalem. Three times each day Daniel got down on his knees and prayed. He prayed and thanked God, just as he always had done.

¹¹Then those men went as a group and found Daniel. They saw him praying and asking God for help. ¹²So they went to the king. They talked to him about the law he had made. They said, "Didn't you write a law that says no one may pray to any god or man except you, our king? Doesn't it say that anyone who disobeys during the next 30 days will be thrown into the lions' den?"

The king answered, "Yes, I wrote that law. And the laws of the Medes and Persians cannot be canceled."

¹³Then those men spoke to the

king. They said, "Daniel is one of the captives from Judah. And he is not paying attention to the law you wrote. Daniel still prays to his God three times every day."

¹⁴The king became very upset when he heard this. He decided he had to save Daniel. He worked until sunset trying to think of a way to save him.

¹⁵Then those men went as a group to the king. They said, "Remember, our king, the law of the Medes and Persians. It says that no law or command given by the king can be changed."

¹⁶So King Darius gave the order. They brought Daniel and threw him into the lions' den. The king said to Daniel, "May

"Three times each day Daniel got down on his knees and prayed."
Daniel 6:10

INCREDIBLE EDIBLES

DANIEL IN THE LIONS' DEN

INGREDIENTS

animal crackers

milk

HERE'S THE SCOOP:

The people wanted Daniel to pray to the king, but Daniel knew he should pray only to God. Daniel did what was right, even when everyone around him did not. Imagine how scared you would be in a lions' den! Daniel's faith in God was so strong he did not even fear the lions.

When Daniel came out of the lions' den the next day, the king declared, "God rescues and saves people. God does mighty miracles in heaven and on earth. God saved Daniel from the power of the lions" (Daniel 6:27). He saw the power of God in Daniel's life.

What "lions" are you facing today? Do you feel left out? Scared? Bullied? Alone? God knows how you feel, and he wants to comfort and protect you. God tells you in his Word about others who have felt just like you do. God has given you your parents, teachers, and leaders in the church for you to learn how to rely on God for everything you need.

INSTRUCTIONS

Talk to God about the lions in your life as you enjoy a glass of milk with animal crackers.

the God you serve all the time save you!" [17]A big stone was brought. It was put over the opening of the lions' den. Then the king used his signet[d] ring to put his special seal[d] on the rock. And he used the rings of his royal officers to put their seals on the rock also. This showed that no one could move that rock and bring Daniel out. [18]Then King Darius went back to his palace. He did not eat that night. He did not have any entertainment brought to entertain him. And he could not sleep.

[19]The next morning King Darius got up at dawn. He hurried

> "My God sent his angel to close the lions' mouths. They have not hurt me, because my God knows i am innocent."
>
> *Daniel 6:22*

to the lions' den. [20]As he came near the den, he was worried. He called out to Daniel. He said, "Daniel, servant of the living God! Has your God that you always worship been able to save you from the lions?"

[21]Daniel answered, "My king, live forever! [22]My God sent his angel to close the lions' mouths. They have not hurt me, because my God knows I am innocent. I never did anything wrong to you, my king."

[23]King Darius was very happy. He told his servants to lift Daniel out of the lions' den. So they lifted him out

and did not find any injury on him. This was because Daniel had trusted in his God.

[24]Then the king gave a command. The men who had accused Daniel were brought to the lions' den and thrown into it. Their wives and children were also thrown into it. The lions grabbed them before they hit the floor of the den. And the lions crushed their bones.

[25]Then King Darius wrote a letter. It was to all people and all nations, to those who spoke every language in the world:

I wish you great wealth.

[26]I am making a new law. This law is for people in every part of my kingdom. All of you must

REAL SUPER HEROES

DANIEL

Never think that your prayers are worthless. God hears every word and answers in some amazing ways. Just look at Daniel.

Daniel loved God and served him with his whole heart, even though he and the Israelites had been taken captive to a foreign land to serve people who didn't love God. The king loved Daniel, but some of his followers didn't. They tricked the king into making a law that said no one could pray to anyone but the king, or else they'd be thrown into the lions' den.

Daniel obeyed God above the king's command. So he continued to pray—three times a day. When he was thrown in with the lions, God kept their mouths shut, and Daniel's life was spared. The king came to believe in Daniel's God, too, and the evil men were killed by the lions.

BiBLe CRitteRS

3-D

FIERCE FELINES

Both David and Samson fought them off. Even in Bible times, **LIONS** were ferocious creatures. Did you know that a lion's roar can be heard more than 5 miles away? It's how they scare off unwanted guests and how they know when to gather together. When lions do get together to eat, the female lions (called lionesses) hunt and catch the meal, only to have the males eat first. Females eat second, and the cubs scramble for what's left over.

> **"God rescues and saves people.... God saved Daniel from the power of the lions."**
>
> *Daniel 6:27*

fear and respect the God of Daniel.

> Daniel's God is the living God.
> He lives forever.
> His kingdom will never be destroyed.
> His rule will never end.

²⁷God rescues and saves people.

> God does mighty miracles[d]
> in heaven and on earth.
> God saved Daniel
> from the power of the lions.

²⁸So Daniel was successful during the time that Darius was king. This was also the time that Cyrus the Persian was king.

BLAST FROM THE PAST

HE WASN'T A WISE OLD PROPHET. Daniel was still very young. He was only in his third year of training in the royal courts when King Nebuchadnezzar called him into his presence. In 604 B.C. young Daniel interpreted the king's dream with God's help and quickly rose in the power ranks among his friends.

STORIES FROM

JONAH

Jonah and the Big Fish

JONAH 1:1–4:11

GOD CALLS AND JONAH RUNS

1 The Lord spoke his word to Jonah son of Amittai: ²"Get up, go to the great city of Nineveh and preach against it. I see the evil things they do."

³But Jonah got up to run away from the Lord. He went to the city of Joppa. There he found a ship that was going to the city of Tarshish. Jonah paid for the trip and went aboard. He wanted to go to Tarshish to run away from the Lord.

⁴But the Lord sent a great wind on the sea. This wind made the sea very rough. So the ship was in danger of breaking apart. ⁵The sailors were afraid. Each man cried to his own god. The men began throwing the cargo into the sea. This would make the ship lighter so it would not sink.

But Jonah had gone down into the ship to lie down. He fell fast asleep. ⁶The captain of the ship came and said, "Why are you sleeping? Get up! Pray to your god! Maybe your god will pay attention to us. Maybe he will save us!"

⁷Then the men said to each other, "Let's throw lots^d to see who caused these troubles to happen to us."

So the men threw lots. The lot showed that the trouble had happened because of Jonah. ⁸Then the men said to Jonah, "Tell us what you have done. Why has this terrible thing happened to us? What is your job? Where do you come from? What is your country? Who are your people?"

DIG THIS!

Nineveh was the capital of the Assyrian Empire and was a great city. Archaeologists uncovered a large temple of Ishtar and other public buildings there. More than 25,000 stone tablets were discovered in the palace of Ashurbanipal. Several of these tablets talk about a worldwide flood.

LIVIN' IT!

HIDE AND SEEK
JONAH 1:1-17

Jonah had spent a lot of energy. He was running hard from the calling he had received from God. On land, onto a boat, into a big fish, and back on land—all of Jonah's efforts were no match for God.

Truth is, we can't escape God. He is everywhere. We can't hide among our friends, our clothes, our money, or our hectic daily routines. God is still with us everywhere we go. Just like he did with Jonah, God chases after us. Instead of avoiding God, we need to turn to him in our hearts and minds as we go about our day, asking him what he would have us to be and do. When we live obedient lives, we discover the true joy of living and fellowshipping with God our Father. Suddenly, we wonder why we ever wasted so much time trying to avoid what is really our life's biggest blessing.

⁹Then Jonah said to them, "I am a Hebrew. I fear the Lord, the God of heaven. He is the God who made the sea and the land."

¹⁰Then the men were very afraid. They asked Jonah, "What terrible thing did you do?" They knew Jonah was running away from the Lord because Jonah had told them.

¹¹The wind and the waves of the sea were becoming much stronger. So the men said to Jonah, "What should we do to you to make the sea calm down?"

¹²Jonah said to them, "Pick me up, and throw me into the sea. Then it will calm down. I know it is my fault that this great storm has come on you."

¹³Instead, the men tried to row the ship back to the land. But they could not. The wind and the waves of the sea were becoming much stronger.

JONAH'S PUNISHMENT

¹⁴So the men cried to the Lord, "Lord, please don't let us die because of taking this man's life. Please don't think we are guilty of killing an innocent man. Lord, you have caused all this to happen. You wanted it this way." ¹⁵Then the men picked up Jonah and threw him into the sea. So the sea became calm. ¹⁶Then they began to fear the Lord very much. They offered a

REAL SUPER HEROES

JONAH

Jonah is a hero, not so much for his actions, but much more for the life lessons he provides for us. Who better than Jonah to show us the silliness of trying to run from God? After receiving his call to preach a message of repentance to the Ninevites, he boarded a ship and headed in the opposite direction. Of course, God stopped him in his tracks with a dangerous storm, and his companions tossed him overboard to end the fury.

Jonah found himself in the belly of a large fish, which three days later landed him on the beach covered in fish vomit. He would have to obey. When he did, it had results. God turned the Ninevites to himself, and they repented. The problem was that their repentance—and God's forgiveness—made Jonah mad. He hated the Ninevites because they were mean to Israel. He didn't want to forgive them.

So Jonah teaches us, too, that no one is past God's forgiveness. God doesn't want us to love only the lovely, but those who make fun of us and are cruel to us, as well. Being a hero isn't about being someone special. A hero is simply someone who understands God's heart and is willing to sacrifice their life to see God work the miracle of love and truth through them.

CONNECT THE DOTS

As Jonah learned, we can never hide from God. God pursues us because he loves us! Connect the dots to see the incredible way God kept Jonah safe, even though he was disobedient.

Write the verses here:

_____

_____

_____

Jonah 2:7, 10

BLAST FROM THE PAST

THERE'S A LOT OF TALK ABOUT TARSHISH IN THE BIBLE. In fact, it's mentioned more than 30 times, but no one today knows exactly where it was located. Some scholars guess that it was a Phoenician colony called Tartessus that was found in Spain, and it was famous for its rich metal resources. The Hebrew word "Tarshish" does refer to a precious stone, so it could be a general word to describe several different places where metalworking took place, instead of just one location.

sacrifice to the Lord. They also made promises to him.

17And the Lord caused a very big fish to swallow Jonah. Jonah was in the stomach of the fish three days and three nights.

2 While Jonah was in the stomach of the fish, he prayed to the Lord his God. Jonah said,

2"I was in danger.
So I called to the Lord,
and he answered me.
I was about to die.
So I cried to you,
and you heard
my voice.
3You threw me
into the sea.
I went down,
down into the
deep sea.
The water was all
around me.
Your powerful waves
flowed over me.

4I said, 'I was driven out of
your presence.
But I hope to see your Holy
Temple^d again.'
5The waters of the sea closed
over me.
I was about to die.
The deep sea was all
around me.
Seaweed wrapped around
my head.
6I went down to where the
mountains of the sea
start to rise.

I thought I was locked in
this prison forever.
But you saved me from
death,
Lord my God.

7"When my life had almost
gone,
I remembered the Lord.
Lord, I prayed to you.
And you heard my prayers
in your Holy Temple.

8"People who worship
useless idols

GET CONNECTED

RELATIONSHIPS WITH GOD

Don't Hide, Just Seek Are you ever afraid of God? Do you worry that he has plans to do something bad to you because you've sinned? If so, you probably try to avoid God or hide from him. But it doesn't need to be that way!

Did you know that, if you belong to God, he loves you as much as he loves his own Son Jesus? That's because when you received Christ into your life, Jesus' blood washed you and made you completely acceptable in God's sight. So next time you sin (and you will!) don't run *away* from God. Run *to* him for forgiveness and help!

give up their loyalty to you.
⁹Lord, I will praise and
thank you
while I give sacrifices to you.
I will make promises to you.
And I will do what I promise.
Salvation comes from
the Lord!"

"Get up. Go to the great city Nineveh. Preach against it what i tell you." *Jonah 3:2*

¹⁰Then the Lord spoke to the fish. And the fish spit Jonah out of its stomach onto the dry land.

GOD CALLS AND JONAH OBEYS

3 Then the Lord spoke his word to Jonah again. The Lord said, ²"Get up. Go to the great city Nineveh. Preach against it what I tell you."

³So Jonah obeyed the Lord. He got up and went to Nineveh. It was a very large city. It took a person three days just to walk across it. ⁴Jonah entered the city. When he had walked for one day, he preached to the people. He said, "After 40 days, Nineveh will be destroyed!"

⁵The people of Nineveh believed in God. They announced they would stop eating for a while. They put on rough cloth to show how sad they were. All the people in the city wore the cloth. People from the most important to the least important did this.

⁶When the king of Nineveh heard this news, he got up from his throne. He took off his robe. He covered himself with rough cloth and sat in ashes to show how upset he was.

"Everyone must turn away from his evil life. Everyone must stop doing harm." *Jonah 3:8*

⁷He made an announcement and sent it through the city. The announcement said:

By command of the king and his important men: No person or animal should eat anything. No herd or flock will be allowed to taste anything. Do not let them eat food or drink water. ⁸But every person and animal should be covered with rough cloth. People should cry loudly to God. Everyone must turn away from his evil life. Everyone must stop doing harm. ⁹Maybe God will change his mind. Maybe he will stop being angry. Then we will not die.

¹⁰God saw what the people did. He saw that they stopped doing evil things. So God changed his mind and did not do what he had warned. He did not punish them.

GOD'S MERCY MAKES JONAH ANGRY

4 But Jonah was very unhappy that God did not destroy the city.

CRAFTS

JONAH
AND THE
BIG FISH

SUPPLIES

waxed paper
shaving cream
Goldfish® crackers

ALL ABOUT IT:

Jonah did not want to obey God when he told him to go to Nineveh. He tried to run from God, but God followed him in an ocean storm. God saved Jonah from the storm in the belly of a big fish. After that, Jonah obeyed God.

What does it take for you to obey God? God wants to use us to accomplish his plans on earth. It is a privilege for us to let God have his way with our lives. Think about God's plans and how he worked to get Jonah to obey as you do the following exercise.

OCEAN WAVES INSTRUCTIONS

1. Place some waxed paper on the kitchen counter.

2. Squirt a handful of shaving cream in the middle of the paper.

3. Use your hands to spread the shaving cream out like a sea, then have fun making waves in the shaving cream.

4. Add more shaving cream to make the waves more violent.

5. When you've had enough fun, make the waves calm down by rubbing them until they disappear.

6. After you've cleaned the mess and washed your hands, enjoy some Goldfish® crackers as a snack.

3-D

JONAH 4:2-10

He was angry. ²He complained to the Lord and said, "I knew this would happen. I knew it when I was still in my own country. It is why I quickly ran away to Tarshish. I knew that you are a God who is kind and shows mercy. You don't become angry quickly. You have great love. I knew you would rather forgive than punish them. ³So now I ask you, Lord, please kill me. It is better for me to die than to live."

⁴Then the Lord said, "Do you think it is right for you to be angry?"

⁵Jonah went out and sat down east of the city. There he made a shelter for himself. And he sat there in the shade. He was waiting to see what would happen to the city. ⁶The Lord made a plant grow quickly up over Jonah. This made a cool place for him to sit. And it helped him to be more comfortable. Jonah was very pleased to have the plant for shade. ⁷The next day the sun rose. And God sent a worm to attack the plant. Then the plant died.

⁸When the sun was high in the sky, God sent a hot east wind to blow.

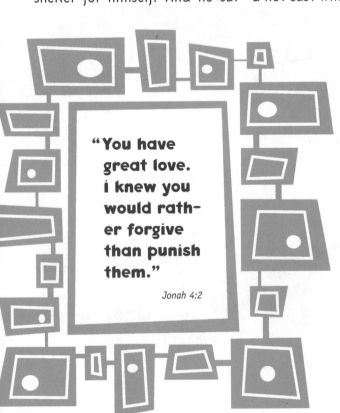

The sun became very hot on Jonah's head. And he became very weak. He wished he were dead. Jonah said, "It is better for me to die than to live."

⁹But God said this to Jonah: "Do you think it is right for you to be angry because of the plant?"

Jonah answered, "It is right for me to be angry! I will stay angry until I die!"

¹⁰And the Lord said, "You

> **"You have great love. I knew you would rather forgive than punish them."**
>
> *Jonah 4:2*

LIVIN' IT!

LOVING ENEMIES
JONAH 4:1-11

Jonah got it all mixed up. He had finally obeyed the Lord and preached to the people of Nineveh—people that the Jews didn't like and who didn't like the Jews. And what did they do? They listened! They repented of their sins and turned to God. So what did Jonah do? He got angry. He didn't like the Ninevites, and he wanted God to punish them. He never thought in a million years that God would change their hearts.

In the end, Jonah was the one learning the difficult lesson. We don't preach to others just to let them know they're doomed to die. We preach because we want them to know and experience God's love. Whether people seem like they deserve to go to heaven or not, we must love them. Whether or not they are kind to us, we are called to love even our enemies. Ask God to fill your heart with his love for the people around you.

showed concern for that plant. But you did not plant it or make it grow. It appeared in the night, and the next day it died. "Then surely I can show concern for the great city Nineveh. There are many animals in that city. And there are more than 120,000 people living there. Those people simply do not know right from wrong!"

Bible Critters
WHALE DONE

Okay, so the Bible doesn't exactly say what kind of fish swallowed Jonah. We only know that it was really big! So it could have been a blue **WHALE.** Blue whales are the largest animals today—and possibly the largest that have ever lived. Today, blue whales can grow up to 85 feet long. Their heart muscle alone weighs about the same as a small car. But if one tries to swallow you, don't worry. Blue whales don't have teeth. Instead, they have baleen plates that act like filters, allowing water to pass through while millions of tiny plankton are ingested as food.

MICAH

The Coming Shepherd

MICAH 5:2-5; 6:6-8; 7:18-19

DIG THIS!

Omri was the king of Israel from 885-874 B.C. He made Samaria the capital of the Israelite kingdom. He grew to be very powerful, and his dynasty lasted for four more generations. The Moabite Stone (a rock slab dating from 850 B.C.) records Omri's military success. Also, ancient documents from Assyria (known as the Annals of Shalmaneser III) relate Omri's powerful position. However, Omri was an evil ruler, and Micah told him and the Israelites that they would be punished for turning away from God.

THE RULER TO BE BORN IN BETHLEHEM

5 "But you, Bethlehem Ephrathah,
are one of the smallest towns in Judah.
But from you will come one who will rule Israel for me.
He comes from very old times,
from days long ago."

³The Lord will leave his people in Babylon
until Jerusalem, who is in labor, gives birth to her children.
Then his brothers who are in captivity will return.
They will come back to the people of Israel living in Judah.
⁴Then the ruler of Israel will stand
and take care of his people.
He will lead them with the Lord's power.
He will lead them in the wonderful name of the Lord his God.
They will live in safety.
And his greatness will be known all over the earth.
⁵ He will bring peace.

• • •

6 You say, "What can I bring with me
when I come before the Lord?

CRAFTS

A PERFECT GIFT

SUPPLIES

construction paper

markers

pencil

ALL ABOUT IT:

"The Lord has told you what is good. He has told you what he wants from you: Do what is right to other people. Love being kind to others. And live humbly, trusting your God" (Micah 6:8).

Micah wanted to give God a gift that would honor him. The gift God asks us to give is the gift of ourselves. He wants us to trust him, not ourselves. He wants us to give ourselves to serve others. He wants us to give him our praise and thanks.

INSTRUCTIONS

Take time today to make a thank-you letter or card for God. Thank him for how he has worked in your life, and give him praise for who he is.

DECEMBER GENEROSITY

1 Make a big pot of chili, and enjoy it with your family

2

3 Save your allowance this month to buy gifts for a needy child.

4

5 Help your dad string lights on the house.

6 Choose—on purpose—to give your brother or sister the bigger piece.

7

8

9 Cut out paper snowflakes, and tape them to your front door.

10

11 PRAYER POINTER: Thank God for giving his only Son to die for you, and ask him to give you the same kind of generous heart.

12

13

14 Hide-It-in-Your-Heart: A child will be born to us. God will give a son to us. . . . His name will be Wonderful Counselor, Powerful God, Father Who Lives Forever, Prince of Peace (Isaiah 9:6).

15 Visit an orphanage, and take bags of candy to the children.

16

17 Go to the gym, and play basketball with your friends.

18 Find three things you own that you think would bless someone else. Wrap them up, and secretly give them away.

19

20  Go caroling in your neighborhood.

21 Invite the neighborhood kids over for hot apple cider and cookies.

22

23 Pile in the car, and go looking at lights while listening to Christmas music.

24

25 Bake a birthday cake for Jesus, and remember to thank him for his wonderful gift to you.

26

27

28 Hide-It-in-Your-Heart: All day long the lazy person wishes for more. But the good person gives without holding back (Proverbs 21:26).

29

30

31 Start a New Year's tradition with your family.

Top Ten

Ways to Study Your Magnify® Biblezine

1. By using with your 3-D glasses
2. By coloring connect-the-dot pictures
3. By answering the quizzes
4. By making your own history timeline
5. By following the calendar suggestions
6. By reading a chapter of Scripture each morning before school
7. By asking God to give you understanding
8. By writing down 3 ways to apply what you've learned
9. By sharing it with a friend
10. By reading it to your younger siblings

What can I bring
when I bow before God
on high?
Should I come before the Lord
with burnt offerings,
with year-old calves?
7Will the Lord be pleased with
1,000 male sheep?
Will he be pleased with
10,000 rivers of oil?
Should I give my first child
for the evil I have done?
Should I give my very own
child for my sin?"
8The Lord has told you what
is good.
He has told you what
he wants from you:
Do what is right to other
people.
Love being kind
to others.
And live humbly,
trusting your God.

• • •

7 There is no God
like you.
You forgive people who are
guilty of sin.
You don't look at the sins of
your people
who are left alive.
You, Lord, will not stay
angry forever.
You enjoy being kind.
19Lord, you will have mercy
on us again.
You will conquer our sins.
You will throw away all
our sins
into the deepest sea.

History Highlights

↗ **334 B.C.**
Alexander the Great begins his quest to destroy the Persian Empire, and the Greek Empire flourishes.

7000 5000 3000 1000 0 1000 NOW

God's Promise of Mercy
MALACHI 3:13-18

THE LORD'S PROMISE OF MERCY

3 The Lord says, "You have said terrible things about me.

"But you ask, 'What have we said about you?'

¹⁴"You have said, 'It is useless to serve God. It did no good to obey his laws. And it did no good to show the Lord of heaven's armies that we are sorry for what we did. ¹⁵So we say that proud people are happy. Evil people succeed. They challenge God and get away with it.'"

¹⁶Then those who hon- ored the Lord spoke with each other. The Lord listened and heard them. The names of those who honored the Lord and respected him were written in a

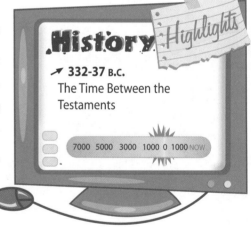

History Highlights

↗ **332-37 B.C.**
The Time Between the Testaments

7000 5000 3000 1000 0 1000 NOW

BLAST FROM THE PAST

IF YOU LIVED IN OLD TESTAMENT TIMES AND NEEDED MONEY, you wouldn't go to the bank! Instead, you would try the Temple or storehouses. Egypt, Greece, and Israel all used their places of worship as places to keep their money. As a result, government and religion were closely linked; and people kept many records of possessions and money that date as far back as the history of writing itself.

WHAT'S HIDDEN IN THE CLOUD?

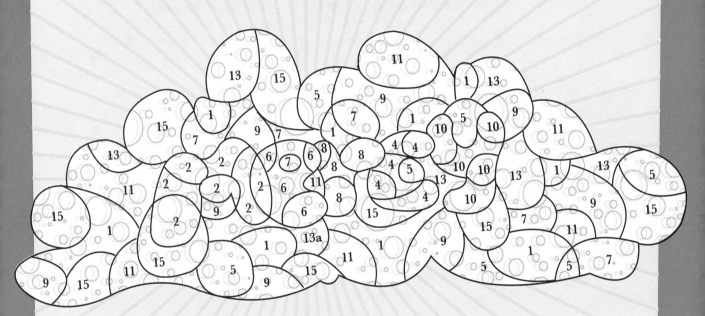

Color in only the even numbers according to the chart below.
You'll discover what God longs to show his people (found in Malachi 3:17).

2 = PURPLE   4 = GREEN
6 = ORANGE   8 = RED   10 =BLUE

10 TOP TEN

Ways To Wake Up

1. By your puppy licking you

2. By your mom scratching your back

3. By listening to music on the radio

4. By your siblings piling in your bed

5. By your dad screaming the wake-up song

6. To the first rays of sunlight

7. By a gentle kiss

8. By the smell of bacon

9. By the sound of laughing

10. By remembering God is with you

POWERFUL PROMISE
MALACHI 3:13-17

From the time of Adam's sin in the garden, people had been waiting. Waiting for God to fulfill the promise of a Savior who would free them from their burden of sin. Finally, after thousands of years had passed, Jesus did come to earth to pay the penalty for our sins. But when he rose again and ascended to heaven, Jesus mentioned another promise that Malachi foretold hundreds of years before. He promised to come again one day to gather his people to himself.

Like the Jews of long ago, we are waiting. Even though it may take a long time, we still wait with hope. God has promised a second coming of his Son that will end sin and pain and enter in a perfect way of life with him for everyone who believes in him. We don't know when that day will be, so we must live each day as if it were the one when Jesus would return.

book. The Lord will remember them.

¹⁷The Lord of heaven's armies says, "They belong to me. On that day they will be my very own. A father shows mercy to his son who serves him. In the same way I will show mercy to my people. ¹⁸You will again see the difference between good and evil people. You will see the difference between those who serve God and those who don't.

MY FAVORITES!

FAVORITE BIBLE STORIES ....
....

FAVORITE BIBLE ANIMALS ....
....

FAVORITE BIBLE RECIPES ....
....

FAVORITE BIBLE GAMES ....
....

PEOPLE I ADMIRE MOST FROM THE OLD TESTAMENT

PERSON ....

WHY I LIKE HIM/HER ....

....

PERSON ....

WHY I LIKE HIM/HER ....

....

PERSON ....

WHY I LIKE HIM/HER ....

....

THINGS I WANT TO PRAY FOR

....

....

....

....

....

....

....

....

....

....

....

THINGS I'M MOST THANKFUL FOR

THINGS I'M MOST THANKFUL FOR

THINGS I'M MOST THANKFUL FOR